A Treasury of Confederate Heritage
A Panorama of Life in the South

Civil War Heritage XIV

Edited by

Walbrook D. Swank

BURD STREET PRESS
SHIPPENSBURG, PENNSYLVANIA

Copyright © 2003 by Walbrook D. Swank

ALL RIGHTS RESERVED—No part of this book may be reproduced in any form without permission in writing from the publisher, except by a reviewer who wishes to quote brief passages in connection with a review.

This Burd Street Press publication
was printed by
Beidel Printing House, Inc.
63 West Burd Street
Shippensburg, PA 17257-0708 USA

The acid-free paper used in this book meets the guidelines for permanence and durability of the Committee on Production Guidelines for Book Longevity of the Council on Library Resources.

For a complete list of available publications
please write
Burd Street Press
Division of White Mane Publishing Company, Inc.
P.O. Box 708
Shippensburg, PA 17257-0708 USA

Library of Congress Cataloging-in-Publication Data

A treasury of Confederate heritage : a panorama of life in the South / edited by Walbrook D. Swank.
    p. cm. -- (Civil War heritage series ; v. 14)
ISBN 1-57249-351-8
  1. United States--History--Civil War, 1861-1865--Personal narratives, Confederate. 2. United States--History--Civil War, 1861-1865--Anecdotes. 3. United States--History--Civil War, 1861-1865--Social aspects--Anecdotes. 4. Confederate States of America--History--Anecdotes. 5. Confederate States of America--Social conditions--Anecdotes. 6. Southern States--History--1775-1865--Anecdotes. 7. Southern States--Social conditions--19th century--Anecdotes. I. Swank, Walbrook D. (Walbrook Davis) II. Series.

E484.T74 2003
975'.03--dc22

2003066165

PRINTED IN THE UNITED STATES OF AMERICA

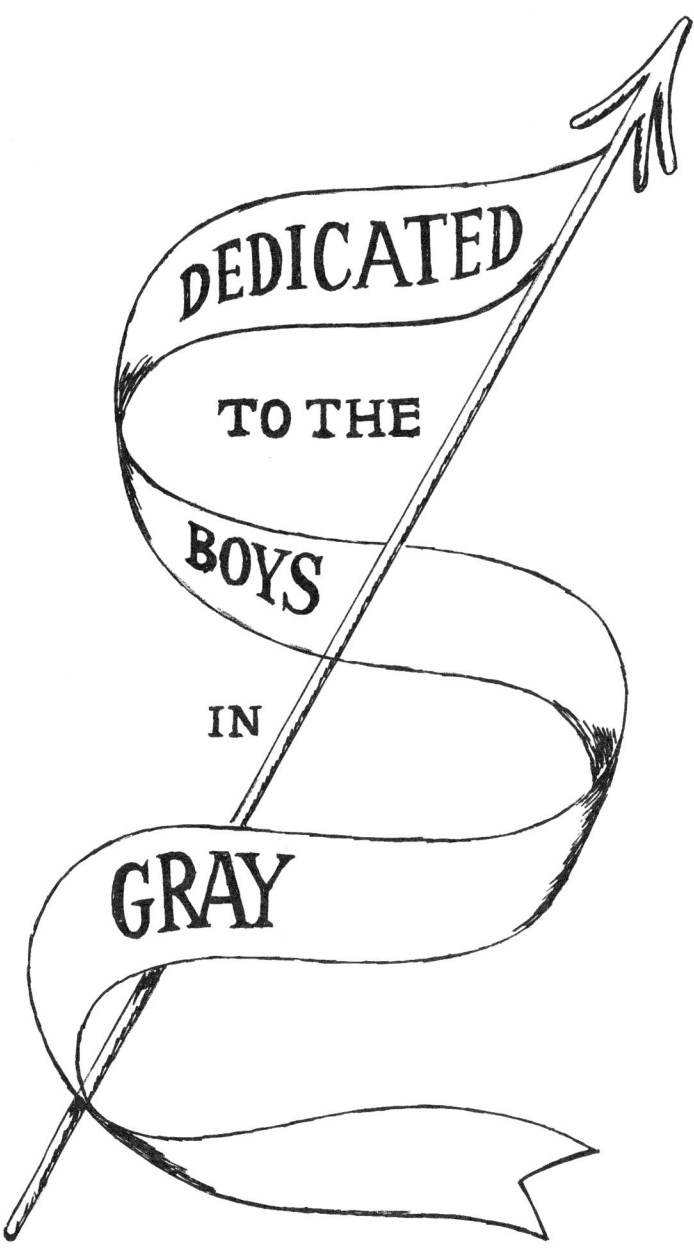

Robert B. Keller

Contents

List of Illustrations and Maps	xiii
Preface	xiv
Acknowledgments	xv
Part I: Narratives of Personal Daring and Adventure	
A Daring Feat	1
In the Wrong Place	2
A Scouting Adventure on the Peninsula	3
How Butler Was Sold	4
Just Heard the News	6
Carrying Despatches to Vicksburg	8
Easily Satisfied	11
Norah McCartey	13
A Modest Request	15
Traveling to Dixie	16
Dixie	25
A Rich Letter to George D. Prentice	26
General Bragg and the Young Officer	27
Anecdotes of General Magruder	30
General Bragg's Army	31
An Incident Under a Flag of Truce	32
A Song of the South	33
Belle Boyd in the Federal Lines	36
Southern Heroism	46
A Contraband's Description of Beauregard	47
Examining Surgeons	49
Love vs. Duty	50
Which Side?	50
Tapping the Telegraph	51
Colonel Menefee's Escape	52

Intrepid Conduct of Two Boys	53
Captain Montgomery's Adventures	54
The Song of the South	55
Negro Heroism	56
The Adventures of George N. Sanders	56
Jackson on a Retreat	59
Execution of Confederate Officers	60
A Touching Incident	66
A Full-Blooded Confederate	67
The Boy-Major	68
Hardee Outdone	68
There's Life in the Old Land Yet!	69
Not down in the "Tactics"	70
General Lee and the Officer	71
A Long Way from Headquarters	71
Belle Boyd in Prison	72
Rosecrans and the Confederate Officer	80
"Call All! Call All!"	81
Black, the Scotchman	82
A New Use for a Shell	83
An Englishman in Mississippi	84
Anecdotes of Stonewall Jackson	87
General Lee	88
Jackson at Kernstown	89
Sidney Johnson's Patriotism	89
A Slight Mistake	90
Crossing the Border	90
A Modest Wish	98
Anecdotes of General Lee	99
Stonewall Jackson and the Farmer	100
A Very Long War	101
Demoralized	101
Zollicoffer	102

Part II: The Grayjackets in Camp, Field, and Hospital

The Angel of the Hospital	103
Heroism of Southern Troops	106

Execution of Captain Webster	107
A War Picture	109
A Spicy Correspondence	113
Carrying Out His Orders	113
The Lone Sentry	114
Conscript Quakers	116
Letters to Soldiers	116
Sharp-Shooting	117
A Night Cruise in Charleston Harbor	118
Preaching Under Fire	121
"Don't Shoot There Any More—That's Father"	122
Badly Sold	123
John Pelham	124
A Just Tribute	125
Don't Belong to Butler's Army	127
Cavalry vs. Infantry	127
Destroying a Railroad	128
A Confederate Heroine	128
A Snow-Ball Battle	129
On the Battle-Field	130
The Fate of a Spy	132
The Private Soldier	134
Falling Back at the Wrong Moment	137
Somebody's Darling	137
Southern Valor	138
Mr. Davis's Trap for Grant	140
A Remarkable Adventure	140
The Closing Scenes at Shiloh	142
A Conscript Story	149
Grand Rounds	149
General Polk in a Very Tight Place	150
A Gallant Lieutenant	151
An Incident at Gettysburg	151
The Fall of Island Number Ten	152
"Stonewall Jackson's Way"	155
The Reserves at Petersburg	156

A Friendly Warning	162
Just for a Sick Man	163
Selling a Parson	164
Under Fire	164
Hard to Move	168
A Review in General Lee's Army	170
An Effort for Freedom	172
Ragged Texans—Boots and Booty	174
An Impudent Reply	175
Sad Death of a Soldier	175
Escaping from Fort Delaware	176
Endurance in Camp Life	177
Sumter in Ruins	178
Looking on at Gettysburg	179
Who Ate the Dog?	189
A Friendly Offer	190
The Neutral Cornfield	191
Life in Battery Wagner	191
Longstreet and the Spy	196
The Bible on the Battle-Field	197
General Cheatham's Escape	197
Camp Life	198
The Confederates in Maryland	201
A Story of Shiloh	204
The Band in the Pines	204
Jackson's Parting with His Old Brigade	205
The Good Samaritan	207
A Full Ration for Once	207
The Man Who Swallowed a Drum	208
The Burial of Stuart	208
The Last Six Days of the Army of Northern Virginia	211
General Green Believes He Was Shot At	220
A Hero	221
The Most Extraordinary Marches on Record	221
All Quiet Along the Potomac	222

Part III: Partisan Life and Adventure
　The Guerrillas 225
　The Capture of Catlett's Station 227
　In the Wrong Place 229
　Lieutenant McNeill's Exploit 230
　A Dutchman's Opinion of Jackson 233
　Insulting Women-Folks 234
　Anecdote of John Morgan 235
　The Marion of the War 235
　Incidents of General Morgan's Career 236
　A Brave Deed 239
　He Wanted to See Morgan 240
　Colonel Morgan Buys a Horse 242
　Quick Work 243
　One of Morgan's Exploits 243
　A Noble Deed 244
　Selling a Federal General 245
　Exploit of One of Morgan's Men 246
　The Kentucky Partisan 246
　An Honest Foe Better Than a False Friend 249
　General Morgan's Escape from the Ohio Penitentiary 250
　The Death of General Morgan 256
　A Patriotic Fellow 258
　Narrow Escape of Van Dorn 259
　Jackson's Strategy 261
　A Thrilling Event 263
　Stuart's Ride Around McClellan 264
　The Mountain Partisan 270
　Anecdote of Mosby 272
　Innocent for Once 272
　A Natural Movement 273
　A Raid into Kentucky 273
　Prompt Settlement of a Claim 284
　Not Wounded 284
　The Return 284
　A Kind of a Sentinel 285

A Friendly Warning 286
Preferred to Die On the Field 286
The Death of Ashby 287
The Romantic Mosby 289
The Bare-Footed Boys 291
Harry Gilmor Attacks the Enemy 292
General Hardee and the Arkansas Soldiers 296
Charging Endways 297
Mosby in the Federal Lines 297
Jackson 299
He Saw Jackson 299

Part IV: The Grayjackets on the High Seas
The Naval Fight on the Mississippi River 301
The Cruise of the Alabama 304
The Fight of the "Hatteras" and "Alabama" 313
The River Devils 314
Cheer Up, My Lads 315
The Attack on the Ironsides 316
The Cruise of the Florida 318
Use for Them 323
Two Things That Sounded Alike 323
A Daring Feat 324
Praise from an Enemy 326
Semmes Outwitting the Vanderbilt 326
Pleasant Hoax All Round 327
A Bold Dash 328
Anecdote of Stonewall Jackson 329
Vicksburg—A Ballad 329
The Wreck of the Vesta 331
A Burial at Sea 335
Capture of Gunboats in the Rappahannock 335
Civille Bellum 341
The Confederate Cruisers 341
Capture of the Underwriter 344
Belle Boyd Runs the Blockade 348
Capture of a Blockade Runner 352

Lucky Moment on Board the Sumter 355
Part V: Home Life in Dixie
Scene in the South Carolina Convention—Ratifying the Ordinance;
    Startling Scene 357
Prepared for It This Time 358
The Fredericksburg Exiles 358
Lines Written on the Back of a Confederate Note 361
A Spartan Dame and Her Young... 362
The Arrest of Marshal Kane 363
A Baltimore Unconquerable 364
Proof Against Federal Gallantry 367
Charleston Women Under Fire 367
Queer Drafting in Maryland 368
A Southern Scene... 368
The Death and Burial of Stuart.. 371
A Girl Worth Having 374
A Romance of the War 375
A Brave Boy 376
Quite the Youngest Recruit in the Service 376
Each For His Own Side 377
Home Life in the South 377
A Strange Resemblance 378
The Rebel Sock 379
Noble Southern Women 382
The Little Girl's Kindness to the Soldiers 383
Spirit of the Women of Virginia 383
Traveling Under a Flag of Truce 384
The Inauguration of President Davis 389
An Impudent Fellow 392
Letter From a Brave Woman 392
Spoken Like Cornelia 393
The Desolation in Tennessee 393
Ben McCulloch and Joe Baxter 395
The Empty Sleeve 396
A Narrow Escape 398
Graphic Picture of a Sacked City 399

Saw the Elephant 400
  Banished From Home 401
  A City Under Fire 401
  A Traveled Lady 406
  Impressment by Women—A Rich Scene 406
  The Evacuation of Savannah 408
  Social Life in Baltimore During the War 410
Epilogue: Postbellum North and South 420
Editor's Note 428

Illustrations and Maps

Confederate Officers	7
Valley of Virginia	28
Richmond and Petersburg to Appomattox Court House	48
Tennessee and Mississippi Area	61
Vicksburg and Port Hudson Defenses	86
Northern Virginia	95
Arkansas, Mississippi, and Louisiana Area	135
Chattanooga, Tenn., to Atlanta, Ga., Area	143
Nashville, Tenn., to Decatur, Ga., Area	169
Areas Occupied in the North by the Confederate Army	203
Mississippi and Louisiana Area	310
Chattanooga, Tenn., and North Georgia Area	334

Preface

This book with two hundred and forty-six stories is a unique and comprehensive historical narrative about the American Civil War. There has been much literature written about the War Between the States, but we are unaware of any complete comprehensive summary or record of the private life of the people of the South during the conflict.

In this volume the writer tells of the daring, the fortitude, the suffering, and heroic endeavors of the citizens, soldiers, and sailors of the South. Here are stories about valor, battlefield, camp, field and hospital incidents, guerilla exploits, home life in Dixie, and action on the high seas. Along with this we must include the wit and humor, the quaint sayings and rough camp jests and pranks that prevailed in the ranks of the armed forces.

Presented in this work are the instances of personal daring, the anecdotes, the words and actions of "The Boys in Gray," the songs and ballads, the home-life events and "internal society" in Dixie land.

The character of the men in military service is reflected in the everyday life and sayings of a society and present a more intimate knowledge of them. Four years of heroic sacrifice, glory, suffering, fortitude, and valor are interwoven in this outstanding anthology about the South and its culture.

This narrative gives the reader a rich synopsis of Southern life during the greatest period of crisis in American history.

In the literature of the Civil War this is one of the finest presentations made about the boys in gray.

Acknowledgments

I express my sincere appreciation to my friend Honorary Kentucky Colonel Quintus Massie and his wife Louise, of Louisa, Virginia, for this anthology by an unknown writer of the nineteenth century that served as the basis for this work.

Part I

Narratives of Personal Daring and Adventure

A Daring Feat

Among the many feats of personal gallantry which marked the campaign of the fall of 1862 is the following, which occurred on the night after the battle of Cedar Run.

After the battle was over for that day, four members of the twenty-seventh Va. regiment, which had participated in the hottest of the fight, took it into their heads to have a little private reconnoissance into the Yankee lines on their own account. Their names are Hospital Steward Patton, of Company D; Color-bearer Powell, of Company G; Lieutenant Edgar, of Company E; and Sergeant Davis, of Company F. The enemy had been driven three miles, and the twenty-seventh regiment was resting for the night on the remote line of the battle-field, next to their rear column. After traveling cautiously for several hundred yards without interruption, these four daring Confederate soldiers, having only two muskets in their possession, passed into the Federal lines. Shortly afterward they heard low talking in some thick underbrush, and immediately demanded: "Who's there?" "Union pickets," was the quick rejoinder. "Advance, Union pickets, throw down your arms, and surrender, or we will fire into you, for you are our prisoners," at once exclaimed Patton. "Who are you—and how many of you?" asked the "Union picket," with evident alarm. "You will soon find out," said Powell. "Wheel into line—cock your guns, and be prepared to fire at the word—steady, boys, steady!" "Hold on!" fairly shrieked the "Union pickets," "we are coming—don't fire, for God's sake!" "Come on then, at once, for we have no time to wait here in idle talk," broke in Edgar and Davis, simultaneously.

Immediately afterwards, one by one, they came forward, throwing their muskets, side arms, etc., at the feet of Powell who received them with dignity, but convulsive laughter concealed. One who seemed to be an officer stepped up to Patton and presented a brace of fine pistols and a ten dollar United States note as a bribe to let him escape.

"No, no," said Patton, "you may keep your money, but we will take both you and your pistols into our custody."

When the last of the "Union pickets" had come forward and found such a disparity in the numbers of captors and captives, for a moment he seemed to hesitate whether to yield or not. Instantly the click of two musket cocks was heard, and two muzzles pointed directly at the doubting and wavering captive. It is needless to add that no one deposited his arms on the heap quicker than he. In a few moments thereafter these four intrepid Confederate "rebels" marched into the camp of the twenty-seventh, *thirteen* captured "Union pickets," and handed them over to be sent to the rear.

IN THE WRONG PLACE

During the battles of the Wilderness, in May 1864, the gallant General Gordon, of Georgia, made a brilliant and successful attack upon the enemy's right wing, and drove it back in disorder for several miles.

When the darkness had put an end to the battle, General Gordon, accompanied only by a single courier, rode to the front to look after his pickets, and, passing them through mistake, rode into the Federal lines. Supposing them to be his own men, he rode on for some distance, when his courier said, in a low tone: "General, these are Yankees." Paying but little attention to this, he still rode on, when the courier said again: "General, I tell you these are Yankees. Can't you see their clothes are too dark for our men?" About this time the general was made aware of his critical situation by hearing all around him such calls as "Rally here, Pennsylvania regiment," etc. Preserving his presence of mind, he whispered to his courier, "Follow me quietly and without a word, Beasely"; but his uniform attracted the attention of the Federals, and they began to call out: "Who are *you*?" "Halt! halt!" etc. Seeing that he was now discovered, General Gordon threw himself upon the side of his horse, called out, "Come on, courier," and putting spurs to his gallant steed, dashed by the men into the woods and made good his escape into his own lines, unharmed by the showers of bullets sent after him.

A Scouting Adventure on the Peninsula

A correspondent of the *Selma (Ala.) Reporter*, relates the following:

I may here mention an act of bravery which is worthy the attention of the historian, whose duty it will be to chronicle the daring and gallant feats accomplished by our soldiery during this bloody struggle. It being of great importance that our Commanding General should be well informed as to the locations and numbers of the enemy's force then landing near West Point, Private Cussons and Sergeant Hartley, of our regiment, readily volunteered for this dangerous service. They were both men universally liked, and well fitted, by some experience of frontier life, for this perilous duty. They left the regiment at dusk on the evening of the 6th, armed with their trusty rifles. The night was clear, and a full moon shone on their figures as they disappeared from my view beneath the dark shadows of the woods. This was the last I saw of poor Hartley.

Pursuing their way cautiously and in silence, they soon reached the enemy's outposts, which they succeeded in safely passing. Once within the enemy's line, their progress was somewhat slow, as greater caution had to be exercised to evade the numerous pickets, which were posted through the woods. It was near midnight, when these two brave scouts reached the bank of the river. From the position they occupied, just below the crest of the bank, and within three hundred yards of the enemy, they had a fine bird's eye view of every thing that was going on. Two boats were rapidly disembarking artillery and wagons, and forty-three were lying off in the river. After remaining in this position for about half an hour, the scouts determined to pass a few hundred yards higher up the river, for the purpose of getting nearer the enemy's forces, and learning something from their conversation. To do this, it was necessary for them to withdraw from the bank, and make a detour through the woods. And while thus changing position, a most lamentable casualty occurred. Passing continuously through the deep shade of a narrow vista in the woods, just as the moon was going down, their attention was attracted by the sharp click of a gun lock, and, at the same instant, they discovered the faint outline of four of the enemy, standing within five paces of them. The scouts halted, side by side, with their guns cocked and at the "ready." After a brief pause, one of the four, who appeared to be in command, ordered the scouts to advance. Cussons replied by a demand to surrender. There was another pause; then a quick motion on the part of the Federals; then four shots, almost simultaneous, and in an instant later two more. At the first fire poor Hartley fell dead, and two of the enemy bit the dust. Cussons reloaded, and stepped behind a tree. While capping his gun at that moment, the four men on the next picket post, attracted by the firing, advanced at a run. Cussons waited until they were within about fifteen paces, and then shot down the foremost one. The others seeing their companion fall, turned and fled without firing. By this time the entire picket was aroused, and Cussons drew off some sixty or seventy yards into the woods, when he lay down and waited until the enemy had formed into squads, and carried the pursuit half a mile beyond him. He then quietly flanked up the river, and passed around them, reaching our camp about sunrise, evidently none the worse for the night's adventure. In the fight of Wednesday, our forces took the remainder of the picket (one company) prisoners, and from them we learned that two were killed and the other mortally wounded. One of the killed was orderly sergeant of the company.

How Butler Was Sold

General Butler had a dandy regiment in New Orleans—one a little nicer in uniform and personal habits than any other; and so ably commanded that it had not lost a man by disease since leaving New England. One day, the colonel of this fine regiment came to headquarters, wearing the expression of a man who had something exceedingly pleasant to communicate. It was just before the fourth of July, and this is Mr. Parton's narration of what followed:

"General," said he, "two young ladies have been to me—beautiful girls—who say they have made a set of colors for the regiment, which they wish to present on the fourth of July."

"But is their father willing?" asked the general, well knowing what it must cost two young ladies of New Orleans, at that early time, to range themselves so conspicuously on the side of the Union.

"Oh, yes," replied the colonel; "their father gave them the money, and will attend at the ceremony. But have you any objections?"

"Not the least, if their father is willing."

"Will you ride out and review the regiment on the occasion?"

"With pleasure."

So, in the cool twilight of the evening of the fourth, the general, in his best uniform, with chapeau and feathers, worn then for the first time in New Orleans, reviewed the regiment amid a concourse of spectators. One of the young ladies made a pretty presentation speech, to which the gallant colonel handsomely replied. The general made a brief address. It was a gay and joyful scene; every thing passed off with the highest *éclat*, and was chronicled with all the due editorial flourish in the *Delta*.

Subsequently, the young ladies addressed a note to the regiment, of which the following is a copy:

"New Orleans, July 5, 1862.

"Gentlemen:—We congratulate and thank you all for the manner in which you have received our flag. We did not expect such a reception. We offered the flag to you as a gift from our hearts, as a reward for your noble conduct. Be assured, gentlemen, that that day will be always present in our minds, and that we will never forget that we gave it the bravest of the brave; but if ever danger threatens your heads, rally under that banner, call again your courage to defend it, as you have promised, and remember that those from whom you received it, will help you by their prayers to win the palm of victory and triumph over your enemies. We tender our thanks to General Butler for lending his presence to the occasion, and for his courtesies to us. May he continue his noble work, and ere long may we behold the Union victorious over its foes and reunited throughout our great and glorious country. Very respectfully."

A few days later, an officer of the regiment came into the office of the commanding general, his countenance not clad in smiles. He looked like a man who had seen a ghost, or one who had suddenly heard of some entirely crushing calamity.

"General," he gasped, "we have been sold. They were Negroes!"

"What! Those lovely blondes, with blue eyes and light hair? Impossible!"

"General, it's as true as there's a heaven above. The whole town is laughing at us."

"Well," said the general, "there's no harm done. Say nothing about it. I suppose we must keep it out of the papers, and hush it up as well as we can."

They did not quite succeed in keeping it out of the papers, for one of the "foreign neutrals" of the city sent an account of the affair to the *Courier des Etats Unis*, in New York, with the inevitable French decorations.

JUST HEARD THE NEWS

When the Union troops under McClellan and Rosecrans, in the summer of 1861, were penetrating the mountain region of West Virginia, as they marched through a quiet nook on the side of Laurel Ridge, they saw a venerable matron standing in the door of a log cabin.

One of the men fell into conversation with her, and found her views on the issues of the day were not very well defined. At length he said:

"You'll not refuse to hurrah for Old Abe, will you, old lady?"

"Who's Old Abe?" asked the dame, growing more astonished every minute.

"Abraham Lincoln, President of the United States."

"Why, hain't General Washington President?"

"No! he's been dead for more than sixty years."

"General Washington dead?" she repeated in blank amazement.

Then, rushing into the cabin, she called, "Yeou Sam!—"

"Well, what is it, Mother?" said a voice within.

In a moment she reappeared with a boy of fifty, whom the men afterward learned was her son.

"Only to think, Sam," she cried excitedly, "General Washington's dead. Sakes alive! I wonder what's going to happen next."

Confederate Officers

N. Orr & Co., N.Y.

Carrying Despatches to Vicksburg

Colonel Fontaine, the father of Lamar Fontaine, the young man whose remarkable adventures are related below, gave the following description of his son's exploit to the Southern press during the war:

Lamar is almost continually in the saddle, and employed in very hazardous enterprises. His last feat of arms was the most daring he has yet performed.

He left my house, under orders from General Johnston, to bear a verbal despatch to General Pemberton, in Vicksburg, and to carry a supply of percussion caps to our troops in that besieged city. I parted with him, hardly hoping ever to see him again alive, for I knew that Vicksburg was closely invested on all sides. The enemy's lines of circumvallation extend from Snyder's Bluff, on the Yazoo, to Warrenton, on the Mississippi, and the rivers and their opposite shores are filled and lined with their forces.

He was well mounted, but was burdened with forty pounds of percussion caps, besides his blanket and crutches. He has no use of his broken leg, and cannot walk a step without a crutch; and, in mounting his horse, he has to lift it over the saddle with his right hand. But he accomplishes this operation with much dexterity, and without assistance. I loaned him a very fine sabre, with wooden scabbard, to prevent rattling, and a very reliable revolver, which has never missed fire when loaded by me.

The family were called together for prayers, and we prayed fervently that the God of our fathers would shield him from all danger, and enable him to fulfill his mission to Vicksburg successfully, and give him a safe return to us all. I then exhorted him to remember that, if it was the will of God for him to live and serve his country, all the Yankees owned by Lincoln could not kill him; but if it was the divine will that he should die, he would be in as much danger at home as in Vicksburg, and death would certainly find him, no matter where he might be. I charged him to use his best endeavors to kill every one of the jackals who should attempt to stop his course, or come within reach of his sword or pistol.

He crossed Big Black river that night, and the next day got between their lines and the division of their army, which was at Mechanicsburg. He hid his horse in a ravine, and ensconced himself in a fallen tree, overlooking the road, during that day. From his hiding place he witnessed the retreat of the Yankees, who passed him in considerable haste and confusion. After their columns had gone by, and the night had made it safe for him to move, he continued his route in the direction of Snyder's Bluff. As he entered the telegraphic road from Yazoo City to Vicksburg, he was hailed by a picket, but dashed by him. A volley was fired at him by the Yankees. He escaped unhurt; but a Minié ball wounded his horse mortally. The spirited animal, however, carried him safely to the bank of the Yazoo river, where he died, and left him afoot. He lost one of his crutches in making his escape. This was jerked from him by the limb of a tree, and he had no time to pick it up.

With the assistance of one crutch, he carried his baggage, and groped along the Yazoo, until he providentially discovered a small log canoe, tied by a rope, within his reach. He pressed this into his service, and paddled down the river, until he met three Yankee gunboats coming up to Yazoo City. He avoided them by running under some willows overhanging the water, and lying concealed until they passed. Soon afterward he floated by Snyder's Bluff, which was illuminated, and alive with Yankees and Negroes, participating in the amusement of a grand ball of mixed races. He lay flat in his canoe, which was nothing but a hollow log, and could hardly be distinguished from a piece of driftwood, and glided safely through the gunboats, transports, and barges of the amalgamationists. He reached the backwater of the Mississippi before day, and in the darkness missed the outlet of the Yazoo, and got into what is called "Old River." After searching in vain for a pass into the Mississippi, day dawned, and he discovered his mistake. He was forced to conceal his boat and himself, and lie by for another day. He had been two days and nights without food, and began to suffer the pangs of hunger.

At night he paddled back into the Yazoo, and descended it to the Mississippi, passing forty or fifty of the Yankee transports. Only one man hailed him, from the stern of a steamboat, and asked him where he was going. He replied that he was going to his fishing lines. In the bend above Vicksburg, he floated by the mortar fleet, lying flat in his canoe. The mortars were in full blast bombarding the city. The next morning he tied a white handkerchief to his paddle, raised himself up in the midst of our picket boats at Vicksburg, and gave a loud huzza for Jeff Davis and the Southern Confederacy, amid the *vivas* of our sailors, who gave him a joyful reception, and assisted him to General Pemberton's headquarters.

After resting a day and a night in the city, he started out with a despatch from General Pemberton to General Johnston. He embarked on his same canoe, and soon reached the enemy's fleet below the city. He avoided their picket boats on both shores, and floated near their gunboats. He passed so near of these that, through an open port-hole he could see men playing cards and hear them converse. At Diamond place he landed, and bade adieu to his faithful "dug-out." After hobbling through the bottom to the hills he reached the residence of a man who had been robbed by the savages of all his mules and horses, except an old worthless gelding and a half-broken colt. He gave him the choice of them, and he mounted the colt, but found that he traveled badly. Providentially he came upon a very fine horse in the bottom, tied by a blind-bridle, without a saddle. As a basket and old bag were lying near him, he inferred that a Negro had left him there, and that a Yankee camp was not far distant. He exchanged bridles, saddled the horse and mounted him, after turning loose the colt.

After riding so as to avoid the supposed position of the Yankees, he encountered one of the thieves, who was returning to it from a successful plundering excursion. He was loaded with chickens and a bucket of honey. He commenced catechizing Lamar in the true Yankee style, who concluded it best to satisfy his curiosity by sending him where he could know all that the devil could teach him. With a pistol bullet through his forehead, he left him, with his honey and poultry lying in the path, to excite the conjectures of his fellow thieves.

He approached with much caution the next settlement. There he hired a guide, for fifty dollars, to pilot him to Hankerson's ferry on Big Black River, which he wished to reach near that point, without following any road. The fellow he hired proved to be a traitor. When he got near the ferry, Lamar sent him ahead to ascertain whether any Yankees were in the vicinity. The conversation and manners of the man had excited his suspicions, and as soon as he left him he concealed himself, but remained where he could watch his return. He remained much longer than he expected; but returned and reported that the way was open, and that no Yankees were near the ferry. After paying him, he took the precaution to avoid the ferry, and to approach the river above it, instead of following the guide's directions. By this he flanked a force of the Yankees posted to intercept him; but as he entered the road near the river bank, one of them, who seemed to be on the right flank of a long line of sentinels, suddenly rose up within ten feet of him, and ordered him to halt. He replied with a pistol shot, which killed the sentinel dead, and, wheeling his horse, galloped through the bottom up the river; but the Yankees sent a shower of balls after him, two of which wounded his right hand, injuring four of his fingers. One grazed his right leg, cutting two holes through his pantaloons, and another cut through one side of my sword scabbard, spoiling its beauty, but leaving a mark which makes me prize it more highly. Seven bullets struck the horse, which reeled under him, but had strength and speed to bear him a mile from his pursuers before he fell and died. Lamar then divided his clothes and arms into packages, and swam Big Black River safely. He did not walk far before a patriotic lady supplied him with the only horse she had—a stray one, which came to her house after the Yankees had carried off all the animals belonging to the place. On this he reached Raymond at two o'clock in the morning, changed his horse for a fresh one, carried his despatch to Jackson that morning, and rejoiced us all by an unexpected visit the same day.

Easily Satisfied

Just after the battle of Prairie Grove, a meeting took place between details of Confederate and Federal officers for the purpose of arranging a cartel for the exchange of prisoners. The meeting was held at Cane Hall, Arkansas.

In a small building close on the only street of that crooked village, three Confederate officers, in their best gray uniform, were sitting on one side of a table, and three Federal officers, in blue, on the other. An old gray-headed and gray-bearded man came to the door, and incontinently walked in, with the query—

"Es this the Provo's offis?"

He was dressed in brown homespun, and had an old white wool hat on his head, tied on with a handkerchief, and he leaned on a brown stick.

"Es this the Provo's offis? I want a pass."

Some one here attempted to explain to the old gentleman that he was in the wrong shop; but the old fellow, who was a little deaf, it seems, mistook this as a hesitation to give him what he wanted.

"I'm a good l'yal citizen. I've got my pertection papers. I've been to get paid for my forage. It's all right."

There was a slight inclination to laugh by several present; but the old gentleman continued to make the most earnest protestations as to his "l'yalty."

"Look here, my friend," said Colonel W——, with a smile, "you had better take care what you say about loyalty. Look at these gentlemen"—pointing over the table—"don't you see they are Southern officers?"

The old man's hand trembled as he now adjusted a dilapidated pair of spectacles to his eyes, and closely examined the gray uniforms with the velvet collars and brass stars. His hands trembled more violently. For the time being he seemed to forget the place and surroundings in his fear and bewilderment. At last, in great distress, he turned to the gentlemen, and began to stammer out his explanations:

"Well, gentlemen, I didn't think. I—I didn't mean any thing. I've allers ben a Southern man. I've jest got one son, and he's with Marmaduke. The only other man grown that's fit for service is my darter's husband and he's with Rector, and—and—"

"Hold on, old fellow!" cried Colonel W——, "what about your being a loyal citizen?"

"Will you inform me," asked Colonel P——, who sat next to Colonel W——, "who paid you for your forage?"

The old man turned to look at t'other side of the table. Again he adjusted his spectacles, and looked at the blue coats, and in an agony of distress he took off his spectacles and his handkerchief and hat, and while he leaned on both hands on the table, the tears ran down the wrinkles of his old face.

"Well, well, gentlemen," he at last found words to say, "you go on an' fight it out among yourselves. I can live in any government."

Norah McCartey

A Reminiscence of the Missouri Campaign

Norah McCartey won by her courage the name of the *Jennie Deans* of the West. She lived in the interior of Missouri—a little, pretty, black-eyed girl, with a soul as huge as a mountain, and a form as frail as a fairy's, and the courage and pluck of a buccaneer into the bargain. Her father was an old man—a secessionist. She had but a single brother, just growing from boyhood to youthhood, but sickly and lamed. The family had lived in Kansas during the troubles of '57, when Norah was a mere girl of fourteen, or thereabouts. But even then her beauty, wit and devil-may-care spirit were known far and wide; and many were the stories told along the border of her sayings and doings. Among other charges laid to her door, it is said that she broke all the hearts of the young bloods far and wide, and tradition does even go so far as to assert that, like Bob Acres, she killed a man once a week, keeping a private church-yard for the purpose of decently burying her dead. Be this as it may, she was then, and is now, a dashing, fine-looking, lively girl, and a prettier heroine than will be found in a novel, as will be seen if the good-natured reader has a mind to follow us to the close of this sketch.

Not long after the Federals came into her neighborhood, and after they had forced her father to take the oath, which he did partly because he was a very old man, unable to take the field, and hoped thereby to save the security of his household, and partly because he could not help himself; not long after these two important events in the history of our heroine, a body of men marched up one evening, whilst she was on a visit to a neighbor's, and arrested her sickly, weak brother, bearing him off to Leavenworth City, where he was lodged in the military guard-house.

It was nearly night before Norah reached home. When she did so, and discovered the outrage which had been perpetrated and the grief of her old father, her rage knew no bounds. Although the mists were falling and the night was closing in, dark and dreary, she ordered her horse to be re-saddled, put on a thick *surtout*, belted a sash round her waist, and sticking a pair of ivory-handled pistols in her bosom, started off after the soldiers. The post was many miles distant. But that she did not regard. Over hill, through marsh, under cover of the darkness, she galloped on to the headquarters of the enemy. At last the call of a sentry brought her to a stand, with a hoarse—

"Who goes there?"

"No matter," she replied. "I wish to see Colonel Prince, your commanding officer, and instantly, too."

Somewhat awed by the presence of a young female on horseback at that late hour, and perhaps struck by her imperious tone of command, the Yankee guard, without hesitation, conducted her to the fortifications, and thence to the quarters of the colonel commanding, with whom she was left alone.

"Well, madam," said the Federal officer, with bland politeness, "to what do I owe the honor of this visit?"

"Is this Colonel Prince?" replied the brave girl, quietly.

"It is, and you are—?"

"No matter. I have come here to inquire whether you have a lad by the name of McCartey a prisoner?"

"There is such a prisoner."

"May I ask why he is a prisoner?"

"Certainly! For being suspected of treasonable connection with the enemy."

"*Treasonable* connection with the enemy! Why, the boy is sick and lame. He is besides my brother; and I have come to ask his immediate release."

The officer opened his eyes; was sorry he could not comply with the request of so winning a supplicant; and must "really beg her to desist and leave the fortress."

"I *demand* his release," cried she, in reply.

"That you cannot have. The boy is a rebel and a traitor, and unless you retire, madam, I shall be forced to arrest you on a similar suspicion."

"Suspicion! I *am* a rebel and a traitor too, if you wish; young McCartey is my brother, and I don't leave this tent until he goes with me. Order his instant release or,"—here she drew one of the aforesaid ivory handles out of her bosom and leveled the muzzle of it directly at him,—"I will put an ounce of lead in your brain before you can call a single sentry to your relief."

A picture that!

There stood the heroic girl; eyes flashing fire, cheek glowing with earnest will, lips firmly set with resolution, and hand outstretched with a loaded pistol ready to send the contents through the now thoroughly frightened, startled, aghast soldier, who cowered, like blank paper before flames, under her burning stare.

"Quick!" she repeated. "Order his release, or you die."

It was too much. Prince could not stand it. He bade her lower her infernal weapon for God's sake, and the boy should be forthwith liberated.

"Give the order first," she replied, unmoved.

And the order was given; the lad was brought out; and drawing his arm in hers, the gallant sister marched out of the place, with one hand grasping one of his, and the other holding her trusty ivory handle. She mounted her horse, bade him get up behind, and rode off, reaching home without accident before midnight.

Now that is a fact stranger than fiction, which shows what sort of metal is in our women of the much abused and traduced nineteenth century.

A Modest Request

"The Land We Love," for January 1867, relates the following rich story, upon the authority of a member of Stonewall Jackson's staff:

During the summer of 1864, while the hospitals in Richmond were crowded with wounded, the ladies of the city visited them daily, carrying with them delicacies of every kind, and vied with each other in their efforts to comfort and cheer up the wounded. On one occasion, a bright-eyed damsel of about seventeen summers was distributing flowers and speaking tender words of encouragement to those around her, when she overheard a young officer, who was suffering from his wounds, exclaim: "Oh, my Lord!" Approaching him rather timidly in order to rebuke his profanity, she said: "I think I heard you call upon the name of the Lord. I am one of his daughters. Is there any thing I can ask him for you?" A hasty glance upon her lovely face and perfect form caused his countenance to brighten, as he instantly replied: "Yes, please ask him to make me his *son-in-law.*"

Traveling to Dixie*

In about ten days I heard from Mr. Symonds. The road was not yet open, but a party was waiting to start. He had secured me a henchman in the shape of a private in an Alabama regiment, who was anxious to accompany any one south, without fee or reward. The man was said to be well acquainted with the country beyond the Potomac, besides being really honest and courageous. * * * It was necessary, of course, that my squire should be mounted, and after some deliberation it was settled that I should furnish him * * * This last negotiation concluded, I had nothing to do but to abide patiently till it pleased others to sound "boot and saddle."

I rode up to Mr. Symonds' in the afternoon of the 19th; he was absent, but his wife informed me that it was possible—though scarcely probable—that our party would start the following night. Then, for the first time, I made acquaintance with my squire for the nonce— "Alick," he was called; I cannot remember his surname—he had a rugged, honest face, and a manner to match; but I was rather disconcerted at hearing that he knew no more of riding or stable work than he had picked up in a fortnight's irregular practice in an establishment where horses as well as men were taught to "rough it" in good earnest.

I found that the party that purposed actually to cross the Potomac was, from one cause or another, reduced to four, including myself and my attendant. A cousin of Symonds', light Walter, with the same surname, was to accompany us only to our first resting place, a farm-house, about eighteen miles off. Our proposed companions were both Maryland men; one had already served for some months in a regiment of Confederate cavalry, and was returning to his duty after one of those furloughs—often self-granted—in which the borderers are prone to indulge; the other was a mere youth, and had never seen a shot fired; but a more enthusiastic recruit could hardly be conceived.

Twilight had melted into darkness long before the rest of the party arrived; then an hour or more was consumed in the last preparations and refreshments. It was fully nine o'clock, on the night of February 21st, when we started from Symonds' door, strengthened for the journey with a warm stirrup-cup, and warmer kind wishes from the family, including two *very*

---

* From *"Berder and Bastile."* By the author of *"Guy Livingstone."*

"sympathizing" damsels who had come in from neighboring homesteads to bid the southward-bound good speed.

Before we had ridden a mile, the Marylanders turned off to a house where they were to take up some letters, promising to rejoin us before we had gone a league. But we traversed more than that distance, at the slowest foot-pace, without being overtaken, and at length determined to wait for the laggards, drawing back about thirty paces off the path, into a glade where there was partial shelter from the icy wind that swept past, laden with coming snow. There we tarried for a long half-hour (told on my watch by a fusee light), and still no signs of our companions. Symonds (the cousin), who abode with us still, began to mutter doubts, and the Alabama man to grumble curses (he had ever a fatal facility in blasphemy), and I own to having entertained divers disagreeable misgivings, though I carefully avoided expressing them. At last our guide thought it best that we should make our way to a lonely farm-house, about seven miles short of our night's destinations, where, in any case, the party was to have called in passing. So we wound on through the narrow wood-paths in single file—sinking, occasionally, pastern-deep, where the thin ice over mud-holes supplanted the safe crackling snow-crests—traversing frequent fords, where rills had swollen into brooks and turbid streams; some of those gullies must have been dark even at noon-day, with overhanging cypress and pine; they were so bitterly black now that you were fain to follow close on the splash in your front, for no mortal ken could have pierced half a horse's length ahead. At length, we left the path altogether, and, pulling down a snake fence, passed through the gap into open fields. It was all plain sailing here, and a great relief after groping through the dim woodland; we encountered no obstacle but an occasional "zigzag," easily demolished, till we came to a deep hollow, where the guide dismounted—evidently rather vague as to his bearings—and proceeded to feel his way. Somewhere about here there was a "branch" (or rivulet) to be crossed, and danger of bog and marsh if you went astray. Once over, that track was easily found, and a barking chorus, performed by half-a-dozen vigilant mongrels, guided us up to the homestead we were seeking, just as the snow began to fall heavily. The stout farmer was soon on foot—men sleep lightly in these troublous times—proffering food, fire, and shelter. Our guide strongly advised our remaining there till we could gain some tiding of our lost companions; it seemed so unlikely that they should have passed or missed us on the road. He could not but fear lest accident or treachery should have detained them. He offered himself to retrace our track, and make all inquiries, which he alone could do safely. So it was settled; and after making the horses as comfortable as rude accommodations would allow, my squire and I betook ourselves to rest, not unwillingly, about three, A.M.

The traveler's first waking impulse leads him straight to the window, or to the weather-glass. I turned away from the look-out in utter disgust. A hundred yards off, through the cloud of driving snow-flakes and a level white mantle, rising up to the lower bars of the snake-fences, merged tillage into pasture undistinguishably.

A visit to the shed which sheltered our horses, did not greatly raise one's spirits. Poor Falcon was hardy as a Shetlander, and in any ordinary weather I never thought of clothing him; but no wonder he shivered there, under a rug, coated inch-deep with snow; the rough-hewn sides and crazy roof gaping with fissures a hand-breadth wide and more, were scanty defense against the furious drifts which swept through, not to be denied. I tried to comfort my horse, by chafing his legs and ears till both were thoroughly warm, setting Alick at the same task with the roan. At last we had the satisfaction of seeing both animals feed, with an appetite that I, for one, could not but envy.

About sundown, Walter returned, sorely travel-worn himself, and with an utterly exhausted horse. He had ascertained that our companions had gone on, probably to our original destination of the previous night; though why they should have passed our present resting-place without calling there, remained a mystery; nor was that point ever satisfactorily explained. To proceed at once was impossible, for a fresh horse had to be found for our guide; this a cousin of our host's offered to provide by the following evening (we could not venture to stir abroad in daylight); he also offered to make his way to the farm where the missing men were supposed to be, early in the morning, and to bring back certain intelligence of their movements. This was only one instance of the cordial kindness and hearty co-operation which I met with at the hands of these sturdy yeomen. Not only would they rise and open their doors at the untimeliest of hours, and entertain you with their choicest of fatlings, corn, and wine, but there was no amount of personal toil or risk that they would not gladly undergo to forward any southward-bound stranger on his way; nor could you have insulted your host more grossly than by hinting at pecuniary guerdon. Before midnight the snow had ceased to fall; the next morning broke bright and sunnily, though the frost still held on sharply. About four, P.M., our good-natured messenger returned; our comrades had duly reached the spot originally fixed for the Saturday night's halt, and had pursued their journey on the Sunday evening to the farm which was to be our last point before attempting the Potomac; their written explanation was very vague, but they promised to wait for us at the house they were then making for. We at once determined to press on thus far that night, though the score or more of miles of crow-flight between would certainly be lengthened at least a third, by the *detours* necessary to avoid probable pickets or outposts, and the deep snow must make the going fearfully heavy. Walter's fresh mount came down—a powerful, active mare, in good working condition, but with weak, cracked hoofs that would not have carried her a day's march on hard, stony roads.

Under the red sunset we started once more, with more good wishes; indeed, I had ridden a mile before my fingers forgot the parting hand-grip of my stalwart host.

We had one thing in our favor—the reflection from the fresh white ground-carpet would have prevented darkness, even without the light of a waxing moon. But it was slow and weary traveling. It would have been cruelty to have forced the horses beyond a walk through snow that in places was over their knees; besides which, we dared not risk a jingle of stirrup or bridle-bit, where an out-lying picket might be within ear-shot. Twice we passed within twenty yards of where the fresh track showed that the patrol had recently turned at the end of his beat; but the guide knew the country thoroughly.

In spite of a warm riding-cloak and a casing of chamois leather from neck to ankle, I felt sometimes chilled to the marrow; my lips would hardly close round the pipe-stem: and even while I smoked, the breath froze on my moustache stiff and hard. Walter himself suffered a good deal in hands and feet; but the Alabama man, utterly unused to the lower extremes of temperature, only found relief from his misery in an occasional drowsiness that made him sway helplessly in his saddle. The last league of our route lay through the White Grounds. The valley of the Potomac widens here toward the north, and six thousand acres of forest stretch away—unbroken, save by rare islets of clearings. There was no visible track; but our guide struck boldly across the woodlands, taking bearings by certain landmarks and the steady moon. It was not dark even here; but low sweeping boughs and fallen trunks, often hidden by snow, made the traveling difficult and dangerous. I ceased not to abjure Alick, who followed close in my rear, to keep fast hold of his horse's head. I doubt if he ever heard me, for he never intermitted a muttered running fire of the most horrible execrations that I ever listened to, even in this hard-swearing country. Whether this ebullition of blasphemy comforted him at the moment I cannot say; but if "curses come home to roost," a black brood was hatched that night, unless one whole page be blotted out from the register of the Recording Angel.

Both men and horses rejoiced, I am sure, when, about two, A.M., we broke out into a wide clearing, and drew rein under the lee of outbuildings surrounding the desired homestead. The farmer was soon aroused, and came out to give us a hearty though whispered welcome. It is not indiscreet to record *his* name, for he has already "dree'd his doom"; he was noted among his fellows for cool determination in purpose and action, and truly, I believe that the yeomanry of Maryland counts no honester or bolder heart than staunch George Hoyle's.

Our last companions were sleeping placidly up-stairs—that was the best intelligence that our host could give us. He laughed at the idea of fording the Potomac, declaring that no living man or horse could stand, much less swim, in the stream. Knowing the character of the man, and his thorough acquaintance with the locality, one ought to have accepted his decision unquestioned; but I was not then so inured to disappointment as I became in later days, and wished to see for myself how the water lay. After a short sleep and hurried breakfast, Hoyle took me to a point whence we looked down on a long reach of the river. At the first glance through my field-glasses, every vestige of hope vanished. The fierce current—its sullen neutral tint checkered with frequent foam clots—washed and weltered high against its banks, eddying and breaking savagely wherever it swept against jut of ground or ledge of rock, while ever and anon shot up above the turbid surface, tossing trunk of uprooted alder or willow.

It was waste of time to look longer, so in no pleasant mood, I returned to the farm-house, where a council of war was incontinently held. The

Marylanders had already arranged their plan; they had a vague idea of some ferry to the northward, and intended to grope their way to it somehow. Before attempting this, it was necessary to divest themselves of any suspicious articles. They meant to assume the character of small cattle-dealers, and as fast as appearance went, succeeded perfectly. Their horses were passably hardy and active, but stunted, mean-looking animals, while the saddle-gear would have been dear, anywhere, at five dollars. The men themselves had the lazy, slouching look peculiar to the hybrid class with which they wished to be identified. They were civil, and sorry enough about the turn affairs had taken, but evidently quite determined that we should part company.

There was no sort of contract between us, nor any promise of remuneration; I only rode by sufferance in that company. I do not think I should have pressed the point, even had I been in a position to do so; as it was, I yielded with good grace, only begging my late companions to let me have the earliest information as to the route, if they succeeded in getting through. This they readily promised; so, with the concurrence of the good Walter, I determined to fall back, for the present, on my original "base," with the consoling reflection that I was only imitating the most renowned Federal commandeers.

All this was scarcely settled, when our host hurried in—rather a blank look on his bold face—to say that one of his contrabands had just come in, after an absence of two hours: he had taken one of his master's horses without leave and absolutely declined to state where, or why, he had gone. As 1,800 Federals, including a regiment of cavalry, occupied Poolsville—only six miles off—it was easy to guess in what direction the "colored person" had wandered. There was no time for argument, and even chastisement was reserved for a more fitting season; in fifteen minutes more, we had ridden swiftly across the cleared lands, and, with Hoyle for our pilot, were winding through the ravines and glades of the White Grounds. The day was dull and cloudy: so, having no sun to guide us, we, the strangers, speedily lost all idea of direction; even Walter, the confident, owned himself fairly puzzled. But our host led on at a steady pace, never pausing to consult landmarks or memory; evidently every bush and brake was familiar to him; there was not the ghost of a track, but we seemed generally to follow the winding of a rapid, shallow stream, up whose channel we often scrambled for forty yard or more.

>We had na ridden a league, a league,
>O' leagues but barely three.

when we struck a path leading straight through the woods to Clarksburg—the first point on the proposed route of the two Marylanders: they meant to feel their way cautiously thence in a northwesterly direction; the elder had one or two acquaintances in the neighborhood of Frederick City that he hoped would assist them. So, with leave-takings, hurried but amicable, our party separated. We, the other three, proposed to make for our quarters of the last Sunday, and for ten miles further our kind host rode in our company, absolutely refusing to turn back till we were in a country that Walter knew right well, and might be considered comparatively safe; then he left us, proposing to return home by another and yet more circuitous route, so as to baffle possible pursuers. He did get home safe, but was arrested within the same week—not, I trust, before he had moderately chastised that treacherous contraband—and we met, two months later, in the Old Capitol.

Three hours more riding, brought us within sight of the town, where we intended to refresh ourselves and our cattle, and perhaps to abide for the night. We relied so implicitly on the hospitality we were certain to find, that we had provided ourselves with no food of any sort; my flask, too, had been emptied on the previous night. Fancy our disgust, when we found the shutters closed, every thing carefully locked up, and no living soul about the place, but two helpless little colored persons of tender age. The whole family had gone out on a "sledging" frolic, and would not return before late at night; it was the past—P.M.; we had breakfasted lightly at seven, and been in the saddle ever since nine o'clock. We did discover some Indian corn for the horses, and left them to feed under their old shed, only removing bridles and loosening girths.

About ten minutes later, we were sitting under the house porch—it was narrow and deep, as is the fashion in those parts, and boarded up the sides breast high—I was lighting a sullen pipe, hoping to deaden the hungry cravings which could not be satisfied, when I felt my arm pulled violently; a hoarse whisper said in my ear, "By G——d , they've got us," and turning, I met the good Walter's face, white, and convulsed with emotions which I care not to define or remember. Alick was already crouching below the boarding, and I stooped too, mechanically; as I did so, I followed the direction of my guide's haggard eyes; by my faith, just where the wood opened on the clearing, about one hundred and eighty yards to our front, there sat on their horses six Federal dragoons, surveying the landscape with some interest. It was very odd to see them gazing straight down upon us, evidently unconscious of our proximity; but they were looking from light into the shadow of the porch; fortunately too, the horses were well under cover. It chanced that close to the gate in the outermost inclosure there was a watering pond; around and from this, tracks of all kinds of cattle crossed and diverged in every direction; as we entered we had remarked many hoof-prints turning abruptly to the right, probably left by the sleighing party. The dragoons halted five minutes or so, in consultation; then they turned and rode off quickly along that same right hand track. The house was so evidently shut up, that I presume they thought it would be wasted time, if they searched it then.

Resistance would have been utterly out of the question; so we prepared for escape instantly. I had to go round to the back of the house to get my hunting cap, which I left there. When I came out I found Walter already mounted; his mare was not in the same shed with our horses. In a few hurried words he explained that it would be best for *him* to make off at once, and wait for us in the woods below, to which the clearing sloped down from the homestead. Though I had before formed my own opinion as to his vaunted valiance, I confess I *was* rather disappointed; but he was not a hireling, and I had no right to prevent him from looking after his own safety first; I only shrugged my shoulders without replying, and went into the other shed to help Alick saddle up. The Alabamian was much less delicate or more determined than myself; when he heard of Walter's intentions, his face darkened threateningly.

"By the ——!" he said, "he ain't going to quit after that fashion" and as he went out toward the corner where Walter still lingered, I saw his hand shift back to the butt of my revolver. Now, I was too sensible of the guide's good intentions and disinterested kindness to wish to press hardly on a temporary loss of nerve, so I busied myself with buckle and curb-link, and refrained from assisting at the debate; it was very brief, nor can I say if Alick's arguments were intimidating or conciliatory; I rather suspected the former, from the expression of his face when he returned, simply remarking, "I've made it all right, Major. He stops with us as long as we want him to."

Ten minutes afterward we gained the shelter of the woods, and, keeping always well down in the gullies or hollows, were picking our way in a direction nearly parallel to that taken by our pursuers. This was our only course, as we dared not show ourselves as yet across open ground or along traveled roads. We might have ridden about a league and a half—it is difficult to judge distance in thick cover and over broken ground, when the pace is so constantly varied—our guide's confidence began to return, and, with it, his weakness for self-laudation. He began once more to recount his many narrow escapes, and was sanguine as to his chance of pulling through this—the closest shave of all. We were halting on the bank of a muddy, swollen stream, in some doubt whether we should try the treacherous bottom there or higher up, when, looking over my shoulder, I saw the figures of four horsemen, looming large against the red evening sky as they passed slowly across the sky line, on the crest of some abrupt rising ground about three hundred yards to our right: soon two or more showed themselves, making the pursuing party complete; they were evidently retracing their steps—for what reason I know not. Almost at the same instant, the Alabamian caught sight of the enemy; but before he could speak I touched our guide on the shoulder with my hunting whip, pointing in the direction of the danger. If you ever saw a wing-tipped mallard's flurry when the retriever comes upon him unawares, you will have a good idea of how the valiant Walter "squattered" through the ford. The twilight was darkening fast, and in the shadow of the ravine, we were almost safe from the eyes of our pursuers; but I marvel that, even at such a distance, their ears were not attracted by the flounder and the splash. My squire and I followed more leisurely.

This was our last look at the dragoons. We learned afterward that, later in the evening, they searched the farm house (the family had just returned), and not only struck our trail through the woods, but held it within three miles of our resting place for the night; there, the numerous cross roads, and the utter confusion of many tracks, baffled our pursuers, probably, too, their horses by that time were in poor condition for following up an indefinite chase.

Alick and I determined to push for our original starting point—the house of Symonds of that ilk. Another two hours riding brought us to where a lane turns off toward Bon Gualtier's home. He was evidently anxious to find himself a free agent, and this time even the Alabamian did not seek to detain him. The rest of the road we had traversed, on the preceding Saturday, and we could hardly miss our way. So there I parted from my honest guide, with many kind wishes on his side, and hearty thanks on mine. I rather repent having alluded to that little nervousness; but, after all, it was hardly a question of physical courage; we sought to avoid imprisonment, not peril to life or limb.

My stout horse, Falcon, strode cheerily over the last of those dark, tiresome miles without a stumble or sign of weariness; but the roan's ears were drooping, and he slouched along heavily on his shoulders long before we saw the lights of Symonds' homestead, where we met a hearty if not a joyful welcome. We had not tasted food for thirteen hours, during which we had scarcely been out of the saddle; so even disappointment could not prevent our relishing to the uttermost the savory supper with which our hostess would fain have comforted us.

DIXIE

BY FANNY DOWNING

Created by a nation's glee,
With jest, and song, and revelry,
We sang it in our early pride
Throughout our Southern borders wide,
While from ten thousand throats rang out
A promise in one glorious shout
    "To live or die for Dixie!"

How well that promise was redeemed,
Is witnessed by each field where gleamed
Victorious—like the crest of Mars—
The banner of the Stars and Bars!
The cannons lay our warriors low—
We fill the ranks and onward go,
    "To live or die for Dixie!"

To die for Dixie! —Oh, how blest
Are those who early went to rest,
Nor knew the future's awful store,
But deemed the cause they fought for sure
As heaven itself, and so laid down
The cross of earth for glory's crown,
    And nobly died for Dixie.

> To live for Dixie—harder part!
> To stay the hand—to still the heart—
> To seal the lips, enshroud the past—
> To have no future—all o'ercast—
> To knit life's broken thread again,
> And keep her mem'ry pure from stain—
> > This is to live for Dixie.
>
> Beloved land! Beloved song,
> Your thrilling power shall last as long—
> Enshrined within each Southern soul—
> As time's eternal ages roll;
> Made holier by the test of years—
> Baptized with our country's tears—
> > God and the right for Dixie!

A Rich Letter to George D. Prentice

The Louisville Journal published the following letter, which it declared to be genuine:

> Lexington, Ky., *Aug.* 4, 1863

George D. Prentice, Esq.

How are you, old George, anyhow? I have just come from a visit to our old city, George, after an absence of two years or more in the Confederate army. Brigadier-General John H. Morgan's command, a particular favorite of yours, I believe. Nothing would have given me more pleasure, old fellow, than to have paid you a call, and have had a social chat with you. After due consideration I thought it would not have been healthy; so I contented myself with a passing look at your noble countenance. How handsome you have grown, George.

"The Captain with his whiskers took a sly glance at me," (old song.) George, your detectives ain't worth a damn. I splurged around in Cincinnati for a week or more before coming to your city. Birney's orders have not killed all the secesh there yet. Didn't they spread themselves to put me through in royal old style! I came to your office, old fellow, bought a newspaper, saw Ellsworth's lightning machine, and several other curiosities you have there; adjourned to Walker's, took a mint julep; went to Hotel de Raine, took several juleps. Mighty refreshing, George, after an absence in Dixie for several years. Mr. Bragg don't allow any such luxuries in his department, you know.

You may want to know what the hell I was doing up there. I will tell you; I will tell you all the particulars. I was gobbled up at Buffington's Island. Having on a very genteel suit of citizen's clothes, on the wharf at Cincinnati, somehow or other I got mixed up with the guard. They knew that I was a citizen, and ordered me back among the crowd—bully!

Now, George, to biz. You have been taunting General John since he had been in prison, about having his head shaved, wearing striped clothes, etc. Now, old fellow, the quieter you keep the better for you; you are going to turn up missing some of these fine mornings—spirited away to Dixie. I will be very sorry to have to do it, but, by the Eternal God, you shall be scalped—no idle threat, George.

You came very near going up awhile back. A little trap was fixed for you so nice, but fortunately for you, you started to New York unexpected to us—mighty mean in you, George. All of your men are not such damn mean fellows; one of them was kind enough to leave his horse standing on the street here for me, fully equipped with saddle, bridle, holsters, etc. I've got him, and by the time you get this, will be far away in Dixie.

Farewell, old boy, until I get you. By-the-by, have you any word for Clarence, or any of your former friends in the Confederacy?

Yours, as ever,   ——F——.
Captain and A.D.C. to General J. H. Morgan,
C.S.A.

GENERAL BRAGG AND THE YOUNG OFFICER

An officer in General Bragg's army had obtained a short leave of absence to permit him to go home and attend to personal interest demanding his presence. Before his time of absence had expired, he requested a further leave of absence for thirty days, and promised to return a better soldier

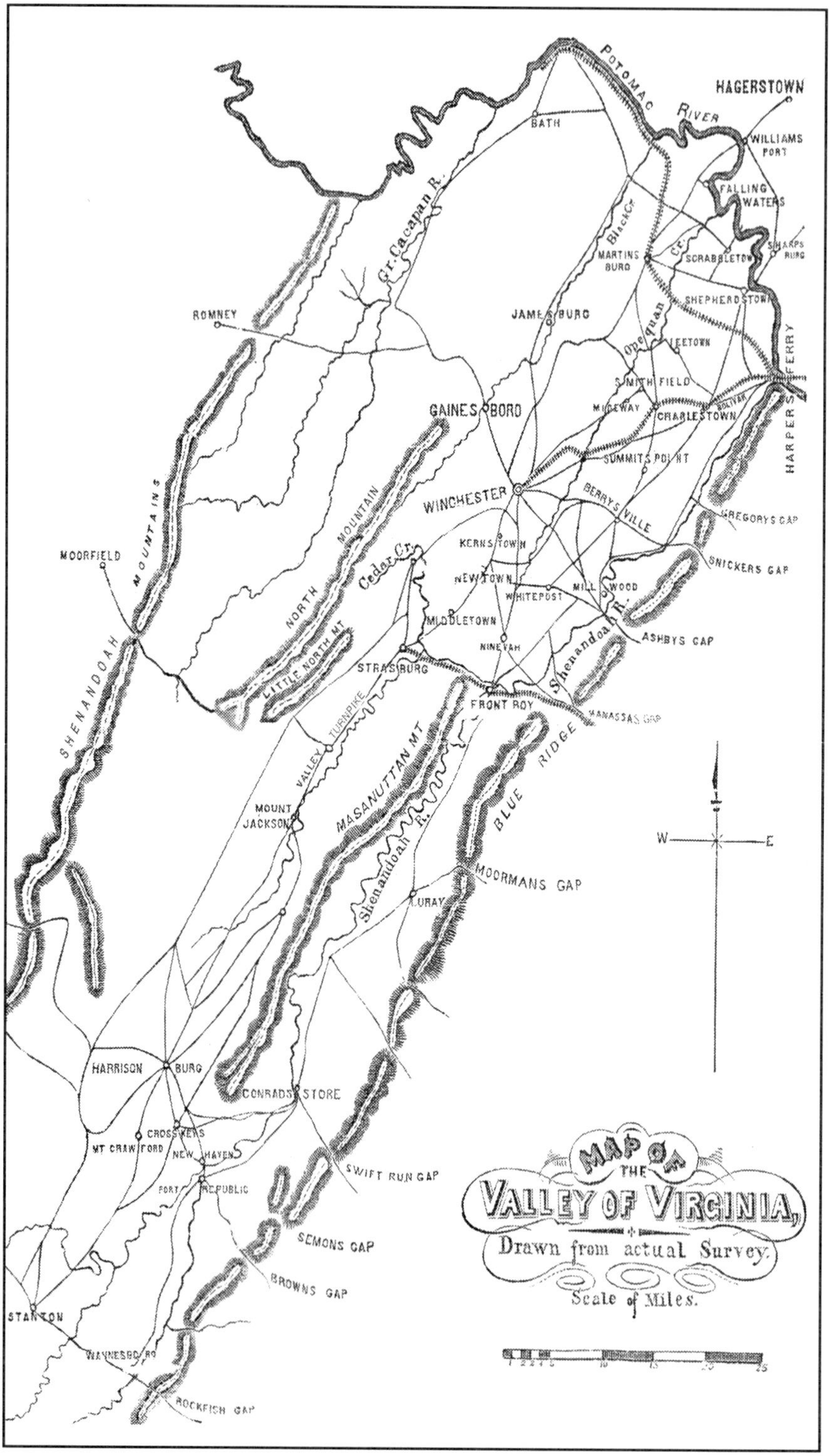
MAP OF
THE
VALLEY OF VIRGINIA,
Drawn from actual Survey.
Scale of Miles.
POTOMAC RIVER
HAGERSTOWN
WILLIAMS PORT
FALLING WATERS
SHARPS BURG
BATH
Gr. Cacapan R.
Black Cr.
MARTINS BURG
SCRABBLETOWN
SHEPHERDSTOWN
HARPERS FERRY
BOLIVAR
ROMNEY
JAMES BURG
Opequan Cr.
LEETOWN
SMITH FIELD
MIDDEWAY
CHARLESTOWN
GAINES BORO
SUMMITS POINT
WINCHESTER
BERRYS VILLE
GREGORYS GAP
SNICKERS GAP
KERNS TOWN
NEW TOWN
WHITEPOST
MILL WOOD
MOORFIELD
MOUNTAINS
NORTH MOUNTAIN
Cedar Cr.
MIDDLETOWN
NINEVAH
ASHBYS GAP
LITTLE NORTH MT
STRASBURG
Shenandoah R.
FRONT ROY
MANASSAS GAP
SHENANDOAH
VALLEY TURNPIKE
MASANUTTAN MT
BLUE RIDGE
MOUNT JACKSON
W
E
MOORMANS GAP
LURAY
Shenandoah R.
HARRISON BURG
CONRADS STORE
CROSS KEYS
MT CRAWFORD
NEW HAVEN
SWIFT RUN GAP
FORT REPUBLIC
SEMONS GAP
BROWNS GAP
STANTON
WAYNESBORO
ROCKFISH GAP

than he had ever been before. His request was approved by the various officers in command over him, who knew him to be a true and faithful man, and finally by General Bragg. Before the thirty days' time had granted expired, he again forwarded a communication desiring a still further leave. His officers were astonished at his impudence and audacity, and each one in turn, through whose hands it passed, marked it "disapproved." Before the communication reached army headquarters, General Bragg was the recipient of a letter from this officer, who stated that he had made application for further leave, and gave as a reason that while our army was further advanced he had become engaged to a young lady from whom he had received a letter, which he enclosed. This delicate missive contained a sad and touching farewell to the young officer who had gained her affections. She explained that since the enemy had gained her homestead they had destroyed her property, taken every thing from her, and well-nigh made her penniless.

When she had engaged herself to her lover, she was the possessor of property, and was in different circumstances. With this state of things existing, hard as she felt would be the trial to her, she had determined to release the object of her affections from an engagement made in her prosperity. This noble missive was couched in such loving and gentle, though prudent and touching language, which it might well have drawn tears from the iron warrior to whom it was presented. The officer added that misfortunes of his affianced had only the more endeared her to him, and this manifestation of her disinterested love and spirit had only inspired a stronger affection for so noble a woman. He desired a still further holiday that he might go to her and marry her, proving that his love was as pure as her own, and by making her his wife, endow his property upon her in case he was made the victim of a bullet. General Bragg sent directions to his bureau officer to send him the communication so soon as it should arrive, and regardless of the endorsement of "disapproved," made by officers unaware of the circumstances, he marked it "Granted for thirty days," and indorsed upon the letter: "The lady is worthy the best and bravest soldier, and from what I learn I believe you are worthy of the lady.
BRAXTON BRAGG."

ANECDOTES OF GENERAL MAGRUDER

Just after the battle of Williamsburg, General Magruder and his staff stopped at the house of a widow lady on the road, and engaged dinner. Soon after their arrival a Louisiana soldier came up, and accosted the landlady with:

"Madam, can I get dinner?"

"Yes, sir," was the reply; "but as I am preparing dinner for General Magruder and staff, and have not room at my table for more, you will have to wait for a second table."

"Very well, ma'am. Thank you," said the soldier, taking his seat in a position to command a view of the dining room. Watching the movement of the servants, he waited until the feast was on the table, and while his hostess proceeded to the parlor to announce dinner to her distinguished guest, he entered the dining room, and, seating himself at the table, awaited further developments, trusting to his impudence to get him out of the scrape.

Upon the entrance of the party of officers, there were found to be seats for all but one, and one politely returned to the parlor to wait. The general took a seat next to the soldier, and, after the first course was finished, turned to him and asked:

"Sir, have you any idea with whom you are dining?"

"No," coolly replied the soldier; "I used to be very particular on that score; but since I turned soldier I don't care whom I eat with, so that the victuals are clean."

The joke was so good that Magruder laughed heartily at it, and even paid for the soldier's dinner and sent him on his way.

Another story, which is not so reliable, is as follows:

Among the men who composed the gallant little "Army of the Peninsula," was one private Winship Stedman, a member of a North Carolina regiment. Stedman being fond of his "glass" and being depressed at the deprivation of it, to which army discipline forced him to submit, several times complained that he did not think it fair that General Magruder should drink all the liquor in Yorktown. One day, after Stedman had performed an act of great gallantry, in the scouting party from Bethel Church, he was commanded to appear before the general, and the order was enforced by a section of soldiers. He was unable to decide whether he was to be shot or reprimanded, until he reached the General's tent, and was sternly addressed thus:

"Private Stedman, I understand that you have said that Old Magruder drinks all the liquor in Yorktown, and wont let you have a drop. You shall say so no longer, sir. Walk in and take a drink. I commend you for your bravery."

General Bragg's Army

General Bragg's rigid discipline and many reverses seriously affected his popularity with his men. While his troops were on the retreat from Murfreesboro', ragged, hungry, and weary, they straggled along the road for miles, with an eye to their own comfort, but a most unmilitary neglect of rules and regulations. Presently one of them espied, in the woods near by, a miserable broken down mule, which he at once seized and proceeded to put to his use, by improvising, from stray pieces of rope, a halter and stirrups. This done, he mounted, with grim satisfaction, and pursued his way. He was a wild Texas tatterdemalion, bareheaded, barefooted, and wore, in lieu of a coat, a rusty-looking hunting shirt. With hair unkempt, beard unshorn, and face unwashed, his appearance was grotesque enough; but, to add to it, he drew from some receptacle his corncob pipe, and made perfect his happiness by indulging in a comfortable smoke.

While thus sauntering along, a company of bestarred and bespangled horsemen—General Bragg and staff—rode up, and were about to pass on, when the rather unusual appearance of the man attracted their notice. The object of their attention, however, apparently neither knew nor cared to know them, but looked and smoked ahead with careless indifference.

"Who are you?" asked the major general.

"Nobody," was the answer.

"Where did you come from?"

"Nowhere."

"Where are you going?"

"I don't know."

"Where do you belong?"

"Don't belong anywhere."

"Don't you belong to Bragg's army?"

"Bragg's army! Bragg's army!" replied the chap. "Why, he's got no army! One half of it he shot in Kentucky, and the other half has just been whipped to death at Murfreesboro'."

Bragg asked no more questions, but turned and spurred away.

An Incident under a Flag of Truce

The late war witnessed many instances in which brother was unwittingly arrayed against brother, and father against son in the same battle. The following is an illustration of this, and is taken from a Northern newspaper:

Lieutenant-Commander H. A. Adams, Jr., United States Navy, has arrived at New Orleans, having been relieved of the command of the United States forces in Mississippi Sound by Lieutenant-Commander Green. He recently sent his boat on shore, and desired the officer in charge to say that if any military officer received the flag, he would be glad to see him on board to arrange the business of the truce. As the boat returned, he saw an officer who appeared to recognize him, but he could not make out who he was. When the boat came alongside he went to the gangway to receive the stranger, and even helped him over the rail on deck, when he immediately found himself clasped in the arms of his own brother—one in command of the Confederate forces on shore, the other in command of the United States forces afloat. The meeting, under such circumstances, was, as you may imagine, a very painful one. After the business was over, and a brotherly chat had, they parted, the Confederate saying, as he got into the boat, "Whatever happens, Hal, recollect one thing—we will always be brothers." Both are sons of Commodore Adams, United States Navy.

A Song of the South

"It may be necessary to put the foot down firmly."—Mr. Lincoln

"Tramp—tramp—tramp."—Burger's Leonora.

  The legion is armed for the battle,
    The charger is hot for the fray,
  The thunders of musketry rattle,—
    You eagle shall feast on the prey;
  The corslets like diamonds are gleaming,
    The standard of blood is unfurled:
  Yes, put the foot down, Mr. Lincoln,
    And trample them out of the world!

  The hosts of the West are in motion,
    The North sends a ravenous pack:
  Like waves on the pitiless ocean,
    When the heavens above them are black,
  They surge over mountain and prairie,—
    Wild billows the tempests has curled:
  Yes, put the foot down, Mr. Lincoln.
    And trample them out of the world!

  The stars in their courses are silent,
    The willows in agony weep,
  The wind o'er the wave murmurs sadly,
    Where the ashes of Washington sleep;
  The cypress is shaken with horror,
    The glory of morning is furled;
  Yes, put the foot down, Mr. Lincoln,
    And trample them out of the world!

In the chambers once vocal with music,
    And drunk with the eloquent word,
The clarion now screams for the conflict,
    And the terrible tocsin is heard:
A torrent is chafing its channel
    Where only a rivulet purled:
So put the foot down, Mr. Lincoln,
    And trample them out of the world!

Weak in the clouds like Antaeus,
    Strong upon touching the earth,
Stormy as Castor and Pollux,
    Twins of Olympian birth;
Blazing with lives like the lightnings
    Jove at Prometheus hurled:
Put the foot down, Mr. Lincoln,
    And trample them out of the world!

What though the land is in sackcloth,
    What though each minstrel is dumb:
And through sweet Wyoming's valleys
    Echoes the roll of the drum;
What though from city and hamlet
    Tears and entreaties are poured;
Put the foot down, Mr. Lincoln,
    Slaughter the dove with the sword!

Attila, fearful destroyer,
    Merciless Genghis Khan,
Veiled like the sage of Khorassan,
    Utter the truculent ban;
Bright as St. George in his armor,
    With blood-red cross unfurled,
Trample the insolent dragon,
    Trample it out of the world.

On the rice-fields of fair Carolina
    The head of the matron is bowed:
And the sire takes down the old flint-lock,
    And back the old memories crowd.
He thinks of the glory of Sumter,
    The valor of Marion's men,
And his heart leaps the gulf in an instant,
    That yawns 'tween the now and the then.

The daughters of Georgia are weeping,
    Though Ramah's sad voices are stilled;
For the earliest violets are peeping
    Where their lovers' hearts' blood shall be spilled:
Her yeomen all chant the bold stanzas,
    Of tyrants to infamy hurled;
But, put the foot down, Mr. Lincoln,
    And trample them out of the world.

The rangers of Texas are mounting,
    And will presently scour the plain;
And, brave for their homes and their kindred,
    Will cover the field with the slain:
Marked you the dark-flashing eye ball,
    And the lip that so scornfully curled?
Then plant the foot firm, Mr. Lincoln,
    And trample them out of the world!

Florida, gem of the ocean,
    Bride of the wondering sea,
Through thy sons' ardent devotion,
    Born to be dauntless and free:
Thy fame is as bright as thy coastland
    With diamond shell impearled,
But put the foot down, Mr. Lincoln,
    And trample her out of the world!

Soft is thy name, Alabama,
    And soft is thy flower-laden gale,
As it breathes over rustling woodlands,
    And whitens the prospered sail,
Like yonder stricken wild-fowl
    With bleeding pinion furled,
The glory is soon to be smitten,
    And trampled out of the world.

Beautiful Louisiana,
    Queen of the river and plain,
Blooming with verdant savannah,
    Rich with the tropical cane;
Over thee floats the proud emblem
    Now on the breezes unfurled,
That dares the unfeeling oppressor
    To trample thee out of the world.

From thy glad fertile realm, Mississippi,
    Where cotton is picked by the slave,
The paean ascendeth to heaven,
    Of liberty won by the brave.
As a sound of tumultuous waters
    Comes the din of the camp and the roar
Of voices that rise on the tempest,
    Shouting *we'll* be slaves nevermore!

BELLE BOYD IN THE FEDERAL LINES*

A few days after my arrival at Front Royal, a battle was fought close by at Keructown… When I found that the Confederate forces were retreating so far down the valley, and reflected that my father was with them, I

---

* From *"Belle Boyd in Camp and Prison,"* written by herself.

became very anxious to return to my mother; and, as no tie of duty bound me to Front Royal, I resolved upon the attempt at all hazards.

I started in company with my maid, and had got safely without adventure of any kind as far as Winchester, when some unknown enemy or some malicious neutral denounced me to the authorities as a Confederate spy.

Before, however, this act of hostility or malice had been perpetrated, I had taken the precaution of procuring a pass from General Shields; and I fondly hoped that this would, under all circumstances, secure me from molestation and arrest; for I was not aware that, while I was in the very act of receiving my bill of "moral health," an order was being issued by the Provost-Marshal which forbade me to leave the town.

When the hour which I had fixed for my departure arrived, I stepped into the railways cars, and was congratulating myself with the thought that I should ere long be at home once more, and in the society of those I loved, when a Federal officer, Captain Bannon, appeared. He was in charge of some Confederate prisoners, who, under his command, were *en route* to the Baltimore prison.

I was more surprised than pleased when, handing over the prisoners to a subordinate, he walked straight up to me and said:——

"Is this Miss Belle Boyd?"

"Yes."

"I am the Assistant-Provost, and I regret to say, orders have been issued for your detention, and it is my duty to inform you that you cannot proceed until your case has been investigated: so you will, if you please, get out, as the train is on the point of starting."

"Sir," I replied, presenting him General Shields's pass, "here is a pass which I beg you will examine. You will find that it authorizes my maid and myself to pass on any road to Martinsburg."

He reflected for some time, and at last said:—

"Well, I scarcely know how to act in your case. Orders have been issued for your arrest, and yet you have a pass from the General allowing you to return home. However, I shall take the responsibility upon my shoulders, convey you with the other prisoners to Baltimore, and hand you over to General Dix."

I played my *role* of submission as gracefully as I could; for where resistance is impossible, it is still left the vanquished to yield with dignity.

The train by which we traveled was the first that had been run through from Wheeling to Baltimore since the damage done to the permanent way by the Confederates had been repaired.

We had not proceeded far when I observed an old friend of mine, Mr. M., of Baltimore, a gentleman whose sympathies were strongly enlisted on the side of the South. At my request, he took a seat beside me, and, after we had conversed for some time upon different topics, he told me, in a whisper, that he had a small Confederate flag concealed about his person.

"Manage to give it me," I said; "I am already a prisoner; besides, free or in chains, I shall always glory in the possession of the emblem."

Mr. M. watched his opportunity, and, when all eyes were turned from us, he stealthily and quickly drew the little flag from his bosom and placed it in my hand.

We had eluded the vigilance of the officer under whose surveillance I was traveling; and I leave my readers to imagine his surprise, when I drew it forth from my pocket and with a laugh waved it over our heads with a gesture of triumph. It was a daring action, but my captivity had, I think, superadded the courage of despair to the hardihood I had already acquired in my country's service.

The first emotions of the Federal officer and his men were those of indignation; but better feelings succeeded, and they allowed it was an excellent joke that a convoy of Confederate prisoners should be brought in under a Confederate flag, and that flag raised by a lady.

Upon our arrival at Baltimore I was taken to the Eutaw House, one of the largest and best hotels in the city, where, I must in justice say, I was treated with all possible courtesy and consideration; and permission to see my friends was at once and spontaneously granted.

As soon as it was known that I was in Baltimore, a prisoner and alone, I was visited not merely by my personal friends, but by those who knew me by reputation only; for Baltimore is Confederate to its heart's core.

I remained a prisoner in the Eutaw House about a week; at the expiration of which time, General Dix, the officer in command, having heard nothing against me, decided to send me home. I arrived safely at Martinsburg, which is now occupied in force by the Federal troops.

Here I was placed under a strict surveillance, and forbidden to leave the town. I was incessantly watched and persecuted; and at last the restriction imposed upon me became so irksome and vexatious, that my mother resolved to intercede with Major Walker, the Provost-Marshal, on my behalf. The result of this intercession was, that he granted us both a pass, by way of Winchester, to Front Royal, with a view to my being sent on to join my relations at Richmond.

Upon arriving at Winchester we had much difficulty in getting permission to proceed; for General Shields had just occupied Front Royal, and had prohibited all intercourse between that place and Winchester. However, Lieutenant Colonel Fillebrowne, of the Tenth Maine Regiment, who was acting as Provost-Marshal, at length relented, and allowed us to go on our way.

It was almost twilight when we arrived at the Shenandoah River. We found that the bridges had been destroyed, and no means of transport left but a ferry boat, which the Yankees monopolized for their own exclusive purposes.

Here we should have been subjected to much inconvenience and delay, had it not been for the courtesy and kindness of Captain Everhart, through whose intervention we were enabled to cross at once.

It was quite dark when we reached the village, and, to our great surprise, we found the family domiciled in a little cottage in the court-yard, the residence having been appropriated by General Shields and his staff.

However, we were glad enough to find ourselves at our journey's end, and to sit down to a comfortable dinner, for which fatigue and a long fast had sharpened our appetite. As soon as we had satisfied our hunger, I sent in my card to General Shields, who promptly returned my missive in person. He was an Irishman, and endowed with all those graces of manner for which the better class of his countrymen are justly famous; nor was he devoid of the humor for which they are no less notorious.

To my application for leave to pass *instanter* through his lines, *en route* for Richmond, he replied that old Jackson's army was so demoralized that he dared not trust me to their tender mercies; but that they would be annihilated within a few days, and, after such a desirable consummation, I might wander whither I would.

This, of course, was mere badinage of his part; but I am convinced he felt confident of immediate and complete success, or he would not have allowed some expressions to escape him, which I turned to account. In short, he was completely off his guard, and forgot that a woman can sometimes listen and remember.

General Shields introduced me to the officers of his staff, two of whom were young Irishmen; and to one of these, Captain K., I am indebted for some very remarkable effusions, some withered flowers, and last, not least, for a great deal of very important information, which was carefully transmitted to my countrymen. I must avow the flowers and the poetry were comparatively valueless in my eyes; but let Captain K. be consoled: these were days of war, not of love, and there are still other ladies in the world besides the "rebel spy."

The night before the departure of General Shields, who was about, as he informed us, to "whip" Jackson, a council of war was held in what had formerly been my aunt's drawing-room. Immediately above this was a bed-chamber, containing a closet, through the floor of which I observed a hole had been bored, whether with a view to espionage or not, I have never been able to ascertain. It occurred to me, however, that I might turn the discovery to account; and as soon as the council of war had assembled, I stole softly up-stairs, and, lying down on the floor of the closet, applied my ear to the hole, and found, to my great joy, I could distinctly hear the conversation that was passing below.

The council prolonged their discussion for some hours; but I remained motionless and silent until the proceedings were brought to a conclusion, at one o'clock in the morning. As soon as the coast was clear I crossed the court-yard, and made the best of my way to my own room, and took down in cipher every thing I had heard which seemed to me of any importance.

I felt convinced that to rouse a servant, or make any disturbance at the hour, would excite the suspicions of the Federals by whom I was surrounded; accordingly, I went straight to the stables myself, saddled my horse, and galloped away in the direction of the mountains.

Fortunately I had about me some passes which I had from time to time procured for Confederate soldiers returning south, and which, owing to various circumstances, had never been put in requisition. They now, however, proved invaluable; for I was twice brought to a stand-still by the challenge of the Federal sentries, and who would inevitably have put a period to my adventurous career had they not been beguiled by my false passport. Once clear of the chain of sentries, I dashed on, unquestioned, across fields and along roads, through fens and marshes, until, after a scamper of about fifteen miles, I found myself at the door of Mr. M.'s house. All was still and quiet; not a light was to be seen. I did not lose a moment in springing from my horse; and, running up the steps, I knocked at the door with such vehemence that the house re-echoed with the sound.

It was not until I had repeated my summons, at intervals of a few seconds, for some time, that I heard the response "Who's there?" given in a sharp voice from a window above.

"It is I."

"But who are you, what is your name?"

"Belle Boyd. I have important intelligence to communicate to Colonel Ashby—is he here?"

"No; but wait a minute, I will come down."

The door was opened, and Mrs. M. drew me in, and exclaimed, in a tone of astonishment:

"My dear, where did you come from, and how on earth did you get here?"

"Oh, I forced the sentries," I replied, "and here I am; but I have no time to tell you the how and the why and the wherefore. I must see Colonel Ashby without the loss of a minute. Tell me where he is to be found."

Upon hearing that his party was a quarter of a mile farther up the wood, I turned to depart in search of them, and was in the very act of remounting when a door on my right was thrown open, and revealed Colonel Ashby himself, who could not conceal his surprise at seeing me standing before him.

"Good God! Miss Belle, is this you? Where did you come from? Have you dropped from the clouds? Or am I dreaming?"

I first convinced him he was wide awake, and that my presence was substantial and of the earth—not a visionary emanation from the world of spirits; then, without further circumlocution, I proceeded to narrate all I had overheard in the closet, of which I have before made mention. I gave him the cipher, and started on my return.

I arrived safely at my aunt's house after a two hours' ride, in the course of which I "ran the blockade" of a sleeping sentry, who awoke to the sound of my horse's hoofs just in time to see me disappear round an abrupt turning, which shielded me from the bullet he was about to send after me. Upon getting home, I unsaddled my horse and "turned in," if I may be permitted the expression, which is certainly expressive rather than refined, just as Auror, springing from the rosy bed of Tithonus, began her pursuit of the flying hour; in plain English, just as day began to break.

A few days afterwards General Shields marched south, laying a trap, as he supposed, to catch "poor old Jackson and his demoralized army," leaving behind him, to occupy Front Royal, one squadron of cavalry, one field battery, and the first Maryland regiment of infantry, under command of Colonel Kenly; Major Tyndale, of Philadelphia, being appointed Provost-Marshal.

My mother returned home, and it was arranged that I should remain with my grandmother until an opportunity of traveling south in safety should present itself. Within a few days after my mother's departure, my Cousin Alice and I applied to Major Tyndale for a pass to Winchester. He at first declined to comply with our request, but afterwards relented, and promised to let us have the necessary passport on the following day. Accordingly, next morning, May 21st, my cousin, one of the servants, and myself, were up betimes, and equipped for the journey, the carriage was at the door, but no passes made their appearance; and when we sent to inquire for the Major, we were informed he had gone "out on a scout," and would probably not be back until late at night. We were of course in great perplexity, when, to our relief, Lieutenant H., belonging to the squadron of cavalry stationed in the village, made his appearance and asked what was the matter.

I explained our case, and said: —

"Now, Lieutenant H., I know you have permission to go to Winchester, and you profess to be a great friend of mine. Prove it by assisting me out of this dilemma, and pass us through the pickets."

This I knew he could easily manage, as they were furnished from his own troop.

After a few moments' hesitation, Lieutenant H. consented, little thinking of the consequences that were to ensue. He mounted the box—my cousin, myself and the servant got inside—and off we set. Shortly before we got to Winchester, Lieutenant H. got down from his seat with the intention of walking the rest of the way, as he had some business at the camp, which was close to the town.

Finding we could not return the same day, we agreed to remain all night with some friends.

Early the next morning, a gentleman of high social position came to the house at which we were staying, and handed me two packages of letters, and these words: —

"Miss Boyd, will you take these letters and send them through the lines to the Confederate army? This package," he added, pointing to one of them, "is of great importance; the other is trifling in comparison. This also," he went on to say, pointing to what appeared to be a little note, "is a very important paper—try to send it carefully and safely to Jackson, or some other responsible Confederate officer. Do you understand?"

"I do, and will obey your orders promptly and implicitly," I replied.

As soon as the gentleman had left me I concealed the most important documents about the person of my Negro servant, as I knew that "intelligent contrabands"—*i.e.*, ladies and gentlemen of color were "non-suspects," and had *carte blanche* to do what they pleased, and to go— where they liked, without hindrance or molestation on the part of the Yankee authorities. The less important package I placed in a little basket, and unguardedly wrote upon the back of it the words, "Kindness of Lieutenant H."

The small note upon which so much stress had been laid I resolved to carry with my own hands; and, knowing Colonel Fillebrown was never displeased by a little flattery and a few delicate attentions, I went to the florist and chose a very handsome bouquet, which I sent to him with my compliments, and with a request that he would be so kind as to permit me to return to Front Royal.

The Colonel's answer was in accordance with the politeness of his nature. He thanked the "dear lady for so sweet a compliment," and enclosed the much-coveted pass. Lieutenant H., having finished his business at the camp, rejoined our party, and we all set out on our return. Nothing happened until we reached the picket lines, when two repulsive-looking fellows, who proved to be detectives, rode up, one on each side of the carriage.

"We have orders to arrest you," said one of them, looking in at the window, and addressing himself to me.

"For what?" I asked.

"Upon suspicion of having letters," he replied; and then turning to the coachman, he ordered him to drive back forthwith to Colonel Beale's headquarters. Upon arriving there, we were desired to get out and walk into the office.

My cousin trembled like a poor bird caught in a snare; and, to tell the truth, I felt very much discomposed myself, although I did not for a moment lose my presence of mind, upon the preservation of which I well knew our only hopes rested. The Negress, almost paralyzed by fear, followed my cousin and myself, and it was in this order we were ushered into the awful presence of our inquisitor and judge.

The first question asked was, had I any letters. I knew that if I said No, our persons would be immediately searched, and my falsehood detected; I therefore drew out from the bottom of the basket the package I had placed there, and which, it will be remembered, was of minor importance, and handed it, with a bow, to the Colonel.

"What!" exclaimed he, in an angry tone—"what is this? 'Kindness of Lieutenant H.!' What does this mean? Is this all you have?"

"Look for yourself," I replied, turning the basket upside-down, and emptying its contents upon the floor.

"As to this scribbling on the letter," I continued, "it means nothing; it was a thoughtless act of mine. I assure you Lieutenant H. knew nothing about the letter, or that it was in my possession."

The Lieutenant turned very pale, for it suddenly occurred to him that he had in his pocket a little package which I had asked him to carry for me.

He immediately drew it out and threw it upon the table, when, to his consternation, and to the surprise of the Colonel, it was found to be inscribed with the very identical words—"Kindness of Lieutenant H."—which had already excited the suspicion of the Federal commander.

This made matters worse; and when the package, upon being opened, disclosed a copy of that decidedly rebel newspaper, *The Maryland News-sheet*, the Colonel entertained no further doubt of Lieutenant H.'s complicity and guilt.

It was in vain I asserted his innocence, and repeated again and again that it was impossible he could know that a folded packet contained an obnoxious journal, and that it was highly improbable, to say the least of it, he could be an accomplice in my possession of the letter.

"What is that you have in your hand?" was the only reply to my remonstrances and expostulations on behalf of the unfortunate officer I had so unintentionally betrayed.

"What—this little scrap of paper? You can have it, if you wish—it is nothing. Here it is"; and I approached nearer to him, with the seeming intention of placing it in his hand; but I had taken the resolution of following the example set by Harvey Birch, in Cooper's well-known novel of "The Spy," in the event of my being positively commanded to "stand and deliver."

Fortunately, however, for me, the Colonel's wrath was diverted from the guilty to the guiltless; he was so incensed with Lieutenant H., that he forgot the very existence of Belle Boyd, and the precious note was left in my possession.

We were then and there dismissed, Colonel Beale contenting himself with giving a hurried order to the effect that I was to be closely watched. He then proceeded to the investigation of Lieutenant H.'s case. Bare suspicion was the worst that could be urged against him, yet, upon this doubtful evidence, or rather in the absence of any thing like evidence, a court-martial, composed of officers of the Federal army, dismissed him from the service.

Some time after the adventure I have just related, the secret of our arrest transpired.

A servant had observed the gentleman to whom I have alluded give me the letter in my friend's house at Winchester. He gave information, and the result was, a telegram was sent to Major Tyndale, who was already incensed against me for having slipped through the pickets and got to Winchester without his pass. He communicated at once with Colonel Beale, and our arrest followed as I have described.

Had it not been for the curious manner in which Lieutenant H. was involved in the affair, and in which that unoffending officer was so unjustly treated, very much to my regret, I should not have escaped so easily.

Southern Heroism

The editor of *"The Land We Love"* relates the following instances of Southern heroism:

At Malvern Hill, a certain division drove the gunners away from a series of guns, but was too weak to hold its ground. The division commander, believing that a single additional regiment would enable him to hold the guns, rode to where he saw a body of men, not under his command, lying down awaiting orders, and briefly explained to them the state of things, and called for volunteers. A young man, with a chin as smooth as a girl's, stepped out and said: "I am here with a portion of the twentieth North Carolina regiment. We all volunteer! We are ready to go anywhere, and to perform any duty." That young man was Colonel Henry K. Burgwyn.

At the first battle of Fredericksburg, Ransom's North Carolina brigade was ordered to reënforce Cobb at the celebrated *stone wall*, which Burnside, like Fremont and Shields, tried to capture, with the same success. As soon as the brigade appeared, more than a division of the enemy opened a terrific fire upon it, and the batteries on the other side rained their shot and shell with the most deadly precision. The men were pushed with all rapidity to the precipice back of the wall, and then, without a moment's hesitation, they sprang down it to find shelter behind the wall. But a dignified mountaineer of the twenty-fifth North Carolina regiment (Rutledge's) refused to run at all, and walked forward with the most leisurely indifference. His hat blew off; he went back and picked it up! his knapsack, probably hit by a ball, fell off; he stooped down, readjusted it, and went on! He was now the solitary target for more than a thousand rifles; but this did not quicken his pace. When he reached the precipice, he determined not to risk the leap, preferring to slide down gently. He did slide down, but it was as a dead man he reached the bottom. He was buried that night, and there was not an inch of his body that was not pierced by a ball.

To prevent reënforcements from reaching the stone wall, which Burnside had selected as the point of attack, the hill above it was swept by thousands of rifles and numerous batteries of artillery. Kershaw's South Carolina brigade was ordered to reënforce the troops at the wall, and had to cross over this terrific hill. An officer went forward to select the safest route for them. He rode to the summit and took a deliberate survey. The firing of the enemy ceased; he raised his cap in acknowledgment, and rode off without having a shot fired at him. That officer was General J. B. Kershaw himself.

A Contraband's Description of Beauregard

After Beauregard's retreat from Corinth, McClellan was much exercised in mind lest he should come to the relief of Lee. McClellan, as a military man, knew this was the move *that ought to be made*, and he believed it *had been made*. However, to make sure on this point, he determined to examine, in person, an intelligent contraband just brought into his lines direct from Richmond.

General McClellan.—"Is Beauregard in Richmond?"

Intelligent Contraband.—"Oh, yes, masser."

General M.—"How many soldiers did he have with him?"

Contraband.—"Hundred tousand! tree tousand! fifty thousand! Cars heaped up with sogers ebery day, two, tree weeks!"

General M.—"Are you sure that Beauregard is there himself?"

Contraband.—"Oh, yes! Him make a speech at de capitol. Hear Marse Letcher call him General Boregar!"

The news was sufficiently confirmatory of McClellan's worst fears, and the intelligent contraband saw plainly that he had "made a sensation." At length some one thought of testing still further the intelligent contraband's accuracy, and the examination was renewed.

General M.—"Did you see General Beauregard yourself?"

Contraband.—"Oh yes, masser, me see him for sartin!"

General M.—"What sort of looking man is he?"

Contraband.—"Him great big fat man—tomack tick out so!" (putting his hands two feet in front of his stomach.)

This was too much for the gravity of McClellan, who laughed heartily with his fears all relieved.

Beauregard's leanness was too well known for the credibility of the contraband's story. It appeared, afterward, that the poor fellow had mistaken the portly Price (who happened to be in Richmond about that time) for the celebrated engineer. The "fifty tousand, tree tousand, hundred tousand" were the troops of Holmes and Huger, from North Carolina and Norfolk.

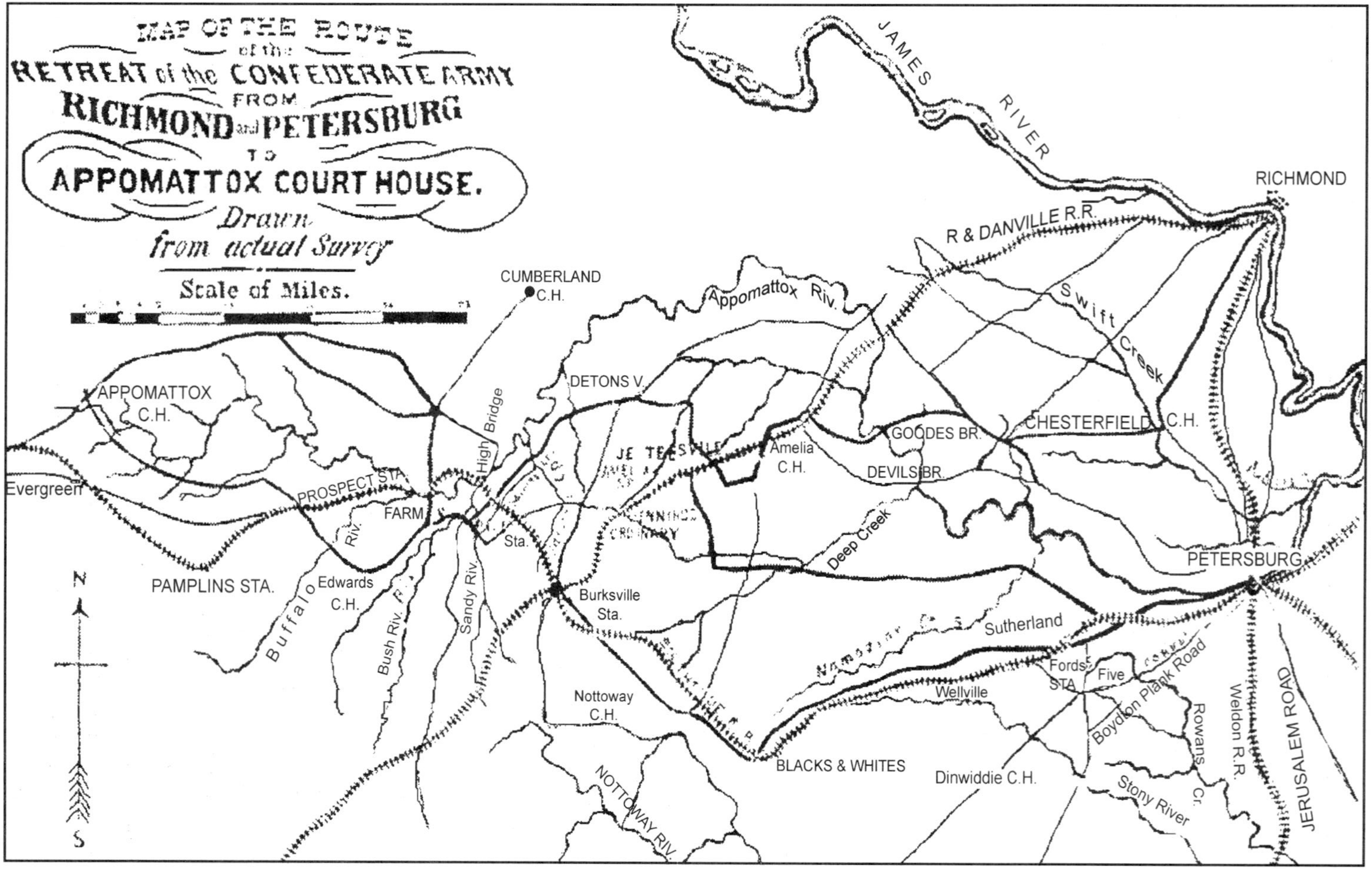
MAP OF THE ROUTE
of the
RETREAT of the CONFEDERATE ARMY
FROM
RICHMOND and PETERSBURG
TO
APPOMATTOX COURT HOUSE.
Drawn
from actual Survey
Scale of Miles.
JAMES RIVER
RICHMOND
R & DANVILLE R.R.
Appomattox Riv.
Swift Creek
CUMBERLAND C.H.
DETONS V.
APPOMATTOX C.H.
High Bridge
CHESTERFIELD C.H.
GOODES BR.
Amelia C.H.
DEVILS BR.
Evergreen
PROSPECT STA.
FARM
Riv.
Sta.
Deep Creek
PETERSBURG
N
PAMPLINS STA.
Edwards C.H.
Buffalo
Bush Riv.
Sandy Riv.
Burksville Sta.
Sutherland
Fords STA
Five
Boydon Plank Road
Wellville
Nottoway C.H.
Rowans Cr.
Weldon R.R.
JERUSALEM ROAD
BLACKS & WHITES
Dinwiddie C.H.
Stony River
NOTTOWAY RIV.
S

Examining Surgeons

After the battle of Shiloh, and the army had fallen back to Tupelo, Mississippi, and was quietly being reorganized preparatory to being transferred to Chattanooga for the campaign into Kentucky, there was an order issued from Richmond that all appointed medical officers were to be examined by a Board, as to their qualifications. Dr. Sandell was President of this Board at Tupelo—and one must know Dr. S. to appreciate the following occurrence. The assistant surgeon of the thirty-ninth Alabama was ordered to appear before the Board. He was naturally a quick-tempered young man, though one of good stern qualities, both of head and heart. The President of the Board took pleasure in touching the young man's testy temper, which he knew was already worked into great excitement by the dread of being rejected; and he perplexed him as much as possible. The young man was soon thrown into such a state of confusion that he could scarcely appreciate the full meaning of the questions propounded. His feeling seemed to be a mixture of rage and diffidence, when the President asked him "what he would do for a man found on the field shot through the knee-joint?" The young man said there were a great many things he would do for such a case, but that he thought the question a very broad one. Dr. S. again asked, "But what would you do *mainly*?" evidently trying to make him say that he would amputate at once. The applicant, by this time was in such a state as not to understand a much more pointed question, and remained perfectly silent. Dr. S. thought he would take him on another tack, and said: "Now, sir, what would you do for me if you found me on the field shot right through there"—holding up his own leg, and pointing to each side of the knee-joint. The applicant hesitated for a moment, and then, his countenance brightening a little, with the light of the spirit of revenge, and of recklessness of the consequences, he broke out slowly, but vindictively through his teeth, "Well, sir, if it was *you* that was shot through there, *I would not do one d——d thing.*" The President of the Board was a *little* put out for the moment, and told the young man he could go; but he went *"by the Board."*—*The Land We Love.*

Love vs. Duty

Colonel Van Brock, chief of staff to General J. E. B. Stuart, in his reminiscences of the war, relates the following incident:

During the night, there came a telegram for General Stuart, which I opened, with his other dispatches, and found to contain the most painful intelligence. It announced the death of little Flora, our chief's lovely and dearly-loved daughter, five years of age—the favorite of her father and of his military family. This sweet child had been dangerously ill for some time, and more than once had Mrs. Stuart summoned her husband to Flora's bedside; but she received only the response of the true soldier: "My duty to my country must be performed before I can give way to the feelings of a father." I went at once to acquaint my General with the terrible tidings: and when I had awakened him, perceiving, from the grave expression of my features, that something had gone wrong, he said, "What is it, Colonel? Are the Yankees advancing?" I handed him the telegram without a word. He read it, and, the tenderness of a father's heart overcoming the firmness of the warrior, he threw his arms around my neck, and wept bitter tears upon my breast. My dear General never recovered from this cruel blow. Many a time afterward, during our rides together, he would speak to me of his lost child. Light-blue flowers recalled her to him. In the glancing sunbeams he caught the golden tinge of her hair; and whenever he saw a child with such eyes and hair, he could not help tenderly embracing it. He thought of her even on his death-bed, when, drawing me toward him, he whispered, "My dear friend, I shall soon be with little Flora again!"

Which Side?

Walking one day on the beach at Biarittz, Louis Napoleon happened to meet an intelligent-looking boy, about eight or nine years old, who took off his hat as he passed. The Emperor courteously returned the salute, and said, "Are you English?" "No," answered the boy, very quickly and drawing himself up, "I'm American." "Oh! American, are you? Well, tell me, which are you for, North or South?" "Well, father's for the North, I believe; but I am certainly for the South. For which of them are you, sir?" The Emperor stroked his moustache, smiled, hesitated a little, and then said, "I'm for both!" "For both, are you? Well, that's not so easy, and it will please nobody!" His Majesty let the conversation drop and walked on.

Tapping the Telegraph

The following was published in a New York paper during the summer of 1862:

The telegraph line between Memphis and Corinth is exceedingly important. General Halleck's messages to Commodore Davis, General Curtis, and the commandant of this post have all passed over it. Little of the line is guarded, but of late the rebels have refrained from cutting the wires. Their unusual amiability is now explained; they found a better use for it.

For a week the Memphis operators have detected something wrong in the working of the instruments, and surmised that some outsider was sharing their telegraphic secrets. They communicated this suspicion to the superintendent at Corinth, who promised to keep a sharp lookout.

Yesterday they discovered that their uninvited confidant could talk as well as listen. The transmission of a message was suddenly interrupted by the ejaculation, "O, pshaw!" A moment after, it was again broken with "Hurrah for Jeff. Davis!"

Individuality shows itself as well in telegraphing as in the footstep, or a handwriting. Mr. Hall, one of the Memphis operators, instantly recognized the performer, not by his tune, but his time, as a young man formerly in Buffalo and other Northern offices, but now employed by the Confederates. Mr. Hall surprised him by replying promptly, "Ed. Saville, if you don't want to be hung you had better leave! Our cavalry is closing in on both sides of you!"

There was a little pause, and then the reply—"How in the world did you know me? However, I've been here four days and learned all we want to know. As this is becoming rather a tight place, I think I *will* leave. You'll see me again when you least expect it. Good-bye, boys!"

The rebel operator made good his escape. He had cut the wire, inserted a piece of his own, and by a pocket instrument had been reading our official dispatches. Some of the utmost importance, giving the very information most desired by the rebels, were passing, and as they were not in cipher he must have received them. One from General Hovey, commandant of this post, in reply to a question from General Halleck, stated the precise number of our available men in Memphis, and their exact location.

Colonel Menefee's Escape

As soon as the loyal men left in this section of the State heard of the appointment of their favorite leader, N. Menefee, as colonel, they flocked to his standard, and fled with him to the mountain-fastnesses, where they lived for months, supported, clothed, armed and furnished at the expense of Colonel Menefee, and with old flint-lock rifles have annoyed the Northern army in this country, and made themselves a terror to the vandal hordes that have been sent here to stain our soil with innocent gore. The name of Menefee is to the enemy, in Eastern Kentucky, what Marion was to the British and Tories in South Carolina.

The gallant Major Thompson, who was left at Sounding Gap with four hundred of the Virginia militia to watch that place, was driven from the gap by an overwhelming force, who attacked him front and rear. But the major brought off all his men safe, I believe.

Colonel Menefee had a fight with the enemy a few days before, and drove the enemy from the field, killing two and wounding four, with the loss of one of his men, who unnecessarily exposed himself. But in a few moments the enemy, reinforced to near three hundred, attempted to surround the colonel and his men. The colonel was too sharp for them, and having only thirteen men, many of whom had failed to get their flint-locks off, had ordered them to the mountain's cliffs. He remained upon the ground for near an hour after his men were gone, watching the enemy.

He was riding his race-mare, "Emma Treadway," who had borne him out of many a close and dangerous chase, and he felt that she was able to flee from all danger and carry him too. After watching the enemy's movements until he saw he must soon be cut off, he turned and rode up the creek, "Elk Horn," which was closely hemmed-in by high bluffs and crags on one side, and the rugged slopes of the Cumberland Mountain on the other. He had not gone far up the creek ere he was apprised of near danger by his watchful mare snorting load and shrill. In an instant, over one hundred cavalry emerged from a wood not more than seventy yards before him.

He saw that his only chance was to climb the Cumberland Mountain. Any other man would have surrendered rather than make the attempt, for the mountain was so steep that it seemed almost impossible for a footman to climb it, much less to ride it. The mountain was one mass of boulder-rocks and hedges covered with laurel. He reined his mare to the bluff, and in an instant was flying up the rugged and dizzy heights, the Yankees rushing on and yelling toward him like so many hungry cannibals sure of a feast. When the enemy reached the foot of the mountain, they had to stop and dismount, and climb up on foot. At this place the Cumberland Mountain is near three miles high. When the colonel had climbed near the top of the first "bench" he was stopped by falling timber. The pause allowed his mare to catch breath. The commander of the enemy, from below, observed the colonel's halt, and mistaking his stop for a surrender, cried out to his men, who were in close pursuit of the colonel, to "hurry on straight up the mountain, we have the G——d d——d Rebel hemmed in at last!" They were so sure of capturing the colonel that they did not fire upon him.

When the colonel's mare had panted a moment, he touched her sides. She leaped the barrier, and in an instant was out of sight behind some bluffs and rocks. After proceeding some distance farther, the colonel dismounted and prepared to fire upon his pursuers; but observing one of his brave comrades approaching him, almost fainting from fatigue, he saw that if he fired, the enemy would come in that direction and perhaps capture and kill his brave soldier. He motioned to the soldier to run on in that direction until he climbed to the top of the bluff. He then stopped and yelled the Osage Indian war-whoop, the most terrific yell known to savage life. He then dashed down a rugged ledge of rocks for near a half a mile, and made his escape.

INTREPID CONDUCT OF TWO BOYS

Two half-grown lads were out hunting in the neighborhood of Newbern, and were discovered and accosted by a Yankee lieutenant.

One of the boys wore the letters "N. C." on his cap, which attracted the Yankee's attention, and he inquired of the boy what they meant. The boy replied, "North Carolina"; whereupon the lieutenant ordered him to remove them. This the boy declined doing, when he was again ordered to take them off, and again refused to do so. The lieutenant then remarked that he would take them off himself, and was in the act of dismounting from his horse to do so, when the boy winked to his comrade, who took his meaning, and in a moment the guns of both the boys were leveled at the head of the Yankee officer, and he was commanded to surrender.

Seeing the utter helplessness of his case, and perfectly astounded at the spirit displayed by the boys, the Yankee gave up his pistol, and on being ordered to dismount, did so. The boys then secured him, and again placing him on his horse, conducted him to Kinston, where he was safely lodged in jail.

Captain Montgomery's Adventures

Captain Montgomery was in command of one of the Confederate vessels engaged in the desperate naval fight before Memphis, Tennessee, when that city was captured. Escaping, after the loss of his vessel, he managed to regain the Confederate lines. His adventures are related as follows, by a Southern paper:

Yesterday evening, Captain J. T. Montgomery arrived here from Corinth, whither he had gone when the wires first flashed the news of Sunday's great fight. After staying there till he desired to return, he left on the Memphis and Charleston Railroad, Wednesday night, and arrived at Huntsville next morning, no one on board dreaming that the Yankees were in the place. He was in the hindmost car and, as the train stopped, he heard some one say, "the Yankees have got us"; and, looking out, he saw them thick as bees around the engine, and coming down along the line of the train. He quickly stepped out, took a back seat, and was soon out of sight. Near the outskirts of the town he entered a house, exchanged his uniform for citizens' clothes, come back into town, hired a horse and buggy and Negro driver, at a livery stable, and started for the Tennessee river at the nearest point. He had proceeded but a little way until a couple of mounted Federal officers, having got scent of him from finding his name on his trunk in the cars, came up and accosted him as Captain Montgomery. He repudiated the name—said his name was Johnson, and that he was going to his home from town. They told him they knew better; that he was Captain Montgomery, of the rebel army, was their prisoner, and must go with them. Quietly remarking that they must know more about him and his business than he did himself, he turned and started back with them.

They stopped on the road-side to chat with some Negroes they found in a field (Yankees will talk to Negroes). They were both very near the captain. Catching the proper moment, when their attention was directed to the Negroes, he drew a pistol from his pocket and instantly put a ball through the heart of one, who fell down dead. Another moment, and he had put a ball through the other, who reeled and clung to his horse a few moments. Meantime the captain was speeding his way back toward the river. Looking back, as he got nearly out of sight, he saw the "Yank" fall from his horse sprawling on the ground. He reached the river safely, turned the Negro driver back with his horse and buggy, and got himself ferried across just as fifty well armed and mounted men approached the bank, and could find no means to cross over after him. They discharged their guns at him, but he managed to gain the mountains, and finally to reach his friends.

THE SONG OF THE SOUTH

BY CAPTAIN R. M. ANDERSON

Another star arisen, another flag unfurled;
Another name inscribed among the nations of the world;
Another mighty struggle 'gainst a tyrant's fell decree,
And again a burdened people have uprisen, and are free.

The Spirit of the fathers in the children liveth yet—
Liveth still the olden blood that hath dimmed the bayonet;
And the fathers fought for freedom, and the sons for freedom fight;
Their God was with their fathers, and is still the God of right.

Behold, the skies are darkened! a gloomy cloud hath lowered!
Shall it break in happy peacefulness, or spread its rage abroad?
Shall we have the smiles of friendship, or feel the fierce, foul blow?
And bare the red right hand of war to meet an insulting foe?

In peacefulness we wish to live, but not in slavish fear,
In peacefulness we dare not die, dishonored on our bier;
To our allies of the northern land we offer heart and hand;
But if they scorn our friendship, then the banner and the brand

Honor to the new-born nation! honor to the brave!
A country freed from thraldom, or a soldier's honored grave!
Every rock shall be a tombstone, every rivulet run red,
And the invader, should he conquer, find the conquered in the dead.

But victory shall follow where the sons of freedom go,
And the signal for the onset be the death-knell of the foe;
And hallowed be the sacred spot where they have bravely met,
And the star that rises yonder shall never, never set.

Negro Heroism

In a raid by the Federals, on the Mississippi river, they took off the son of a Negro man belonging to Senator Henry. The boy was about ten years old; and when Jenkins ascertained that his son was on board the Yankee boat, he immediately repaired to the boat, foaming at the mouth, like an enraged tiger. He went on board, knife in hand, and demanded his boy. "Give me back my boy!" exclaimed he, in those terrible, fierce tones that electrify with fear all who hear them, "or I will make the deck of this boat slippery with your blood. You are nothing but a set of vile robbers and plunderers, and I will spill the last drop of my blood but I will have my child. Give him to me, or I will plunge my knife into the heart of the first man I reach." The captain on the boat seeing the desperate determination of Jenkins, told the soldier they had better give him up, or some of them would be killed, and he was given up. Hurrah for Jenkins! He had previously resisted all appeals to him to desert his master, and he took his boy back to his contented home in triumph. He is one amongst a thousand.

The Adventures of George N. Sanders

George N. Sanders having been entrusted with an important mission to Europe, by the Confederate Government, made his way through the Loyal States to Canada, and sailed thence to Europe. A Northern paper contains the following account of his entrance into Canada:

There have been several brief accounts of the successful passage across the Canada frontier of George N. Sanders, rebel emissary to Europe, but the following statement, gathered from those who personally witnessed the adventure in its various stages, gives the fullest details.

A few days ago a man dressed in well-worn working clothes presented himself to the United States Provost Marshal on the United States side of the Suspension Bridge. He wore a pair of very short trousers of striped Kentucky jean, and a seedy coat of the same material. A coarse, not over clean shirt, and a jagged straw hat completed the costume. The man had no collar or cravat, and his face was apparently greatly tanned by exposure to the weather.

He wanted to go over the river, he said, but had no pass and did not know that any would be needed. He stated that he was an Englishman from Cornwall, and a miner by trade. He had been working for some time in Pennsylvania, but had lately received a letter from his brother, a farmer, near London, Canada West, stating that he was short of help, and urging his miner relatives to come on to his assistance at least, till the harvest time was over.

The miner held his tools in one hand, and in the other carried an old carpet bag of the black glazed style in common use. The glazing in many places had come off, and the outside was, moreover, spotted and soiled with dirt.

The carpet bag, more valuable than the famous one of John Brown, for it contained the papers, despatches and money of the rebel emissary Sanders.

The marshal pondered awhile, but the poor miner gave such a consistent story, and seemed so disappointed at his unexpected trouble in crossing, that the official's heart was melted, and he gave him the required pass.

The toll man of the Suspension Bridge then demanded a quarter of a dollar toll.

"Two shillings!" said the miner, "why, I can't give it. I've only got one shilling."

This plea of poverty completely disarmed whatever shadow of suspicion may have existed in regard to the poor workman. After the proper degree of hesitation the "fellow" was allowed to pass over at half price.

Thanking the toll-keeper for his liberality, the miner walked on wearily across the bridge. As he neared the Canada side his step became lighter—just as Christian (pardon the comparison) felt when the burden dropped off his back. A decided burden had dropped off George N. Sanders' mind—he was safe in Canada.

Arriving at the Canada side of the bridge, the miner, with his tools and carpet-bag, jumped into the Clifton House omnibus, and was quickly driven to that famous hotel. He went to the desk and registered on the book the initials S. N. G.—his own initials reversed.

The clerk looked at the shabby working man a moment, and then coldly said:

"We can't give you a room here, sir."

"But I must have a room," said Sanders.

"None to spare to-night," replied the clerk.

The miner thrust his hands in his pocket and drew forth a great roll of "greenbacks."

"Here," said he to the clerk, "take these as security. Put them in your safe; but give me a room at once."

Of course money has its effect in Clifton House, as everywhere else. Still the clerk hesitated.

"Is there any place about here where I can get a respectable suit of clothes?" asked the miner, dropping his Cornish dialect.

There was no place nearer than the Bridge, a mile distant. So the miner again insisted on having the room; and as it was obvious that "things were not as they seem," he was shown to a suitable apartment.

A few minutes afterward a guest strolled out on the piazza, where ex-Governor Morehead, of Kentucky, was sitting. "By the way, Governor," said he, "what a singular old fellow that was in the office. He registered his name on the book only in initials!"

"Good God! in initials!" cried Morehead, starting up, "he's come then"; and rushing past the astonished guest, he demanded to be shown to the room of the mysterious S. N. G.

Other Secessionists also hastened thither. Sanders was provided with a suit of clothes at once, the clerks and servants altered their deportment to the quondam miner, and the guests had a rare piece of gossip to talk about. Sanders is by this time half way across the ocean; and whatever is thought of him or his cause, it is generally acknowledged that his journey from Richmond to Canada is one of the "cutest" specimens of rebel "strategy" the war has produced. It shows that our blockade is so stringent, that a Rebel emissary prefers a long land journey in disguise to attempting to break it.

Of course, the adventure has been the chief topic of gossip in the Niagara hotels; and miners will henceforth be viewed with a very profound suspicion in the neighborhood of the Suspension Bridge.

Jackson on a Retreat

Captain Cooke, in his "Life of Stonewall Jackson," gives the following account of the great soldier when he retreated from Winchester in the early Spring of 1862:

Jackson still occupied his position in advance of the town, with the determination not to retire before the enemy without engaging them, when, late in the afternoon, he received an order from Richmond directing him to evacuate Winchester and fall back up the valley. This was a bitter disappointment to him. All his dreams of defending Winchester were at once dispelled; and with a heavy heart he prepared to obey. There was nothing in his orders, however, which forbade him to fight as he fell back, and he resolved that, before retiring, he would attack his adversary.

On the night of the 11th of March he visited the family of the Rev. Mr. Graham, a Presbyterian clergyman of the town, with whom he was intimate, and the whole family were struck with the unusual buoyancy of his bearing. His manner was animated; his countenance smiling, almost gay; and he came in with a rapid, elastic tread, which indicated high spirits. As the hour for evening prayers had arrived, he asked permission to read a chapter in the Bible, and offer a prayer, as he frequently did; and every one took notice of the eloquence and feeling in his voice. When the family rose from their knees, Jackson remained for a moment silent, and then said: "My good friends, I can tell you what I am going to do to-night. I shall attack the enemy, and defeat him!"

After a few more words he left the house, but, to their great surprise, returned toward midnight, looking haggard and dispirited. He came in slowly, almost dragging himself along, and said, in accents of the greatest depression, "I have come to tell you that I must leave you, and to say farewell!" His head sank as he spoke, and he seemed to fall into a gloomy reverie. From this he suddenly roused himself, and starting to his feet, with flushed cheeks and flashing eyes, he half drew his sword from the scabbard, and exclaimed—"I will never leave Winchester without a fight! Never! never!"

He stood looking at the astonished auditors for some moments without uttering another word, and then his excitement disappeared. His sword was driven back with a ringing clash into the scabbard, and, in tones of profound discouragement, he said:

"No, I cannot sacrifice my men! I intended to attack the enemy on the Martinsburg road, but they are approaching on the flanks too, and would surround me. I cannot sacrifice my men—I must fall back!"

He then bade his friends farewell, and left the house. On the same night he recalled his troops from their position in front of the enemy, left the cavalry to guard his rear, and silently evacuated Winchester.

Execution of Confederate Officers

The sad fate of Colonel Orton and Lieutenant Peters, who were hung as spies by the Federals at Franklin, Tennessee, aroused a deep sympathy in the South. The following is the Federal account of the execution:

Headquarters Post,
Franklin, Tennessee, June 9, 1863.

Last evening, about sundown, two strangers rode into camp and called at Colonel Baird's headquarters, who presented unusual appearances. They had on citizens' overcoats, Federal regulation pants and caps. The caps were covered with white flannel havelocks. They wore side-arms, and showed high intelligence. One claimed to be a colonel in the United States army, and called himself Colonel Austin; the other called himself Major Dunlap; and both representing themselves as inspector-generals of the United States army. They represented that they were now out on an expedition in this department, inspecting the outposts and defenses, and that day before yesterday they had been overhauled by the enemy and lost their coats and purses. They exhibited official papers from General Rosecranz, and also from the War Department at Washington, confirming their rank and business. These were all right to Colonel Baird, and at first satisfied him of their honesty. They asked the colonel to loan them fifty dollars, as they had no coats, and no money to buy them. Colonel Baird loaned them the money, and took Colonel Austin's note for it. Just at dark they started, saying they were going to Nashville, and took that way. Just so soon as their horses' heads were turned, the thought of their being spies struck Colonel Baird, he says, like a thunderbolt; and he ordered Colonel Watkins, of the sixth Kentucky cavalry, who was standing by, to arrest them immediately. But

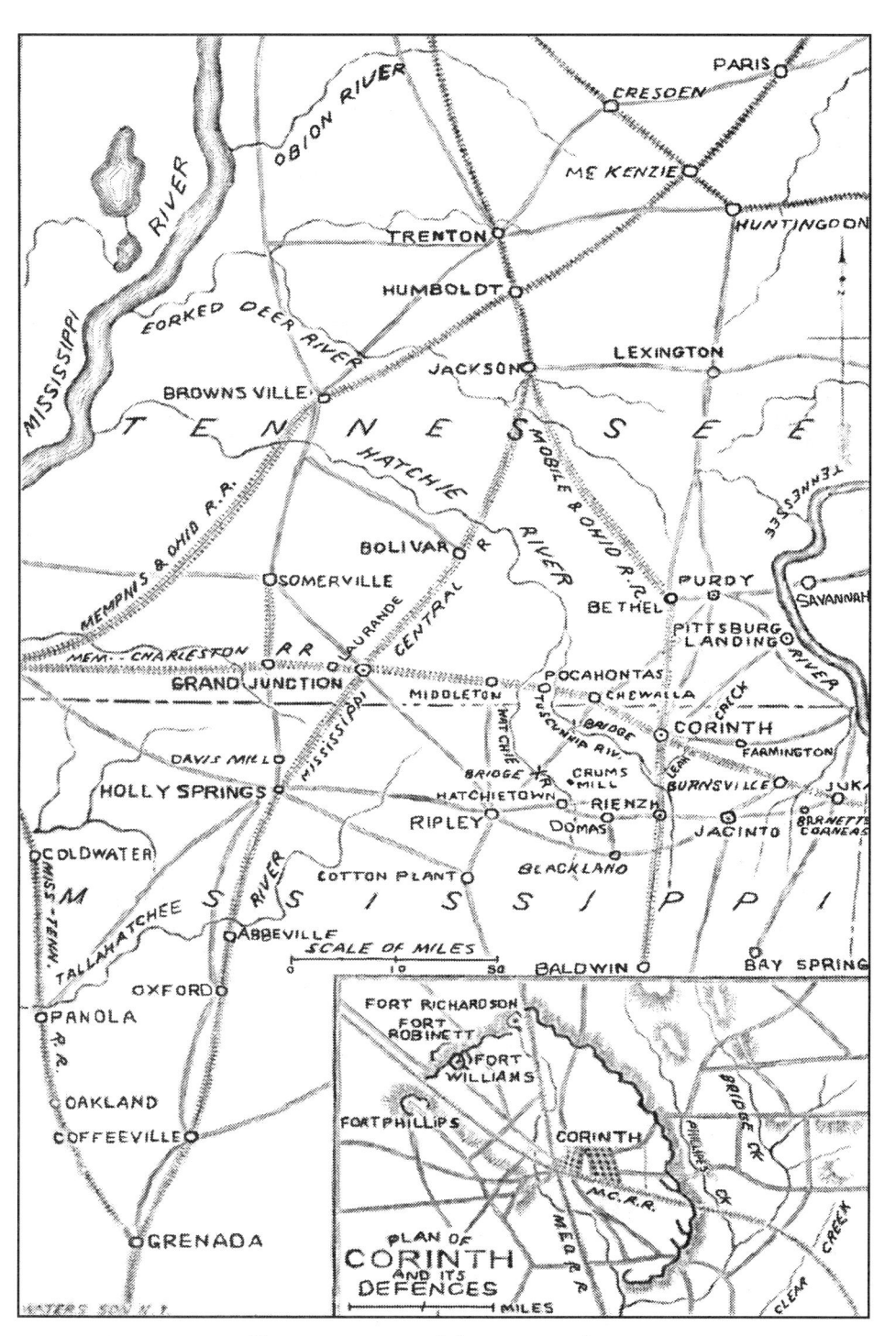

TENNESSEE AND MISSISSIPPI AREA

they were going at lightning speed. Colonel Watkins had no time to call a guard, and, only with his orderly, he set out on the chase. He ordered the orderly to unsling his carbine, and if, when he (the colonel) halted them, they showed any suspicious motions, to fire on them without waiting for an order. They were overtaken about one third of a mile from here. Colonel Watkins told them that Colonel Baird wanted to make some further inquiries of them, and asked them to return. This they politely consented to do, after some remonstrance on account of the lateness of the hour, and the distance they had to travel, and Colonel Watkins led them to his tent, where he placed a strong guard over them. It was not until one of them attempted to pass the guard at the door that they even suspected they were prisoners. Colonel Watkins immediately brought them to Colonel Baird under strong guard. They at once manifested great uneasiness, and pretended great indignation at being thus treated. Colonel Baird frankly told them that he had his suspicions of their true character, and that they should, if loyal, object to no necessary caution. They were very hard to satisfy, and were in a great hurry to get off. Colonel Baird told them that they were under arrest, and he should hold them prisoners until he was fully satisfied that they were what they purported to be. He immediately telegraphed to General Rosecranz, and received the answer that he knew nothing of such men; that there were no such men in his employ, or had his pass.

Long before the dispatch was received, however, everyone who had an opportunity of hearing their conversation was well satisfied that they were spies; smart as they were, they gave frequent and distinct evidence of duplicity. After this dispatch came to hand, which it did about twelve o'clock (midnight), a search of their persons was ordered. To this the major consented without opposition, but the colonel protested against it; and even put his hand to his arms. But resistance was useless, and both submitted. When the major's sword was drawn from the scabbard, there were found etched upon it these words: "Lt. W. G. Peter, C. S. A." At this discovery, Colonel Baird remarked, "Gentlemen, you have played this d——d well." "Yes," said Lieutenant Peter, *"and it came near being a perfect success."* They then confessed the whole matter, and upon further search various papers showing their guilt were discovered upon their persons. Lieutenant Peter was found to have on a rebel cap, secreted by the white flannel havelock.

Colonel Baird immediately telegraphed the facts to General Rosecranz, and asked what he should do, and in a short time received an order "to try them by a drum-head court-martial, and, if found guilty, *hang them immediately.*" The court was convened, and before daylight the case was decided, and the prisoners informed that they must prepare for immediate death by hanging.

At daylight men were detailed to make a scaffold. The prisoners were visited by the chaplain of the seventy-eighth Illinois, who, upon their request, administered the sacrament to them. They also wrote some letters to their friends, and deposited their jewelry, silver cups, and other valuables for transmission to their friends.

The gallows was constructed by a wild cherry tree not far from the depot, and in a very public place. Two ropes hung dangling from the beam, reaching within eight feet of the ground. A little after nine o'clock, A.M., the whole garrison was marshaled around the place of execution in solemn sadness. Two poplar coffins were lying a few feet away. Twenty minutes past nine the guards conducted the prisoners to the scaffold—they walked firm and steady, as if unmindful of the fearful precipice which they were approaching. The guards did them the honor to march with arms reversed.

Arrived at the place of execution, they stepped upon the platform of the cart, and took their respective places. The provost marshal, Captain Alexander, then tied a linen handkerchief over the face of each, and adjusted the ropes. They then asked the privilege of bidding a last farewell, which being granted, they tenderly embraced each other. This over, the cart moved from under them, and they hung in the air. What a fearful penalty! They swung off at 9:30—in two minutes the lieutenant ceased to struggle. The colonel caught hold of the rope with both hands and raised himself up at three minutes, and ceased to struggle at five minutes. At six minutes, Dr. Forrester, Surgeon sixth Kentucky cavalry, and Dr. Moss, seventy-eighth Illinois infantry, and myself, who had been detailed to examine the bodies, approached them and found the pulse of both full and strong. At seven minutes, the colonel shrugged his shoulders. The pulse of each continued to beat seventeen minutes, and at twenty minutes all signs of life had ceased. The bodies were cut down at thirty minutes, and encoffined in full dress. The colonel was buried with a gold locket and chain on his neck. The locket contained the portrait and a braid of hair of his intended wife—her portrait was also in his vest pocket—these were buried with him, at his request. Both men were buried in the same grave—companions in life, misfortune, and crime, companions in infamy, and now companions in the grave.

I should have stated, in another place, that the prisoners did not want their punishment delayed, but, well knowing the consequences of their acts, even before their *trial*, asked to have the sentence, be it hanging or shooting, quickly decided and executed. But they deprecated the idea of death by hanging, and asked for commutation of the sentence to shooting.

The elder and leader of these unfortunate men was Lawrence Williams, of Georgetown, D.C. He was as fine-looking a man as I have ever seen; and six feet high, and perhaps thirty years old. He was son of Captain Williams, who was killed at the battle of Monterey. He was one of the most intellectual and accomplished men that I have ever known. I have never known any one who excelled him as a talker. He was a member of the regular army, with the rank of captain of cavalry, when the rebellion broke out, and at that time was aide-de-camp and private secretary to General Winfield Scott. From this confidence and respect shown him by so distinguished a man, may be judged his education and accomplishments. He was a first cousin of General Lee, commanding the Confederate army on the Rappahannock. Soon after the war began, he was frank enough to inform General Scott that all his sympathies were with the South, as his friends and interests were there, and that he could not fight against them. As he was privy to all of General Scott's plans for the campaign, it was not thought proper to turn him loose, hence he was sent to Governor's Island, where he remained three months. After the first Bull Run battle he was allowed to go South, where he joined the Confederate army; and his subsequent history I have not been able to learn much about. He was awhile on General Bragg's staff, as chief of artillery; but at the time of his death was inspector general. When he joined the Confederate army, he altered his name, and now signs it thus: "Lawrence W. Orton, Col. Cav. P. A. C. S. A."—(Provisional Army Confederate States of America.) Sometimes, he writes his name "Orton," and sometimes "Auton," according to the object which he had in view. This we learn from the papers found on him. These facts in relation to the personal history of Colonel Orton, I have gathered from the colonel himself and from Colonel Watkins, who knows him well, they having belonged to the same regiment of the regular army, second United States cavalry. Colonel Watkins, however, did not recognize Colonel Orton until after he had made himself known, and now mourns his apostacy and tragic death.

The other victim of this delusive and reckless daring, was Walter G. Peter, a lieutenant in the rebel army and Colonel Orton's adjutant. He was a tall, handsome young man of about twenty-five years, that gave many signs of education and refinement. Of his history I have been unable to gather any thing. He played but a second part. Colonel Orton was the leader, and did all the talking and managing. Such is a succinct account of one of the most daring enterprises that men ever engage in. Such were the characters and the men who played the awful tragedy.

History will hardly furnish its parallel, in the character and standing of the parties, the boldness and daring of the enterprise, and the swiftness with which discovery and punishment were visited upon them. They came into our camp and went all through it, minutely inspecting our position, works, and forces, with a portion of their traitorous insignia upon them, and the boldness of their conduct made their flimsy subterfuges almost successful.

To the last, however, they denied being spies. They claimed that they were endeavoring to get through our lines in order to visit friends in the North and in Europe. But this story was so poorly matured, that, when either told it, it would not hang together, and there was little resemblance between the accounts which the two gave. The arrest so completely confounded them that they were never afterward able to recover from it.

The unfortunate men made no complaint at the severity of their punishment, except they deprecated the ignominy of being hung. They were too well informed not to know that, upon conviction of being spies, they must suffer death; and hence they expected it, and made no complaint.

Colonel Orton, who recognized Colonel Watkins as soon as he saw him, told him that he barely saved his life when the arrest was made—that he had his hand on his pistol, to kill him and escape; that, had it been any one else here, he would have done so.

Colonel Orton delivered his sword and pistols to Colonel Watkins, and told him to keep and wear them. He also presented him his horse, valued at five thousand dollars, and asked him to treat it kindly for his sake.

We are all sad over this event. There is a gloom upon every face. Although we are fully satisfied that the mission of these men was to plan our destruction, and that even they recognized their punishment just, according to the accepted rules of war among all nations, still, to see them suffer such a penalty, has filled our garrison with sadness.

A Touching Incident

One of the most affecting incidents of the brilliant and successful recapture of Galveston, by the forces under Major General Magruder, was the meeting between Major Lea, of the Confederate army, and his eldest and fondly-loved son, who was first-lieutenant of the Harriet Lane. The *Houston Telegraph* narrates the incident as follows:

Nearly two years ago the father, then residing in Texas, had written repeatedly to the son, then on the coast of China, suggesting the principles that should determine his course in the then approaching struggle between the North and the South of the United States, and saying that he could not dictate to one so long obligated to act on his own judgment and that, decide as he might, such was his confidence in his high conscientiousness, he would continue to regard him with the respect of a gentleman, and the affection of a father; but that, if he should elect the side of the enemy, they would probably never meet on earth, unless perchance they should meet in battle.

The father had served nearly eighteen months eastward of the Mississippi, and, through unsolicited orders, arrived late at night at Houston, *en route* for San Antonio, to report there for duty, when, hearing of the intended attack on the Harriet Lane, on board of which he feared his son was, he solicited permission to join the expedition, in the hope of nursing or burying him, for well he knew his son's courage would expose him to the resistless daring of our Texas boys.

During the fight, Major Lea was ordered by the general to keep a lookout from a house-top for all movements in the bay. As soon as daylight enabled him to see that the Lane had been captured, by permission of the general, who knew nothing of the expected meeting, he hastened aboard, when he was not surprised to find his son mortally wounded. Wading through blood, amidst the dying and the dead, he reached the youth, pale and exhausted.

"Edward, 'tis your father!"

"I know you, father—I know you, father, but cannot move!" he said, faintly.

"Are you mortally wounded?"

"Badly, but I hope not fatally."

"Do you suffer pain?"

"Cannot speak!" he whispered. A stimulant was given him. "How came you here, father?"

When answered, a gleam of surprise and gratification passed over his fine face. He then expended nearly his last words in making arrangements for his wounded comrades. His father knelt and blessed him, and hastened ashore for a litter, and returned just after life had fled.

When told by the surgeon that he had but a few minutes to live, and asked to express his wishes, he answered, confidingly, "My father is here!" and spoke not again. He was borne in procession to the grave from the headquarters of General Magruder, in company with his captain; and they were buried together, with appropriate military honors, in the presence of many officers of both armies, and many generous citizens, all of whom expressed their deep sympathy with the bereaved father, who said the solemn service for the Episcopal Church for the burial of the dead, and then added this brief address:

"My friends: The wise man has said, that there is a time to rejoice, and a time to mourn. Surely, this is a time when we may weep with those that weep. Allow one, so sorely tried in this his willing sacrifice, to beseech you to believe, whilst we defend our rights with strong arms and honest hearts, that those we meet in battle may also have hearts brave and honest as our own. We have here buried two brave and honest gentlemen. Peace to their ashes! tread lightly o'er their graves! Amen."

A Full-Blooded Confederate

A Massachusetts chaplain, Rev. Mr. Hepworth, writes from Louisiana:

Just beyond Carrollton is an immense and magnificent estate, owned by one of those Creoles. His annual yield of sugar is fifteen hundred hogsheads. He might have taken the oath of allegiance, and thus saved his property. But he would not. The work of depredation commenced, but he bore it without a murmur.

First, we took his wagons, harness, and mules. He said nothing, but scowled most awfully! Next we emptied his stables of horses, for the cavalry service. He did not have a pony left, and was compelled to trudge along on foot! Still, nothing was said. Next, we took his entire crop; ground it in his own sugar-house; used his barrels for the molasses, and his hogsheads for the sugar, and marked the head of each, "U. S." Not a murmur! Then came his Negroes—three hundred and more, home-servants and all—who took it to come within our camp lines. The Creole was most completely stripped. Still, he stood in the midst of the ruins, cursing Abe Lincoln, and wishing that he had eight, instead of four sons, in the rebel army!

THE BOY-MAJOR

Among the mortally wounded at Gettysburg, was Major Joseph W. Latimer, of Prince William county, Virginia, who was better known among his comrades as the "Boy-Major"; for he was under twenty years of age when he died. When the war began, he was in the Lexington Military Institute. He entered the army as second-lieutenant, and rapidly advanced until, at Gettysburg, he commanded a battalion of artillery in General Ewell's corps. In this battle he lost an arm. He reached Harrisonburg, on his way to Richmond, when he was arrested by a disease produced by his wound, which, in a few days, terminated his short but useful and honorable career.

He gave rare promise of future greatness; and, though so young, was known as one of the most skilful officers in the army. General Ewell declared he was proud of him, and called him his "Little Napoleon!" Nor was this empty praise, for the brave soldier showed his confidence in him by constantly giving him the post of danger and of honor.

HARDEE OUTDONE

A well-known Confederate major-general was stopping for a while in a Georgia village, which circumstance coming to the knowledge of the "Home Guard" of that vicinity, the captain resolved to give the general an opportunity of witnessing the "revolutions" of his superb corps. In due time, Captain ——'s company, having "fell in," were discovered by the general in front of his quarters, in the execution of his command, "In two ranks, git," etc. During the exhibition, by some dexterous double-quick movement, only known among militia officers, the captain, much to his surprise and chagrin, found the company in a "fix," best described, I reckon, as a "solid circle." In stentorophonic tones he called them to "halt!" The general became interested, and drew near, in order to see in what way things would be righted. The captain, in his confusion, turned his head to one side, like a duck when she sees the shadow of a hawk flit past, and seemed to be in the deepest thought. At last an idea seemed to strike him; a ray of intelligence mantled his face, and straightening himself up, he turned to the company, and cried out; "Company, disentangle to the front, march." The company was "straightened," and the general gave it as his opinion that it was the best command he had ever heard given.

THERE'S LIFE IN THE OLD LAND YET!

BY JAS. B. RANDALL

By blue Patapsco's billowy dash,
    The tyrant's war-shout comes,
Along with the cymbal's fitful clash,
    And the growl of his sullen drums,
We hear it! we heed it, with vengeful thrills,
    And we shall not forgive or forget;
There's faith in the streams, there's hope in the hills,
    There's life in the old land yet!

Minions! we sleep, but we are not dead;
    We are crushed, we are scourged, we are scarred;
We crouch—'tis to welcome the triumph tread
    Of the peerless Beauregard
Then woe to your vile, polluting horde
    When the Southern braves are met,
There's faith in the victor's stainless sword,
    There is life in the old land yet!

Bigots! ye quell not the valiant mind,
    With the clank of an iron chain,
The spirit of freedom sings in the wind,
    O'er Merryman, Thomas and *Kane;*
And we, though we smite not, and are not thralls,

We are piling a gory debt;
While down by McHenry's dungeon-walls,
There's life in the old land yet!

Our women have hung their harps away,
And they scowl on your brutal bands,
While the nimble poignard dares the day,
In their dear defiant hands.
They will strip their tresses to string our bows,
Ere the Northern sun is set;
There's faith in their unrelenting woes,
There's life in the old land yet!

There's life, though it throbbeth in silent veins,
'Tis vocal without noise,
It gushed o'er Manassas' solemn plains,
From the blood of the Maryland Boys!
That blood shall cry aloud, and rise
With an everlasting threat,—
By the death of the brave, by the God in the skies,
There's life in the old land yet!

Not Down in the "Tactics"

While on a forced march in some of the army movements in Mississippi, General Hardee came up with a straggler who had fallen some distance in the rear of his command. The general ordered him forward, when the soldier replied that he was weak and broken down, not having had even half rations for several days.

"That's hard," replied the general, "but you must push forward, my good fellow, and join your command, or the provost guard will take you in hand."

The soldier halted, and, looking up at the general, asked:

"Are you General Hardee?"

"Yes," replied the general.

"Didn't you write Hardee's Tactics?"

"Yes."

"Well, General, I have studied them tactics and know 'em by heart. You've got a order to double column at half distance, ain't you?"

"Well," asked the general, "what has that got to do with your case?"

"I am a good soldier, General, and obey all that is possible to be obeyed; but if your orders can show me a order in your tactics to double distance on half rations, then I'll give in."

The general, with a hearty laugh, admitted that there were no tactics to meet the case, and putting spurs to his horse, rode forward.

GENERAL LEE AND THE OFFICER

The day after the battle of Spottsylvania Court House, General Lee was standing near his lines, conversing with two of his officers, one of whom was known to be not only a hard fighter, and a hard swearer, but a cordial hater of the Yankees. After a silence of some moments, the latter officer, looking at the Yankees with a dark scowl on his face, exclaimed most emphatically: "I wish they were all dead." General Lee, with the grace and manner peculiar to himself, replied, "How can you say so, General? Now I wish they were all at home, attending to their own business, leaving us to do the same." He then moved off, when the first speaker, waiting until he was out of earshot, turned to his companion and in the most earnest tone, said, "I would not say so before General Lee, but I wish they were all dead, and *in hell!*" When this amendment to the wish was afterward reported to General Lee, in spite of his goodness, he could not refrain from laughing heartily at the speech, which was so characteristic of one of his *favorite* officers.

A LONG WAY FROM HEADQUARTERS

A Texian soldier, trudging along one day all alone, met a Methodist circuit rider, and at once recognized him as such but affected ignorance of it.

"What army do you belong to?" asked the preacher.

"I belong to the ——th Texas regiment, Van Dorn's army," replied the soldier. "What army do you belong to?"

"I belong to the army of the Lord," was the solemn reply.

"Well then, my friend," said the soldier dryly, "you've got a very long way from Headquarters!"

BELLE BOYD IN PRISON[*]

I was thrust into a carriage; and the order, "Drive to the Old Capitol," was promptly given; but, before it could be obeyed, Lieutenant Steele, who had been very unceremoniously dismissed from further attendance upon me, stepped up and politely begged permission to wait upon me to prison. To a gruff refusal he firmly rejoined—

"I am determined to see her out of your hands, at least."

The carriage was driven at a rapid pace, and we soon came within sight of my future home—a vast brick building, like all prisons, somber, chilling, and repulsive.

Its dull, damp walls look out upon the street: its narrow windows are further darkened by heavy iron stanchions, through which the miserable inmates may soothe their captivity by gazing upon those who are still free, but whose freedom hangs but by a slender thread.

Such is the calm retreat provided by a free and enlightened community, for those of its citizens who have the audacity to express their convictions of public justice.

Upon my arrival at the prison, I was ushered into a small office. A clerk, who was writing at a desk, looked up for a moment, and informed me the superintendent would attend to my business immediately. The words were hardly uttered when Mr. Wood entered the room, and I was aware of the presence of a man of middle height, powerfully built, with brown hair, fair complexion, and keen, bluish-gray eyes.

Mr. Wood prides himself, I believe, upon his plebeian extraction; but I can safely aver that beneath his rough exterior there beats a warm and generous heart.

"And so this is the celebrated rebel spy," said he. "I am very glad to see you, and will endeavor to make you as comfortable as possible; so whatever you wish for, ask for it and you shall have it. I am glad I have so

---

[*] From *"Belle Boyd in Camp and Prison,"* written by herself.

distinguished a personage for my guest. Come, let me show you to your room."

We traversed the hall, ascended a flight of stairs, and found ourselves in a short, narrow passage, up and down which a sentry paced, and into which several doors opened. One of these doors, No. 6, was thrown open; and behold my prison cell!

Mr. Wood, after repeating his injunction to me to ask for whatever I might wish, and with the promise that he would send me a servant, and that I should not be locked in as long as I "behaved myself," withdrew, and left me to my reflections.

At the moment I did not quite understand the meaning of the last indulgence, but within a few minutes I was given a copy of the rules and regulations of the prison, which set forth that if I held any communication whatever with the other prisoners, I should be punished by having my door locked.

There was nothing remarkable in the shape or size of my apartment, except that two very large windows took up nearly the whole of one side of the wall.

Upon taking an inventory of my effects, I found them to be as follows:—A washing-stand, a looking-glass, an iron bedstead, a table, and some chairs.

From the windows I had a view of part of Pennsylvania Avenue, and far away in the country the residence of General Floyd, ex-United States Secretary of War, where I had formerly passed many happy hours.

At first I could not help indulging in reminiscences of my last visit to Washington, and contrasting it with my present forlorn condition; but rousing myself from my reverie, I bethought myself of the indulgence promised me, and asked for a rocking-chair and a fire; not that I required the latter, for the room was already very warm, but I fancied a bright blaze would make it look more cheerful.

My trunk, after being subjected to a thorough scrutiny, was sent up to me, and, having plenty of time at my disposal, I unpacked it leisurely.

The first night in prison was a trying one to me. I rose from my bed and walked to the window. The moon was shining brightly. How I longed that it were in my power to spring through the iron bars that caught and scattered her beams around the room!

The city was asleep, but to my disordered imagination its sleep appeared feverish and perturbed. Far away the open country, visible in the clear night, looked the express image of peace and repose.

"God made the country, and man made the town," I thought, as I contrasted the close atmosphere of my city prison with the clear air of the fields beyond.

What would I not have given to exchange the sound of the sentry's measured tread for the wild shriek of the owl and the drowsy flight of the bat!

The room which was appropriated to me had formerly been the committee-room of the old Congress, and had been repeatedly tenanted by Clay, Webster, Calhoun, and other statesmen of their age and mark.

A thousand strange fancies filled my brain, and nearly drove me mad. The phantoms of the past rose up before me, and I fancied I could hear the voices of the departed orators as they declaimed against the abuses and errors of the day, and gave their powerful aid to the cause of general liberty. They never dreamed that the very walls which reechoed the eloquence of freedom would ere long confine the victims of an oligarchy. Theirs was the bright day—ours is the dark morrow, of which the evil is more than sufficient. Those great men (for great they unquestionably were) lacked not the gift of prophecy, for they did not fail to discern the little cloud, then no bigger than a man's hand, which was gathering in the horizon—that dark speck which was so soon to generate a tempest far blacker than that from which the chariot of Ahab made haste to escape.

Throughout that long dreary night I stood at the window watching, thinking, praying. It seemed to me that morning would never come.

> Methought that streak of dawning gray
> Would never dapple into day,
> So heavily it rolled away
> Before the estern flame.

But the morning came at last—the herald, let me hope, from a brighter world of another morrow to us. No sooner did the first faint light find its way through the windows, than I threw myself again upon my bed, and almost immediately sank into a deep sleep.

It was about nine o'clock, I believe, when I was aroused by a loud knocking at my door.

"What is it?" I cried, springing up.

"The officer calling the roll, to ascertain that no one has escaped."

"You do not expect me to get through these iron bars, do you?"

"No, indeed!" was the chuckling rejoinder; and immediately afterward I heard the officer's retreating footsteps as he passed on in the execution of his duty.

Soon after, the servant who had been assigned to me came to make preparations for breakfast; and, as my morning meal was no less ample and choice than my dinner of the preceding evening, I will not detain my readers with a second prison bill-of-fare.

It was but a few minutes after breakfast, when the sentry directly outside my door was relieved.

I listened attentively, to catch the orders given to the relief. They were—

"You will not allow this lady to come outside her door, or talk to any of those fellows in the room opposite; and if she wants any thing, call the corporal of the guard. Now don't let these —— rebels skear yer!"

There was no more information to be gained for the moment; so, I sat down and amused myself with the morning papers, which had been brought to me with my breakfast.

They all contained an account of my capture, and a summary of my career. The subject-matter was, of course, personally interesting, although in every instance my motives were misconstrued, and my character was aspersed. I must however admit, that many of the most bitter calumnies then published of me were contradicted, not many days afterward, in the very same journals which had originally circulated them.

There was a narrow space behind the prison, which was reserved for the prisoners' exercise—an indulgence they were granted at stated hours. On their way to their play-ground most of them had to pass my door, and in the procession I recognized, on the second day of my imprisonment, several of my old friends and acquaintances who had formerly belonged to the army of Virginia.

The tedious day wore on, and a shudder passed over me as I recalled the hideous thoughts which had banished sleep throughout the previous night.

Late in the evening, when my servant came with my tea, she told me that many prisoners had been brought in during the day, and that two of the newly arrived captives had been consigned to the room adjoining mine.

By this time it had become known throughout the length and breadth of the prison-house that I was no other than the persecuted young lady, "Belle Boyd."

Acting upon this knowledge, my neighbors, who were the friends of happier days, devised a scheme by means of which they were enabled to make themselves known to me.

At about eleven o'clock I sat down and opened my Bible. I selected a chapter, the promises contained in which are peculiarly consoling to the captive; but I had not read more than two or three verses, when my attention was distracted by a knock against the wall. I listened with attention, and presently felt sure that the next sound which reached my ears was that made by a knife scooping out the plaster of the wall.

Within a few minutes, the point of a long case-knife was visible; and I was not slow to co-operate with those pioneers of free communication, the inmates of the next room.

I made use of the knife that remained on my supper-tray; and before long the two knives had conjointly made an aperture large enough to admit of the transmission of notes, rolled tight, and of the circumference of a man's forefinger. The clandestine correspondence that was thus carried on was, on either side of the wall, a source of much pleasure, and served to beguile many a tedious hour.

In the room immediately above mine, and in which Mrs. Greenhow had been incarcerated, and suffered so much for five long weary months, were confined some gentlemen of Fredericksburg. They had contrived to loosen a plank in the floor, and to make an aperture through which the occupant of the room beneath them might receive and return letters.

Whenever I desired to communicate with the prisoners whose rooms were on the opposite side of the passage, I adopted the expedient of wrapping my note round a marble, which I rolled across, taking care that the sentry's back was turned when my missive was started on its voyage of discovery.

I have described how I established a post between my room and the room on my right. The same system was applied, with equal success, to the one on the left, which was the abode of Major Fitzhugh, of Stuart's staff, and Major Morse, of Ewell's. This room, which joined with many others, became a medium of communication with all; and we were soon enabled to transmit intelligence to each other throughout the prison.

It was on the fourth morning of my imprisonment, as I was watching from my door the prisoners going down to breakfast, that a little Frenchman handed me, unobserved, a half-length portrait of Jefferson Davis. This I forthwith hung up in my room over the mantel-piece, with this inscription below it:—"Three cheers for Jeff. Davis and the Southern Confederacy!"

One of the prison officials, Lieutenant Holmes, passing by my door, caught sight of the hostile President's likeness, and the words with which I had decorated it. Rushing like a madman into my room, he tore it down, with many violent oaths. "For this," he said, "you shall be locked in! " And he was as good as his word, for he turned the key in the door as he left the room.

My offence was severely punished. I was kept a close prisoner; and so little air was stirring, in the sultry month of July, that I grew very ill and faint, and at times I really thought I should have died from the oppressive heat of the room. And this misery I had to endure for several weeks. At last Mr. Wood paid me a visit, and, observing how pale and ill I had become under such rigorous treatment, took pity upon me, and gave orders that my door should be once more left open. Soon after, I was granted the further indulgence of half an hour's walk, daily, in that portion of the prison-yard which had been assigned to ladies for exercise.

One day, whilst standing in the doorway, my attention was attracted to an old gentleman almost bent double with age; his long white hair hung down to his shoulders, whilst his beard, gray with the heavy touch of old Father Time's fingers, reached nearly to his waist.

A feeling of pity took possession of my soul, and I could not but help thinking, as I gazed upon him, "Poor old man! what an unfit place for you; even I, the delicate girl, can better stand the hardships of this dreary, comfortless place, than you." And what was his crime? This—he was designated a traitor to the Northern Government because he firmly believed that the Constitution as it was should remain unaltered. I afterward learned that he was Mr. Mahoney, the editor of the *Dubuque* (Iowa) *Crescent*, and who, when released, published a book, "The Prisoner of State," which was, however, suppressed by the Secretary of War, Stanton.

The rules of the prison, of course, interdicted all intercourse between the prisoners, but alas! I was on one occasion taken so completely by surprise as to obey my first impulse and commit a flagrant breach of orders.

I was walking up and down my "seven feet by nine" promenade, when I suddenly recognized one of my cousins, John Stephenson, a young officer in Mosby's cavalry. So glad was I to see him that I never thought of consequences, but rushed up to exchange a few words with him. The charged bayonet of the sentry soon checked my impetuosity, and I was summarily sent back to my room, although "playtime" had not expired. My unfortunate cousin was at once removed to the guard-room.

It was late one evening, and I was sitting reading at my open door, when Mr. Wood came down the stairs, exclaiming—

"All you rebels get ready; you are going to 'Dixie,' tomorrow, and Miss Belle is going with you."

At this joyful news, all the prisoners within hearing of the tidings of their approaching liberation, joined in three hearty cheers. For my part, I actually screamed for joy, so suddenly had my return to freedom been announced.

The next day all the prisoners whose turn for exchange had come were drawn up in line in the prison yard.

Soldiers were stationed from the door of the prison halfway across the street, which was thronged by a dense crowd, brought together by curiosity to witness the departure of the rebel prisoners.

Two hundred captives, inclusive of the officers and myself, were then passed beyond the prison walls, and formed in line on the opposite side of the street.

I stepped into an open carriage, followed by Major Fitzhugh, who had been "told off" to convey me to Richmond.

I carried concealed about me two gold sabre-knots, one of which was intended for General Jackson, the other for General Joe Johnston.

As we drove off, the Confederate prisoners cheered us loudly; their acclamations were taken up by the crowd, so that the whole street and square resounded with applause. When we arrived at the wharf, we were sent on board the steamer *Juniata*, which lay at her moorings all that night.

I shall conclude this chapter with two or three prison reminiscences, which will, I hope, give my reader some idea of the *ménage* of the "Old Capitol."

On one occasion my servant had just brought me a loaf of sugar, when it occurred to me that the Confederate officers in the opposite room across the passage were in want of this very luxury. Accordingly, I asked the sentry's permission to pass it over to them, and received from him an unequivocal consent, in these plain words: "I have no objection."

This, I thought, was sufficient; and it will hardly be believed that, while I was in the very act of placing the sugar in the hand of one of the officers, the sentry struck my left hand with the butt-end of his musket, and with such violence was the blow delivered that my thumb was actually broken. The attack was so unexpected, and the pain so excruciating, that I could not refrain from bursting into tears.

As soon as I could master my feelings, I demanded of the sentry that he should summon the corporal of the guard; and upon his refusing my just demand, I stepped forward with the intention of exercising my undoubted right *in propriâ personâ*.

But my tyrant was now infuriated; he charged bayonet, and actually pinned me to the wall by my dress, his weapon inflicting a flesh-wound on my arm.

At this moment, fortunately for me, the corporal of the guard came rushing up the stairs to ascertain the cause of the disturbance. The sentry was taken off his post, and, unless I am grievously mistaken, a short confinement in the guard-room was considered sufficient punishment for such outrageous conduct.

Not long after this adventure, my aunt called to see me. Permission was given to me to pass down-stairs for the purpose of an interview with my relation, and I was proceeding on my way, when one of the sentries, with a volley of oaths, commanded me to "halt."

"But I have permission to go down and see my relation."

"Go back, or I'll break every bone in your body"; and a bayonet was presented to my breast.

I produced the certificate which authorized me to pass him; and I think, from his manner, he would have relented in his intentions toward me, and returned to a sense of his own duty, but he was encouraged in his mutinous behavior by the cheers of a roomful of Federal deserters, who called upon him to bayonet me. In this predicament I was saved by Major Moore, of the Confederate States Army, and the timely arrival of Captain Higgins and Lieutenant Holmes, two prison authorities, who secured me from further molestation.

This man's crime, which was neither more nor less than open mutiny, was visited by a slight reprimand. This leniency was perhaps intended for a personal compliment to me. If so, let me assure the Yankee officers, I duly appreciate both its force and delicacy.

Mr. Wood, the superintendent, will, I am sure, forgive me for relating one characteristic anecdote of him.

It was Sunday morning when he came stalking down the passage into which my room opened, proclaiming in the tones and with the gestures of a town-crier—

"All you who want to hear the Word of God preached according to 'Jeff. Davis' go down into the yard; and all you who want to hear it preached according to 'Abe Lincoln' go into No. 16."

This was the way in which he separated the goats from the sheep. I need not say which party was considered the goats within the walls of the Old Capitol.

ROSECRANS AND THE CONFEDERATE OFFICER

The following interview took place, during the progress of the battle of Chickamauga, between General Rosecrans and a Captain Rice, of the First Texas regiment. The captain was made prisoner on Saturday afternoon, and taken immediately to Rosecrans, who was two hundred and fifty yards in the rear of the portion of his army which was engaged by Hood's division. Rosecrans appeared, dressed in black breeches, white vest, and plain blouse, and was surrounded by a gorgeous staff. The general is short and thick-set, with smooth face, rosy cheeks and lips, brilliant black eyes, and is very handsome. He is exceedingly affable and pleasant in conversation. On the approach of Captain Rice, he dismounted, tapped him familiarly on the shoulder and said: "Let us step aside and talk a little." Seated on a fallen tree, some thirty yards from the staff, the general, *à la* genuine Yankee, picked up a stick and commenced whittling, and the following conversation ensued:

Rosecrans.—"Where are your lines?"

Rice.—"General; it has cost me a great deal of trouble to find your lines; if you take the same amount of trouble, you will find ours."

Rose.—(Wincing slightly.) "What brigade do you belong to?"

Rice.—"Robertson's."

Rose.—"What division?"
Rice.—"I don't know."
Rose.—"What corps?"
Rice.—"I don't know."
Rose.—"Do you belong to Bragg's army?"
Rice.—"O, yes, sir."

Rosecrans looked at him, and smiled at his ingenuous manner, so perfectly open and candid the captain seemed, then again commenced, blandly:

Rose.—"How many of Longstreet's men got here?"
Rice.—"About forty-five thousand."
Rose.—"Is Longstreet in command?"
Rice.—"O, no, sir! General Bragg is in command."
Rose.—"Captain, you don't seem to know much, for a man whose appearance seems to indicate so much intelligence."
Rice.—"Well, General, if you are not satisfied with my information, I will volunteer some. We are going to whip you most tremendously in this fight."
Rose.—"Why?"
Rice.—"Because you are not ready to fight."
Rose.—"Were you ready?"
Rice.—"Yes; we were ready."
Rose.—"How do you know we were not ready?"
Rice.—"You sent a brigade to burn a bridge. General Bragg sent a brigade to drive yours back. You were forced to reënforce; then General Bragg reënforced, and forced you into an engagement."
Rose.—"I find you know more than I thought you did. You can go to the rear."

"CALL ALL! CALL ALL!"

BY "GEORGIA"

Whoop! the Doodles have broken loose,
Roaring round like the very deuce!
Lice of Egypt, a hungry pack;
After 'em boys, and drive 'em back.

Bull-dog, terrier, cur and fice,
Back to the beggarly land of ice,
Worry 'em, bite 'em, scratch and tear
Everybody and anywhere.

Old Kentucky is caved from under,
Tennessee is split asunder,
Alabama awaits attack,
And Georgia bristles up her back.

Old John Brown is dead and gone!
Still his spirit is marching on,
Lantern-jawed, and legs, my boys,
Long as an ape's from Illinois!

Want a weapon? Gather a brick!
Club or cudgel, or stone or stick,
Anything with a blade or butt!
Anything that can cleave or cut!

Anything heavy, or hard, or keen!
Any sort of slaying-machine!
Anything with a willing mind,
And the steady arm of a man behind.

Want a weapon? Why, capture one!
Every Doodle has got a gun,
Belt and bayonet, bright and new:
Kill a Doodle and capture *two!*

Shoulder to shoulder, son and sire!
All, call all! to the feast of fire!
Mother and maiden, and child and slave,
A common triumph or a single grave.

Black, the Scotchman

One of the Confederate soldiers in the Virginia army was a rough Scotchman, named Black. His relatives were at the South, and, desiring to get to them, he had joined the Northern army, with the intention of deserting at the first opportunity. When on picket-guard at the river, therefore, he pretended to bathe, and being a good swimmer, dexterously struck out for the Virginia shore. When midway, the rogue turned and shouted—"Good-bye, boys; I'm bound for Dixie!" "Come bock, or we'll shoot!" answered the guard. "Shoot and be d——, you white-livered nigger thieves!" shouted Black; and in the midst of a shower of Minié balls he reached his destination. He entered at once the Confederate ranks, and proved an active fighter. During the battle he performed many feats of daring, and at night formed one of a corporal's guard who escorted a full company of captured Federals off the hotly-contested ground. As Black was laughing and joking, the captain of the Federals remarked to him:

"I ought to know that voice! Is that you, Black?"

"That's me!" jocosely replied the renegade Scotchman. "I couldn't stay with you, you see; it wasn't because I feared to fight, but I like to fight in the right cause always."

Singular enough, Black was escorting his old company, officers and all!

A New Use for a Shell

Captain T. J. Adams, of the army of Northern Virginia, relates the following incident:

"Private William Guffey, of my company, while rubbing-up his 'field-piece,' as he was pleased to call his rifle, had the misfortune to have it smashed by a mortar shell. He was more enraged than frightened by the occurrence, and uttered a very uncomplimentary expression against the whole Yankee race. When he saw the shell, with the fuse burning rapidly, and almost ready to explode the dreadful missile, he cried out, 'Why, there's the darned old thing frying now!' And immediately seizing it, he threw it over the works."

An Englishman in Mississippi[*]

On reaching Crystal Springs, half way to Jackson, we found General Loring's division crossing the railroad, and marching east. It had been defeated, with the loss of most of its artillery, three days before, and was now cut off from General Pemberton.

At five in the afternoon the conductor stopped the engine, and put us out at a spot nine miles distant from Jackson; and as I could procure no shelter, food, or conveyance there, I found myself in a terrible fix.

At this juncture, a French boy rode up on horseback, and volunteered to carry my saddlebags as far as Jackson, if I could walk and carry the remainder. Gladly accepting this unexpected offer, I started with him to walk up the railroad, as he assured me the Yankees had really gone; and during the journey he gave me a description of their conduct during the short time they had occupied the city.

On arriving within three miles of Jackson, I found the railroad destroyed by the enemy, who, after pulling up the track, had made piles of the sleepers, and put the rails in layers on the tops of these heaps. They had then set fire to the sleepers, which had caused the rails to bend when redhot. The wooden bridges had also been set on fire, and were still smoking.

When within a mile and a half of Jackson, I met four men, who stopped and questioned me very suspiciously, but they at length allowed me to proceed, saying that these "were curious times." After another mile, I reached a mild trench, which was dignified by the name of the "Fortifications of Jackson." A small fight had taken place there four days previous, when General Johnston had evacuated the city. When I got inside this trench, I came to the spot on which a large body of Yankees had recently been encamped. They had set fire to a great quantity of stores and arms which they had been unable to carry away with them, and which were still burning and were partially destroyed. I observed also a great number of pikes, and pike-heads, among the debris.

At the entrance to the town, the French boy took me to the house of his relatives and handed me my saddlebags. I then shouldered my saddlebags and walked through the smoking and desolate streets toward the Bowman House hotel.

---

[*] From the Diary of Lieutenant Colonel Fremantle.

I had not proceeded far, before a man with long gray hair, and an enormous revolver, rode up to me and offered to carry my saddlebags. He then asked me who I was. And after I told him, he thought a few moments, and then said, "Well, sir, you must excuse me, but if you are a British officer, I can't make out what on earth you are doing at Jackson just now!" I could not but confess that this was rather a natural idea, and that my presence in this burning town must have seemed rather odd, more especially as I was obliged to acknowledge that I was there entirely of my own free will, and for my own amusement.

Mr. Smythe, for so this individual was named, then told me, that if I was really the person I represented myself, I should be well treated by all; but that, if I could not prove myself to be an English officer, an event would happen which it was not difficult to foresee. And the idea caused a disagreeable sensation about the throat!

Mr. Smythe gave me to understand that I must remain a prisoner for the present. He conducted me to a room in the Bowman House hotel, where I found myself speedily surrounded by a group of eager and excited citizens, who had been summoned by Smythe *to conduct my examination.*

At first they were inclined to be disagreeable. They examined my clothes, and argued as to whether they were of English manufacture. Some, who had been in London, asked me questions about the streets of the metropolis, and about my regiment. One remarked that I was *"mighty young for a lootenant-colonel."*

When I suggested that they should treat me with proper respect until I was proved to be a spy, they replied that their city had been brutally pillaged by the Yankees, and that there were many suspicious characters about.

Every thing now looked very threatening, and it became evident to me that nothing would relieve the minds of these men so much as a hanging match. I looked in vain for some one to take my part, and I could not even get any one to examine my papers.

At this critical juncture, a new character appeared on the scene, in the shape of a big, heavy man, who said to me, "My name is Doctor Russell; I am an Irishman by birth, and I hate the British Government and the English nation; but if you are really an officer in the Coldstream Guards, there is nothing I won't do for you; you shall come to my house, and I will protect you."

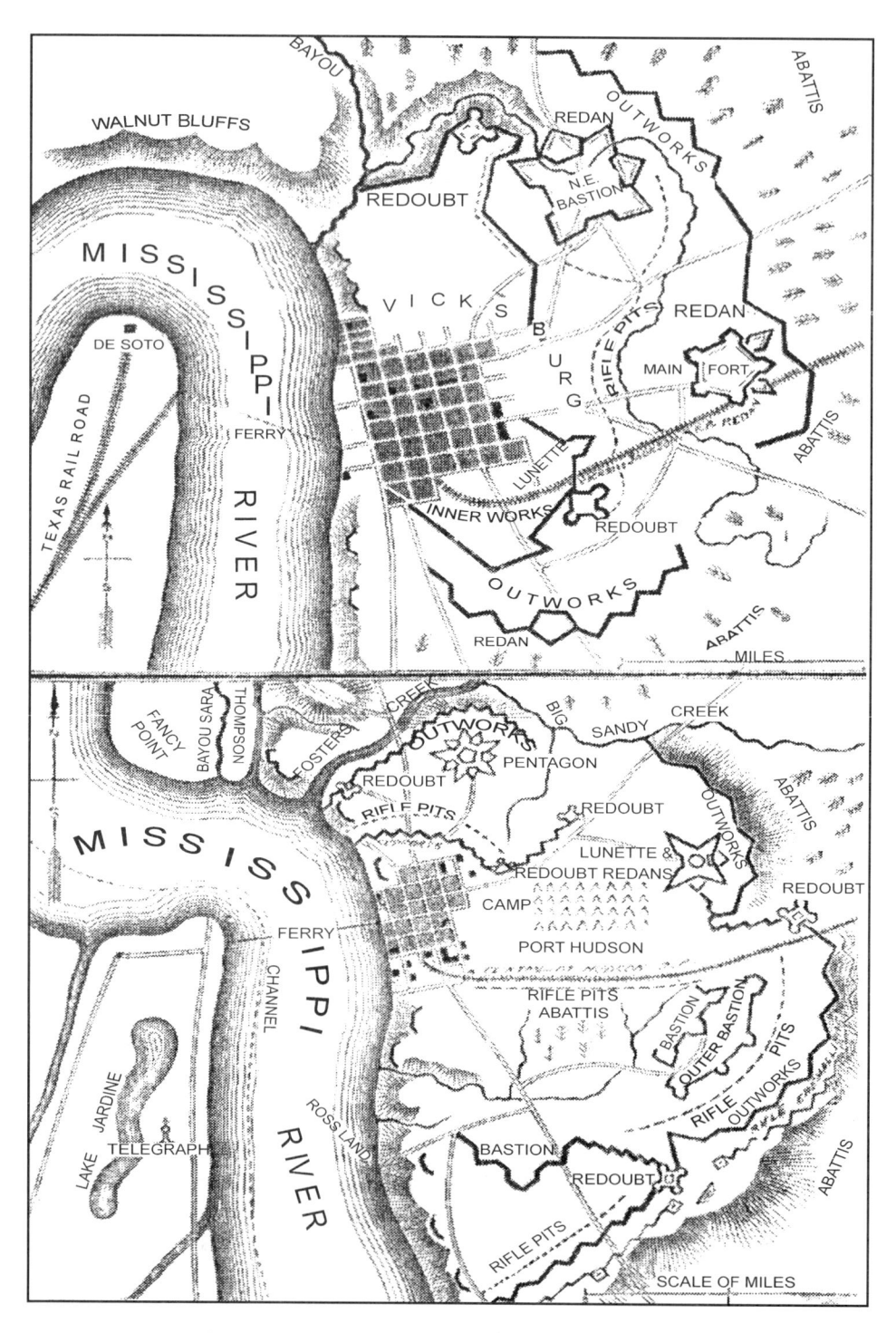

VICKSBURG AND PORT HUDSON DEFENSES

I immediately showed Doctor Russell my passport and my letters of introduction to General Johnston and the other Confederate officers; he pronounced them genuine, promised to stand by me, and wanted to take me away with him at once.

But observing that the countenances of Smythe and his colleagues did not by any means express satisfaction at this arrangement, I announced my determination to stay where I was until I was released by the military authorities, with whom I demanded an immediate audience.

A very handsome cavalry officer, called Captain Yerger, shortly afterward arrived, who released me at once—asked me to his mother's house, and promised that I should join a brigade which was to march for General Johnston's camp on the following morning.

All the citizens seemed to be satisfied by the result of my interview with Captain Yerger, and most of them insisted on shaking hands and "liquoring up" in horrible whisky. Smythe, however, was an exception to this rule. He evidently thought he had effected a grand capture, and was not at all satisfied with the turn of affairs. I believe, to his dying day, he will think I am a spy.

Anecdotes of Stonewall Jackson

A Yankee captain, captured in the battles beyond Richmond, was brought to some brigadier's headquarters. Being fatigued, he laid down under a tree to rest. Pretty soon, General Lee and staff rode up. The Yankee asked who he was, and when told, praised his soldierly appearance in extravagant terms. Not long after, Jackson and his staff rode up. When told that that was Jackson, the Yankee bounced to his feet, in great excitement, showing that he was much more anxious to see Old Stonewall than Lee. He gazed at him a long time. "And that's Stonewall Jackson?" "Yes." "Waal, I swan he ain't much for looks"; and with that he laid down and went to sleep.

During the same battles, a straggler who had built a nice fire in the old field and was enjoying it all to himself, observed what he took to be a squad of cavalry. The man in front seemed to be reeling in his saddle. The straggler ran out to him and said, "Look here, old fellow, you are mighty happy.

Where do you get your liquor from? Give me some, I'm as dry as a powder-horn." Imagine his feelings when he found it was Jackson—the most ungraceful rider in the army, and who naturally swayed from side to side.

General Lee

"General Lee is, almost without exception, the handsomest man of his age I ever saw," says an English writer, who passed some time with him in the field. "He is fifty-six years old, tall, broad-shouldered, very well made, well set up—a thorough soldier in appearance; and his manners are most courteous, and full of dignity. He is a perfect gentleman, in every respect. I imagine no man has so few enemies, or is so universally esteemed. Throughout the South, all agree in pronouncing him to be as near perfection as a man can be. He has none of the small vices, such as smoking, drinking, chewing, or swearing; and his bitterest enemy never accused him of any of the greater ones. He generally wears a well-worn, long gray jacket, a high black felt hat, and blue trousers, tucked into his Wellington boots. I never saw him carry arms, and the only mark of his military rank are the three stars on his collar. He rides a handsome horse, which is extremely well groomed. He himself is very neat in his dress and person, and, in the most arduous marches, he always looks smart and clean.

"In the old army he was always considered one of its best officers, and at the outbreak of these troubles he was Lieutenant-Colonel of the second cavalry. He was a rich man, but his fine estate was one of the first to fall into the enemy's hands. I believe he has not slept in a house since he has commanded the Virginian army, and he invariably declines all offers of hospitality, for fear the person offering it may afterward get into trouble for having sheltered the rebel General. The relations between him and Longstreet are quite touching. They are almost always together. Longstreet's corps complain of this sometimes, as, they say, they seldom get a chance of detached service, which falls to the lot of Ewell. It is impossible to please Longstreet more than by praising Lee. I believe these two Generals to be as little ambitious, and as thoroughly unselfish, as any men in the world. Both long for a successful termination of the war, in order that they may retire into obscurity. Stonewall Jackson (until his death the third in command of their army) was just such another simple-minded servant of his country. It is understood that General Lee is a religious man, though not as demonstrative, in that respect, as Jackson; and, unlike his late brother-in-arms, he is a member of the Church of England. His only faults, so far as I can learn, arise from his excessive amiability."

Jackson at Kernstown

Jackson was watching the progress of the action, from a point near at hand, when suddenly, to his inexpressible chagrin, he saw the lines of his old brigade fall back. He galloped to the spot—stern, fiery, and menacing as Washington at Monmouth—and imperatively ordering General Garnett to hold his ground, pushed forward to stop and rally the men. Seeing a drummer retreating like the rest, he seized him by the shoulder, dragged him to a rise in the ground, in full view of all the troops, and said in his curt quick tones: "Beat the rally!"

The drum rolled at his order, and with his hand on the frightened drummer's shoulder, amid a storm of balls, Jackson saw that the disordered lines were reformed and brought into something like order.—*Cooke's "Life of Stonewall Jackson."*

Sidney Johnson's Patriotism

Lieutenant-Colonel Jack, of the late General Johnson's staff, relates the following incident:

It was after a conversation on the subject of the war, on a bright morning when the winter's sun was shining out, and nature was assuming the smiles of spring, that, looking around upon the surrounding landscape of beauty, General Johnson burst forth, with the enthusiasm of an ardent nature: "Who could be a coward when called to the defence of a country like this!"

A Slight Mistake

"Not long since," wrote a soldier, "a lot of us—I am a H. P., 'high private,' now—were quartered in several wooden tenements, and in the inner room of one lay the *corpus* of a young Confederate officer awaiting burial. The news soon spread to a village not far off, and down came a sentimental, not bad-looking specimen of a Virginia dame.

"'Let me kiss him for his mother!' she cried, as I interrupted her progress. 'Do let me kiss him for his mother!'

"'Kiss whom?'

"'The dear little Lieutenant, the one who lies dead within. I never saw him, but, O'——,

"I led her through a room in which Lieutenant ——, of New Orleans, lay stretched out in an up-turned trough, fast asleep. Supposing him to be the article sought for, she rushed up, exclaiming: 'Let me kiss him for his mother,' and approached her lips to his forehead. What was her amazement, when the 'corpse' clasped his arms around her, and exclaimed: 'Never mind the old lady, miss; go it on your own account. I haven't the slightest objection.'"

Crossing the Border*

We were in the saddle again an hour before sunset, our next point being a log-hut on the very topmost ridge of the Alleghenies, wherein dwelt a man said to be better acquainted than any other in the country round, with the passes leading into the Shenandoah Valley. We ascertained, beyond a doubt, that a company was stationed at Greenland Gap, close to which it was absolutely necessary we should pass; but with a thoroughly good local guide, we might fairly count on the same luck which had brought us safe round Oakland.

Night had fallen long before we came down on the South River, a mere mountain torrent, at ordinary seasons; but now, flowing along with the broad dignity of a swift, smooth river. My guide's mare wanted shoeing, and there chanced to be a rude forge close to the ford, which is the only crossing-place since the bridge was destroyed last autumn by the

---

* From *"Border and Bastile."* By the author of *"Guy Livingstone."*

Confederates. It was important that the local pilot should be secured as soon as possible (he was constantly absent from home), so I rode on alone, with directions that were easy to follow.

The smith, whose house stood but three hundred yards or so off, had told me that I had to strike straight across the ford, for a gap in the dense wood cloaked by the opposite bank. It was disagreeably dark at the water's edge, for the low moon was utterly hidden behind a thicket of cypress and pine; but I did make out a narrow opening *exactly* opposite; for this I headed unhesitatingly. We lost footing twice; but a mass of tangled timber above broke the current—nowhere very strong—and the water shoaled quickly under the further shore; the bottom was sound, too, just there, though the bank was steep; and Falcon answered a sharp drive of the spurs with a gallant spring, that landed him on a narrow shelf of slippery clay, hedged in on three sides by brush absolutely impenetrable. There was not room to stand firm, much less to turn safely; before I had time to think what was to be done, there was a backward slide, and a flounder; in two seconds more, I had drawn myself with some difficulty from under my horse, who lay still on his side, too wise, at first, to struggle unavailingly. If long hunting experience makes a man personally rather indifferent about accidents, it also teaches him when there is danger to the animal he rides; looking at Falcon's utter helplessness and the constrained twist of his hind legs, which I tried in vain to straighten, I began to have uncomfortable visions of ricked backs and strained sinews: I was on the wrong side of the river, too, for help; though even the rope of a Dublin Garrison "wrecker" would have helped but little then. Thrice the good horse made a desperate attempt to stand up, and thrice he sank back again with the hoarse sigh, between pant and groan—half breathless, half despairing—that every hunting man can remember, to his cost. It was impossible to clear the saddle-bags without cutting them; I had drawn my knife for this purpose, when a fourth struggle (in which his fore-hoofs twice nearly struck me down), set Falcon once more on his feet—trembling, and drenched with sweat, but materially uninjured. I contrived to scramble into the saddle, and we plunged into the ford again, heading up stream, till we struck the real gap, which was at least thirty yards higher up. It is ill trusting to the accuracy of a native's *carte du pays*. Another league brought me to the wayside but where I was instructed to ask for fresh guidance.

"Right over the big pasture, to the bars at the corner—then keep the track through the wood to the 'improvements'—and the house was close by." Such were the directions of the good-natured mountaineer, who offered himself to accompany me; but this I would by no means allow.

Now, an up-country pasture, freshly cleared, is a most unpleasant place to cross, after nightfall: the stumps are all left standing, and felled trees lie all about—thick as boulders on a Dartmoor hillside; then, however, a steady moon was shining, and Falcon picked his way daintily through the timber, hopping lightly, now and then, over a trunk bigger than the rest, but never losing the faint track; we got over the high bars, too, safely, hitting them hard. The wood-path led out upon a clearing, after a while: here I was fairly puzzled. There was no sign of human habitation, except a rough hut, some hundred yards to my right, that I took to be an outlying cattle-shed: there was not the glimmer of a light anywhere.

I have not yet written the name of the man I was seeking: contrasts of time and place made it so very remarkable, that I venture to break the rule of anonyms. Mortimer Nevil—who would have dreamed of lighting on, perhaps, the two proudest patronymics of baronial England, in a log hut crowning the ridge of the Alleghenies?

While I wandered hither and thither in utter bewilderment, my ear caught a sound as of one hewing timber; I rode for it, and soon found that the hovel I had passed thrice was the desired homestead; truly, it was fitting that the possible descendant of the king-maker should reveal himself by the rattle of his axe.

It is needless to say that I was received courteously and kindly. The mountaineer promised his services readily; albeit, he spoke by no means confidently of our chances of getting through; the company of Western Virginians that had recently marched into Greenland was said to be unusually vigilant; only the week before, a professional blockade runner had been captured, who had made his way backward and forward repeatedly, and was thoroughly conversant with the ground. The attempt could not possibly be made till the following evening; till then, Nevil promised to do his best to make Falcon and me comfortable.

I shall not easily forget my night in the log hut; it consisted of a single room, about sixteen feet by ten; in this lived and slept the entire family—numbering the farmer, his wife, mother, and two children. When they spoke confidently of finding me a bed, I fell into a great tremor and perplexity; the problem seemed to me not more easily to solve than that of the ferryman who had to carry over a fox, a goose, and a cabbage; it was physically impossible that the large-limbed Nevil and myself should be packed into the narrow nonnuptial couch; the only practicable arrangement involved my sharing its pillow with the two infants or with the ancient dame; and, at the bare thought of either alternative, I shivered from head to heel. At last, with infinite difficulty, I obtained permission to sleep on my horse-rug spread on the floor, with my saddle for a bolster; when this point was once settled, I spent the evening very contentedly, basking in the blaze of the huge oaken logs; if stinted in all else, the mountaineer has always large luxury of fuel. I was curious to find out if my host knew any thing of his own lineage; but he could tell me nothing further than that his grandfather was the first colonist of the family. Oddly enough, though, in his library of three or four books, was an ancient work on heraldry; his father had been much addicted to studying this, and was said to have been learned in the science.

At about ten, P.M., Shipley knocked at the door, fearfully wet and cold. The smith had accompanied him to the ford, so that he could not go astray, but his filly hardly struggled through the deep, strong water. Our host found quarters for him in the log hut of a brother who dwelt a short half-mile off.

I spent all the forepart of the next day in lounging about, watching the sluggish sap drain out of the sugar-maple, occasionally falling back on the female society of the place; for the Nevil had gone forth on the scout. It was not very lively. My hostess was kindness itself, but the worn, weary look never was off her homely face. Nor did I wonder at this, when I heard that, beside their present troubles and hardships, they had lost four children in one week of the past winter from diphtheria. It was sad to see how painfully the mother clung to the two that death had left her. She could not bear them out of her sight for an instant. A very weird-looking comer was the grand-dame—with a broken, piping voice, tremulous hands, and jaws that, like the stage-witch's wife, ever munched and mumbled. She seldom spoke aloud, except to groan out a startlingly-sudden ejaculation of "Oh, Lord!" or "Oh dear!" These widow's mites, cast into the conversational treasury, did not greatly enhance its brilliancy.

The blue sky grew murky white before sundown, and night fell intensely cold. The Nevil, who guided us on foot, had much the best of it, and I often dismounted to walk by his side. If he who sang the praises of the "wild northwester," had been with us then, I doubt if he would not have abated of his enthusiasm. The bitter snow-laden blast, even where thick cover broke its vicious sweep, was enough to make the blood stand still in the veins of the veriest Viking. After riding about ten miles, we left the rough paths we had hitherto pursued and struck across the country. For two hours or more we forced our way slowly and painfully through bush and brake—through marshy rills and rocky burns—demolishing snake-fences whenever we broke out on a clearing. Shipley led his mare almost the whole way ; and I, thinking the saddle the safest and pleasantest conveyance over ordinarily rough ground, was compelled to dismount repeatedly.

It was about one o'clock in the morning of Sunday, the 5th of April. We were then crossing some tilled lands, intersected by frequent narrow belts of woodland. Our course ran parallel to the mountain-road leading from Greenland to Petersburg. The former place was then nearly three miles behind us, and our guide felt certain that we had passed the outermost pickets. It was very important that we should get housed before break of day; so we were on the point of breaking into the beaten track again, and had approached it within fifty yards, when suddenly, out of the dark hollow on our left, there came a hoarse shout:—"Stop! Who are you? Stop! Or I'll fire!"

Now, I have heard a challenge or two in my time, and felt certain at once that even a Federal picket would have employed a more regular formula. The same idea struck Shipley too.

"Come on!" he said, "they're only citizens."

So on we went, disregarding a second and third summons in the same words. We both looked round for the Nevil, but keener eyes would have sought for him in vain. At the first sound of voices he had plunged into the dark woods above us, where a footman, knowing the country, might defy any pursuit. Peace and joy go with him! By remaining he would only have ruined himself, without profiting us one jot.

Then three revolver-shots were fired in rapid succession. To my question if he was hit, my guide answered cheerily in the negative. Neither of us guessed that one bullet had struck his mare high up in the neck; though the wound proved mortal the next day, it was scarcely perceptible; and bled altogether internally. One of those belts of woodland crossed our track

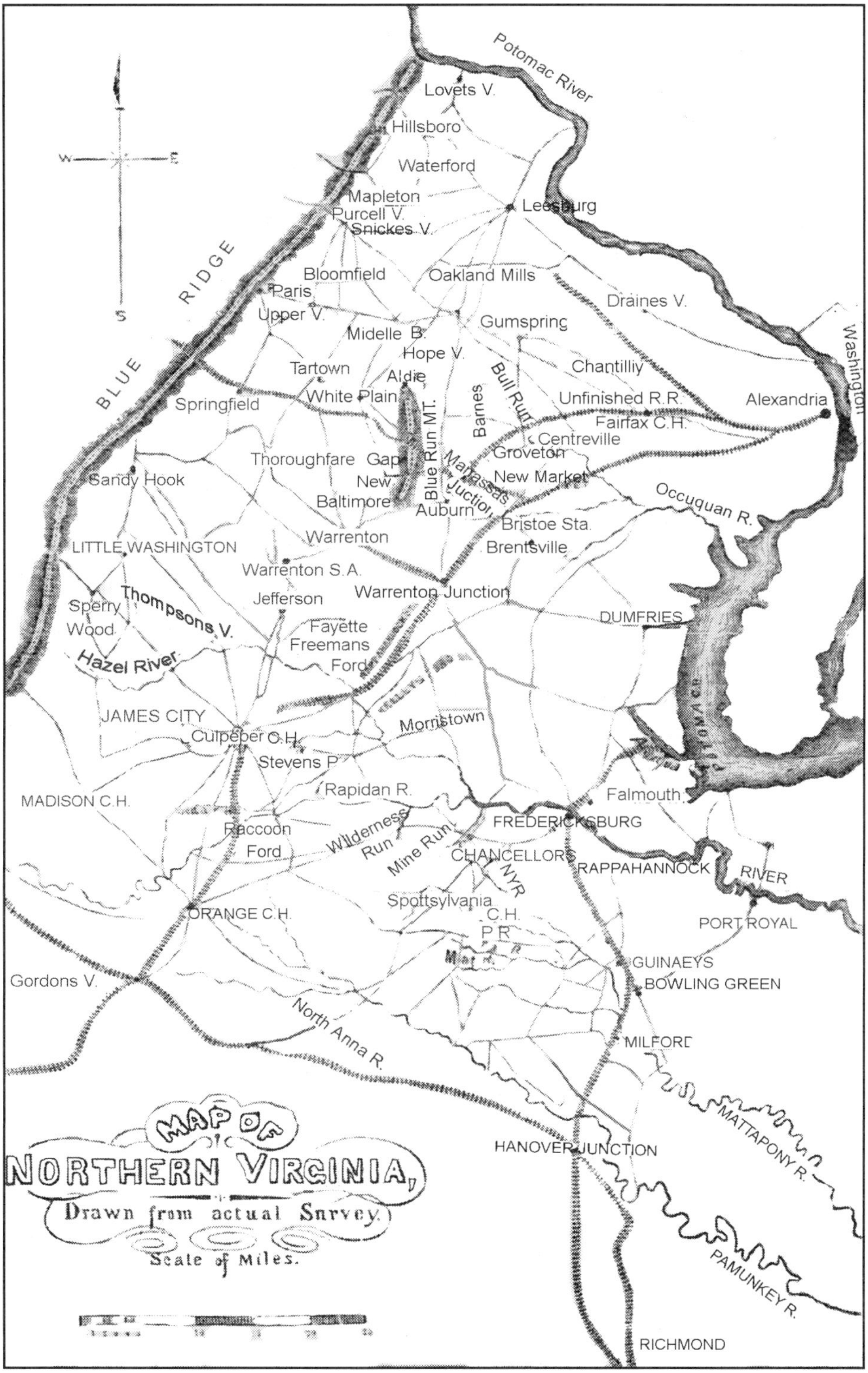

MAP OF
NORTHERN VIRGINIA,
Drawn from actual Snrvey.
Scale of Miles.
Potomac River
Lovets V.
Hillsboro
Waterford
Mapleton
Purcell V.
Snickes V.
Leesburg
BLUE RIDGE
Bloomfield
Oakland Mills
Paris
Upper V.
Draines V.
Midelle B.
Gumspring
Hope V.
Tartown
Aldie
Chantilliy
White Plain
Bull Run
Barnes
Unfinished R.R.
Alexandria
Washington
Springfield
Blue Run MT.
Fairfax C.H.
Centreville
Groveton
Thoroughfare
Gap
Manassas Junction
New Market
Sandy Hook
New Baltimore
Auburn
Occuquan R.
Bristoe Sta.
Warrenton
Brentsville
LITTLE WASHINGTON
Warrenton S.A.
Warrenton Junction
Jefferson
Sperry
Thompsons V.
Wood
DUMFRIES
Fayette
Freemans
Ford
Hazel River
POTOMAC R.
JAMES CITY
Morristown
Culpeper C.H.
Stevens P
Rapidan R.
MADISON C.H.
Falmouth
FREDERICKSBURG
Raccoon
Ford
Wilderness
Run
Mine Run
CHANCELLORS
NYR
RAPPAHANNOCK
RIVER
Spottsylvania
C.H.
ORANGE C.H.
PORT ROYAL
P R
GUINAEYS
Gordons V.
BOWLING GREEN
North Anna R.
MILFORD
MATTAPONY R.
HANOVER JUNCTION
PAMUNKEY R.
RICHMOND
W
E
S

about two hundred yards ahead. We crashed into this over a gap in the snake-fence; but the barrier on the further side was high and intact. Shipley had dismounted, and had nearly made a breach by pulling down the rails, when the irregular challenge was repeated directly in our front, and we made out a group of three dark figures about thirty-five yards off.

"Give your names, and where you are going, or I'll fire!"

"He's very fond of firing!" I said in an undertone to Shipley, and then spoke out aloud—(I saw at once the utter impossibility of escape, even if we could have found our way back, without quitting our horses, which I never dreamed of):

"If you'll come here, I'll tell you all about it."

I could not have advanced if I had wished it. In broad day, the fence would have been barely practicable. I spoke those exact words in a tone purposely measured and calm, so that they should not be mistaken by our assailants. I have good reason to remember them, for they were the last I ever uttered on American ground as a free agent. They had hardly passed my lips, when a rifle cracked. I felt a dull numbing blow inside my left knee, and a sensation as if hot sealing-wax was trickling there! At the same instant, Falcon dropped under me—without a start, or struggle, or sound, beside a horrible choking sob—shot right through the jugular-vein!

Before I had struggled clear of my horse, Shipley's hand was on my shoulder, and his hurried whisper in my ear: "What shall we do? Will you surrender?"

Now, though I knew already that I had escaped with a flesh-wound from a spent bullet, I felt that I could not hope to make quick tracks that night. Certain reasons—wholly independent of personal convenience—made me loth to part with my saddlebags. Besides this, I own I shrank from the useless ignominy of being hunted down like a wild beast on the mountains. So I answered, rather impatiently: "What the deuce would you have one do, with a dead horse and a lamed leg? Shift for yourself as well as you can."

Without another word, I walked toward the party in our front, with an impulse I cannot now define. It could scarcely have been seriously aggressive, for a hunting-knife was my solitary weapon. But, for one moment, I *was* idiot enough to regret my lost revolver. I was traveling as a neutral and civilian, with no other object than my private ends. The slaughter of an American citizen, on his own ground, would have been simply murder, both by moral and martial law, and I heard afterward that our Legation could not have interfered to prevent condign punishment. But reason is dumb sometimes, when the instincts of the "old Adam" are speaking. I suppose I am not more truculent than my fellows; but, since then, in all calmness and sincerity, I have thanked God for sparing me one strong temptation.

Before I had advanced ten paces, the same voice challenged again.

"Stop where you are! If you come a step nearer, I'll shoot!"

I was in no mood to listen to argument, much less to an absurd threat.

"You may shoot and be d——d!" I said. "You've got the shooting all your own way to-night—I carry no fire-arms"; and walked on.

Now, I record these words, conscious that they were thoroughly discreditable to the speaker, simply because I mentioned them in my examination before the judge-advocate (after he had insisted on the point of verbal accuracy); and from his office emanated a paragraph, copied into all the Washington journals, stating that I had cursed my captors fluently. I affirm, on my honor, that this was the solitary imprecation that escaped me from first to last.

So I kept on advancing: they did *not* fire, and I don't suppose they would have done so, even if they had had time to reload. I soon got near enough to discern that, among the three men, there was not a trace of uniform; they were evidently farmers, and roughly dressed "at that." So I opened parley in no gentle terms, requiring their authority for what they had done, and promising that they should answer it, if there was such a thing as law in these parts.

"Well, if we ain't soldiers," the chief speaker said, "we're Home Guards, and that's the same thing here; we've as much authority as we want to back us out. Why didn't you stop, and tell us who you are, and where you're going?"

By this time I was cool enough to reflect and act with a purpose. For my own as well as for his sake, I was most anxious that Shipley should escape. I knew they would not find a scrap of compromising paper on me; but he was a perfect post-carrier of dangerous documents, and a marked man besides—altogether a suspicious companion for an innocent traveler. So I began to discuss several points with my captors in a much calmer tone—demonstrating that from the irregularity of their challenge we could not suppose that it came from any regular picket—that there were many horse thieves and marauders about, so that it behooved travelers to be cautious—that it would have been impossible to have explained our names, object, and destination in a breath, even if they had given more time for such reply. Finally, making a virtue of necessity, I consented to accompany them to the regular outpost of Greenland, stipulating that I should have a horse to carry me and my saddle-bags; for my knee was still bleeding, and stiffening fast.

All this debate took ten minutes at least, during which time my captors seemed to have forgotten my companion's existence, though they must have seen his figure cross the open ground when they first fired. Long before we got back to the horses, Shipley had "vamosed" into the mountain, carrying his light luggage with him; only some blank envelopes were lying about, evidently dropped in the hurry of removal.

I knelt down by Falcon's side, and lifted his head out of the dark-red pool in which it lay. Even in the dim light I could see the broad, bright eye glazing: the death-pang came very soon; he was too weak to struggle, but a quick, convulsive shiver ran through all the lower limbs, and, with a sickening hoarse gurgle in the throat, the last breath was drawn.

A Modest Wish

At the battle of Kinston, the Junior Reserves (made up of lads under eighteen) were sent to force the crossing of Southwest creek, and drive the enemy away, to make good the passage of the other troops. This they did very handsomely, but encountering a severe fire, a portion of one regiment sought a safer place. As they were streaming to the rear, they met the Alabama boys, and were greeted with shouts of laughter. A general officer, in no laughing mood at their behavior, took steps to stop the disorder, and, with his own hands, seized one of the fugitives.

General.—"What are you running for?"

Junior.—"Oh! General, the Yankees were shooting at us."

General.—"Why didn't you shoot back again? Ain't you ashamed of yourself? You are crying like a baby."

Junior.—(Blubbering)— "I wish I was a baby! Oh, I wish I was a *gal* baby!"

ANECDOTES OF GENERAL LEE

"The Land We Love," relates the following anecdotes of General Lee:

Our noble old commander-in-chief was always so occupied with his many cares and responsibilities, that he had but little time, during the war, for social intercourse, and yet he very much enjoyed a quiet joke. Witness the following:

Upon one occasion, while inspecting the lines near Petersburg, with several general officers, he asked General —— if a certain work which he had directed him to complete as soon as possible, had been finished. General —— looked rather confused, but answered that it was. General Lee at once proposed to ride in that direction. On getting to the place, it was found that no progress had been made on the work since General Lee was last there. General —— at once apologized, and said that he had not been on that part of the line for some time, but that Captain —— had told him that the work was completed. General Lee made no reply, at the moment, but not long after began to compliment General —— on the splendid horse he rode. " Yes, sir," replied General —— , "he is a very fine animal. He belongs to my wife." "A remarkably fine horse," returned General Lee, "but not a safe one for Mrs. —— . He is too mettlesome by far, and you ought to take the mettle out of him before you permit her to ride him. And let me suggest, General —— , that an admirable way of doing that *is to ride him a good deal along these trenches.*" The face of the gallant General —— turned crimson, and General Lee's eyes twinkled with mischief. No further allusion was made to the matter, but General —— adopted the suggestion.

Late one night General Lee had occasion to go into a tent where several officers were sitting around a table, on which was a stone jug and two tin-cups, busily engaged in the discussion of a mathematical problem. The general obtained the information he desired, gave a solution of the problem, and retired—the officers hoping he had not noticed the jug. The next day, one of these officers, in the presence of the others, related to General Lee a very strange dream he had had the night before. "That is not at all surprising," replied the general, "when young gentlemen discuss, at midnight, mathematical problems, the unknown quantities of which are a stone jug and two tin-cups, they may expect to have strange dreams."

STONEWALL JACKSON AND THE FARMER

There lived, in the summer of 1862, on the Mechanicsville turnpike, near Richmond, a generous, hospitable, whole-souled Virginia gentleman, who, however, was very passionate and excitable, and who, when flurried, was apt to mix up the reverential and the profane, the sublime and the ridiculous, in a very odd kind of way. He had given up all his crop, pasture-fields, and every thing he could spare, to the Confederate States Government; but he had reserved one ten-acre lot of corn for his own use, and this he guarded with unceasing vigilance. One day, while on watch, he discovered a group of horsemen approaching, and, instead of going round his fence; they took the most direct road right through. His wrath was instantly aroused, and supposing that they belonged to that class of individuals whom a well-known French officer in our service used to call "de damn cavelree," he rushed out in great rage. "How dare you go through my field? Damn you, I'll report you to President Davis."

"We are on urgent business, and took the shortest cut," mildly replied the leading horseman, in an old faded-gray suit.

Gentleman.—"Do you command this company?"

Horseman.—"Yes, sir."

Gentleman.—"I'll teach you not to ride through my field, damn you! What's your name?"

Horseman.—"My name is Jackson."

Gentleman.—"What Jackson?"

Horseman.—"T. J. Jackson."

Gentleman.—"What is your rank?"

Horseman.—"I am a major-general in the Provisional army!"

Gentleman (raising his hat).—"Bless my soul! you ain't *Stonewall* Jackson?"

Horseman. —"I am sometimes called by that name."

Gentleman (rushing eagerly up to him and shaking his hand). —"God bless you, General Jackson! I am so glad to see you! Go back and ride all over my field, damn you, ride all over my field! Get down, and come into my house. I am so glad to see you. Ride all over my field, all over it—all over it! Bless your soul, I'm so glad to see you."

A Very Long War

Some good, but rather hard stories, are told by the Northern papers in connection with the occupation of the Southern coast towns by their forces. Among them is the following:

In the month of February 1862, when the United States troops occupied Jacksonville, Florida, some Confederate soldiers were captured. A motley crew they were, whose picturesque variety of raggedness bore here and there some indications of aim at military style, but nothing of what could be called "uniform." Two men claimed exemption from capture as being civilians. One of the two owned to having been impressed into the Confederate army, but alleged that he had got his discharge, and was then a civilian.

"How long were you a soldier?" asked Captain Randolph.

"Three years!" replied the prisoner.

"The Confederate army has been three years in the field, eh?" asked the captain.

"No," answered the 'cracker,' "but I was in the State of Florida service part of the time."

"How long were you a soldier for Florida?"

"Two years," said the ex-conscript.

"And how long has the war been going forward?" asked the captain again.

"Well, I suppose going on fifteen years !" replied the prisoner.

"Are you sure of that?" his captor inquired.

"Now, I hain't kept no strict tally," the Floridan veteran answered, "but this I do know sarten—we've been hangin' the darned Ab'lishnists a darned sight longer time nor that well, 'bout's longs I kin remember!"

Demoralized

At the battle of Sharpsburg, General Lee met a straggler going to the rear at full speed. Stopping him, the general sternly ordered him to return to his duty immediately.

"I can't, General! I can't!" replied the man, his face paling, and his teeth chattering at the very thought of going back; "I'm wounded!"

"You are not wounded, sir," cried the general, indignantly. "You are as sound as I am."

"Well, Gen'ral," stammered the fellow, "to tell you the truth, *I was stung by a bung* (bomb) *just now, and I'm what you call demoralized, badly demoralized, sir!*"

Zollicoffer

First in the fight, and first in the arms
    Of the white-winged angels of glory,
With the heart of the South at the feet of God,
    And his wounds to tell his story.

For the blood that flowed from his hero heart,
    On the spot where he nobly perished,
Was drunk by the earth as a sacrament,
    In the holy cause he cherished!

In Heaven a home with the brave and bless'd,
    And for his soul's sustaining
The apocalyptic eyes of Christ—
    And nothing on earth remaining,

But a handful of dust in the land of his choice,
    A name in song and story—
And Fame to shout, with her brazen voice.
    He died on the field of glory!

Part II

The Grayjackets in Camp, Field, and Hospital

THE ANGEL OF THE HOSPITAL

'Twas nightfall in the hospital. The day,
As though its eyes were dimmed with bloody rain
From the red clouds of war, had quenched its light,
And in its stead some pale, sepulchral lamps
Shed their dim lustre in the halls of pain,
And flaunted mystic shadows o'er the walls.

No more the cry of Charge! On, soldiers, on!
Stirred the thick billows of the sulphurous air;
But the deep moan of human agony,
From pale lips quivering as they strove in vain
To smother mortal pain, appalled the ear,
And made the life-blood curdle in the heart.
Nor flag, nor bayonet, nor plume, nor lance,
Nor burnished gun, nor clarion call, nor drum,
Displayed the pomp of battle; but instead
The tourniquet, the scalpel, and the draught,
The bandage, and the splint were strewn around—
Dumb symbols, telling more than tongues could speak
The awful shadows of the fiend of war.

Look! Look! What gentle form with cautious step
Passes from couch to couch as silently
As yon faint shadows flickering on the walls,
And bending o'er the gasping sufferer's head,
Cools his flushed forehead with the icy bath,

From her own tender hand, or pours the cup
Whose cordial powers can quench the inward flame
That burns his heart to ashes, or with voice
As tender as a mother's to her babe,
Pours pious consolation in his ear

She came to one long used to war's rude scenes—
A soldier from his youth, grown gray in arms,
 Now pierced with mortal wounds. Untutored, rough,
Though brave and true, uncared for by the world.
His life had passed without a friendly word,
Which timely spoken to his willing ear,
Had wakened godlike hopes, and filled his heart
With the unfading bloom of sacred truth.
 Beside his couch she stood, and read the page
Of heavenly wisdom, and the law of love,
And bade him follow the triumphant chief
Who bears the unconquered banner of the cross.
 The veteran heard with tears, and grateful smile,
Like a long frozen fount whose ice is touched
By the resistless sun, and melts away,
And fixing his last gaze on her and heaven,
 Went to the Judge in penitential prayer.

She passed to one in manhood's blooming prime,
Lately the glory of the martial field,
But now sore scathed by the fierce shock of arms,
Like a tall pine shattered by the lightning's stroke.
Prostrate he lay, and felt the pangs of death,
And saw its thickening damps obscure the light
Which makes our world so beautiful. Yet these
He heeded not. His anxious thoughts had flown
O'er rivers and illimitable woods,
To his fair cottage in the Western wilds,
Where his young bride and prattling little ones—
Poor hapless little ones, chafed by the wolf of war—
Watched for the coming of the absent one
In utter desolation's bitterness.

O, agonizing thought! which smote his heart
With sharper anguish than the sabre's point.
The angel came with sympathetic voice,
And whispered in his ear: Our God will be
 A husband to the widow, and embrace
 The orphan tenderly within his arms;
For human sorrow never cries in vain
To His compassionate ear. The dying man
 Drank in her words with rapture; cheering hope
Shone like a rainbow in his tearful eyes,
And arched his cloud of sorrow, while he gave
The dearest earthly treasures of his heart,
In resignation to the care of God.

A fair man-boy of fifteen summers, tossed
His wasted limbs upon a cheerless couch.
Ah! how unlike the downy bed prepared
By his fond mother's love, whose tireless hands
No comforts for her only offspring spared,
From earliest childhood, when the sweet babe slept
Soft, nestling in her bosom all the night,
Like a half-blown lily sleeping on the heart
Of swelling summer wave, till that sad day
He left the untold treasure of her love
To seek the rude companionship of war.

The fiery fever struck his swelling brain
With raving madness, and the big veins throbbed
A death-knell on his temples, and his breath
Was hot and quick, as is the panting deer's,
Stretched by the Indian's arrow on the plain.
"Mother! Oh, mother!" oft his faltering tongue
 Shrieked to the cold bare walls, which echoed back
His wailing in the mocking of despair.
Oh! angel-nurse, what sorrow wrung thy heart
For the young sufferer's grief! She knelt beside
The dying lad, and smoothed his tangled locks

Back from his aching brow, and wept and prayed
With all a woman's tenderness and love,
That the good Shepherd would receive this lamb,
Far wandering from the dear maternal fold,
And shelter him in His all-circling arms,
In the green valleys of immortal rest.
And so the Angel passed from scene to scene
Of human suffering, like that blessed One,
Himself the Man of sorrows and of grief,
Who came to earth to teach the law of love,
And pour sweet balm upon the mourner's heart,
And raise the fallen and restore the lost.
Bright vision of my dreams! thy light shall shine
Through all the darkness of this weary world—
Its selfishness, its coldness, and its sin,
Pure as the holy evening star of love,
The brightest planet in the host of Heaven.

Heroism of Southern Troops

General Bradley T. Johnston, of Maryland, thus describes the gallantry of the North Carolina troops in the battles of Jackson's Valley campaign:

You know it was my fortune to fight the battle of Front Royal by myself, having only Wheat's Tigers with me—we, in all, not three hundred; they, eight hundred, and two pieces of artillery. Not a shot was fired by infantry, except my regiment and Wheat's men; and after a three hours' fight we drove the enemy, and the cavalry captured those we left. Forty escaped; the rest were killed or captured. Of course we had quite a number of congratulations; and the capture of one first Maryland regiment, by another, was considered, in our army, a capital joke. However, early Sunday morning, just at daylight, I was ordered to the front again. There I found Kirkland, and the twenty-first North Carolina, who had occupied a hill overlooking Winchester since midnight. He was deployed on our (Ewell's) right, as skirmishers. I was to take the same position on our left, and open communication with Jackson, who was approaching by the

Strasburg road. The crest of hills we occupied sweeps along in a semicircle southeast of Winchester; overlooking the town, and half a mile from its suburbs. As the mist of the morning melted before the advancing light, I looked over toward the North Carolinians, who were feeling their way down the hill slowly, but with the regularity and precision of veterans. Soon they formed line-of-battle, and, with a "huzza!" charged, in a run. I did the best I could to beat them; but just as I got on their flank, some hundred of yards to their left, a brigade of Yankees rose from behind a stone wall, and poured into them a sheet of lead and fire which nothing could withstand. Kirkland went down; the lieutenant-colonel fell; the front rank was shattered, as a wave on a rock; but still, many kept on, with a shout, and gained the wall, only to meet death there at the muzzles of the guns of the concealed foe. I ran on to turn the flank of their position; got there just in time to be seen; and in the smoke, which was then so thick you could see nothing ten yards off, the enemy retired. All firing ceased for fifteen minutes; and when the curtain raised from the field, the wall was clear, and the Yankees had gone. Banks's adjutant-general, in an address to Massachusetts, said, "It (the second Massachusetts) retired because a large force suddenly appeared behind them to their right." It was only my small regiment; but the truth is, they had no stomach for another charge from the North Carolinians. That charge was the closest I have ever seen. Some of the men were not ten yards from the enemy.

Execution of Captain Webster

One of the Richmond papers of April 30th, 1862, contained the following account of the execution of a Federal spy:

On the second of April, the court-martial convened for the trial of Timothy Webster, as an alien enemy; Colonel Nat. Tyler being President of the same. Charge—Lurking about the armies and fortifications of the Confederate States of America. 1st *Specification*—That on the 1st of April, being an alien enemy, and in the service of the United States, he lurked about the armies and fortifications of the Confederate States in and near Richmond. 2nd *Specification*—That about the 1st of July, 1864, prisoner being an alien enemy, and in the service of the United States, did lurk in, around, and about the armies and fortifications of the Confederate States, at Memphis, in the State of Tennessee.

The prisoner was defended by Nance and Williams, who introduced a number of witnesses in his behalf.

The court, having maturely considered the evidence adduced, and two thirds concurring therein, they found the prisoner, guilty of the charge on the first specification; not guilty, on the second.

Whereupon, two thirds of the court concurring, it was adjudged that the accused "suffer death by hanging."

On the 25th of April, the proceedings, findings, and sentence of the court, were approved by the commanding-general of the Department of Henrico, who ordered that the sentence should be executed, under the direction of the provost-marshal, on the 29th of April, between the hours of six and twelve o'clock, A.M.

On the announcement of his approaching fate, the prisoner grew defiant, thinking no doubt that he would not be hung. He also said he could make several parties in the War Department "shake in their jackets" by his revelations. But he made none up to his last hour. Learning on Monday night that there was no show for him, he became completely unnerved. He was carried to the Fair grounds by Captain Alexander, but had previously received a visit from Rev. Mr. Woodbridge. He asked the clergyman to read the Psalm of David invoking vengeance on his enemies. He refused, and Webster grew indignant, causing the clergyman to take an early departure. When brought to the gallows, the prisoner was visibly affected by the sight of the prepararations observable, and shuddered when he looked at his coffin. After the rope was adjusted round his neck, prayer was offered up by Rev. M. D. Hoge. At the conclusion, a black cap was drawn over his eyes, he having previously bid farewell to several persons standing by. The signal being given, the trigger that sustained the drop was drawn, and it struck against the uprights with a loud sound. Owing to a defect in the knot, the noose slipped, and Webster fell on his back to the ground. The half-hung and partially stunned man was speedily raised, and assisted up, and a new rope being ready, he was soon swinging in accordance with his sentence. He died in about one minute.

Webster, who had plenty of gold and Confederate treasury notes, gave it all to his wife the night before his execution. He was in the employment of one of the Departments here as a letter-carrier between this city and Maryland. He was said to take the letters received here to Washington, where they were copied, and the answers received were served in the same way—thus being used as evidence against the parties, as many of them have found to their cost by subsequent arrest and incarceration in Northern forts. Suspicion was first excited against the prisoner by the style of his evidence against Lewis and Scully; and they let the cat out of the bag on him after their conviction. Mrs. Webster was arrested along with her husband as a spy, and sent to Castle Godwin. Webster was the first man executed here as a spy.

A War Picture

A correspondent of the *Richmond Sentinel* wrote the following graphic letter from the battle-field of Chickamauga:

When setting out for the West from your city a few weeks ago, a friend said to me at parting, "If you write from the West, be sure and give us the truth!" Having been accustomed to look upon 'news from the west' with the same suspicion, I promised to exercise due caution.

Judge of my chagrin, when the first message I sent by telegraph, on getting to Atlanta, turned out to be false. Arriving a few days after the fight, a rumor that Chattanooga had been evacuated by the Yankees was very current. I did not believe it. It happened, however, during the day, that I was introduced to a gentleman of high position among the railroad men of the town, and, on inquiry, I was informed that the report was true—that General Bragg had telegraphed for a train to leave next morning for that point, via Cleveland, and that the train would certainly go. These data even my cautious friend in your city would have regarded as satisfactory. I have no doubt but that such a message was received, and the general, for the second time at least in his life, telegraphed too soon.

I have seen about fifteen hundred of our wounded, and have also been to the battle-field. The wounded I saw were among the worst cases. They had been sent down to the (then) terminus of the railroad on Chickamauga river—many of them after being operated upon, and many others where further attempts would be made to save the limb. Some of these poor fellows were terribly hurt. Many were wounded in two and three places, sometimes by the same ball. Though suffering much for food and attention, they were in remarkably good spirits. It would sicken many of your readers were I to describe minutely the sufferings of these men—exposed, first, for four days upon the field, and in the field-hospitals; then hauled in heavy army-wagons over a rocky road for twelve miles, and afterward to lie upon straw, some in the open air, and others under sheds, for two and three days more, with but one blanket to cover with, and none to lie upon. Nothing that I have seen since the war began has so deeply impressed me with the horrors of this strife as frequent visits to this hospital at Chickamauga. God forbid that such a spectacle may be witnessed again in this Confederacy! I did not visit the entire battle-field, but only that part of it where the strife was most deadly. It being a week after the fight, I saw only about fifteen unburied Yankees, and two Confederates, and about twenty dead horses, nine lying upon a space thirty feet square. They had belonged to one of our batteries which attempted to go into action within one hundred and twenty yards of a Yankee battery, the latter being masked. The chief evidences of a severe engagement were the number of bullet-marks on the trees. The ground on which this severe conflict took place was a beautiful wood with but little undergrowth.

I never saw a more beautiful place for skirmishing, and I have understood from men in the fight that the Yankees favored this mode of warfare greatly, the men taking to the trees. But our boys dashed upon them and drove them from this cover. I had heard that the battle-ground was like that of Seven Pines, but that part I visited had no such resemblance. It was open and gently undulating. Here and there you would find a small, cleared field. Very little artillery was used, though some correspondents say the "roar was deafening." It has been also said that the enemy were driven from behind "strong breastworks" on Sunday. The works I saw were mean, consisting of old logs, badly thrown together. I saw in one collection thirty-three pieces of captured artillery, and nineteen thousand muskets, in very good order. These latter will be of great service in arming the exchanged Vicksburg prisoners. But before closing I must tell you of a little affair in which Longstreet's artillery took a part. Chattanooga, as you know, lies in a deep fold of the Tennessee River. In front of the town, and three miles east of it, Missionary Ridge runs from north to south, completely investing the town in this direction. On the west of the town Lookout Mountain, with its immense rocky "lookout" peak, approaches within three miles, and rests upon the river which winds beneath its base. The Yankee line (the right wing of it) rests about three fourths of a mile from the base of the mountain. Our pickets occupy the base.

The river makes a second fold just here, and in it is "Moccason Ridge," on the opposite side, where the Yankees have several casemated batteries, which guard their right flank. When on the mountain this ridge is just beneath you, say twelve hundred yards, but separated by the river. From this mountain you have one of the grandest views, at present, I ever beheld. You see the river far beneath you in six separate and distinct places, like six lakes. You see the mountains of Alabama and Georgia and Tennessee in the distance, and just at your feet you see Chattanooga and the Yankee army, and in front of it you see the "Star" fort, and also two formidable forts on the left wing, north of the town. You see their whole line of rifle pits, from north to south. Along the base of Missionary Ridge the Confederate tents are seen forming a beautiful crescent; and perched high upon the top of this ridge, overlooking this grand basin, you see four or five white tents, where General Bragg has his headquarters. Our army is strongly fortified upon the rising ground along the base of the ridge. I have ridden three miles along these fortifications, and think they are the best of the kind I ever saw. Now for the little affair I spoke of. Colonel E. P. Alexander, General Longstreet's active and skillful Chief of Artillery, hoped he might be able to shell Chattanooga, or the enemy's camps, from this mountain, and three nights ago twenty long-ranged rifle pieces were brought up, after great difficulty. It was necessary to bring them up at night, because the mountain road is in many places commanded by the batteries on Moccason Ridge. We used mules in getting our heaviest pieces up. They pull with more steadiness than horses. Every gun was located behind some huge rock, so as to protect the cannoneers from the cross-fire of the "Ridge". The firing was begun by some guns upon the right in General Polk's corps. Only one gun in that quarter (twenty-four pound rifle gun) could reach the enemy's line. At one P. M., order was given to open the rifles from the mountain. Parker's battery, being highest up the mountain, opened first, and then down among the rocky soils of the mountain. Jordan, Woolfolk's, and other batteries spoke out in thunder tones. The reverberations were truly grand. Old Moccason turned loose upon us with great fury; but "munitions of rocks" secured us.

All their guns being securely casemated, we could do them little or no injury; so we paid little or no attention to them. Colonel Alexander, with his glass and signal flag, took position higher up in the mountain, and watched the shots. Most of our fuses (nine tenths of them, indeed) were of no account, and hence there was great difficulty to see where our shot struck, only a few exploding. The Yankees in their rifle pits made themselves remarkably small. They swarmed before the firing began, but soon disappeared from sight. We fired slowly, every cannoneer mounting the rocks and watching the shot. After sinking the trail of the guns, so as to give an elevation of twenty-one degrees, the shots continued to fall short of the camps and the principal works of the enemy, and the order was given to cease firing. It has been reported we killed and wounded a few men in the advanced works. Last night at nine, four shots, at regular intervals and for special reasons, were fired at the town, and it was amusing to see the fires in the camps go out. The pickets, poor fellows, were the first to extinguish their little lights, which, like a thread of bright beads, encircled the great breast of the army. We have spent two nights upon the mountain. It is hard to say which is the most beautiful—the scene by night, when thousands of camp fires show the different lines of both armies with a dark, broad band between them, called "neutral ground," and when the picket by his little fire looks suspiciously into this dark *terra incognita* the livelong night, or the view after sunrise before the fog rises, when the valley northward and eastward, as far as the eye can reach, looks like one great ocean. The tops of the trees of Missionary Ridge, in the east, are seen above the great waste of water, and here and there in the great distance some mountain peak rears its head. I have seen celebrated pictures of Noah's deluge, but nothing comparable to this.

The view by clear daylight is also very grand and beautiful. The Yankees and their lines are seen with great distinctness, and appear so near that you think you could almost throw a stone into their camps. You see every wagon that moves, and every horse carried to water.

A Spicy Correspondence

During the march of General Lee's army through Northern Virginia to Maryland, General Jackson chanced to notice a number of stragglers from General Early's division. That night he caused the following note to be sent to his gallant subordinate:

"Head-Quarters, Left Wing.

General:—General Jackson desires to know why he saw so many of your stragglers in rear of your division to-day?

(Signed,) A. S. Pendleton, A. A. G."

To Major-General Early.

Old Jubal at once replied:

"Head-Quarters, Early's Division.

Captain:—In answer to your note, I would state that I think it probable that the reason why General Jackson saw so many of my stragglers on the march to-day is, that he rode in rear of my division.

Respectfully,

J. A. Early, Major-General."

Captain A. S. Pendleton, A. A. G."

The word "saw" was duly underscored with the general's boldest dash. Contrary to general expectation, General Jackson only smiled, and made no further inquiries about the curious investigators whom small-pox could not terrify.

Carrying Out His Orders

Hugh Mc———, a son of the Emerald Isle, who had volunteered in the sixth regiment of South Carolina infantry, was stationed on the beach of Sullivan's Island, with strict orders to walk between two points, and to let no one pass him without the countersign, and that to be communicated only in a whisper. Two hours afterward, the corporal, with the relief, discovered, by the moonlight, Hugh up to his waist in water, the tide having set in since he was posted.

"Who goes there?" "Relief." "Halt, relief. Advance, corporal, and give the countersign."

Corporal. —"I'm not going in there to be drowned. Come out here, and let me relieve you."

Hugh. —"Divil a bit of it. The lieutenant tould me not to lave me post."

Corporal. —"Well, then, I'll leave you in the water all night" (going away as he spoke).

Hugh. —"Halt! I'll put a hole in ye, if ye pass without the countersign. Them's me orders from the leftenant" (cocking and leveling his gun).

Corporal. —"Confound you, every body will hear it if I bawl out to you."

Hugh. —"Yes, me darlin'; and the leftenant said it must be given in a *whasper*. In with ye, me finger's on the trigger, and me gun may go off."

The corporal had to yield to the force of the argument and wade in to the faithful sentinel, who exclaimed: "Be jabers, it's well ye've come, the bloody tide has a most drowned me."

The Lone Sentry

By James R. Randall

The Rev. Dr. Moore, of Richmond, in a sermon in memory of the much-loved and lamented Stonewall Jackson, narrates the following incident:

Previous to the first battle of Manassas, when the troops under Stonewall Jackson had made a forced march, on halting at night they fell on the ground exhausted and faint. The hour arrived for setting the watch for the night. The officer-of-the-day went to the general's tent, and said:

"General, the men are all wearied, and there is not one but is asleep. Shall I wake them?"

"No," said the noble Jackson, "let them sleep, and I will watch the camp to-night."

And all night long he rode round that lonely camp, the one lone sentinel for that brave but weary and silent body of Virginia heroes. And when glorious morning broke, the soldiers awoke fresh and ready for action, all unconscious of the noble vigils kept over their slumbers.

> 'Twas in the dying of the day,
> The darkness grew so still;
> The drowsy pipe of evening birds
> Was hushed upon the hill;
> Athwart the shadows of the vale

Slumbered the men of might,
And one lone sentry paced his rounds,
    To watch the camp that night.

A grave and solemn man was he,
    With deep and sombre brow;
The dreamful eyes seemed hoarding up
    Some unaccomplished vow.
The wistful glance peered o'er the plains,
    Beneath the starry light—
And with the murmured name of God,
    He watched the camp that night.

The Future opened unto him
    Its grand and awful scroll:
Manassas and the Valley march
    Came heaving o'er his soul—
Richmond and Sharpsburg thundered by,
    With that tremendous fight
Which gave him to the angel hosts
    Who watched the camp that night.

We mourn for him who died for us,
    With one resistless moan;
While up the Valley of the Lord.
    He marches to the throne!
He kept the faith of men and saints
    Sublime and pure and bright—
He sleeps—and all is well with him
    Who watched the camp that night.

Brothers! the Midnight of the Cause
    Is shrouded in our fate;
The demon Goths pollute our halls
    With fire, and lust and hate.
Be strong—be valiant—be assured—
    Strike home for Heaven and Right;
The soul of Jackson stalks abroad,
    And guards the camp to-night!

Conscript Quakers

An amusing incident occurred at the Provost Marshal's office at Gen. Lee's head-quarters at Orange Court House, Va. Four Quakers were brought in as conscripts from Loudon. They were ordered to fall in the ranks, in order to be marched to the command to which they were to be assigned. They refused, saying, "We will not fall in, but will follow whithersoever thou leadest." A few persuasive arguments, however, in the shape of thrusts with bayonets, changed their opinions; and they fell in and marched off to camp.

Letters to Soldiers

The army correspondent of the Atlanta "Intelligencer," relates the following incident to show how welcome a letter from home was to the soldier, and how depressing it was when those at home neglected to write to him:

I witnessed an incident yesterday which goes far to show how welcome a letter is to the soldier, and how sad he feels, when those at home neglect to write to him. As I was riding to town I heard a man on horseback hail another in a wagon, and going up, handed him a letter. Another man in the same wagon inquired if there was no letter for him, and the reply was "none." It was at that moment I noted the feelings of the two men by their changed countenances. The features of one lit up with pleasure, as he perused the epistle in his hand,—doubtless the letter of some dear wife, or mother,—and as he read it, a smile of joy would illuminate his weather-beaten face. This was happiness. It was an oasis on the desert of his rough life of danger and suffering, and no doubt was welcomed by him as the dearest gift a relative could send. With the other the opposite effect was observed; as soon as the word "none" had passed the lips of the man addressed, the look of anxiety with which the question was put faded away, and an appearance of extreme sorrow could have been plainly seen stamped on his features, while a feeling of envy at his fortunate comrade was very apparent. This was unhappiness. The song of hope that had illuminated his heart when he inquired if there was any letter for him had died away, and a feeling of loneliness and regret at the neglect of those at home took possession of him. Happy are they who have homes and loved ones to hear from! While it is the cruelest of all neglects not to write to those relatives in the army, if it makes them sad and unhappy, how much more must those feel whose homes are in possession of the enemy, and they cannot hear from their relatives.

Sharp-Shooting

A gentleman informs us of the death of one of McClellan's sharpshooters, on the Peninsula, under circumstances which possess interest sufficient to give them to the public. Several of our men, it seems, were killed while going to a spring near by, but by whom no one could imagine. It was at last determined to stop this inhuman game, if possible, even at the cost of killing the hireling himself, who was thus, in cold blood, butchering our men. So, a sharp look out was kept for this sharpshooter, and the next time he fired, the smoke of his rifle revealed the locality of his pit. That night a pit was dug by the Confederate soldiers, commanding the position of the Yankee sharpshooter, and arrangements made to get rid of the annoying creature. For this purpose a young Kentuckian was placed in our pit, with a trusty rifle, and provisions enough to last him until the next night. Next morning early, a man was dispatched as usual, with two buckets, to go to the spring. He had proceeded about two hundred yards, when the Yankee marksman elevated himself, and placing his rifle to his shoulder was about to pull trigger, but the Kentuckian was too quick for him, for he pulled his trigger first, and simultaneously therewith the Yankee fell. Upon repairing to the spot—which the Kentuckian did immediately—he discovered the rifle pit, and a sturdy Yankee in it, in the last agonies of expiring nature. The pit was provided with a cushioned chair, pipes and tobacco, liquor and provisions. But the rifle which had been used was really a valuable prize. It was of most superb manufacture, and supplied with the latest invention—an improved telescopic sight upon its end. The pit had been dug at night, and its occupant had been provisioned at night, so but for a sharp look out for the smoke of his gun there is no saying how long this Yankee vandal would have enjoyed the luxury of killing Southern men, without even a chance of losing his own worthless life. We are gratified to know that he at last met with so righteous a fate.

A Night Cruise in Charleston Harbor

Steamer Seabrook, Stono Inlet, *April* 12, 1861.

About seven o'clock on Thursday evening, two of the South Carolina vessels, under command of Commodore Hartstene, left Charleston for a cruise off the bar.

The squadron consisted of the steamers Clinch and Seabrook. The former was the flag-ship. Both have been fitted up with a view to service in the harbor, and are furnished with twelve-pounder howitzers, and a force sufficient to serve them. There was no want of ammunition. In short, every preparation was made for a successful cruise. The following are the officers of the Clinch: Lieutenant Pelot, Commanding; Lieutenant Porcher; Midshipmen R. H. Bacot and G. D. Bryan. The Seabrook was commanded as follows: Lieutenant Commanding, J. M. Stribling; Lieutenant Evans; First Assistant Engineer, J. H. Loper; Assistant Surgeon R. W. Gibbes; Gunner Cuddy, and Midshipmen Ingraham and Wilkinson. The Lady Davis, also, forms a part of the squadron, but she was not on duty last night. Her officers consist of Lieutenant Dozier, Commanding; Lieutenant Grimble; First Lieutenant Henry A. Mullins, acting Pilot; First Assistant Engineer Geddes; Third Assistant Engineer Yates, and Midshipman Thomas. The Clinch had taken her position near the bar early in the afternoon, and accordingly it was the Seabrook that left Charleston at seven o'clock, cheered by the large crowd at the wharf. About half past seven, under easy head of steam, the various conjectures in regard to what would be the probable reply of Major Anderson to the summons to surrender, were suddenly cut short by the lookout reporting a rocket seaward. All eyes were instantly turned in that direction, and two red rockets burst in the air, followed by the burning of a blue light. Fort Johnson promptly recognized the signal that our enemy had made his appearance, sending up the answering rocket almost the instant the blue light, displayed by the Clinch, disappeared. Excitement and preparation for whatever might occur immediately succeeded. The howitzers were manned, the decks were stripped, guns, revolvers, and ammunition were distributed. When all that could be had been done, silently sped the steamer on her course, steadily she approached Fort Sumter, all blackness in the distance. Suddenly a hail was heard, and a hoarse voice shouted, "The pirates are off the bar." "What steamer?" was asked. "The Harriet Lane, twelve miles out," shouted the same gruff voice, and we were then informed that she alone, of all the expected cruisers, had been seen. Great eagerness was at once manifested to reach our destination. It was fully expected an attempt would be made to land troops in boats. This it was the purpose of the expedition to prevent. Finally, at eight o'clock, the Seabrook lay off the Clinch, when a pilot boat brought a confirmation of the approach of the Harriet Lane. Commodore Hartstene then took possession of the flag-ship, and twenty men were transferred from the Clinch to the Seabrook. The hour at which Major Anderson was to indicate his decision by the firing of a shell, having arrived, all eyes were strained in the direction of Fort Sumter. As minute after minute elapsed, and the stillness and blackness of Fort Sumter remained unbroken, the belief became general that Major Anderson had surrendered.

In the meantime the squadron lost not sight of its duty. Both vessels cruised all night in search of the expected war boats, just within the bar. It was the original intention of the commanding officer to have proceeded out to sea, but as the wind increased, and there was every indication of a "heavy blow," the pilots said it could not be done with safety. In this manner an hour passed, supper was eaten—ten o'clock arrived, and yet Fort Sumter had given no signal, nor had the slightest appearance of hostilities been noticed on the part of our batteries. Belief now became certainty, and not one of us but expected to steam into Charleston for breakfast, after saluting the Palmetto waving over that much coveted "four acres of land." The expedition, however, redoubled its vigilance, in order to prevent the possibility of surprise. Lieutenant Stribling sleeplessly paced the deck all night. His energy and perseverance overcame all obstacles. Lieutenant Evans took the first watch as officer of the deck; Midshipman Ingraham took the second; First Assistant Engineer Loper the third; Gunner Cuddy the fourth; and Midshipman Wilkinson the morning watch. Scarcely, however, had the latter officer entered upon the discharge of his duties, before he made a report that cleared up all doubt as to the decision of Major Anderson and the determination of General Beauregard.

At 4.40 A.M., the signal shell was thrown from Fort Johnson, and shortly afterwards the contest—a contest that will make the 12th of April, 1861, a memorable day in history—for the possession and occupation of Fort Sumter commenced. Shell followed shell in quick succession; the harbor seemed to be surrounded with miniature volcanoes belching forth fire and smoke. Still Major Anderson gave no sign of resentment, save the defiance expressed at his flag-staff. But a shell from Cummings' Point bursts on the parapet—the brave Cummings' Pointers are getting the range! Another falls quite within; and now Fort Moultrie seems to have got the range; and the floating battery, which the North believed a humbug, begins to indicate her position. She's not exactly at her wharf in Charleston, nor is it positive she will not take a position nearer still to Fort Sumter. It is getting to be warm work for Major Anderson. There, I see a flash—there goes the first shot from Fort Sumter, right plump at Cummings' Point. A considerable interval elapses, which is improved by all the batteries within range of Fort Sumter, and then the question of whether Major Anderson will keep up the fire is definitely settled. Casemate follows casemate with dogged deliberation. But whilst all this was transpiring, we were rapidly steaming out to sea. There goes the whistle of the General Clinch, and we haul up close and receive orders to follow in her wake. We come to anchor, and presently Lieutenant Stribling starts from his seat, seizes a glass, and looks eagerly eastward. He reports a steamer, and what he supposes to be a brig, standing straight in. The vessels are at a great distance, however; but when we see them more plainly, we are almost satisfied that we have had a sight of the Lincoln squadron, or at least a portion of it. The General Clinch makes another signal, and we haul in our anchor and steam toward Cummings' Point. As we go by battery after battery, we can see the men on the beach waving their hands to us, and distinguish a faint cheer. At last we come to anchor close in, where an excellent view of the firing was obtained. In a brief period the steamer which had been seen off the bar became plainly visible at Cummings' Point. She was taken for the Harriet Lane. The squadron immediately steamed out to sea, and as we neared the strange steamer, she ran up the Palmetto flag. It is believed to have been the Nashville, Captain Murray, from New York. At first she made for the squadron, but afterwards changed her course, and when last seen was heading for Charleston.

Stono was reached about ten o'clock, A. M.; without any further adventure, and as the vessel came to anchor, Fort Palmetto fired a gun. Commodore Hartstene went on shore, and made a report. It appears that this was the first intelligence of the commencement of hostilities that had been received; the firing of the guns not being audible at this distance, in consequence of the wind.

At seven o'clock we left Fort Palmetto. All was quiet there. No steamers were in sight, and the Edisto had arrived with Captain Shedd's command, consisting of eighty tall, stout, fighting men. The men are in the best of spirits, and have made up their minds to fight to the death. Captain Pope and the Lafayette Artillery have been at this fortress for the last three months, and they have made it almost impregnable. Their battery fully commands Stono Inlet, and woe to the unlucky vessel with Yankee colors that escapes the breakers and gets within range.

The firing of our batteries was audible for miles, and the large volume of smoke issuing from Fort Sumter created almost universal belief that Major Anderson had surrendered.

Preaching under Fire

An Incident of Chattanooga

One of the most impressive scenes ever witnessed occurred in the Presbyterian church. The services were being held by the Rev. Dr. Palmer, of New Orleans, and the pews and aisles were crowded with officers and soldiers, private citizens, ladies and children. A prayer had been said and one of the hymns sung. The organist was absent. "I will be thankful," continued the minister, "if some one in the congregation will raise the tune." The tune was raised; the whole congregation joined in singing as in days gone by; the sacred notes rose in humble melody from the house of God, swelling their holy tribute to His glory, and dying away at last like echoes of departed days: the second, or what is known as the long prayer, was begun, when out upon the calm still air there came an alien sound—the sullen voice of a hostile gun—ringing from the north bank of the river, and echoing back and back among the far-off glens of Lookout peak. It was sudden: it took every one by surprise; for few if any expected the approach of an enemy. The day was one of fasting and prayer; the public mind was upon its worship. Its serenity had not been crossed by a shadow. And it was not until another and another of these unchristian accents trembled in the air, and hied away to the hills, that it was generally realized that the enemy were shelling the town.

Without a word of warning, in the midst of church services, whilst many thousands of men and women thronged the several places of public worship, the basest of human foemen had begun an attack upon a city crowded with hospitals and refugees from the bloody pathway of their march, and in no wise essential to a direct assault.

There was a little disturbance in the galleries; the noise in the streets grew louder; near the doors several persons, who had other duties, military or domestic, to look to, hastily withdrew; the mass of the congregation, however, remained in their places, and the man of God continued his prayer. It was impressive in the extreme. There he stood, this exile preacher from the far South, with eyes and hands raised to Heaven, not a muscle or expression changed, not a note altered, not a sign of confusion, excitement, or alarm, naught but a calm, Christian face uplifted and full of unconsciousness to all save its devotions, which beams from the soul of true piety. Not only the occasion, but the prayer was solemnly, eloquently impressive. The reverend doctor prayed, and his heart was in his prayer; it was the long prayer and he did not shorten it; he prayed it to the end, and the cannon did not drown it from those who listened, as they could not drown it from the ear of God. He closed, and then, without panic or consternation, although excited and confused, the dense crowd separated whilst shells were falling on the right and left.

All honor to this noble preacher, and to those brave women and children.

"Don't Shoot There Any More—That's Father"

An eye and ear witness relates an occurrence at the battle of Shiloh, which shows, by one of innumerable similar instances, the peculiar frightfulness of the late war. Two Kentucky regiments met face to face, and fought each other with terrible resolution. It happened that one of the Federal soldiers wounded and captured a man who proved to be his brother, and, after handing him back, began firing at a man near a tree, when the captured brother called to him and said: "Don't shoot *there* any more—*that's* father."

BADLY SOLD

Shortly after the arrival of a certain Federal regiment in the suburbs of Martinsburg, Virginia, the squad messing in one of the tents near a dwelling, were listeners to most beautiful music. The unknown vocalist sang in tones so soft, so pathetic, and so melodious, that the volunteers strained their ears to drink in every note of the air. In daytime they went by squads past the dwelling, but saw no soul. Once they pursued a sylph-like figure to the very gate, but, alas! she was not the lady sought for. And so they lived on, each night hearing the music repeated, and, when it ceased, ambition and worldly interest went out with them, so that their dreams were filled with fancies of the unseen face.

One night, gathered together, the voice struck up again.

"By jove," said one, "this is agonizing. I can't stand it. She must be discovered!"

A dozen eager voices took up the remark, and a certain amorous youth was delegated to reconnoitre the place. He crept on tiptoe toward the dwelling, leaped the garden pales, and finally, undiscovered, but very pallid and remorseful, gained the casement.

Softly raising his head, he peeped within. The room was full of the music. He seemed to grow blind for the moment.

Lo! prone upon the kitchen hearth, sat the mysterious songstress—an ebony-hued Negress, scouring the tin kettles!

The soldier's limbs sank beneath him, and the discovered, looking up, said, "Go way dar, won't ye, or I'll shy de fryin' pan out o' de winder!" The soldier left—but not to dream, perchance!

John Pelham

By James R. Randall

Kelley's Ford, March 17, 1863

Just as the Spring came laughing through the strife,
    With all its gorgeous cheer;
In the bright April of historic life
    Fell the great canoneer.

The wondrous lulling of a hero's breath
    His bleeding country weeps—
Hushed in the alabaster arms of Death
    Our young Marcellus sleeps.

Nobler and grander than the Child of Rome,
    Curbing his chariot steeds;
The knightly scion of a Southern home
    Dazzled the land with deeds.

Gentlest and bravest in the battle brunt,
    The champion of the Truth;
He bore his banner to the very front
    Of our immortal youth.

A clang of sabres 'mid Virginian snow,
    The fiery pang of shells—
And there's a wail of immemorial woe
    In Alabama dells.

The pennon drops that led the sacred band
    Along the crimson field;
The meteor blade sinks from the nerveless hand
    Over the spotless shield.

We gazed and gazed upon that beauteous face,
    While 'round the lips and eyes,
Couched in the marble slumber, flashed the grace
    Of a divine surprise.

> O, mother of a blessed soul on high!
>   Thy tears may soon be shed—
> Think of thy boy with princes of the sky,
>   Among the Southern dead.
>
> How must he smile on this dull world beneath,
>   Fevered with swift renown—
> He—with the martyr's amaranthine wreath
>   Twining the victor's crown!

A Just Tribute

Mr. A. M. Keiley, in his famous little volume, "In Vinculis," pays the following well-deserved tribute to the Maryland boys serving in the Confederate armies:

This house was occupied by Marylanders; and the mention of the name suggests to me that I will not have a better opportunity to challenge for these exiles from that noble State, a reversal of the unjust reproach which has been cast upon her from various quarters, and in various forms, in the South. It is doubtless true that there are cowards and knaves in Maryland, and it is not less true, that every Southern State and Northern could furnish many a sample to place by the side of those who have earned so much reproach for her. But it is quite true, that no people, in any part of the world, have furnished more illustrious examples of pure, unselfish, uncompromising, all-sacrificing devotion, than now distinguishes the citizens of that gallant State. I knew much of this before I had seen her brave sons suffering a long and bitter exile from all that was dear to them—uncheered by hope of speedy return—cut off from their families—hurled, in many cases, from affluence to poverty—condemned to the disheartening spectacle of witnessing their possessions enjoyed, their friends imprisoned, and their State controlled, by an abhorred race, imported from New England to colonize and *convert* Maryland. And yet, I had seen them gallantly bearing a banner, which no hand of ours has been able to maintain on any spot of Maryland's soil, for thirty days, hoping against hope, while the weary years rolled on, for the day of deliverance, and faltering not, nor failing, though their hearts sank in the pain and palsy of that hope for ever deferred. So have I seen her daughters—many of them tenderly and delicately raised—forced to choose exile as the alternative of a jail—perchance for some act of common humanity—or voluntarily embracing the perils and hardships, because in their generous, loyal hearts, approving the principles and sympathizing with the sufferings of our beleaguered Confederacy, spending their days near the hospital cot, and devoting their nights to the tolls of the busy needle, for an army that has never yet been strong enough to give them an escort for one short day to their hospitable city of monuments. All this have I seen, and have seen it oftentimes repeated, and I have placed it to the credit of that noble State against the recreancy of the few Marylanders who have skulked among us, and the many *not Marylanders,* who have counterfeited the name to cloak their cowardice. But it was not till I became a prisoner that I appreciated to the full the devotion of her children. When I saw them cheerfully enduring the privations of a long imprisonment, almost within sight of their own homes, many of them persecuted with solicitations from their nearest relatives to come out, take the oath, and enjoy every comfort that wealth and society can offer, all of them conscious that a word would unlock the prison gates and send them forth to their families, with no one to question or reproach them; and then learned, that of the many hundred Marylanders, at various periods, who were tenants of that pen,* some of whom are prisoners of over a year's standing, *not five in all* had taken the oath of allegiance to the Yankee Government, I felt that the best of us might take a lesson from their patriotic constancy. And when, a few months later, I saw some of these very men marched like felons through their own fair city, without permission to whisper a word—scarcely cast a look at mothers and sisters standing by, who were heart-hungry for the poor privilege of a mere greeting, and yet saw no cheek blanch, no muscle quiver, no weakening of their proud resolve to fight the fight out for principle, through every sacrifice and every peril—calmly, nay, with a smile on their lips, half of triumph, half of scorn, answering the taunts of their keepers—they marching from prison to exile, while I was marching from prison to my home—I felt, as I now feel, the wish that the Confederacy was peopled by such men. Let not their names nor their deeds die—let some pen, meet for the task, gather now, while the events are fresh, the memorials of her children in this

---

* Point Lookout Prison.

war for freedom where they have so little to hope, so much to fear—and though the fortune of war should separate them and the Confederacy from their beloved State, let history do justice to the faithful living, and let a nation's gratitude lay immortal laurels o'er

> —The sacred grave
> Of the last few who, vainly brave,
> Die for the land they cannot save.

Don't Belong to Butler's Army

"When our brigade (Hagood's)," writes a soldier, "was sent with other brigades, under General D. H. Hill, on a flanking expedition below Kingston, on the 8th of March 1865, one of my men was examining the dead and wounded left by the enemy in the open field which we passed on our right. On attempting to turn over what he took to be a dead Federal, the aforesaid dead man exclaimed: 'What do you want?' The grayback answered, 'I only wanted to swap spoons with you.' (This expression, in our division, signifying the exchanging of canteens etc., with prisoners.) The almost dying man replied indignantly, 'I have no *spoons;* you must think I belong to Butler's army.'"

Cavalry vs. Infantry

The cavalry and infantry were generally at daggers' points, and never failed to improve an opportunity for talking very plainly to each other. One day a dragoon was stopped by a foot soldier, and the following dialogue took place:

Infantry—"Mister, did you ever see a Yankee?"
Cavalry. —(Sharply.) "Yes."
Infantry. —"Did he have on a blue coat?"
Cavalry. —(More sharply.) "Yes."
Infantry.—"Did you stop to look at him?"
Cavalry.—(More sharply.) "Yes."
Infantry.—(Very earnestly.) "Mister, please tell me if your hoss woz lame, or if your spurs woz broke?"

Destroying a Railroad

The Lynchburg *"Republican"* publishes a letter from Jackson's army, from which we extract the following. The letter is dated Bunker Hill, October 23d, 1862.

****Yesterday I took a ride to see the destruction done by our troops to the Baltimore and Ohio Railroad, I left our camp near Martinsburg early in the morning, expecting to go about five or six miles, but kept following the numerous columns of smoke encircling the atmosphere, until I had gone about fifteen miles, and yet I could see smoke arising from the burning timbers along the road as far as the eye could reach. Falling in with one of General Jackson's aids, I learned that my brigade had been ordered back to this place, they having completed their work of destruction at Martinsburg. I turned my course in this direction, where I arrived at dark, and spent the night with Lieutenant Warwick, of the Wise Troop. I am now at General Jackson's headquarters, where I learned that the road was destroyed on yesterday to within three miles of Harper's Ferry, the Yankee fastness. About twenty-five or thirty miles of the road has been destroyed, and also many valuable buildings belonging to the company. The manner of destroying a railroad is thus: The track is torn up and the cross-ties piled up, then the iron rails are laid across the ties and fire communicated to the whole. When the iron becomes hot it falls at both ends and bends in the shape of the letter V. This renders the iron worthless until it is taken to the foundry and worked over.

A Confederate Heroine

A Northern correspondent writes:

When the fight commenced we sent a shell directly through the roof of Mrs. Crittenden's house, when most of the family decamped. A Miss Crittenden, said to be comely and fair to look upon, refused, however, to absent herself and insisted upon remaining with the wounded Confederates, who were rapidly being carried to the house. Directly a shell came hurtling down through the roof and floors into the very apartment where the young lady was pouring in oil and wine. It did not burst, however, and she remained till the end, doing good.

A Snow-Ball Battle

Colonel Van Borcke, in his "memories," gives the following description of a snow-ball engagement in General Lee's army:

We were enlivened by snow-ball fights, which commenced as skirmishes near our headquarters, but extended over the neighboring camps, and assumed the aspect of general engagements. In front of our headquarters, beyond an open field of about half a mile square, Hood's division lay encamped in a piece of wood; in our immediate rear stretched the tents and huts of a part of M'Law's division. Between these two bodies of troops animated little skirmishes frequently occurred whenever there was snow enough on the ground to furnish the ammunition; but on the morning of the 4th, an extensive expedition having been undertaken by several hundred of M'Law's men against Hood's encampments, and the occupants of those finding themselves considerably disturbed thereby, suddenly the whole of the division advanced in line of battle, with flying colors, the officers leading the men, as if in real action, to revenge the insult. The assailants fell back rapidly before this overwhelming host, but only to secure a strong position, from which, with reënforcements, they might resume the offensive. The alarm of their first repulse having been borne with the swiftness of the wind to their comrades, sharpshooters in large numbers were posted behind the cedar bushes that skirt the Telegraph Road, and hundreds of hands were actively employed in erecting a long and high snow wall in front of their extended lines. The struggle had now the appearance of a regular battle, with its charges and counter-charges; the wild enthusiasm of the men and the noble emulation of the officers finding expression in loud commands and yet louder cheering while the air was darkened with the snow-balls as the current of the fight moved to and fro over the well contested field. Nearer and nearer it came, toward our headquarters, and it was soon evident to us that the hottest part of the engagement would take place on our neutral territory. Fruitless were the efforts of Stuart and myself to assert and maintain the neutrality of our camp, utterly idle the hoisting of a white flag: the advancing columns pressed forward in complete disregard of our signs and our outspoken remonstrances. Clouds of snow-balls passed across the face of the sun, and ere long the overwhelming wave of the conflict rolled pitilessly over us. Yielding to the unavoidable necessity which forbade our keeping aloof from the contest, Stuart and I had taken position, in order to obtain a view over the field of battle, on a big box, containing ordnance stores, in front of the general's tent, where we soon became so much interested in the result, and so carried away by the excitement of the moment, that we found ourselves calling out to the men to hold their ground, and urging them again and again to the attack, while many a stray snow-ball, and many a well directed one, took effect upon our exposed persons. But all the gallant resistance of M'Law's men was unavailing. Hood's lines pressed resistlessly forward, carrying every thing before them, taking the formidable fortifications, and driving M'Law's division out of the encampments. Suddenly, at this juncture, we heard loud shouting on the right, where two of Anderson's brigades had come up as reënforcements. The men of M'Law's division, acquiring new confidence from this support, rallied, and in turn drove, by a united charge, the victorious foe in headlong flight back to their own camps and woods. Thus ended the battle for the day, unhappily with serious results to some of the combatants, for one of Hood's men had his leg broken, one of M'Law's men lost an eye, and there were other chance wounds on both sides. This sham-fight gave ample proof of the excellent spirits of our troops, who, in the wet, wintry weather, many of them without blankets, some without shoes, regardless of their exposure and of the scarcity of provisions, still maintained their good humor, and were ever ready for any sort of sport or fun that offered itself to them.

ON THE BATTLE-FIELD

A correspondent of a Southern paper gives the following description of the feelings of a soldier for the first time on a battle-field:

No person who was not upon the ground, and an eyewitness of the stirring scenes which there transpired, can begin to comprehend, from a description, the terrible realities of a battle. And even those who participated are competent to speak only of their own personal experience. Where friends and foes are falling by scores, and every species of missile is flying through the air, threatening each instant to send one into eternity, little time is afforded for more observation or reflection than is required for personal safety.

The scene is one of the most exciting and exhilarating that can be conceived. Imagine a regiment passing you at "double-quick," the men cheering with enthusiasm, their teeth set, their eyes flashing, and the whole in a frenzy of resolution! You accompany them to the field. They halt. An aid-de-camp passes to or from the commanding general. The clear voices of officers ring along the line, in tones of passionate eloquence, their words hot, thrilling, and elastic! The word is given to march; and the body moves into action. For the first time in your life you listen to the whizzing of iron. Grape and canister fly into the ranks; bombshells burst overhead, and the fragments fly all around you. A friend falls; perhaps a dozen or twenty of your comrades lie wounded or dying at your feet. A strange, involuntary shrinking steals over you, which it is impossible to resist. You feel inclined neither to advance nor recede, but are spell-bound by the contending emotions of the moral and physical man. The cheek blanches, the lip quivers, and the eye almost hesitates to look upon the scene.

In this attitude you may, perhaps, be ordered to stand an hour inactive, havoc meanwhile marking its footsteps with blood on every side. Finally, the order is given to advance, to fire, or to charge. And now, what a metamorphosis! With your first shot you become a new man. Personal safety is your least concern. Fear has no existence in your bosom. Hesitation gives way to an uncontrollable desire to rush into the thickest of the fight. The dead and dying around you, if they receive a passing thought, only serve to stimulate you to revenge. You become cool and deliberate and watch the effect of bullets—the shower of bursting shells—the passage of cannon-balls, as they rake their murderous channels through your ranks—the plunging of wounded horses—the agonies of the dying—and the clash of contending arms—which follows the dashing charge, with a feeling so calloused by surrounding circumstances, that, our soul seems dead to every sympathizing and selfish thought.

Such is the spirit which carries the soldier through the field of battle. But when the excitement has passed, when the roll of musketry has ceased, the noisy voices of the cannons are stilled, the dusky pall of sulphurous smoke has risen from the field, and you stroll over the theatre of carnage, hearing the groans of the wounded—discovering here, shattered almost beyond recognition, the form of some dear friend whom only an hour before you met in the full flush of life and happiness—there, another perforated by a bullet—a third with a limb shot away—a fourth with his face disfigured—a fifth almost torn to fragments—a sixth a headless corpse—the ground ploughed up and stained with blood—human brains splashed around—limbs without bodies, and bodies without limbs, scattered here and there, and the same picture duplicated scores of times—then, you begin to realize the horrors of war, and experience a reaction of nature. The heart opens its floodgates, humanity asserts herself again, and you begin to feel.

Friend and foe alike now receive your kindest ministerings. The enemy whom but a short time before, full of hate, you were doing all in your power to kill, you now endeavor to save! You supply him with water to quench his thirst, with food to sustain his strength, and with sympathizing words to soothe his troubled mind. All that is human or charitable in your nature now rises to the surface, and you are animated by that spirit of mercy "which blesseth him that gives and him that takes." A battle-field is eminently a place that tries men's souls.

The Fate of a Spy

"Personne," the correspondent of the *Charleston Courier,* writes, in a letter from the Rappahannock, in the summer of 1862:

To-day has been further signalized by the hanging of a spy, a man named Charles Mason, of Perrysville, Pennsylvania. It appears that as one of the couriers of General Longstreet was carrying an order, he was met by this man, who inquired, "Whose division do you belong to?" "Longstreet's." The courier then asked, "Whose division do you belong to?" "Jackson's," was the reply. A gray Confederate uniform favored this idea, and a conversation ensued. As the two traveled together the courier observed that there was a disposition on the part of his companion to drop behind; and, finally, he was astonished by a pistol presented at his breast, and a demand for the delivery of the papers he carried in his belt. Having no other resource, the latter surrendered the documents, when the spy deliberately shot him in the back and ran. Soon afterward the courier was found by some of his friends, and narrated the particulars of the affair, describing the man so minutely, that when subsequently arrested he was known beyond a peradventure. He had, for instance, two defective front teeth—was a pale-faced, determined-looking, and quick-spoken person.

A search was at once instituted, but fortunately he fell into our hands by his own foolishness. It is stated that the spy rode up to General Jones, who was at the head of his column, and said—"General, I am the chief courier of General Jackson; he desires me to request you to order your column to be reversed at once." The order was of course given, and the pretended courier rode away. His next exploit was to ride up to the colonel of one of our regiments and give him the same command he had given to Jones. The colonel was a shrewd officer, however, and remarked, "I am not in the habit of receiving my orders from General Jackson." "Well, sir, those were my orders from him to you." "What cavalry are you from?" The courier hesitated a moment, and said "from the Hampton Legion." "In whose division and brigade is that?" asked the colonel. This confused him still more, and he could only reply, "I don't know—I have forgotten!" Being then taken into custody and examined, several papers were found upon his person written in short-hand and an abbreviated long-hand, embracing the information he had obtained. A pair of lieutenant's shoulder-straps were also concealed in his pocket. These discoveries being made, the man confessed that he was a Yankee, and belonged to the Union army, but in the capacity of an independent scout. He admitted, further, that he had observed and reported the movements of our army, but denied having killed the courier. He claimed that it was done by a party of Texans with whom he was traveling.

These various facts being conclusive, the court-martial by which he was tried had little hesitation in finding him "guilty," and sentencing him to be hung. The execution took place this afternoon, under the direction of General Evans, in the presence of his brigade and a large number of soldiers. The prisoner was mounted on a horse, his hands tied behind him, and he was driven beneath a tree. The rope, which was a little larger than an ordinary bed cord, then being adjusted, he was ordered to stand upon the saddle. As he did so, a soldier gave a sharp cut to the animal, and in a second more the spy was jerking convulsively from the limb above him. He met his fate with great stoicism, and appeared perfectly satisfied with what he had accomplished, but to the last denied all participation in the act of shooting Longstreet's courier. He said that he had an uncle and aunt living in Clarke county, Virginia, and that the latter had made him the Confederate uniform which he wore.

The Private Soldier

The "*Jackson* (Mississippi) *Crisis,*" pays the following just tribute to the much neglected private soldier:

Justice has never been done him. His virtuous merit and unobtrusive patriotism have never been justly estimated. We do not speak of the regular soldier, who makes the army his trade for twelve dollars per month. We do not include the coward, who skulks; nor the vulgarian, who can perpetrate acts of meanness; nor the laggard, who must be forced to fight for his home and country. These are not the subjects of our comment. We speak of the great body of citizen soldiery who constitute the provisional army of the Confederacy, and who, at the sound of the trumpet and drum, marched out with rifle or musket to fight—to repel their country's invaders, or perish on that soil which their fathers bequeathed, with the glorious boon of civil liberty. These are the gallant men, of whom we write, and these have saved the country; these have made a breastwork of their manly bosoms to shield the sacred precinct of altar-place and fireside. Among these private soldiers are to be found men of culture, men of gentle training, men of intellect, men of social position, men of character at home, men endeared to a domestic circle of refinement and elegance, men of wealth, men who gave tone and character to the society in which they moved, and men who, for conscience sake, have made a living sacrifice of property, home, comfort, and are ready to add crimson life to the holy offering. Many of these, if they could have surrendered honor and a sense of independence, could have remained in possession of all these elegancies and comforts. But they felt like the Roman who said, "Put honor in one hand and death in the other, and I will look on death indifferently." Without rank, without title, without anticipated distinction, animated only by the highest and noblest sentiments which can influence our common nature, the private labors, and toils, and marches, and fights; endures

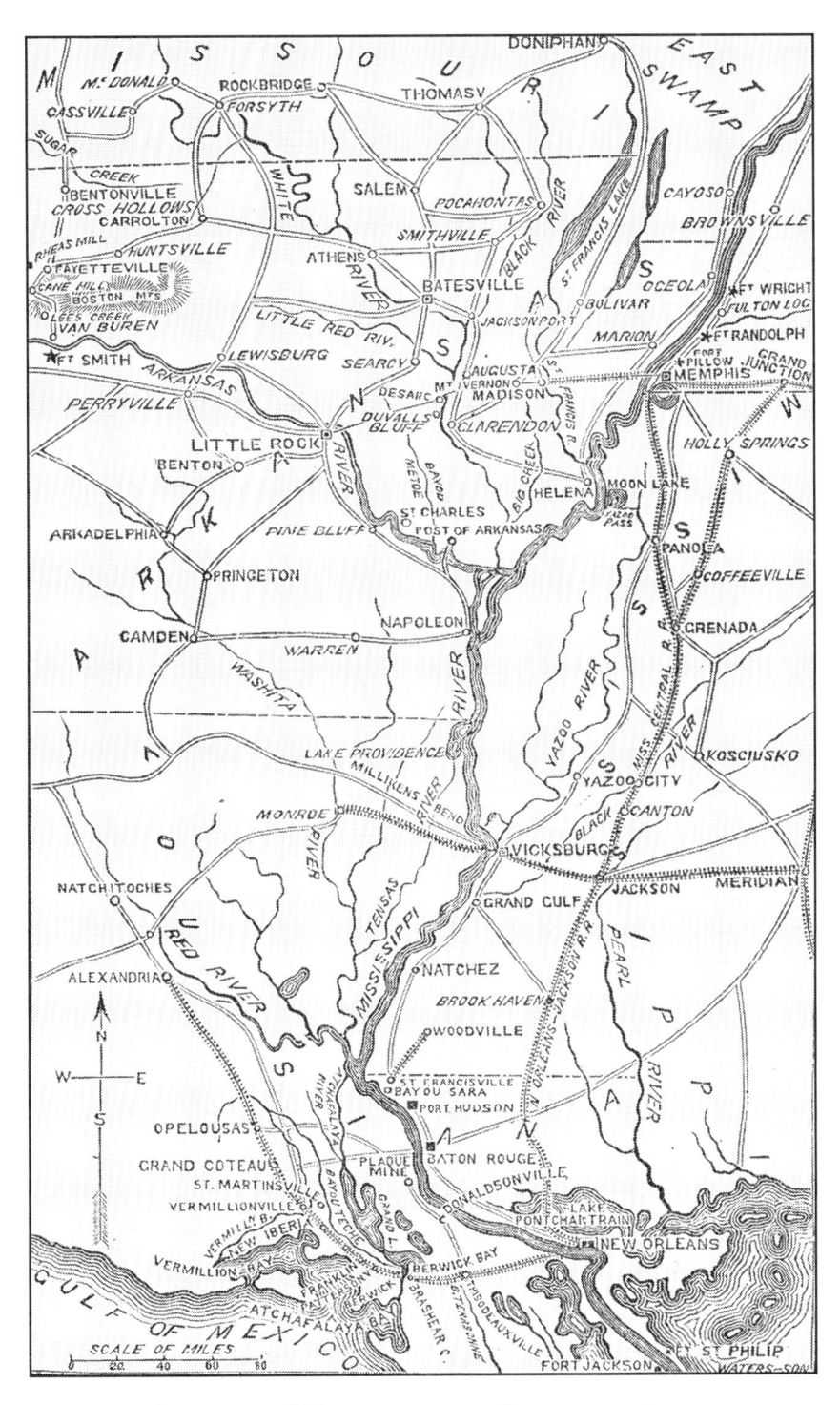

ARKANSAS, MISSISSIPPI, AND LOUISIANA AREA

hunger, and thirst, and fatigue; through watchings, and weariness, and sleepless nights and cheerless, laborious days, he holds up before him the one glorious prize—"Freedom to my country"; "Independence and my home!" If we can suppose the intervention of less worthy motive, the officer, and not the private, is the man whose merit must commingle such alloy. The officer may become renowned—the private never reckons upon that; the officer may live in history—the private looks to no such record; the officer may attract the public gaze—the private does not look for such recognition; the officer has a salary—the private only a monthly stipend, the amount of which he has been accustomed to pay to some field laborer on his rich domains; the officer may escape harm in battle by reason of distance—the private must face the storm of death; the officer moves on horseback—the private on foot; the officer carries a sword, the emblem of authority, and does not fight—the private carries his musket, and does all the fighting. The battle has been fought—the victory won; and Lee, or Longstreet, or others, have achieved a glorious success; but that success was attained by the private soldier, at the cost of patriot blood, of shattered bones, and torn and mangled muscle and nerves! We do not mean to under-estimate the officer, or disparage his courage, or his patriotism. We draw the parallel for another purpose, and that is, to show, if other than the highest human motive prompts the soldier to action, it is the officer, and not the private, who is not liable to feel its influence.

We have often felt pained and annoyed at the flippant reference to the privates, while the unreasoning speaker seemed to regard the officers as the prime and meritorious agents of all that is done. Why, in those ranks is an amount of intellect which would instruct and astonish a statesman. In those ranks the merit of every officer and every action is settled unappealably. In those ranks there is public virtue and capacity enough to construct a government, and administer its civil and military offices. The opinion of these men will guide the historian, and fix the merits of generals and statesmen. The opinion of these men will be, and ought to be, omnipotent with the people and government of the Confederacy. Heaven bless those brave, heroic men! Our hearts warm to them. Our admiration of their devotion and heroism is without limit. Their devotion to principle amounts to moral sublimity. We feel their sufferings, and share their hopes and desires to be identified in our day and generation with such a host of spirits, tried and true, who bend the knee to none but God, and render homage only to worth and merit.

Falling Back at the Wrong Moment

Two old ladies were one time conversing on the battle of Chickamauga. Said one,

"I wish, as General Bragg is a Christian man, that he were dead and in heaven; I think it would be a god-send to the Confederacy."

"Why, my dear," said the other, "if the general were near the gates of heaven, and invited in, at that moment he would fall back."

Somebody's Darling

> Into a ward of the whitewashed halls,
>   Where the dead and dying lay,
> Wounded by bayonets, shells, and balls,
>   Somebody's Darling was borne one day—
> Somebody's Darling, so young and so brave,
>   Wearing yet on his pale, sweet face,
> Soon to be hid by the dust of the grave,
>   The lingering light of his boyhood's grace.
>
> Matted and damp are the curls of gold,
>   Kissing the snow of the fair young brow
> Pale are the lips of delicate mould—
>   Somebody's Darling is dying now.
> Back from his beautiful blue-veined brow,
>   Brush all the wandering waves of gold:
> Cross his hands on his bosom now—
>   Somebody's Darling is still and cold.
>
> Kiss him once for somebody's sake,
>   Murmur a prayer both soft and low;
> One bright curl from its fair mates take—
>   They were somebody's pride, you know;

Somebody's hand hath rested there—
  Was it a mother's, soft and white?
And have the lips of a sister fair
  Been baptized in the waves of light?

God knows best! he has somebody's love:
  Somebody's heart enshrined him there;
Somebody wafted his name above,
  Night and morn, on the wings of prayer.
Somebody wept when he marched away,
  Looking so handsome, brave, and grand;
Somebody's kiss on his forehead lay,
  Somebody clung to his parting hand.

Somebody's waiting and watching for him—
  Yearning to hold him again to her heart;
And there he lies with his blue eyes dim,
  And the smiling child-like lips apart.
Tenderly bury the fair young dead,
  Pausing to drop on his grave a tear
Carve in the wooden slab at his head,
  "Somebody's Darling lies sleeping here."

Southern Valor

A Northern writer, in describing the battle of Corinth, Mississippi, which was fought on the 3d of October, 1862, between the Confederate army, under Generals Price and Van Dorn, and the Federal army, under General Rosecrans, and which is famed as one of the hardest fought battles of the war, thus describes the behavior of the Confederate troops:

By the time this line was driven back, the other line with their reserves were well advanced in the direction of battery Robinett.

During the period of seeming inaction when the Confederates had withdrawn to the cover of the timber, while preparing to make the two charges in question, General Price and his principal officers held a consultation to devise ways and means to take the battery. The importance of its capture was admitted, and the risk and danger of the attempt thoroughly canvassed. General Price would not undertake the responsibility of ordering the attack, but called for volunteers. Colonel Rogers, of Arkansas, immediately tendered his brigade as the forlorn hope, and Colonel Ross his brigade as a support.

They massed their troops eight deep, and advanced under a heavy fire of double charges of grape and canister. A terrible enfilading and flanking fire was poured upon them from every battery bearing in that direction, aided by incessant volleys of musketry from the supports of the batteries and the Union regiments drawn up in line parallel with them.

The first shell from Battery William exploded in the centre of the advancing column, sending thirty or forty to their long home. Every discharge caused huge gaps in their ranks. The effect of the Federal fire was like the falling of grain before the scythe. But this tremendous mortality did not affect their irresistible onward march. As fast as one man fell, his comrade stepped forward in his place. Twice did they approach almost to the outer works of the battery, and twice they were compelled to fall back. The third time they reached the battery and planted their flag upon the edge. It was shot down—raised again—again shot down. They swarmed about the battery; they climbed over the parapets; they fired through the escarpments, and for a time it seemed as if they had secured the victory their valor had so richly earned.

When they obtained the battery, the Federals who were working it fell back behind the projecting earth-works, out of reach from the Federal shell, and immediately all the batteries bearing upon the position were turned upon Battery Robinett, and soon a shower of missiles was falling like hail upon the brave intruders. No mortal man could stand the fire, and they retreated. Slowly the brave remnant turned their unwilling steps toward the forest from which they started, when the order was given to the two regiments supporting the battery to charge. This order was splendidly executed. The miserable remnant of troops which the batteries had nearly destroyed was now almost annihilated. A few scattering troops were all that remained of the column which so valiantly attacked the battery scarcely an hour before. The dead bodies of rebels were piled up in and about the intrenchments, in some places eight and ten deep. In one place directly in front of the point of assault, two hundred and sixteen dead bodies were found within a space of a hundred feet by four, among them the commanders of both brigades making the assault—Colonel Rogers and Colonel Ross. This was the termination of the engagement.

Mr. Davis's Trap for Grant

The following event is related as having occurred during the visit of President Davis to Bragg's army, just before the reverses at Missionary Ridge:

Looking down one day from the summit of Lookout Mountain, and commanding a clear view into four States, and a very distant view into a fifth, Mr. Davis saw Grant's army almost beneath his feet, across the valley, working like beavers on their fortifications.

"I have them now," said he, "in just the trap I set for them!"

To which Lieutenant-General Pemberton, who was sitting on horseback beside him, replied:

"Mr. Davis, you are commander-in-chief, and you are here. You think the enemy in a trap, and can be captured by vigorous assault. I have been blamed for not having ordered a general attack on the enemy when they were drawing around me their lines of circumvallation at Vicksburg. Do you now order an attack on those troops down there below us, and I will set you my life that not one —— man of the attacking column will ever come back across that valley, except as a prisoner."

A Remarkable Adventure

Brigadier-General Roger A. Pryor, during the battle between General Pope and the Confederates near Manassas, in August 1862, had the misfortune to be taken a prisoner, but the corresponding good fortune to escape.

He had started off on foot to call up two or three regiments for reënforcements, and on his return found his command moved from the position in which he had left it. Thinking it had gone ahead, he too went on, wondering all the time where his men were, until he suddenly encountered two Yankee soldiers sitting at the foot of a hay-rick.

His uniform being covered by a Mexican *poncho*, they did not observe that he was not one of their own men; nor was there any mark visible upon his person to indicate that he was an officer.

They, accordingly, familiarly inquired how every thing was going on in front. He replied, "Very well"; and in the conversation which ensued, learned that he was a mile and a half within the Federal lines! They asked him numerous questions, under some of which he began to quake and grow uneasy, fearing his inability, good lawyer though he is, to cope successfully with a cross-examination of such a dangerous character. He accordingly began to look about him to discover some means of escape. There was apparently none. He observed standing near him, however, the two muskets of the men, one of them with a bayonet, and the other without.

The colloquy had not proceeded much further before one of them, looking at him keenly, asked him to what regiment, brigade, and division he belonged. And as Pryor hesitated and stammered out his reply, the Yankee sprang to his feet and exclaimed, "You are a —— Rebel, and my prisoner!" In an instant, the general, who is a powerful man, and as active as a squirrel, seized the gun with the bayonet, and, before his antagonist could turn, ran him through the body twice. The other now jumped to his feet, apparently as if to escape, but he also received from Pryor a lunge that left him helpless on the field. Throwing down the musket, the general moved rapidly away in the direction from whence he came, and after dodging Federal stragglers for an hour or two, had the satisfaction of finally regaining his command.

Anxious to know the fate of the two men whom he had so summarily disposed of, he sent one of his aids the next day to examine the hospitals in that neighborhood and ascertain if possible whether any men were present wounded with a bayonet. The aid returned with the information that he had found one so injured. Whereupon, Pryor mounted his horse and went in person to see him. The man was asleep when he entered the hospital, but the surgeon awoke him, and the general asked if he recognized him. "Yes, sir, I do," was the reply; "you're the man who struck me." The wounded man was not less surprised when he learned that the author of his misery was the redoubtable Roger A. Pryor.

The Closing Scenes at Shiloh

The rest and refreshments in the inglorious camps of the enemy, so greatly needed and so fondly anticipated, by our exhausted troops on the night of the 6th of April, were rudely interrupted. Early in the night that invariable effect of a severe battle and great cannonading followed the prolonged struggle of the day. A heavy shower came up and continued the greater part of the night. The heavens had been clear and cloudless, the air warm and balmy during that day, but now, at night, dark clouds hung heavily in the sky, and the rain fell in torrents, and the atmosphere became suddenly chilly. Our men huddled in the enemy's tents without blankets, or any other covering but their ordinary uniforms. There was another source of trouble and anxiety.

The enemy's gunboats continued firing all night, throwing conical shells into the camps, which exploded with destructive effect, scattering small fragments of iron in every direction, and frequently wounding men and horses. Under these depressing circumstances, our army passed the night. To our generals it was a night of special anxiety. General Beauregard and staff had established their headquarters in the midst of the Yankee camps near the old log and boarded church, or rather meeting house, which had given a name to the battlefield. Long and anxious consultations were held at these headquarters. General Polk, in apprehension of the enemy making an effort to get in on our left flank, had established his quarters some distance in the rear and on the left. Here he and staff passed the night in the midst of what was intended as the amputating hospital, but which had soon become a general hospital. This hospital quickly became overcrowded with the wounded. To the kind-hearted and sympathetic general, that must have proved a terrible, sleepless night, which was passed amid such harrowing scenes—the constant groans of agony, the throat-rattle, the pitiful moans, and heroic utterances, and last gentle words, for home and friends, of the dying.

Before seeking a place of retirement and rest for the night, we made the rounds of several of our largest hospitals. We have no heart to revise the harrowing scenes they presented. We had already, during the prolonged conflict of the day, witnessed enough of suffering to have left impressions, which a life-time could not efface. The unbroken processions of those mournful ambulances—the continual current of poor, bleeding, mutilated, but still heroic soldiers, making their way to the rear, had banished from our minds all pride, exultation and enthusiasm for our brilliant success.

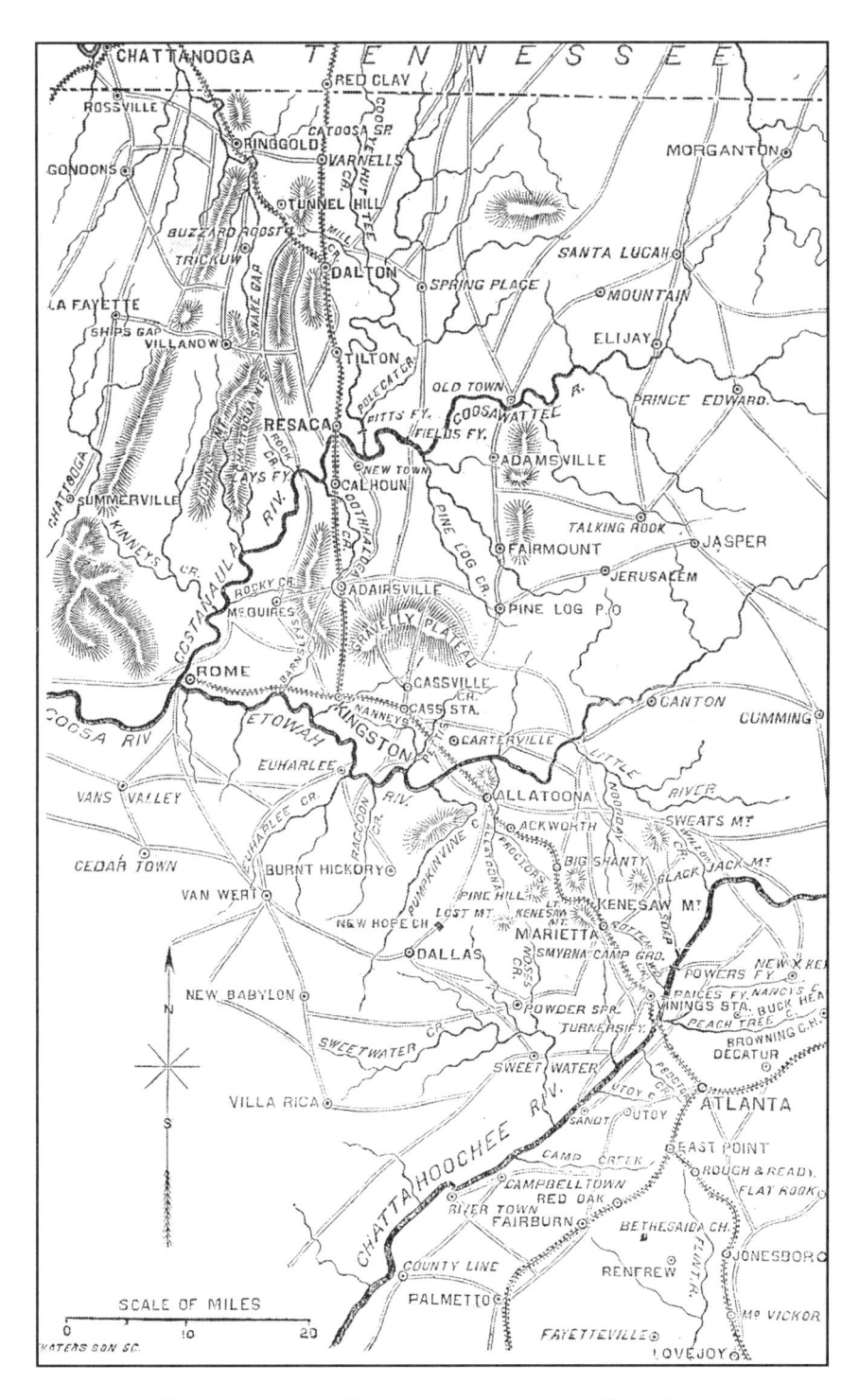

CHATTANOOGA, TENN., TO ATLANTA, GA., AREA

The most agreeable emotions that ever thrilled our heart were those we experienced in affording many of these wounded the grateful relief of a drink from our canteen. The earnest thankfulness with which they received this little comfort was indescribably eloquent and touching. But even these harrowing scenes were somewhat relieved and lightened by the heroic bearing, cheerful resignation, and wonderful fortitude with which our wounded bore up under their afflictions. This was especially conspicuous in the younger soldiers. Mere striplings, who were badly wounded—many of them mutilated or mortally hurt—seemed to have as little heed of their pains and danger as if returning from the playground. Every where it was apparent that the older class of the wounded manifested far more gravity and solicitude, more sensibility to pain, and more anxiety as to the character of their wounds, than the younger soldiers, many of them boys from our high schools.

All the hospitals were soon crowded. There were few buildings near the battle-field. These had been appropriated as hospitals, but were quite inadequate, and all the tents that had been brought by our army were devoted to hospital purposes. Still there were hundreds who had no shelter. Many remained in the wagons; many, alas! were left in the air, exposed to the cold rain. All that could be done for them was done. The surgeons were diligent and indefatigable. Their labors were incessant. By dim lights and in the open air, they were compelled to perform the most delicate surgical operations. It was cheering, indeed, to observe the universal spirit of brotherly love, the earnest humanity, the entire absence of selfishness, which were displayed by all classes in attendance on the wounded.

The constant shelling of the Yankee camps by the gun-boats early in the night, induced us to shift our quarters, and creeping into a wagon—already pretty well filled with sleepers—near one of the hospitals, we sought a few hours of sleep. But, exhausted as we were, we could only snatch a few minutes of broken and unsatisfying slumber. The groans of the suffering, the cries of those undergoing operations, and, more than all, the awful gurgling sound made by a poor fellow who had been shot through the lungs, and had been laid out to die, under the wagon in which we lay, was terribly trying to our nerves and sensibilities.

Thus the night passed—a night of continual rain. We were aroused before daylight by a rapid and irregular fire, extending along the whole line and over the whole area occupied by our troops. We soon learned that this was the firing of our own men, whose guns had become wet and foul from exposure during the rain. We now proceeded to the front, to learn what was to be the order of the day. Repairing to the headquarters of General Beauregard, we found that ever cool and vigilant chief sitting in front of one of the enemy's tents with his aids, Colonel Jacob Thompson, Colonel Jordan, Colonel Chisolm, and several of his staff. The general was receiving reports from couriers and scouts. It was obvious that he intended to renew the fight. It was cheering and inspiring to observe his calm self-possession and thoughtful precision and alertness. There came to him every minute the most conflicting accounts of the enemy's movements. First, it was reported the enemy was flanking our right. The general quickly gave an order to send a brigade in that direction. The order had hardly issued before another courier contradicted this report, and stated that no enemy was visible in that direction. The general, smiling, remarked to one of his aids: "This is one of Morph's blind games. I wish I had him here to help me play it out." Presently rode up Colonel Beard, of Florida, an acting aid of General Beauregard, holding his left arm, which was bleeding. Dismounting, he reported the reconnoissance he had been ordered to make that the enemy's outposts were not nearer than three quarters of a mile from our lines—that from the strength of his advance parties it was obvious that he intended to renew the battle. In making this reconnoissance, the colonel had been fired at by about fifty skirmishers, and one of the balls had struck his left arm.

The general now issued a number of orders, which were rapidly carried off by his couriers and aids. One order, which was found the most difficult to enforce, directed several of his aids to proceed to the rear, and with such of our cavalry as could be found to occupy all the roads and prevent straggling parties from leaving the field, and to capture and drive back to their posts those who were leaving. In this way a great many stragglers were reclaimed. Many were induced to return by the appeals of officers, but a great number excused themselves by the plea of utter exhaustion, by wounds, and sickness; others set up the still weaker excuse of having lost their officers, and not knowing where to find their regiments. These reductions and the casualties of the day before had greatly thinned our army. But the spirit of those who remained to fight was unbroken. Regiments and brigades were now made up of all the fragments that could be marched to the front. In many cases the commanders of these newly organized corps were extemporized, the authority of any gallantly bearing officer being cheerfully recognized by subordinates and privates. It was now light. The heavens were still hung with murky clouds, and the air was cold. We were sitting in the enemy's camp, near the staff of General Beauregard, when the familiar but never to us agreeable whistle of Minié balls began to strike unpleasantly upon the ear. "The enemy must be near," coolly remarked the general. "We will mount, gentlemen, and go to the front."

The general arrived in front in time to witness the advance of the enemy. Here the indefatigable Bragg had already busied himself in making the best formation that could be made to meet the advancing foe. Hardee, with the remnant of his corps, with Wood's, Hindman's, Chalmer's, and Gladden's brigades—the latter no longer led by the gallant Colonel Adams, of Louisiana, who had been severely wounded on Sunday—still held the right. Breckinridge, with what remained of his division, with Trabu's, Statham's, and Bowen's brigades, stood as firm as Gibraltar on the left of Hardee, while Bragg and Ruggles held the extreme left of our line with the remainder of their fine divisions, eked out by a portion of Cheatham's and Clark's divisions of Polk's corps; while General Polk, with the remainder of his corps, brought up a strong reserve to support either division in the front that might need aid. The several batteries were placed in the most favorable positions, with little regard to brigades.

General Beauregard, riding to the right, was everywhere received with huzzas. A few words of cheer and encouragement were uttered by him to the several commanders as he passed. It was no time now for speeches or cheers. The enemy was bearing down on our greatly weakened line with a confidence and boldness which satisfied everybody who observed them that they had been reënforced. It was apprehended that Buell's whole army had reached the Tennessee. The conclusion was confirmed by previous intelligence of the advance of his army from Columbia. We have no reliable information even now that such reënforcements had reached him. It was regarded more probable that he should be reënforced by Wallace's division, which had abundant time to come up from Crump's Landing, where it had arrived from a scout toward Purdy. Even this division of eight or ten thousand men would have been a most valuable reënforcement, competent to turn the scale of battle between two armies which had already been engaged in the exhausting and prolonged conflict of the day before. A much smaller reënforcement of fresh troops for our army would have enabled us to complete the work of the day before—indeed, would have made one day's job of it. Many thought it the best strategy to have pushed the fight to a conclusion on the first day, and that our army might easily have been induced to advance under the fire of the enemy's batteries and gunboats, and thus have accomplished the end much more efficiently than by the long and furious bombardment of the artillery. It was pretty evident that that bombardment had not produced the effects anticipated from it. From the quantity of shot and shell fired by our thirty-six pieces, we concluded that the enemy was annihilated. But we had not learned what a great quantity of ammunition may be wasted in a battle. We did learn on this occasion how little effective the best artillery is without being followed up by that weapon which determines the results of battles, the invincible musket. The enemy did not give Hardee, the ever reliable, observant, and careful Hardee, long to complete and strengthen his division. They began the attack near the river, with a large force of infantry and several batteries. The vigor, spirit, and resolution of this assault surpassed any of their efforts of the day before. Hardee met them with unbroken energy and unexhausted valor. The batteries opened terribly, and the whole line, on both sides, seemed to be wrapped in a bright flame, from the constant fire of the musketry. This was one of the severest conflicts of the two days. It was maintained with great obstinacy by both parties. The two opposing lines oscillated with the varying results of the conflict. Now the enemy—and now our lines would be pressed backward. Some of the batteries changed hands several times.

At one time the enemy would overpower and drive back the infantry support of a battery, and obtain possession of it; and then, by a like advance of our infantry, would be despoiled of his trophies and routed. Thus our own fifth company Washington Artillery, was twice rescued from them—once by the first Missouri under Colonel Rich, who was himself badly wounded. At the same time fell that gallant young officer, so well known and so much beloved, Captain Sprague. On the second occasion, the Washington Artillery, which was always getting into dangerous places, and often too near the covers of the enemy's sharpshooters, who seemed to take a special grudge against our gallant boys, was saved by a timely charge of the Crescents, who, pouring a heavy volley into the enemy, enabled the artillerists to limber up and haul off their pieces to the rear. The losses of both the fifth company and the Crescents, on this occasion, were heavier than on the day before. It was in this conflict that noble officer and gentleman, Captain Graham, of the Louisiana Guards, Company C, of the Crescent regiment, fell at the head of his company. By his side fell young Arthur

R. Clark, son of Dr. Clark, of Richmond, one of the most interesting and noble youths we ever knew. He was just seventeen—a delicate, graceful, gentle, but brave and manly youth as ever bore a musket. Even now, we can not recall our last interview with this noble boy without an inexpressible feeling of anguish. He was an only son, the idol of his family and of all who knew him. He said to us, gaily marching to the field of combat, "I want you to tell my father how I fight to-day; and if I am killed, take my body back to him." "I have no better man in my company than that boy," remarked Captain Graham. Alas! that such a man, and such a youth could not have been spared as examples and models for our volunteer soldiers. In this same conflict fell that tall and martial-looking officer, Captain Campbell, of the Sumter Rifles—a most promising commander, who had left a sick bed to take his post in the march and battle. So, too, fell young Todd—the brother of the "Lady of the White House," who holds high revelry after the recent decease of her own son, and while her own brothers are pouring out the blood they derived from a common parent in the defence of the soil of her and their ancestors, against the hired mercenaries of her husband. Then, too, fell, either killed or wounded, others of the best blood of our city—young men, who had left homes of ease and wealth, and doting relatives and friends, in response to the call of our gallant Louisiana chief. Among the wounded there was not one who excited greater anxiety and alarm than that heroic and dashing officer, Lieutenant Slocomb, of the fifth company Washington Artillery. His bearing during the two days had drawn upon him the admiration of the whole army. He had shown something even more valuable than the most brilliant courage and daring. That was no rare virtue in our army. But with it Slocomb united the most careful attention to every detail of duty—a perfect knowledge of all the appliances and rules for the efficient use of artillery, and wonderful quickness in seizing every advantage and in controlling his men and even his horses. Struck by a ball in the breast, it was believed that the wound was mortal. But he would not leave the field until his guns were all limbered up and borne safely out of the reach of the enemy's infantry. He then galloped to a hospital. His faithful horse, pierced by a half dozen bullets, bore him some distance—indeed to the very hospital tent; and when he was lifted from the saddle, the noble animal lay quietly down and breathed his last.

A Conscript Story

"In my regiment," writes Colonel T——, of Tennessee, "was a fellow (I will not say soldier) named Aikin. He was a strange looking creature every way, with his eyes cut the wrong way of the leather. He was fit for nothing but to play poker, and acquainted with little beyond the slaying phrases of the card-table. After the battle of Harper's Ferry, in which he behaved badly, he renewed a former application to be discharged under the Conscript Act, alleging that he was over thirty-five years old. His proofs upon his first application were against him, and his attempt to make the surgeon believe that he was blind, was equally unsuccessful.

"He came to me this time, saying: 'Colonel, I've got the proof now, sure enough, that I'm over thirty-five.' I said, 'It is too late, Aikin, your conduct has been such that I cannot believe any thing you say; besides the newspapers report that Congress has raised the conscript age to forty five'. He looked at me with much surprise expressed in his countenance, at this Congressional blow to all his hopes.

"Then rolling his eyes round in the reverse direction to all other human eyes, he said: 'Colonel, do I understand you to say that Congress has seen my *blind* and *raised me ten?*'"

Grand Rounds

"While I was serving on the staff of Brigadier General Tappan, of Arkansas," writes an ex-officer of the C.S.A., "I was ordered one night to superintend the grand rounds. There happened to be on post that night, a Frenchman by the name of Victor Pedron, as gallant a soldier as ever shouldered a musket. He was on the second relief, and toward the close of his tour was getting tired and sleepy, when to his great joy he saw a body of men approaching, which he did not doubt was the third relief. He challenged promptly, 'Who comes dere?' Answer 'Grand Rounds.' 'Begar, I tought it was ze tird relief.' Nothing was said on either side for some time, when we, getting tired of waiting, again advanced. 'Who comes dere?' 'Grand Rounds.' 'Oh, go vay vid your grand rounds. I have ze grand sommeil too much (am too sleepy) zat I cannot receive grand rounds proprement.'"

General Polk in a Very Tight Place

An English officer, Colonel Freemantle, who served for some time in the Confederate army, and lived long enough in the South to make the acquaintance of a number of the prominent men there, afterward published a book relating his experience. In this book he tells the following story, as it was told him by Lieutenant-General Polk:

Well, sir, it was at the battle of Perryville, late in the evening—in fact, it was almost dark, when Lindell's battery came into action. Shortly after the arrival, I observed a body of men, whom I thought to be Confederates, standing at an angle to this brigade, and firing obliquely at the newly arrived troops. I said, "Dear me, this is very sad and must be stopped"; so I turned round, but could find none of my young men, so I determined to ride myself and settle the matter. Having cantered to the colonel of the regiment that was firing, I asked him, in angry tones, what he meant by shooting his own friends. He answered with surprise:

"I don't think there can be any mistake about it; I am sure they are the enemy."

"Enemy! Why, I have only just left them myself. Cease firing, sir. What is your name?"

"My name is Colonel ——, of the —— Indiana; I pray, sir, who are you?"

Then I saw, to my astonishment, that I was in the rear of a regiment of Yankees. Well, I saw there was no hope but to brazen it out; my dark blouse and the increasing obscurity befriended me; so I approached quite close to him, and shook my fist in his face, saying:

"I'll show you who I am, sir! Cease firing, sir, at once!"

I then turned my horse and cantered slowly down the line, shouting authoritatively to the Yankees to cease firing; at the same time I experienced a disagreeable sensation, like screwing up my back, and calculating how many bullets would be between my shoulders every minute. I was afraid to increase my pace till I got to a small copse, when I put the spurs in and galloped back to my men. I went up to the nearest colonel, and said: "Colonel, I have reconnoitered those fellows pretty closely, and there is no mistake who they are; you may get up and go at them." And I assure you, sir, that the slaughter of that Indiana regiment was the greatest that I have seen in this war.

A Gallant Lieutenant

During the battle near Spottsylvania Court House, Virginia, on the 14th of May, 1864, Major-General Wright's brigade was ordered to charge the Union works. In doing so, the third Georgia regiment passed through a heavy fire of Minié balls, losing seventy-eight men in killed and wounded. The color-bearer of the regiment, being wounded, planted the colors in the ground, and retired to the rear. At this moment the skirmish line was ordered to halt, which was understood by many as an order for the regiment to halt, which they did. Perceiving that a crisis was at hand, Lieutenant R. G. Hyman sprang forward, seized the colors from amid a pile of slain, and waving them in the face of the foe, called upon the old third to rally to it, which they did, with a yell, and the Yankee breastworks were taken. Lieutenant Hyman was at least fifty yards in advance of the regiment all the time.

An Incident at Gettysburg

A surgeon of the Virginia army relates the following incident: "As I was pushing my way through a crowd of idle spectators, at the second corps hospital, Gettysburg, one of our wounded, from a North Carolina regiment, called to me in feeble voice. I went to him, and he said: 'You are a Confederate surgeon—are you not?' I answered him, 'Yes; what can I do for you?' He caught me nervously by the arm, and, in a manner very striking and very eloquent, he uttered: 'What do you think, doctor? I am wounded and dying in defense of my country, and these people are trying to persuade me to take the oath of allegiance to theirs!'

"The crowd around him scattered as if a bomb had fallen into their midst, whilst I, overcome by the fervent eloquence of his words, could only bow in silence over the gallant fellow, upon whose brow the damp shadow of death was already gathering."

The Fall of Island Number Ten

On Tuesday, April 1st, the guns of Rucker's battery were spiked; on the succeeding Friday evening the enemy's gunboat and tug passed the island during a storm. On Saturday night the enemy, with a gunboat, engaged Rucker's battery, the guns of which had been restored to fighting condition; while attention was engaged with this boat, a second gunboat slipped down unperceived, except by the men at one of the batteries, who fired two shots at her without effect. Things were now getting serious; the enemy had possession of the river below the island. General Mackall, therefore, on Sunday, April 6th, moved the infantry and Stewart's battery to the Tennessee shore, to protect the landings from anticipated attacks. The artillerists, numbering about four hundred, alone remained on the island.

On the succeeding day, Monday, the enemy assumed the offensive below the island. They first silenced the battery manned by a detachment of Southern Guards, the guns were spiked and the limbers cut. Other batteries we had on this side below the island were successively silenced. At ten o'clock in the morning they landed troops on the Tennessee side. This, of course, made the continuance of our men on the island no longer possible for any useful purpose, and measures were taken with a view to deserting a spot that will ever be memorable for the bold stand made there against the attacks of the enemy's gunboats. The guns, seventy in number, were spiked with rat-tail files softened at one end; balls were then rammed in at the muzzle—they would turn the soft end of the file and clinch it.

The transports and wharf boats at the landing, of which we gave a list on Tuesday evening, last, were scuttled and sunk in deep water; the Yazoo and De Soto were kept until dusk to convey the artillerists to the main land, and when that service was performed they, too, were ordered to be sunk; but it was rumored that their captains had refused to scuttle them. The floating battery was scuttled and cut loose; some of the Federals boarded her, but they found their prize in a sinking condition. The ammunition in the magazines was wholly or partially destroyed. On the two wharf boats lying at the shore were provisions for one month—the whole was sunk and destroyed. A considerable quantity of small arms, and the private baggage of the officers and others, suffered the same fate as the other property.

These important matters being arranged, the time had arrived to secure personal safety. The number of sick was very large; there was no help for them; they must necessarily fall into the hands of the foe. The greater portion of them marched down the Tiptonville road; these fell into the hands of the invading troops, and were compelled to stack arms and surrender. The number of persons taken prisoners is estimated at two thousand. General Mackall and staff, except Major Davis and Lieutenant-Colonel Henderson, fortieth Confederate, were among them. Ex-Major Baugh was sick on Monday afternoon; he procured a mule and cart in the afternoon to take him away, since which time he was seen safe on this side the lake. Captain Rucker and Colonel T. J. Finnie got off safely. We learned that all the Southern Guards escaped, except Frank Harrison, who was left in the hospital; also Captain Hoadley and ten of his men; Lieutenant Torrey and thirty-nine men; Lieutenant M. Trezevant, fortieth regiment; Robert Pitman and John Ginnis, of Baker's regiment; Captain Robert Lewis and seven men. Captain Jackson, Lieutenant McClure, and their commands, are supposed nearly all to be safe. The same is believed of Captains Strelling, Hume, and Caruthers.

The adventures of many that escaped were of great interest. A gentleman, from whom we have received many of the above particulars, after starting from the island with his party, in the direction of Tiptonville, became suspicious that there was danger in that direction, and a detour was made by wading through the overflowed country. Thus the town was avoided, and the river gained below. Here the company, consisting of four persons, constructed a raft with which to float down the Mississippi. The raft was difficult to manage, the wind high, and the party, after floating down a considerable distance, found themselves in the middle of the Mississippi; under circumstances of extreme peril. They contrived at length to arouse the attention of some one on land, and a skiff put out and took them ashore. Here they were treated with great kindness, and on the rest of their way along the river they received readily the most hospitable attentions from the country people.

We also learned something of the adventure of a gentleman who took a different direction from the party above. Distrusting the state of things below the island, he, with many others, started up the river, with the intention of skirting the north shore of Reelfoot Lake, crossing the Ohio river, and thus reaching the interior. After traveling some distance up the river, when it became quite dark—for it was dark when they started—they turned into the canebrake. There they wandered about for some time until they became completely lost, and had no idea whether they were traveling toward the lake or the river, or to or from the enemy, whose scouting parties were occasionally heard. Toward morning one of the company was sent in search of a guide; after long wandering about, he returned with a man, who, for a mule one of the party offered him, agreed to put them in the right direction.

They had passed the night with little rest and no food, but the way before them required all their energies. The country was covered with water, and miles had to be waded. At times, as a descent in the ground or a little run was reached, a step would sink the travelers from the knees to the neck. Two places, especially, sank the party nearly overhead. In places the current was rapid, and so dangerous were some parts of the route that one or two individuals lost their footing and were drowned; some, thinking they could find a better route, wandered off and became lost in the flooded and tenantless woods.

Thus the day passed without food and in a severe toil Tuesday night came on raining, and so continued. On Wednesday morning some snow fell. At a place where some scows and dugouts were found, a large party of stragglers had collected, perhaps between two and three hundred, and here they crossed the lake. It was necessary to wade into the water to get to the scows, and there was immense disorder, all struggling to get aboard. After this, some further traveling brought the men to Obion River, which was crossed in a ferry; then Dyersburg was reached. Here our informant, and many others, got their first meal from the time of leaving the island. Men and women turned out and set before the escaped soldiers all they had in their houses, showing a warm-hearted hospitality, that speaks nobly for Dyersburg. From this place the travelers made their way to Bell's station, on the Ohio railroad, and reached Memphis.

"Stonewall Jackson's Way"

Come, stack arms, men! Pile on the rails,
    Stir up the camp-fire bright;
No matter if the canteen fails,
    We'll make a roaring night.
Here Shenandoah brawls along,
There burly Blue Ridge echoes strong,
To swell the brigade's rousing song
    Of "Stonewall Jackson's way."

We see him now—the old slouched hat
    Cocked o'er his eye askew,
The shrewd, dry smile, the speech so pat,
    So calm, so blunt, so true.
The "Blue-Light Elder" knows 'em well;
Says he, "That's Banks—he's fond of shell
Lord save his soul we'll give him"—well,
    That's "Stonewall Jackson's way."

Silence! ground arms! kneel, all! caps off!
    Old Blue-Light's going to pray.
Strangle the fool that dares to scoff!
    Attention! it's his way.
Appealing from his native sod,
In *forma pauperis* to God—
"Lay bare thine arm, stretch forth thy rod!
    Amen!" That's "Stonewall's way."

He's in the saddle now. Fall in!
    Steady the whole brigade!
Hill's at the ford, cut off—we'll win
    His way out ball and blade!
What matter if our shoes are worn?
What matter if our feet are torn?
"Quick-step! we're with him before dawn!"
    That's "Stonewall Jackson's way."

> The sun's bright lances rout the mist
>   Of morning, and, by George!
> Here's Longstreet struggling in the lists,
>   Hemmed in an ugly gorge.
> Pope and his Yankees, whipped before,
>   "Bay'nets and grape!"near Stonewall roar;
> "Charge, Stuart! Pay off Ashby's score!"
>   Is " Stonewall Jackson's way."
>
> Ah maiden, wait and watch, and yearn
>   For news of Stonewall's band!
> Ah widow, read, with eyes that burn,
>   That ring upon thy hand!
> Ah. wife, sew on, pray on, hope on!
>   Thy life shall not be all-forlorn.
> The foe had better ne'er been born
>   That gets in "Stonewall's way."

THE RESERVES AT PETERSBURG[*]

    I was sitting in my office, peacefully engaged in endeavoring to extract from the Richmond papers, just received, something like an idea of the "situation," when, as though our city were blessed with a patent fire-telegraph, all the available bell metal in the corporation broke into chorus with so vigorous a peal, and a clangor so resonant, as to suggest to the uninitiated a general conflagration. Not being connected with the fire brigade, and being otherwise totally disinterested on the subject of inflammable real estate, I might have remained absorbed in my inquiries, and thus escaped my fate (and you these pages), but for the general understanding, if not orders, that this signal, theretofore consecrated to the annunciation of fire, should thenceforth, in Petersburg, serve the purpose further of heralding the approach of another "devouring element," the Yankees. Thus it came to pass, that in most indecent haste I let fall my journals and hastened into the street, to learn from the first

---

[*] From "In Vinculis." By A. M. Kelley.

excited passer-by that the enemy's cavalry to the number of twenty thousand—so ran the tale—were approaching the city, and already within two miles of where my informants stood! The "usual discount" of seventy-five per cent still left the tale uncomfortable to a degree.

"What forces have we on the Jerusalem plank road (the road by which they were approaching), do you know?"

"Not a d——n man (we had not had—I remark parenthetically—a revival of religion in our town for some time, and Confederate whisky would make a nun swear) except Archer's Battalion, and not a hundred and fifty of them."

Archer's Battalion was an organization of militiamen, armed for local defence, and formed of the non-conscribable population. It was, therefore, composed of citizens least fitted for military service, but in preparation for the gigantic struggle, which, General Lee foresaw, the vast Federal superiority of numbers would impose on him, he could spare no young arm well from his ranks.

Here was what the gentleman of the prize ring would call "another bloody go."

Military criticism was, however, obviously out of place just then, though, like all my fellow Americans, I affirm my competence, and claim my right to hold forth on that theme as the spirit moves, so I turned the key in my office door—destined, alas! to remain untouched by hand of mine for many a moon—and calling by my home to replenish my commissariat, I sallied forth prepared (morally speaking let it be understood) to do battle *à l'outrance,* against all comers of the Yankee persuasion, though they had been as numerous as Abe's jokes, Ben. Butler's thieveries, or the leaves in that umbrageous Spanish valley which has done such incalculable service to simile-mongers since the days of our greatest great grandmothers.

Admonished by the example of Tristam Shandy, whose amiable desire to acquaint his friends and the world with every thing possible to be known of himself, leads him into most indecorous developments in the first three chapters of his autobiography, I shall not undertake to explain, but only state the fact that I was, at that time, not in "active service" in any capacity—though it is due to my family, to say that I was *not* in the Nitre and Mining Bureau, a member of the society of Friends, nor the editor of a newspaper. One result of this unattached condition was, that like "Black

Dan" in the halcyon days after Tippecanoe was *translated,* I was somewhat puzzled to know "whither I should go." Another difficulty was, the vagueness of my idea what to do when I got there; but as the place to be useful was obviously the line of the enemy's approach, I turned my face thither and soon found myself in the camp of Major Archer's Battalion, where all was preparation. This was about two miles from the city, or a mile southeast of the Blandford cemetery, and exactly at the point known in the subsequent operations around Petersburg as Rives' House—not very far from "The Mine."

I found here a very stimulating degree of excitement. The battalion, understanding perfectly well that a fight, at very great odds, was before it, and being so small that the accession of a single volunteer was not to be slighted, was marching by companies to assigned positions in the little earthwork before its tents; and breathless couriers, racing at the highest speed possible to Confederate steeds, were momently arriving with news of the leisurely advance of General Kautz.

Reporting to the first captain I met, he made the obvious suggestion that I should get a musket; and I hastened to the ordnance officer to supply myself. This gentleman courteously invited me to make intelligent choice between three specimens of smooth-bore military architecture universally known in the army as "altered percussions"; guns originally with flint locks, and therefore demonstrably a quarter of a century old, but modernized by the substitution of the percussion hammer and tube. These hybrids, without bayonets, were the weapons with which that handful of militia were to resist (or fly before) the picked cavalry (and many regiments of them) of the Yankee army.

One of those formidable arquebuses had a trigger with so weak a spring, that the tenderest cap ever turned out of a laboratory would successfully resist its pressure; the second was so rusty that its ramrod shrank from sounding its oxydized depths; while the third, which had the "spic and span" appearance of an assistant-surgeon, or a regimental-adjutant on dress-parade, proved on examination to be so bent and wrenched, that you could not see light through it when the breech-pin was unscrewed! I now began to be overwhelmed with apprehensions that I was destined to act exclusively as a lay figure in the drama about to be put on the boards, and my vanity not a little recoiled from the prospect of playing dummy in the game, when a friend, commiserating my perplexity, handed me a gun left in his tent by a comrade who had gone to town "on leave" that morning, and who was not likely to return. I soon balanced the "provant" which filled one of my pockets with ammunition enough to fill the other; and, accounting myself "armed and equipped as the law directs," I stepped forward to the earthwork.

Several months had elapsed since I quit soldiering proper, leaving behind me at Orange Court-House the noblest company of gentlemen that ever perilled their lives as private soldiers in any cause or country; and I longed for them that day, with the immortal "Twelfth Virginia," in which they marched, that they might stand by their sires at the portal of their home, and "keep the gate."

Glorious boys! There is not an acre in the long line of the circumvallation of Petersburg that is not vocal with some gallant deed of their achieving; and when the death-struggle came, they abandoned their city, not their cause, fought their weary way to Appomattox Court House, dealt the last successful blows at the foe, and ere they stacked arms for the last time, divided among them the tatters of their untarnished flag, that memory might never want a souvenir of a career glorious and unsullied from its first hour to its last.

The fairy days are passed, and my comrades came not for my wishing; and I, who had been proud to stand amid the sons, was content to stand that day amid their sires. *Sang azul* I suspect, for, as that morning's work showed, as stout hearts beat beneath gray locks as beneath gray jackets.

The sun was clambering up the sky—a figure which astronomy has perpetually but vainly tilted against since the great Italian's day—and the town-clock had struck ten, many minutes before, when a pair of frantic videttes, one of them without his hat, tore into camp on foaming steeds, with the news that the enemy, not more than a half a mile away, were rapidly approaching in a body, consisting of several regiments of cavalry, and at least four pieces of artillery. Our "position" was an open earthwork, the front face of which was cut at right angles by the Jerusalem plank-road—a thoroughfare which, some outside barbarians may not know, opens up to deserving Petersburgers, in times of peace, the beatific vision of Sussex hams and Southampton brandy. This work, intended to accommodate two pieces of artillery—but then all innocent of ordnance—was accompanied by a line of low breastworks running out on either flank, to afford shelter to such infantry as might be destined to support the guns; while beyond, on each side, lay a level and accessible country, inviting easy approach to man or beast.

There was nothing in the character of the position to give the assailed any advantage other than that which the breastwork offered in case of a direct attack, the ground being almost a dead level in every direction, and when Major Archer, our commandant, disposed of his little force of about one hundred and twenty-five men along the extended line six—hundred yards, I presume—it was perfectly evident that twenty thousand cavalry, or any respectable minority of the same, would make short work of us. In conformity to universal civilized precedent, the major addressed us a word of cheer and counsel before he assigned us our position; but there was eloquence incomparably superior to all the witchery of words in the hundred homes which stood but a scant cannon-shot behind us, and in the reflection that, according as we did our devoir, there might be, then and thenceforth, grief or rejoicing to them and to many more. Small marvel then, that as I looked down our little band, sparsely stretched over our extended and exposed front, and noticed how well the best of my townsmen were represented in its ranks, I felt that they would give an account of themselves that no wife or mother, sweetheart or sister, would blush to hear or remember, though every Cossack that ever swam the Don should charge our line that day—an account that the brave boys keeping watch and ward before Grant's legions would toss their tattered caps in air to hear.

We expended a few moments in closing our lines at the point at which the road cut them, with an old wagon and a score or two of fence-rails disposed *â la chevaux de frise*, and *waited*.

We had not long to wait: a cloud of dust in our front told of the hurried advance of cavalry, and the next instant, the glitter of spur and scabbard revealed to us a long line of horsemen, rapidly deploying under cover of a wood that ran parallel to our line, and about half a mile in front of us. *Then we missed our cannon!* Our venerable muskets were not worth a tinker's imprecation, at longer range than a hundred yards, and we were compelled, *per force*, to watch the preparations for our capture or slaughter, much after the fashion that a rational turtle may be presumed to contemplate the preliminaries of a civic dinner in London. A little of that military coquetry called reconnoissance, determined our enemy to feel us first with a small portion of his command, and on came, at a sweeping gallop, a gallant company of troopers with as confident an air as though all that was necessary was that they should "come" and "see" in order to "conquer." Every one saw that this was a party we could easily manage, and we possessed, therefore, our souls in great patience, till we could see the chevrons on the arm of the non-commissioned officer who led them—a brave fellow—and then there broke forth (from such amiable muskets as could be induced to go off) a discharge that scattered the cavaliers like chaff—three riderless horses being all of the expedition that entered our lines.

The incident was trifling in the extreme, but it saved Petersburg, and probably prolonged for months the surrender.

The Federals now became convinced that no cavalry charge would frighten these uninformed and half-armed militiamen from their posts, and that a regular attack *au pied* must be made. For this purpose two regiments of their cavalry were dismounted and deployed on either side of the road, in a line double the length of our own, and it was evident that they had determined to flank us on both sides.

The welcome rattle of artillery horses brought now a cheer to every lip as they observed a field-piece falling into position on our right, and the sharp shriek of a shell curvetting over the Yankee line, was an agreeable variation of the monotonous silence in which, to the right and left, their skirmish line was stretching away to encompass us. This occasioned another check, and provoked an artillery response, which continued for twenty minutes, with about the effect currently attributed to sacred melodies chanted in the hearing of a certain useful hybrid, deceased. But these were all golden moments for Petersburg—cannon and horses were pouring into town. Graham's and Sturdivant's batteries were wheeling into position, and Dearing was hastening to the scene with his cavalry—Dearing, the gallant trooper, who gave away his noble life in the gathering gloom of the last hours of the Confederacy. "Green be the turf above thee!"

Meanwhile, the long line of foemen was stretching around us—manifold more than we in numbers, and, as we soon found, armed with the Spencer rifle, repeating sixteen times. And there we fought them; fought them till we were so surrounded, that the two nearest men to me were shot *in the back* while facing the line of original approach; till both our guns were captured; till our camp, in the rear of our works, was full of the foe; till the noblest blood of our city stained the clay of the breastwork as they gave out their lives, gun in hand and face foeward, on the spot where their officers placed them. Their faces rise before me now: the calm, grave countenances of Bannister and Staubley; the generous, joyous frankness of Friend and Hardee; the manly, conscientious fire of patriotism in all—Bellingham and Blanks, Jones, Johnson, and the rest—all gallant gentlemen and true; one of whose lives was well worth a hecatomb of the bummers and bounty jumpers before them; and I could but ask myself then as now, the prophetic question whose answer has in all ages sustained the martyrs of freedom as of faith, *"Can such blood fall in vain?"*

Truly, the cause is lost; but no man, in all the ages, died for what he thought the right and true, in absolute fruitlessness.

One by one, my comrades of an hour fell around me—Bellingham the last; and as I turned, at his request, and stooped to change his position to one of greater comfort, the enemy trooped over the earthwork behind me, and the foremost, presenting his loaded carbine, demanded my surrender with an unrepeatable violence of language that suggested bloodshed. All avenue of escape being cut off, I yielded with what grace I could to my fate, captive to the bow and spear of a hatchet-faced member of the First District Cavalry, greatly enamored of this honorable opportunity of going to the rear.

A Friendly Warning

During the retreat of the Confederates through South Carolina, Sergeant McD———, of Western North Carolina, was sent on detail to the town of M———, where a regiment of home guards were stationed. These valorous heroes, seeing a soldier from the front, gathered around him eagerly, inquiring the news. "News!" said Mack, solemnly; "I believe there is none. Yes, there is a little, too, but it's not of much importance. *Old Hardee burnt up a regiment of home guards at Florence the other day, to keep them from falling into the enemy's hands.*" Mack walked coolly on, leaving his auditors in a state of semi-bewilderment.

Just for a Sick Man

During General Lee's advance upon Manasses, in the fall of 1863, the musicians of Cook's and Kirkland's North Carolina brigades were left behind to attend to and nurse the wounded of their commands. When the army commenced to retire to the Rappahannock, these men were moved forward to rejoin their commands. They had been so much bedeviled, and hooted at by the troops, that they tried to avoid them by going through the fields, and away from the road, but go where they would, they were sure to meet some of the much dreaded arms bearing men; till, at last, they betook themselves to the road in despair, assuming a sullen, indifferent air, never daring to turn their heads to any of the hailing appeals of " I say, mister," "I say, you man with the horn," etc., etc. The most shining mark, and apparently the most sullen and worst worried of them, was the bass drummer of the band of the twenty-seventh infantry (Cook's brigade), who was a tall, handsome; dignified looking man, carrying one of the largest drums in the army. He was greeted on all sides, but heeded nothing, till attracted by a most pitiful and doleful sound of "Mister! Oh mister!" several times repeated very near him. He turned, and discovered that it proceeded from a most woe-begone, tall, cadaverous-looking Georgia soldier, standing about half bent, his hands resting on the muzzle of his gun, and his chin on his hands, his uncombed hair hanging over his eyes, and his under lip (from which dripped saliva) hanging about half an inch below his chin—altogether, looking such a picture of misery and bodily suffering, that said musician's sympathies were at once enlisted, and he asked in a tone of commiserating kindness: "What can I do for you?" With a very beseeching air and trembling voice, the Georgian said: "Won't you please be so kind as to pick a tune on that ar' thing for a sick man."

The poor musician went on his way supremely disgusted, amid the shouts and laughter of all within hearing. So long as the war lasted, he never heard the last of it, and many were the applications made to him for the soothing tones of "that ar' thing."

Selling a Parson

At the depot in ——, a clergyman had an affecting and earnest conversation with some soldiers *en route* to ——. He gave them a good deal of wholesome advice and wholesome warning, to which they listened most respectfully. At length, the whistle blew, and the soldiers ran and sprang upon the flat cars. Just as the train began slowly to move, one of them cried out to the preacher: "Oh, parson, I have left my oven behind. We can't cook without it. Please throw it up here." Picking up the oven pointed out, the good minister ran after the cars, and succeeded in pitching it aboard. Coming back a good deal jaded by the race, but with a countenance beaming with satisfaction at having done a good deed, he was accosted by an indignant old Negro, with: "Marser, what for you throw dat uben to de soger. *Dat my uben!*" The mortified clergyman never after denied the doctrine of the total depravity of human nature, at least, of *soldier* nature.

Under Fire

A correspondent of the *Fayetteville (N.C.) Observer,* gives the following account of the bombardment of Fort Fisher, when General Butler tried and failed to take that work:

About twelve o'clock the fleet had formed in line-of-battle and commenced to move up. On they came, the huge frigates leading the way; then, the grim, ugly Ironsides; then the monitors, and the great line of smaller vessels, stretching away out almost as far as the eye could see. Nearer and nearer they approach! All is calm and quiet in the fort. The men are at their guns. Our colonel stands on the parapet, watch in hand, to note the time they commence firing. Closer still they come! And now they are in position. A flash—a curl of smoke, and a loud report, followed by the shrieking noise of the shell from one of the frigates—announces the fight commenced, twenty minutes before one o'clock. And now the fight progresses in earnest. Thick fly the shell; loud sounds the thunder of artillery; lurid are the flashes of great guns, as they vomit forth their missiles of death and destruction. And oh, nobly stand our men to their guns! From Shepherd's battery to the Mound, they stand unquivering and defiant, loading and firing coolly and calmly, the gunners sighting their guns as if they were practicing at a target.

The scene is grand and awful. From every vessel can be seen the white curl of smoke, and high up in the air hundreds of smoky rings are formed from the explosion of shells. The firing does not abate in the least; it increases as the fight progresses, and the noise is deafening. The enemy have concentrated their fire on our flag, and the halyards are cut; and now the noble staff is struck in several places, and falls. The flag at the Mound still floats, and now they fire on it thick and fast. At last they strike it, and down it comes. But it is immediately raised again. Bang, bang, bang! whiz, whiz, whiz! clash, clash, clash! all the time. The quarters have caught fire, and the bright flames stretch out their tongues, while the heavens are enveloped with dark clouds of smoke. The air is sulphurous from burned powder. Still all goes well.

About five o'clock the fire of the enemy begins to slacken, and the intervals between the firing are longer. Still gradually it slackens; and at half past five o'clock the fight ceases. The vessels haul off and return to their anchorage. The damage to the fort has been very slight—hardly any—and our weary, gallant soldiers rest from their struggle for the while, as they expect another attack at night. The casualties are twenty-three—one mortally, three severely, and nineteen slightly wounded.

Sunday's fight will always be memorable to the men who garrisoned Fort Fisher.

The expectation of the garrison that we would have a night fight was not realized. The night was spent in watchfulness, and repairing the slight damage sustained by the fight. Our noble General Whiting had arrived, and all was confidence and cheerfulness. As the morning dawned, the fleet could be discerned in the distance getting ready to renew the attack; but it was not expected that operations would commence before high tide, which would be about half past twelve o'clock. However, every man was at his post, ready at any moment to again engage the fleet.

About ten o'clock the fleet commenced moving in, their extreme right resting near Gatlin's battery, about six miles up the beach, and their left extending down to the fort. The Ironsides led the attack, the frigates resting on her right and left, and the monitors to the right of the frigates. I counted fifty-two vessels in all—the Ironsides, three or four monitors, four frigates, and forty-seven other vessels. They steamed in very slowly, two of the frigates going round to the seafront of the fort, and the Ironsides and monitors lying abreast of the centre front. The Ironsides and monitors came up within a mile; the rest of the fleet remained out about one and a half miles. At 10:34 A.M. the first gun was fired by the Ironsides, followed by the rest of the fleet, firing very slowly and deliberately for the while. The fort reserved its fire, thinking that the wooden fleet would be tempted to come in closer range. Finding, however, that they would not come closer, our guns opened; also firing very slowly. The day was quite foggy, and the smoke from the guns rendered it more so.

About twelve o'clock the fire commenced to increase with great rapidity. The dull, heavy, thumping sounds of the enemy's guns as they were fired could be heard first, and then the whistling, shrieking sound of the shells as they came whizzing and buzzing through the air. Their explosion and the myriad fragments that went rattling by, thick almost as hail, were terrible to listen to. Terrific continued the bombardment—no slow firing now from the enemy—no deliberation—away they would shoot their hell balls, not caring where they threw them—faster and faster comes the iron hail, louder and louder sounds the terrible thunder—the air is hot with the fire, such as you would experience from the heat of a furnace; the earth shakes; no interval of quiet; all is noise—crash, bang, and bang, crash, all the time. Will it ever cease? Will it ever stop? No lull. Bang, bang, bang, quicker than you can count. The sand flies all about. There goes a shell whistling by, close to General Whiting; it buries itself, exploding, covering him all over with the wet sand. He does not even move, not even take his pipe from his mouth, and only remarks coolly, "Well, it spattered me."

Still no intermission; the evening goes on; the time passes slowly. The men stand to their guns nobly. Some have been, yesterday, fighting all day, and still fighting; there is no lag in them; they fight as men never fought before with heavy guns. Colonel Lamb and General Whiting are everywhere along the lines encouraging them; from battery to battery they go; the men look at them and smile, and bang away again; the commanders of the companies are all at their posts.

The bombardment continued terrific till about five o'clock, when the firing suddenly slackened from the fleet. It was then discovered that the enemy had succeeded in landing a force at Anderson and Holland batteries, and that their line of skirmishers were advancing on the fort. All is excitement now. Our infantry man the parapets; and now the sharp crack of the rifle can be heard instead of the heavy booming of guns. Faison and

Parker have engaged them. But the lull is of short duration—the most terrific bombardment now commences; the fleet have seen their land forces, and they open with greater vim than ever to keep our men from engaging the skirmishers. Colonel Lamb comes rushing up the parapets; he calls for his men to man the line of palisades; with a cheer for him they answer to his call. Away they went after him, and soon they are in line, ready to meet the enemy. The sharp crack of the rifle is mixed in with the loud noise of the cannon. The Yankees can be seen creeping away on their bellies, like crawling worms. Lieutenant Hunter, with his Whitworth rifle, is doing good service; Colonel Tansill and Major Saunders are among the junior reserves, encouraging them on; fainter grows the cannonade; the musket firing has ceased; the fleet is drawing off; the land attack has been repulsed. The day's fight is over; and, thank God, all is well.

Every thing about the land front was now got in readiness with the expectation that a night attack would be made by the land force to storm the fort. A bright lookout was kept up and our pickets were thrown out. Every thing was quiet, however, until about twelve o'clock, when our pickets discovered the Yankees landing on the extreme right of the fort, near the mound. The night was dark and a heavy rain had set in—Colonel Lamb, at the head of his infantry, engaged them, and, for awhile the rattle of musketry was heavy; but the enemy are at last driven off, and quiet is again resumed. Our casualties to-day were thirty-nine—four killed and thirty-five wounded.

Monday, 26th.—The morning was very foggy, and the fleet was hardly visible. The tall, tapering masts of the frigates could be discerned in the fog looming up like phantom ships. The booming of cannon could be heard in the distance up the beach, and it was supposed that the enemy were landing their forces, which turned out to be true. About ten o'clock, by looking through a glass, could be seen a column of the enemy stretched out across the land front near Anderson. The long roll was beat, and the men lined the palisades and manned the guns. From some cause, however, the enemy made no advance, and nothing happened about the fort during the day. The men were all in fine spirits; and Colonel Tait, with his fine battalion, had arrived to take part in the fray. The firing up the beach continued all day, and also during the night. The men were hard at work to-day in repairing the damages to the fort.

Tuesday, 27th.—The morning opened brightly. The glorious sun came forth from great old ocean in all its splendor. The rippling waves, crowned with their white caps, rushing on each other as in a playful gambol sparkled in its light. All nature seemed lovely. And lo! there on the bar is the blockade-runner Banshee. The fleets see her, and two of them start after her, but she is too quick, and proudly she comes in the inlet, while the men crowd the curtains, and cheer after cheer greets her, which are answered with a vim by her crew. During the night another had come in, whose name I have not learned. I wonder how Mr. Admiral Porter felt at that time, with a fleet of upwards of sixty vessels, not able to *effectually* blockade New inlet.

About twelve o'clock M. the fleet stood out; the Ironsides, which had been lying nearer the fort, got up steam and started out, and soon the whole fleets were out some distance, where they anchored. A bright lookout was kept up at night, but nothing of importance occurred.

Wednesday, December 28.—Another beautiful morning. Half of the fleet has disappeared; the rest are going off.

Twenty minutes after five o'clock, P.M. —The rest have disappeared; nothing but the usual blockade squadron are now visible.

Hard to Move

William McG——, of the thirty-sixth Virginia infantry, was a good shot. At the battle of Fort Donnelson, Bill saw a Yankee's head peering above a stump. Pointing his gun in that direction he fired. The Yankee remains with his gun leveled across the stump. Bill reloaded, fired, once, twice, thrice, four times, with the same result. Turning to his brother, he said,—"Charlie, do you see that Yankee behind that stump? I have fired five shots at his head, and cannot make him remove it. Do you give him a shot." Just then the line was advanced, and Bill made for the stump.

The Yankee still held his position, *with five holes in his cranium.*

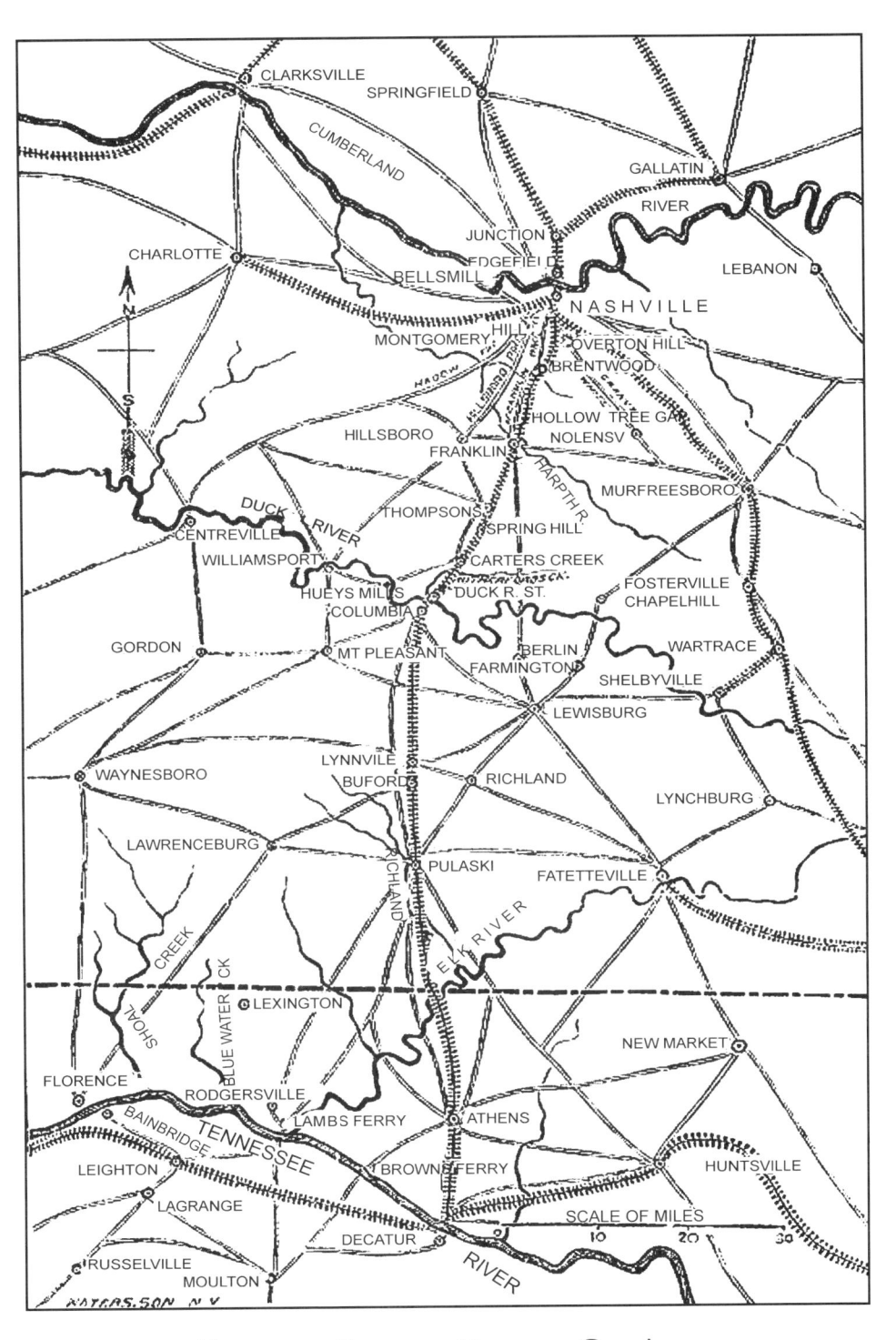

NASHVILLE, TENN., TO DECATUR, GA., AREA

A Review in General Lee's Army

A correspondent of the *"Petersburg Express,"* writing from Orange C.H., on the 11th of September 1863, thus describes a review of the 2d corps, of the army of Northern Virginia:

I witnessed, on Wednesday evening, the grandest military display that I have ever before seen. In a large and beautiful field just east of the courthouse, General Ewell's entire corps, consisting of three divisions, commanded respectively by Major-Generals Early, Rhodes and Johnson was reviewed by General Lee, in person. About noon, large bodies of troops could be seen wending their way across the field to the place designated for them, and wishing to be in at the commencement of the show, I immediately repaired thither, and wishing to hear what was going on, as well as to see, I took my stand immediately by the large flag, designating the general's stand point. By this time three lines of troops, each some mile and a half in length, and one behind the other, was stretching out to the right and left, and now they are halted, arms stacked, and the men are lying down awaiting the movements of the generals. The crowd around my stand point was now augmenting rapidly, and on looking around I beheld a large body of ladies on horseback, and in carriages and buggies, who had been drawn thither to witness the scene. Just then a number of officers came dashing up, who proved to be Generals Ewell, Early and Rhodes, and a number of their respective staffs. Never having seen General Ewell before, my eyes were riveted upon him. He is a tall, slim individual, with extremely sharp features, and his Frenchified moustache and whiskers make him look the warrior that he is; but the most remarkable feature about him is his restless eyes, which were constantly wandering over the field, and ever and anon some courier would be hastily dispatched to some point to order some movement or other. General Early is a most husky looking person, and seemed as one who would not be brooked in any thing he wished, while General Rhodes is one of the most pleasant looking men that I have seen for many a day.

The bugle soon announced all in readiness, and General Lee was despatched for, who soon came riding up, and now the cavalcade, composed of General Lee and staff, General Ewell and staff, and the division commanders, started off at a swift gallop to the right of the first division, and soon they are seen coming down the front of the line, each brigade coming to a present as the cavalcade passed, and as they swept by us the strains of music were swelling up all along the line. They passed around the left of the line, dashed back to the right of the second division, and reviewed the second and third divisions in the same manner as the first, and once more came back to the original starting point, the riders and horses both looking much jaded, the distance they had gone so swiftly over being fully nine miles.

General Lee immediately dismounted and came to his carriage, which was only a few steps distant, and in which were two of his daughters, and in a few minutes he called to his side many of his generals, among them Generals Ewell, Longstreet, Hill, Stuart, Wilcox and others, and gave his daughters an introduction to them. His daughters, though not over handsome, have exceedingly pleasant and intelligent countenances, both having dark and piercing eyes, and both bearing some resemblance to their father.

The generals now took a stand just by the flag, and the troops commenced passing in review before General Lee, and as each flag in passing would be lowered as a salute, the general in response would take his hat off. And now I got a close view of the men composing this gallant corps. Here passed those men who had so often followed General Jackson in his numerous battles, and who had won for him that renown which will live through ages to come; and now passes Jackson's old division, at present commanded by the gallant General Johnston, and here comes the "Stonewall Brigade," which was composed of veteran looking soldiers. Many of the banners of the corps bore evidence of having been often borne to the breeze amid the whistling of bullets, and all of them contained some dozen or fifteen names to mark the different battles the respective regiments had distinguished themselves in. One stand of colors, belonging to the twenty-first Virginia regiment, was carried by Color-Sergeant John Brent, formerly of Richmond city, who is at present performing one of the most gallant acts that has yet exhibited itself in the Confederate army, for notwithstanding he lost his right arm at the battle of Chancellorsville last May, he has returned to his regiment, and being offered a discharge refused to receive it, but asked of his colonel permission to again carry those colors that had oft before proudly waved over his head. His colonel consented, and the affair being mentioned to General Johnston, he took the colors and presented them to the young man in person as a reward for the noble patriotism which prompted him to such an act of self-denial and love of country.

The review being now over, the crowd of spectators dispersed, and the troops, with three hearty cheers for General Lee, commenced wending their way back to their camps.

Among the ladies in attendance, other than the Misses Lee already mentioned, were General Ewell's lady and daughter. Mrs. Ewell is a handsome and agreeable looking lady, and the general's daughter is almost a beauty.

While General Ewell is on his horse, one can hardly notice that he is minus one of his original nether limbs, his cork leg being hardly noticeable.

It is surprising to see how eager the men of this army are always, to get a good view of General Lee, for though a person may have seen him a hundred times, yet he never tires looking at him, and this was noticeable as the many thousands passed by, to see how eagerly they would peer to the right to get a glance at him.

I witnessed last Sunday a scene of a different nature, but which was of no less interest. About three in the afternoon, it having been announced that the ordinance of baptism was to be administered a short distance from here to a good number of those who had recently joined the Baptist church, a large crowd repaired thither, and some thirty young men of this brigade were immersed, the Rev. Andrew Broaddus, of Caroline, officiating. As many more have since been received into the Methodist and other churches by other ministers, the ordinance of baptism being administered according to the creed of the several churches.

An Effort for Freedom

The *Sandusky* (Ohio) *Register* gives the following account of an unsuccessful attempt of a party of Confederate prisoners of war to escape from the Federal pen on Johnson's Island:

About one o'clock in the morning, by a preconcerted arrangement, a rush was made by twenty-four prisoners upon the centre of the guard line on the northwest side of the prison on Johnson's Island. The prisoners had improvised eight scaling ladders by attaching cleats to boards and strips; very light, easily carried, and just the thing for scaling the high prison fence.

The rush upon the guard at once occasioned the proper cry, "Turn out the guard!" accompanied by quite a rattling fire from the guard line. But the rush was so impetuous, and by so many prisoners, that, in spite of the guard, four men out of the twenty-four scaled the fence, passed the guard, escaped from the island, crossed the north channel of the bay, and went some distance upon the peninsula. Of the others who did not get through, one received a shot cutting away his coat at the waist, and was knocked down and captured. Another, Lieutenant John B. Bowles, son of the president of the Louisville Bank, Kentucky, was shot twice through the body, about the same instant, and killed. The other eighteen found the work too hot and retreated to their barracks.

The rush on the guard was immediately followed by the long-roll, and the proper signal gun. By the way, this is the first "long-roll" occasioned by any demonstration of the prisoners since last March; and the only other one was on the night of the 23rd of September, when at least one third of the prison fence was swept away in an instant by a tornado.

Under a standing order, all the troops were promptly in position, ready to give proper attention to the rebels should any further efforts be made within the enclosure. To make sure of any who might be lurking on the island awaiting better opportunities to elude observation, three companies of the Sixth Veteran Reserve Corps were ordered out to patrol the island and make a thorough search. At the same time, several detachments of the one hundred and twenty-eighth regiment were ordered off in pursuit of the escaped prisoners, who had passed the picket on the northwest side of the island, receiving a fire from them at long range. The flying rebels made the best time possible, but were hotly pursued; and with soldiers on their rear and both flanks, and the loyal citizens of the peninsula (who had been aroused by the discharge of the twenty-pounder Parrott) in their front, their escape soon terminated in recapture.

The morning roll-call and muster of prisoners showed that but four of them had left the prison. They were all back and returned to their home in the "bull pen" next morning. The unwilling denizens of that locality are full of their schemes and threats, and seem disposed to make the very most of their opportunities while the ice is practicable as a highway.

Three of the fugitives were seen running across the peninsula by Mr. G. B. Wright, a gentleman who has a vineyard there. As soon as he heard the firing he got out with his gun, and seeing the three escaped prisoners, called to them—"Stop, or I'll put a hole through you as big as my hat!" At this they halted, and he marched them back to quarters. Another was brought in by the guard.

RAGGED TEXANS—BOOTS AND BOOTY

In one of the frightful contests near Yorktown, Virginia, some noble instances of bravery and reckless daring occurred. Nor was this confined to one of the great armies only. Conspicuous among these cases was the conduct of a tall, hard-fisted, and very ragged Texan soldier, who was hunting up, very cautiously, a pair of boots and pants. He was warned by his Confederate comrades not to show his head above the parapet, for the Yankee sharpshooters, armed with rifles of a long range, with telescopic "sights," were "thick as blackberries" in the woods to the front, and were excellent shots. "Darn the blue skins, any how! who's scared of the bluebellies? (That is, eastern men.) Let all the Yankees go to —— , for all *I* care. Let 'em shoot and be —— ! I'm bound to have a pair of boots any how!" And so saying, the rash fellow passed over the parapet, down its face, and returned with the body of a Federal which he had fished out of the water. He first pulled off the boots, which proved to be an excellent pair; then, proceeding to rifle the pockets, he found the handsome booty of sixty dollars in gold! He was much astonished and delighted at these discoveries; but when he examined the haversack, and found it well stored with capital rations, including a canteen full of fine rye whisky, he was electrified with sudden joy, dropped boots, haversack and money, upon the ground, and half-emptied the canteen at a draught. Setting down the can, he smacked his lips, and thus soliloquized upon his rare adventure:

"Well, poor devil, he's gone, like a mighty big sight of 'em; but *he* was a gentleman, and deserved better luck. If he'd been a Massachusetts Yankee, I wouldn't cared a darn! but these fellows are the right kind. They come along, as they should, with good boots and pants, lots to eat, money in their pockets, and are no mean judges of whisky. These are the kind of fellows I like to fight."

An Impudent Reply

The chaplain of a Texas regiment tells the following story of an incident of the retreat of the Confederates from Yorktown, in May, 1862:

Late in the afternoon of May 8th, the brigade was drawn up in line of battle, in the lawn, in front of Dr. Tyler's residence, five miles west of New Kent Court House, as the enemy were threatening to attack us. They did not, however, come up, and we remained here until the following evening, when we moved one mile up the road, and formed a new line of defense, to be held until our army could reach and take its position in front of Richmond. About noon, on ——, we decamped, and, though constantly in motion, only reached the Chickahominy, about six miles, by one o'clock at night. This was owing to the fact that the road was blocked up by the rear of our artillery and baggage train, and not daring to lie down or rest, we could only "mark time" in the rain and mud until the hour above mentioned, when all others having passed over, we reached the bridge. Here we found several generals, with their attendant aids and couriers, all exhorting us to "close up," and for God's sake to hurry. This was more easily said than done, for the roads had been cut by artillery and wagons, until a perfect mortar had been formed from one to three feet deep, and through this below, and a heavy, soaking rain above, the men floundered on. At length, losing all patience, General Whiting dashed upon the bridge. "Hurry up, men, hurry up! don't mind a little mud." "Do'ye call this a *little mud?* S'pose you git down and try it, stranger; I'll hold your horse." "Do you know whom you address, sir? I am General Whiting." "General ——, don't you reckon I know a *general* from a long tongued courier?" says the fellow, as he disappeared in the darkness. This, repeated with sundry variations several times, at length discouraged the general, and leaving the Texans, whose spirits he had threatened to subdue, to cross as best they might, he rode away.

Sad Death of a Soldier

The *Rockingham* (Virginia) *Register* gives the following account of the sufferings and death of a Confederate soldier, caused by the brutal conduct of an ambulance driver:

The case to which we refer is that of Henry Wagoner, a member of Company F., North Carolina Volunteers, who died in an ambulance near Harrisonburg on Sunday night or Monday morning last. This poor fellow, we have learned, died from the neglect, or something worse, of the man or men in whose care he was placed. He is thought to have perished from cold whilst the man who drove the ambulance was too much under the influence of strong drink to hear or heed his cries for relief—Sabbath night our readers in this part of the valley will remember was exceedingly inclement, a cold rain falling, and keen autumnal winds blowing, so that any one much exposed would necessarily suffer. Whether this poor soldier had been wounded, or whether he was suffering from disease, we have not learned; but at all events, he was unable to help himself, and his feeble cries for relief grew fainter and fainter as they fell upon the dull, cold ear of the wailing night storm, until finally the merciful angel Death, came, and his poor, shivering body ceased to suffer! His dead body was found in our court-house on Monday morning, stark and cold, with his eyes wide open, as though he was looking for the cruel man who permitted him to perish. He was decently buried on Monday afternoon, in Woodbine Cemetery.

Escaping from Fort Delaware

The *Richmond Dispatch* for August 28th, 1863, contains the following:

Yesterday afternoon five Confederate prisoners: A. L. Brooks and C. J. Fuller, company G, 9th Georgia; J. Marian, company D, 9th Ga.; Wm. E. Glassey, co. B, 18th Miss., and Jno. Dorsey, co. A, Stuart's Horse Artillery, arrived here from Fort Delaware, having escaped therefrom on the night of the 12th inst. The narrative of their escape is interesting. Having formed the plan to escape, they improvised life preservers by tying four canteens, well corked, around the body of each man, and on the night of the 12th inst. proceeded to leave the island. The night being dark they got into the water and swam off from the back of the island for the shore. Three of them swam four miles and landed about two miles below Delaware City; the other two, being swept down the river, floated down sixteen miles, and landed at Christine Creek. Another soldier (a Philadelphian) started with them, but was drowned a short distance from the shore. He said he was not coming back to the Confederacy, but was going to Philadelphia. He had eight canteens around his body, but was not an expert swimmer.

The three who landed near Delaware City laid in a cornfield all night, and the next evening, about dark, started on their way south, after first having made known their condition to a farmer, who gave them a good supper. They traveled that night twelve miles through Kent county, Delaware, and the next day lay concealed in a gentleman's barn. From there they went to Kent County, Maryland, where the citizens gave them new clothes and money. After this their detection was less probable, as they had been wearing their uniforms the two days previous. They took the cars on the Philadelphia and Baltimore railroad at Townsend and rode to Dover, the capital of Delaware. Sitting near them in the cars were a Yankee colonel and captain, and the provost guard passed through frequently. They were not discovered, however, though to escape detection seemed almost impossible. They got off the train at Delamar and went by way of Barren Creek Springs and Quantico, Maryland, to the Nanticoke river, and got into a canal.

Here they parted company with five others, who had escaped from Fort Delaware some days previous, as the canoe would not hold ten of them. In the canoe they went to Tangier's Sound, and, crossing the Chesapeake, landed in Northumberland county below Point Lookout, a point at which the Yankees were building a fort for the confinement of prisoners. They met with great kindness from citizens of Heathsville, who contributed a hundred and twenty dollars to aid them on their route. They soon met with our pickets, and came to this city on the York River railroad. These escaped prisoners express in the liveliest terms their gratitude to the people of Maryland and Delaware, who did every thing they could to aid them. There was no difficulty experienced in either State in finding generous people of Southern sympathies, who would give them both money and clothing, and put themselves to any trouble to help them on their journey.

ENDURANCE IN CAMP LIFE

A writer in the Washington *Chronicle*, says that the greatest power of endurance of such hardships as belong to a soldier's life, belongs to men over thirty-five years of age; that men from eighteen to thirty are ten times on the sick list where those older are only once; that the hospitals around Washington develop the fact that, aside from surgical cases, the patients there under thirty-five are forty to one over that age. Consequently a sound man of forty, and of temperate habits, will endure more fatigue and hard treatment than one equally sound at the age of twenty.

Sumter in ruins

By W. Gilmore Sims, Esq.

I.

Ye batter down the lion's den,
    But yet the lordly beast goes free;
And ye shall hear his roar again,
From mountain height, from lowland glen,
From sandy shore, and reedy fen,
Where'er a band of freeborn men
    Rear sacred shrines to liberty.

II.

The serpent scales the eagle's nest,
    And yet the royal bird, in air
Triumphant, wins the mountain's crest,
And, sworn to strife, yet takes his rest,
And plumes, to calm, his ruled breast,
Till, like a storm-bolt from the west
    He strikes the invader in his lair.

III.

What's loss of den, or, nest, or home,
    If, like the lion, free to go,—
If, like the eagle, wing'd to roam,
We span the rock and breast the foam,
Still watchful for the hour of doom,
When, with the knell of thunder-boom,
    We bound upon the serpent-foe!

IV.

Oh, noble sons of lion heart!
    Oh, gallant hearts of eagle wing!
What though your batter'd bulwarks part,
Your nest be spoiled by reptile art,—
Your souls, on wings of hate, shall start
For vengeance, and with lightning-dart
    Rend the foul serpent ere he sting!

V.

Your battered den, your shattered nest.
    Was but the lion's crouching place,—
It heard his roar, and bore his crest,
His, or the eagle's place of rest:
But not the soul in either breast!—
This arms the twain, by freedom bless'd,
    To save and to avenge their race!

LOOKING ON AT GETTYSBURG[*]

At two in the afternoon (July 1st), firing became distinctly audible in our front; but although it increased as we progressed, it did not seem to be very heavy. A spy who was with us insisted upon there being "a pretty tidy bunch of *Blue-Bellies* in or near Gettysburg," and he declared that he was in their society three days ago.

After passing Johnson's division we came to a Florida brigade, which is now in Hill's corps; but as it had formerly served under Longstreet, the men knew him well. Some of them, after the general had passed, called out to their comrades—"Look out for work now, boys, for here's the old bull-dog again!"

At three o'clock we began to meet wounded men coming to the rear, and the number of these soon increased most rapidly—some hobbling along, others on stretchers carried by the ambulance corps, and others in the ambulance wagons. Many of the latter were stripped nearly naked,

---

[*] From Colonel Fremantle's Diary.

and displayed very bad wounds. This spectacle, so revolting to a person unaccustomed to such sights, produced no impression whatever upon the advancing troops, who certainly go under fire with the most perfect nonchalance. They show no enthusiasm or excitement, but the most complete indifference. This is the effect of two years' almost uninterrupted fighting.

We now began to meet Yankee prisoners coming to the rear in considerable numbers. Many of them were wounded, but they seemed already to be on excellent terms with their captors, with whom they had commenced swapping canteens, tobacco, etc. Among them was a Pennsylvania colonel, a miserable object, from a wound in his face. In answer to a question, I heard one of them remark, with a laugh, "We're pretty nigh whipped already." We next came to a Confederate soldier carrying a Yankee color, belonging, I think, to a Pennsylvania regiment, which he told us he had just captured.

At half past four we came in sight of Gettysburg, and joined General Lee and General Hill, who were on the top of one of the ridges which form the peculiar feature of the country round Gettysburg. We could see the enemy retreating up one of the opposite ridges, pursued by the Confederates with loud yells.

The position into which the enemy had been driven was evidently a strong one. His right appeared to rest on a cemetery, on the top of a high ridge to the right of Gettysburg, as we looked at it.

General Hill now came up and told me he had been very unwell all day, and in fact he looks very delicate. He said he had had two of his divisions engaged and had driven the enemy four miles into his present position, capturing a great many prisoners, some cannon, and some colors: he said, however, that the Yankees had fought with a determination unusual to them. He pointed out a railway cutting, in which they had made a good stand; also, a field in the centre of which he had seen a man plant the regimental color, round which the regiment had fought for some time with much obstinacy, and when at last it was obliged to retreat, the color-bearer retired last of all, turning round every now and then to shake his fist at the advancing Rebels. General Hill said he felt quite sorry when he saw this gallant Yankee meet his doom.

General Ewell had come up at 3.30, on the enemy's right (with part of his corps), and completed his discomfiture.

General Reynolds, one of the best Yankee generals, was reported killed. Whilst we were talking, a message arrived from General Ewell, requesting Hill to press the enemy in the front, whilst he performed the same operation on his right. The pressure was accordingly applied in a mild degree, but the enemy were too strongly posted, and it was too late in the evening for a regular attack.

The town of Gettysburg was now occupied by Ewell, and was full of Yankee dead and wounded.

I climbed up a tree in the most commanding place I could find, and could form a pretty good general idea of the enemy position, although, the tops of the ridges being covered with pine woods, it was very difficult to see any thing of the troops concealed in them.

The firing ceased about dark, at which time I rode back with General Longstreet and his staff to his headquarters at Cashtown, a little village eight miles from Gettysburg. At that time troops were pouring along the road, and were being marched toward the position they are to occupy tomorrow.

In the fight to-day nearly six thousand prisoners had been taken, and ten guns. About twenty thousand men must have been on the field on the Confederate side. The enemy had two corps d'armée engaged. All the prisoners belong, I think, to the first and fourteenth corps. This day's work is called a "brisk little scurry," and all anticipate a "big battle" to-morrow.

I observed that the artillerymen in charge of the horses dig themselves little holes like graves, throwing up the earth at the upper end. They ensconce themselves in these holes when under fire.

At supper this evening General Longstreet spoke of the enemy's position as being "very formidable." He also said that they would doubtless intrench themselves strongly during the night.

The staff officers spoke of the battle as a certainty, and the universal feeling in the army was one of profound contempt for an enemy whom they have beaten so constantly, and under so many disadvantages.

Thursday, July 2d.—We got up at 3.30 A.M., and breakfasted a little before daylight. Lawley insisted on riding, notwithstanding his illness. Captain —— and I were in a dilemma for horses, but I was accommodated by Major Clark (of this staff), whilst the stout Austrian was mounted by Major Walton.

Colonel Sorrell, the Austrian, and I arrived at 5 A.M. at the same commanding position we were on yesterday, and I climbed up a tree in company with Captain Schreibert, of the Prussian army.

Just below us were seated Generals Lee, Hill, Longstreet and Hood, in consultation—the two latter assisting their deliberations by the truly American custom of *whittling* sticks. General Heth was also present: he was wounded in the head yesterday, and although not allowed to command his brigade, he insisted upon coming to the field.

At 7 A.M., I rode over part of the ground with General Longstreet, and saw him disposing McLaws' division for today's fight. The enemy occupied a series of high ridges, the tops of which were covered with trees, but the intervening valleys between their ridges and ours were mostly open, and partly under cultivation. The cemetery was on their right, and their left appeared to rest upon a high rocky hill. The enemy's forces, which were now supposed to comprise nearly the whole Potomac army, were concentrated into a space apparently not more than a couple of miles in length.

The Confederates enclosed them in a sort of semicircle, and the extreme extent of our position must have been from five to six miles at least. Ewell was on our left: his headquarters in a church (with a high cupola) at Gettysburg; Hill in the centre; and Longstreet on the right. Our ridges were also covered with pine woods at the tops, and generally on the rear slopes. The artillery of both sides confronted each other at the edges of these belts of trees, the troops being completely hidden. The enemy was evidently entrenched, but the Southerns had not broken ground at all. A dead silence reigned till 4.45 P.M., and no one would have imagined that such masses of men and such powerful artillery were about to commence the work of destruction at that hour.

Only two divisions of Longstreet were present to-day, viz: McLaws' and Hood's—Pickett being still in the rear. As the whole morning was evidently to be occupied in disposing the troops for the attack, I rode to the extreme right with Colonel Manning and Major Walton, where we ate quantities of cherries, and got a feed of corn for our horses. We also bathed in a small stream, but not without some trepidation on my part, for we were almost beyond the lines, and were exposed to the enemy's cavalry.

At 1 P.M. I met a quantity of Yankee prisoners who had been picked up straggling. They told me they belonged to Sickles' corps (third, I think), and had arrived from Emmetsburg during the night.

About this time skirmishing began along part of the line, but not heavily.

At 2 P.M., General Longstreet advised me, if I wished to have a good view of the battle, to return to my tree of yesterday. I did so, and remained there with Lawley and Captain Schreibert during the rest of the afternoon. But until 4.45 P.M. all was profoundly still, and we began to doubt whether a fight was coming off to-day at all. At that time, however, Longstreet suddenly commenced a heavy cannonade on the right. Ewell immediately took it up on the left. The enemy replied with at least equal fury, and in a few moments the firing along the whole line was as heavy as it is possible to conceive. A dense smoke arose for six miles, there was little wind to drive it away, and the air seemed full of shells—each of which seemed to have a different style of going and to make a different noise from the others. The ordnance on both sides is of a very varied description.

Every now and then a caisson would blow up—if a Federal one, a Confederate yell would immediately follow. The Southern troops, when charging, or to express their delight, always yell in a manner peculiar to themselves. The Yankee cheer is much more like ours; but the Confederate officers declare that the rebel yell has a particular merit, and always produces a salutary and useful effect upon their adversaries. A corps is sometimes spoken of as a "good yelling regiment."

So soon as the firing began, General Lee joined Hill just below our tree, and he remained there nearly all the time, looking through his field glass—sometimes talking to Hill, and sometimes to Colonel Long of his staff. But generally he sat quite alone on the stump of a tree.

What I remarked especially was, that during the whole time the firing continued, he only sent one message, and only received one report. It is evidently his system to arrange the plan thoroughly with the three corps commanders, and then leave to them the duty of modifying and carrying it out to the best of their abilities.

When the cannonade was at its height, a Confederate band of music, between the cemetery and ourselves, began to play polkas and waltzes, which sounded very curious, accompanied by the hissing and bursting of the shells.

At 5.45 all became comparatively quiet on our left and in the cemetery; but volleys of musketry on the right told us that Longstreet's infantry were advancing, and the onward progress of the smoke showed that he was progressing favorably; but about 6.30 there seemed to be a check, and even a slight retrograde movement. Soon after seven General Lee got a report by signal from Longstreet, to say, "we *are doing well.*"

A little before dark, the firing dropped off in every direction, and soon ceased altogether.

We then received intelligence that Longstreet had carried every thing before him for some time, capturing several batteries, and driving the enemy from his positions; but when Hill's Florida brigade and some other troops gave way he was forced to abandon a small portion of the ground he had won, together with all the captured guns, except three.

His troops, however, bivouacked during the night on ground occupied by the enemy in the morning.

Every one deplores that Longstreet will expose himself in such a reckless manner. To-day, he led a Georgia regiment in a charge against a battery, hat in hand, and in front of everybody. General Barksdale was killed, and Semmes wounded; but the most serious loss was that of General Hood, who was badly wounded in the arm early in the day. I heard that his Texans are in despair. Lawley and I rode back to the general's camp, which had been moved to within a mile of the scene of action. Longstreet, however, with most of his staff, bivouacked on the field.

Major Fairfax arrived at about ten P.M., in a very bad humor. He had under his charge about one thousand to one thousand five hundred Yankee prisoners, who had been taken to-day, among them a general, whom I heard one of his men accusing of having been "so drunk that he had turned his guns upon his own men." But, on the other hand, the accuser was such a thundering blackguard, and proposed taking such a variety of oaths in order to escape from the United States army, that he is not worthy of much credit. A large train of horses and mules, etc., arrived to-day, sent in by General Stuart, and captured, it is understood, by his cavalry, which had penetrated to within six miles of Washington.

Friday, July 3d.—At 6 A.M. I rode to the field with Colonel Manning, and went over that portion of the ground, which, after a fierce contest, had been won from the enemy yesterday evening. The dead were being buried, but great numbers were still lying about; also many mortally wounded, for whom nothing could be done. Amongst the latter were a number of Yankees dressed in bad imitations of the Zouave costume. They opened their glazed eyes as I rode past, in a painfully imploring manner.

We joined Generals Lee and Longstreet's staff; they were reconnoitering, and making preparations for renewing the attack. As we formed a pretty large party, we often drew upon ourselves the attention of the hostile sharpshooters, and were two or three times favored with a shell. One of these shells set a brick building on fire which was situated between the lines. This building was filled with wounded, principally Yankees, who, I am afraid, must have perished miserably in the flames. Colonel Sorrell had been slightly wounded yesterday, but still did duty. Major Walton's horse was killed, but there were no other casualties amongst my particular friends.

The plan of yesterday's attack seems to have been very simple—first a heavy cannonade all along the line, followed by an advance of Longstreet's two divisions and part of Hill's corps. In consequence of the enemy's having been driven back some distance, Longstreet's corps (part of it) was in a much more forward situation than yesterday. But the range of heights to be gained was still most formidable, and evidently strongly entrenched.

The distance between the Confederate guns and the Yankee position—*i.e.* between the woods crowning the opposite ridges—was at least a mile—quite open, gently undulating, and exposed to artillery the whole distance. This was the ground which had to be crossed in to-day's attack. Pickett's division, which had just come up, was to bear the brunt in Longstreet's attack, together with Heth and Pettigrew in Hill's corps. Pickett's division was a weak one (under five thousand), owing to the absence of two brigades.

At noon all Longstreet's dispositions were made; his troops for attack were deployed into line, and lying down in the woods; his batteries were ready to open. The general then dismounted and went to sleep for a short time.

Captain —— and I, now rode off to get, if possible, into some commanding position from whence we could see the whole thing without being exposed to the tremendous fire which was about to commence. After riding about for half an hour without being able to discover so desirable a situation, we determined to make for the cupola, near Gettysburg, Ewell's headquarters. Just before we reached the entrance to the town, the cannonade opened with a fury which surpassed even that of yesterday.

Soon after passing through the tollgate at the entrance of Gettysburg, we found that we had got into a heavy crossfire—shells both Federal and Confederate passing over our heads with great frequency.

At length two shrapnel shells burst quite close to us, and a ball from one of them hit the officer who was conducting us. We then turned round and changed our views with regard to the cupola—the fire of one side being bad enough, but preferable to that of both sides. A small boy of twelve years was riding with us at the time: this urchin took a diabolical interest in the bursting of the shells, and screamed with delight when he saw them take effect. I never saw this boy again, or found out who he was. The road at Gettysburg was lined with Yankee dead, and as they had been killed on the 1st, the poor fellows had already begun to be very offensive. We then returned to the hill I was on yesterday. But finding that, to see the actual fighting, it was absolutely necessary to go into the thick of the thing, I determined to make my way to General Longstreet. It was then about half past two. After passing General Lee and his staff, I rode on through the woods in the direction in which I had left Longstreet. I soon began to meet many wounded men returning from the front; many of them asked in piteous tones the way to a doctor or an ambulance. The further I got, the greater became the number of the wounded. At last I came to a perfect stream of them flocking through the woods in numbers as great as the crowd in Oxford street in the middle of the day. Some were walking alone on crutches composed of two rifles, others were supported by men less badly wounded than themselves, and others were carried on stretchers by the ambulance corps; but in no case did I see a sound man helping the wounded to the rear, unless he carried the red badge of the ambulance corps. They were still under a heavy fire; the shells were continually bringing down great limbs of trees, and carrying further destruction amongst this melancholy procession. I saw all this in much less time than it takes to write it, and although astonished to meet such vast numbers of wounded, I had not seen *enough* to give me any idea of the real extent of the mischief.

When I got close up to General Longstreet, I saw one of his regiments advancing through the woods in good order; so, thinking I was just in time to see the attack, I remarked to the general that *"I wouldn't have missed this for any thing."* Longstreet was seated at the top of a snake fence at the edge of the wood, and looking perfectly calm and unperturbed. He replied, laughing, *"The devil you wouldn't! I would like to have missed it very much; we've attacked and been repulsed: look there!"*

For the first time I then had a view of the open space between the two positions, and saw it covered with Confederates slowly and sulkily returning toward us in small broken parties, under a heavy fire of artillery. But the fire where we were was not so bad as further to the rear; for although the air seemed alive with shell, yet the greater number burst behind us.

The general told me that Pickett's division had succeeded in carrying the enemy's position and capturing his guns, but after remaining there twenty minutes, it bad been forced to retire on the retreat of Heth and Pettigrew on its left.

No person could have been more calm or self-possessed than General Longstreet, under these trying circumstances, aggravated as they now were by the movements of the enemy, who began to show a strong disposition to advance. I could now thoroughly appreciate the term bull-dog, which I had heard applied to him by the soldiers. Difficulties seem to make no other impression upon him than to make him a little more savage.

Major Walton was the only officer with him when I came up—all the rest had been put into the charge. In a few minutes Major Latrobe arrived on foot, carrying his saddle, having just had his horse killed. Colonel Sorrell was also in the same predicament, and Captain Goree's horse was wounded in the mouth.

The general was making the best arrangements in his power to resist the threatened advance, by advancing some artillery, and rallying the stragglers.

He asked for something to drink: I gave him some rum out of my silver flask, which I begged he would keep in remembrance of the occasion; he smiled, and, to my great satisfaction, accepted the memorial. He then went off to give some orders to McLaws' division.

Soon afterward I joined General Lee, who had in the meanwhile come to the front on becoming aware of the disaster. If Longstreet's conduct was admirable, that of General Lee was perfectly sublime. He was engaged in rallying and in encouraging the broken troops, and was riding about a little in front of the wood, quite alone, the whole of his staff being engaged in a similar manner further to the rear. His face, which is always placid and cheerful, did not show signs of the slightest disappointment, care, or annoyance; and he was addressing to every soldier he met a few words of encouragement, such as "All this will come right in the end—we'll talk it over afterward; but, in the mean time, all good men must rally—we want all good and true men just now," etc. He spoke to all the wounded men that passed him, and the slightly wounded he exhorted "to bind up their hurts and take up a musket" in this emergency. Very few failed to answer his appeal, and I saw many badly wounded men take off their hats and cheer him.

He said to me, "This has been a sad day for us, colonel, a sad day; but we can't expect always to gain victories." He was also kind enough to advise me to get into some more sheltered position.

Notwithstanding the misfortune which had so suddenly befallen him, General Lee seemed to observe every thing, however trivial. When a mounted officer began whipping his horse for shying at the bursting of a shell, he called out, "don't whip him, captain, don't whip him; I've got just such another foolish horse myself, and whipping does no good."

I happened to see a man lying flat on his face in a small ditch, and I remarked, that I didn't think he seemed dead. This drew General Lee's attention to the man, who commenced groaning dismally. Finding appeals to his patriotism of no avail, General Lee had him ignominiously set on his legs by some neighboring gunners.

I saw General Wilcox (an officer who wears a short round jacket and a battered straw hat) come up to him, and explain, almost crying, the state of his brigade. General Lee immediately shook hands with him and said, cheerfully, "Never mind, general, *all this has been MY fault;* it is *I* that have lost this fight, and you must help me out of it in the best way you can."

In this manner I saw General Lee encourage and reanimate his somewhat dispirited troops, and magnanimously take upon his own shoulders the whole weight of the repulse. It was impossible to look at him or to listen to him without feeling the strongest admiration, and I never saw any man fail him except the man in the ditch.

It is difficult to exaggerate the critical state of affairs as they appeared about this time. If the enemy or their general had shown any enterprise, there is no saying what might have happened. General Lee and his officers were evidently fully impressed with a sense of the situation; yet there was much less noise, fuss, or confusion of orders, than at an ordinary field-day. The men, as they were rallied in the wood, were brought up in detachments, and lay down quietly and coolly in the positions assigned to them.

We heard that Generals Garnett and Armistead were killed, and General Kemper mortally wounded; also, that Pickett's division had only one field officer unhurt. Nearly all this slaughter took place in an open space about one mile square, and within one hour.

At 6 P.M. we heard a long and continuous Yankee cheer, which we at first imagined was an indication of an advance; but it turned out to be their reception of a general officer, whom we saw riding down the line, followed by about thirty horsemen.

Soon afterward I rode to the extreme front, where there were four pieces of rifled cannon almost without any infantry support. To the non-withdrawal of these guns is to be attributed the otherwise surprising inactivity of the enemy.

I was immediately surrounded by a sergeant and about half a dozen gunners, who seemed in excellent spirits, and full of confidence in spite of their exposed situation. The sergeant expressed his ardent hope that the Yankees might have spirit enough to advance and receive the dose he had in readiness for them. They spoke in admiration of the advance of Pickett's division, and of the manner in which Pickett himself had led it. When they observed General Lee, they said, "We've not lost confidence in the old man. This day's work won't do him no harm. 'Uncle Robert' will get us into Washington yet; you bet he will," etc.

Whilst we were talking, the enemy's skirmishers began to advance slowly, and several ominous sounds in quick succession told us that we were attracting their attention, and that it was necessary to break up the conclave. I therefore turned round and took leave of these cheery and plucky gunners.

At 7 P.M., General Lee received a report that Johnson's division of Ewell's corps had been successful on the left, and had gained important advantages there. Firing entirely ceased in our front about this time, but we now heard some brisk musketry on our right, which I afterward learned proceeded from Hood's Texans, who had managed to surround some enterprising Yankee cavalry, and were slaughtering them with great satisfaction. Only eighteen out of four hundred are said to have escaped.

Who Ate the Dog?

During Hood's unfortunate march into Tennessee, most rigid orders were given against taking sheep, hogs, poultry, etc. The better to enforce these orders, General S—— organized a special provost guard, with specific instructions to arrest all plunderers. As an incentive to the more efficient performance of duty, the guard was promised half the booty taken from stragglers. The jolly "goobers" soon got wind of this, and planned for revenge. They killed a certain animal, and removing the hide, feet and ears, converted him into quite respectable mutton. They next sent one of their own numbers to inform the provost that some of the "goobers" were killing and dressing a sheep out in the woods. Away posted the guard in hot haste, eager to do their duty, and eager to have some nice mutton. The "goobers" and their prey were captured. The guard had a savory mess of mutton, and in the grateful emotions excited by it, sent a goodly portion to General S——, who enjoyed it exceedingly. The next day, as he was riding by the famous "Fifth Confederate," composed of all nationalities, but all of them "goobers," a voice on the right cried, "Who killed the dog?" The answer came from the left—"Bill Jones!" Then from the rear, "Who captured the dog?" Answer from the front—"The provost guard!" Question from the centre, "Who *ate* the dog?" Answer from all sides—"General S——! General S——! Bow-wow! Bow-wow!"

Until the surrender at Greensboro, the gallant general would sometimes hear an unpleasant barking of curs when he rode near that regiment.

A Friendly Offer

On Hood's retreat from Nashville, a broken-down infantryman dropped out of the ranks, hoping that he might get a lift from some merciful trooper in the rear guard. As the cavalry began to pass, he made known his wants, but got the same reply from each and every one— "Have but one horse, and he don't carry double!" One benevolent "man on horseback" stopped, however, and kindly asked the weary man what was the matter. "Most gone up the spout!" said the footman; "I'm broke down walking, and want some fellow to give me a lift."

Trooper.—"Does it tire you to walk?"

Infantry (very pitifully).—"Yes, I'm m-o-s-t gone up; it breaks me down to walk."

Trooper.—"Well, then, give me five dollars and I'll teach you how to *pace!*"

The broken-down man recovered his wind sufficiently to pursue the trooper at 2.40 speed!

The Neutral Cornfield

A Federal writer gives the following account of the neutral cornfield in front of Petersburg:

There was a cornfield between the Union and Confederate lines at a certain point before Petersburg, during Grant's autumn campaign,—a little to the left of Cemetery Hill. The opposing pickets of the two great confronting armies would, in spite of all, occasionally creep into that field for a friendly chat, or for a barter, or for a game of cards! Two of them were playing a game one day, with Abe Lincoln and Jeff Davis as imaginary stakes. The Lincolnite lost. "There," says the winner, " Old Abe belongs to me." "Well, I'll send him over by the 'Petersburg express,' " responded the defeated Yank. At another time there had been lively shelling and some musketry firing during the afternoon—of course but little talking. After dinner there was a slack of hostilities. A gray jacket rose up on the parapet of his line, and shook a paper as a sign of truce, then sprang over into the cornfield. At once a hundred men from either line were over their works and side by side, swapping papers for papers, tobacco for coffee or jack-knives, hard tack or sugar for corn cake. New acquaintances were made. In some instances old acquaintances were revived. A Connecticut sergeant found a townsman and schoolmate in a sergeant from over the way. A Connecticut officer found a kinsman in a rebel officer. A Federal Maryland regiment was *vis-a-vis* with a Maryland Confederate regiment. Many links of union were there. One found a brother on the other side, and yet another his own father! After a little time the swapping of the day was done, and officers and men returned to their respective lines. All was quiet again until the artillery re-opened fire. Then a half score of loiterers sprang up from their concealment in the corn, and scrambled back to their places behind the works. Thus the fighting and the chatting alternated.

Life in Battery Wagner[*]

I was chaplain of one of the regiments selected to garrison the fort in rotation, and had danced attendance for some time upon the orders which were to send us thither. Getting tired of the delay, however, I took a short

---

[*] From "The Land We Love," for March 1867.

furlough, at last, and went home—exacting a promise that I should be recalled at once if the orders came. A day after my arrival, came the news—the regiment was gone to Morris' Island. The night train carried me down, of course, but too late to run the gauntlet before sunrise, and, the fire of the enemy forbade the attempt to go, except under cover of the night.

Night came at last, however. Two small casks of coffee had been entrusted to me by ladies in the city, one for their own relatives, and one for general distribution. And I never shall forget the odd shock it gave me—rather romantically strung up as I was for the adventure,—when an officer of the boat said to me—"Mister, you had *better sit on them kegs* if you want to carry over your coffee; those black rascals (the boat hands) will steal every drop before you get away." Most vigilantly I guarded my treasure on the steamboat which silently bore us to Fort Johnson, (James' Island,) carried them in my own arms to the row boat which made the rest of the passage, and resigned them on shore to the commissary for safe keeping.

A rapid walk along the beach toward the glow of a fire—itself carefully hidden amid the hillocks of sand—an angry buzz or two about my ears of sharpshooters' balls,—a dive through what seemed a perfect labyrinth of burrows, crowded with men and reeking with foul air, and my hands were caught by the hands of glad friends. They were smirched and haggard already, though all they had borne was as nothing to what was to come, for, as it turned out, we had the honor of being the *last garrison*.

In a few minutes I was hurried out, to take a hasty glance at the works by a Bade-light. We struck across to the extremity of the works nearest the enemy, and looked thence back. What a magical effect, to be so cruelly meant as it was. The brilliant light transfigured those gray mounds of sand, gave to them the resemblance of snow. It proved, however, ineffectual for the purpose it was meant to answer—guiding the artillery fire at night, and preventing our fatigue parties from repairing damages.

At this time there was quite a lull in the contest, the Federal forces, preparing, as it proved, for their last advance. But, weary as I was, I postponed my study of the works, to get a little rest, and thus, as so often happens in life, threw away my only opportunity.

The bomb-proofs, where my duty and the surgeons' lay, and where all remained when off duty, were large cells, constructed of pine logs,—some of them round, some roughly hewn—set upright, close together, and roofed with similar logs—the whole then buried under mounds of sand, from twelve to twenty feet thick. The constant drip, drip, drip of salt water from this sand, into the room below, was one of the mysteries, and one of the great annoyances of the place; all the greater because drinking water was very scarce, very bad, and only to be obtained at the risk of life. Going down to the sally-port next morning, I was struck with the eager faces turned outward, watching for something. Presently a young fellow hove in sight, literally dressed in canteens, and running at the top of his speed, to shorten his perilous passage back to the fort. He had been sent for water, and got back safe.

Presently I heard my name on a good many lips, inquiring where I was. Soon, somebody with glistening eyes informed me that the coffee had come. Poor fellows, how they enjoyed it! But a mouthful or two apiece, yet it was an event.

The day wore away with few casualties, and a good deal of hard work for the garrison. But next morning, with the earliest glimpse of day, began the awful tornado; "blood, and fire, and vapor of smoke." Ironsides, monitors, wooden vessels, land batteries, sharpshooters—booming, whizzing, cracking, crashing; the solid ground throbbing under the impact of thirteen inch mortar shells, dropping as out of the iron sky upon the roofs and bursting there—great cannon struck in the throat and knocked down like men; fifteen inch shells, rolled by; the monitors into open spaces, exploding and raining the fragments everywhere; ramparts cut down by Parrott shells, and rebuilt in the face of that infernal fire. Yesterday wore out, to-day burns out!

Now come the litters with their woeful burdens, often dripping blood as they come. Wounds of every conceivable and unimaginable character; right arms torn off, not cut off, like a bird's wing with all the muscles and organs that are closely connected with it—deadening sensation, thank God; the skull over the cerebellum completely blown away—and yet the man will not die! There are few groans, except from men unconscious, or from men injured by concussion. Now and then a man whose nervous system has been prostrated in this way—viz: by the explosion of a shell close by—stung by a bung, as the soldier in the army of Northern Virginia said—comes in crying like a child; a half hour's rest, and a drop of spirits, and his manhood is restored.

The sickening smell of blood, as from some foul shambles in a dungeon; the reeking, almost unbreathable air, away from the skylight; the bare-armed surgeons, operating by candle-light; the floor crowded with anguish and death; the grim, low walls, and the steady drip, drip, drip, ticking aloud; all these must come into the picture of the hospital bombproof of Battery Wagner. Then you must draw out these horrors from Saturday morning until Sunday night; and you will be measurably prepared to admire the courage that gave not an inch, though hungry, thirsty, sleepy, worked almost to death to repair injuries, and without a breath of fresh air that was not obtained at the risk of being torn to pieces.

Six men were ordered out on fatigue; as they left cover a shell exploded among them, killing and wounding all but one. That one picked up his sand bag, and walked up to the breach without an instant's hesitation; while the steady voice of the officer called out, "second relief!" and the gap was filled. That gallant fellow was afterwards left disabled in a retreat of pickets, at Petersburg, and died on the field of battle.

Being anxious to see how the men were prospering at a distant part of the work, I started across, and presently found an officer sitting in the heart of that terrible commotion, calmly writing in his note book. He was off duty, but preferred—as experience taught many to do—to keep his place outside, rather than be weakened by the heat and foul air of the bomb-proofs, and dazzled, on his return, by the glare on his eyes. Then an enthusiastic sharp-shooter called out to me: "Come up here, sir! here's a first rate shot," which I thankfully declined, as not in my line.

Many curious incidents occurred, of course. A captain took the place of a sharp-shooter for a little while; soon he was whirled round and thrown to the ground. His men ran to him, but he picked himself up, *not* killed. It proved that a minie ball had grazed his ear. A sentinel outside the Battery was standing in a rifle-pit, with not much room to spare, when lo! a large shell dropped into the pit. He shut his eyes, as he told me afterwards, thinking it idle to attempt an escape. The shell exploded, and "only shocked him a little."

Saturday afternoon, my lieutenant colonel proposed to me that he and I should go through the bomb-proofs and hold short religious services with the men. I carried my Testament and hymn book, and he the indispensable candle. I am satisfied that the flame of the candle was at times three inches long, and of a dirty yellow—so dreadfully impure had the air become. Shall I ever forget that horrible gloom, or the spectral faces in the background, or the faces that the struggling flame made visible—ghastly squalid, smirched—lips parched, tangled hair, eyes glittering with fever, watching, and toil. How they drank in every word. Faint and husky voices joined fitfully in the hymn, or faltered amen to the prayer. They were the farewell prayer meetings in Battery Wagner.

Saturday night, the Federals determined to attack Battery Gregg and take it by surprise. This would have hemmed us in and compelled the surrender of the whole command. But our signal men read their signal, as they had often done before; proper preparations were made, and the surprise reversed. The attacking party hardly fired a volley before they pushed back to sea.

Sunday noon brought the Chief Engineer of the Department, to examine if the last hour had indeed come, to which the defense could be protracted. After a careful survey, and a conference with the officers, he returned with his report, and soon there came up the order, by telegraph, from General Beauregard, commanding the evacuation, followed directly by the full written order, adjusting the details, and concluding with the remark that if the evacuation were accomplished, it would be equal to a victory.

Then I got my *mittimus*. My commanding officer assured me I had done all that could be done in my department, and that it would be a relief to him, if I would go in advance of the mass.

Little preparation was needed, as you may suppose. Soon I was standing at the sally port, dozed by my long stay in the darkness, and weakened even to exhaustion by the toils and griefs of my work; head throbbing loud and hard, mental faculties almost benumbed. "Now, sir," said a gallant fellow on duty there, "I've watched these fellows until I can almost certainly tell when they are slacking off; just wait till I give the word, and then run about two hundred yards, and you'll be pretty nearly safe." Nothing loath to live and see home once more, I waited the word of command, and then started as fast as I could. So far from lulling, the fire grew; in about twenty yards, instead of two hundred, my strength gave way completely, and I had to *walk* along in such company as I hope never to keep again. Minie balls, scraps of shells, whole shells bursting, shells overhead on their way to Battery Gregg—why, they positively *swarmed*. My mind was too torpid with weariness to be alarmed, and I watched the display with wonderfully little interest. But I shall ever regret that I had not at the moment energy enough to scramble to the edge of the hillocks, and look out, upon the fleet, engaged in its terrible work. I trust in the mercy of God that I shall never have such another opportunity; which makes it the greatest pity not to have improved that.

In the same profound apathy of exhaustion, I climbed over the face of Battery Gregg, then being scarred and ploughed with shell and ball, instead of going round it. And when, the boat being ready, I was warned to *run* for it, I answered "yes," and walked stupidly out; when a friend, whom I teach my children to thank and love, threw his arms round me, and ran me down to the boat. He got back safely.

My narrative properly ends at this point; but it may be well to add a word about the evacuation. South Carolina troops were accorded the honor of leaving the fort last. Men were kept on the works to the very last moment to keep up the appearance of a fight and mislead the enemy. Proper arrangements were made for blowin' up the magazine. They failed, of course; they always do. But it was not for lack of care or coolness that time. One of the bravest of brave men went back alone, and went into the magazine, making sure that all was working well. Yet the drips from the roof, or some other unlooked-for accident, extinguished the fuse, and saved the trophy for the enemy. They pounded away nearly all night, however; we had that satisfaction; pounded away at the empty walls, while the eight hundred men who had held it were safe in the harbor, or on shore.

LONGSTREET AND THE SPY

The following incident occurred during the campaign against Pope, in 1862:

While Longstreet's corps was hurrying forward to Jackson's relief, several brigades in advance, on different roads, were observed to halt, thereby stopping all further progress of the corps. Very angry at this, Longstreet trotted to the front, and was informed that a courier had brought orders from General Lee to that effect!

"From General Lee!" said Longstreet, his eyes glowing with rage; "where *is* that courier?"

"There he goes now, General, galloping down the road."

"Keep your eyes on him. Overtake him and bring him here!" Which was soon accomplished.

"By whose orders did you halt my brigade?" asked a brigadier.

"As I have already told you, by General Lee's. I have orders for Longstreet, and must be off to the rear!"

"Here is Longstreet," said that general, now moving forward; "where are your orders?"

The spy was caught! He turned red, and pale—his lip quivered—he was self-condemned.

"Give this man ten minutes, and hang him! Let the columns push forward immediately."

In fifteen minutes the spy was lifeless, hanging from a tree by the roadside; but, before death, confessed that, although a Virginian and a Confederate soldier, he had been in communication with the enemy over ten months, and was then acting for General Pope.

The Bible on the Battle-Field

Among the dead of one of the battle-fields before Richmond, was a Confederate soldier who lay unburied several days after the conflict. Already the flesh had been eaten by the worms from his fingers, but underneath the skeleton-hand lay an open copy of the Bible, and the fingers pressed upon those precious words of the twenty-third Psalm—*"Thy rod and thy staff they comfort me:"*

General Cheatham's Escape

The following story was told by General Cheatham, of the manner in which he escaped capture at the battle of Belmont, Missouri:

Just as the opposing armies were approaching one another, General Cheatham discovered a squadron of cavalry coming down a road near his position. Uncertain as to which force it belonged, accompanied only by an orderly, he rode up to within a few yards of it, and inquired,

"What cavalry is that?"

" Illinois cavalry, sir," was the reply.

"O, Illinois cavalry; all right. Just stand where you are!"

The cavalry obeyed the order, and, unmolested by them, who supposed he was one of the Federal officers, the general rode safely back, directly under the guns of another Federal regiment which had by that time come up, but who, seeing him coming from the direction of the cavalry, also supposed that he was one of them. Some of the national officers remembered the incident, and agreed with the hero of it that if they had known who he was, it was very probable that there would have been one general less that night.

Camp Life

"Cock-a-doodle-doo-oo!" sounded the "shrill clarion" of a neighboring hen roost *before* day this morning. A wakeful soldier caught up the strain, and he and a hundred others forthwith repeated bogus cock-a-doodle-doos, until they had effectually "murdered sleep" throughout the entire regiment, To pass the time till breakfast (!)—i.e., till some "solid shot biscuit" and leather steaks of lean kind be cooked—I will 'retaliate' on you and your readers.

The campaign having apparently ended, there are no moving accidents by flood or field of interest, and therefore, nothing left to record but the routine of daily camp life; this shall be true to history, however, to let the old folks at home know how we live "sure enough" while here. At this particular season, though, it is particularly dull—

> No mail, no post,
> No news from any foreign coast;
> No warmth, no cheerfulness, no healthful ease,
> No comfortable feel in any member,
> No shade, no sunshine, no butterflies, no bees,
> November!

Our camps not being regulated by military rule for want of material in tents, etc., is left to illustrate the variegated, architectural and domestic tastes of the thousand different individuals concerned. Hence, although a wall tent or Sibley graces an occasional locality, the most of the men ensconce themselves in bush-built shelters of various shapes, in fence-corners, under gum blankets eked out by cedar boughs, or burrow semi-subterraneously, like Esquimaux. If, as is said, the several styles of architecture took their origin from natural circumstances and climate, etc., as the curving oriental roofs, from the long reeds originally in use—the slanting Egyptians from the necessity of baking their unburnt bricks in the hot sun—the Corinthian from its own flowery clime, etc., etc.—an architectural genius might find enough original designs in this camp to supply a century to come.

The only "useful occupation" of this brigade for sometime past has been to destroy all the railroads in reach; apparently, too, for no better reason than the fellow had for killing the splendid Anaconda in the museum, because it was his "rule to kill snakes wherever found." A soldier just said, "Old Jack intends us to tear up all the railroads in the state, and with no tools but our pockets knives." They have so far destroyed the Baltimore and Ohio from Hedgesville to near Harper's Ferry, the Winchester and Potomac almost entirely, and now the Manassas Gap from Piedmont to Strasburg.

It is when idle in camp that the soldier is a great institution, yet one that must be seen to be appreciated. Pen cannot fully paint the air of cheerful content, care-hilarity, irresponsible loungings and practical spirit of jesting that obtains, ready to seize on any odd circumstance in its licensed levity. A cavalryman comes rejoicing in immense top-boots, for which in fond pride, he had invested full forty dollars of pay; at once the cry from a hundred voices follows him along the line: "Come up out o' them boots!—come out!—too soon to go into winter quarters! I know you're in thar!—see your arms stickin' out!" A bumpkin rides by in an uncommonly big hat, and is frightened at the shout: "Come down out o' that hat! Come down! 'Taint no use to say you ain't up there; I see your legs hanging out!" A fancy staff officer was horrified at the irreverent reception of his nicely twisted moustache—as heard from behind innumerable trees—"take them mice out o' yer mouth!—take 'em out!—no use to say they aint thar—see their tails hanging out!" Another, sporting immense whiskers, was urged to "Come out of that bunch of har! I know you're in thar! I see your ears a working!" Sometimes a rousing cheer is heard in the distance, it is explained—"Boys, look out!—here come 'old Stonewall' or an old hare, one or tother"—they being about the only individuals who invariably bring down the house.

And yet there are no better specimens of the earnest, true soldier, than the men of this brigade. It is known in the army, if not in print, as "the fighting brigade." It is now constituted of the thirteenth, twenty-fifth, thirty-first, forty-fourth, forty-ninth, fifty-second and fifty-eighth Virginia regiments—the twelfth Georgia, one of the most gallant regiments in the service, having, to the regret of all their old comrades of "the mountain brigade," been transferred. The brigade has been represented by some of its regiments, in nearly every battlefield in Virginia—in Northwest Virginia, in the Valley, on the Peninsula, around Richmond from Cedar Run to Manassas Plains, at Harper's Ferry, and when reduced to scarce five hundred men and surrounded by overwhelming numbers, it fought a bloody way clear out through the Yankee lines at Sharpsburg. Four of its brigadiers have been wounded in the service—Generals Ed. Johnson, Ellzey, Stuart and Early. Five of the regiments above named were united in one command under General Ed. Johnson, whose conspicuous bravery at Greenbrier, Alleghany and McDowell, has never lost its example upon his men. The thirteenth and forty-ninth Virginia have been since united with it. It is at present commanded by Colonel J. A. Walker, of the thirteenth, a gallant officer and courteous gentleman, who has well deserved a brigadier's commission.

But the whole day of camp life is not yet described; the light remains, and latterly it is no unusual scene, as the gloaming gathers, to see a group quietly collect beneath the dusky shadows of the forest trees—"God's first temples"—whence soon arise the notes of some familiar hymn, awaking memories of childhood and of home. The youthful chaplain, in earnest tones, tells his holy mission; another hymn is heard, and by the waning light of the pine torches the weird-like figures of the grouped soldiers are seen reverently moving to the night's repose. The deep bass drum beats taps—the sounds die out in all the camps, save at times the sweet strains from the band of the fifth Stonewall regiment, in a neighboring grove, till they, too, fade away into the stilly night, and soon

> The soldiers lie peacefully dreaming,
>   Their tents in the rays of the clear Autumn moon,
>   Or the light of the watch fires are gleaming,
>   A tremulous sigh as the gentle night wind
>   Thro' the forest leaves slowly is creeping,
>   While the stars up above with their glittering eyes
>   Keep guard, for the army is sleeping.

THE CONFEDERATES IN MARYLAND

A correspondent of one of the southern papers wrote from Frederick City, Maryland, in September, 1862:

Frederick to-day presents a busy scene more like that of a fourth of July festival than a gathering of armed invaders. A majority of the stores are closed to general admission, because of the crowds eager to press and buy, but a little diplomacy secures an entrance at the back door, or past the sentinel wisely stationed to protect the proprietor from the rush of anxious customers. Prices are going up rapidly. Every thing is so cheap, that our men frequently lay down a five dollar bill to pay for a three dollar article, and rush out without waiting for the change. The good people here don't understand it. Bitter complaints are uttered against those who refuse Confederate money, and it is understood that the authorities will insist upon its general circulation.

The people are beginning to recover from their surprise at our sudden appearance, and to realize the magnitude of our preparations to advance through and relieve Maryland from her thraldom. Some are still moody, and evidently hate us heartily, but we are more than compensated by the warm welcome of others, who now begin to greet us from every quarter. Only a few moments ago I met a lady who confessed that although she had Confederate flags ready to expose in her windows as we passed, she was afraid to wave them, lest being discovered by her Union neighbors she should be reported to the Federals in case of our retreat, and be thereby subjected to insult if not imprisonment at their hands. To assure me how true were her sentiments, she introduced me to a large room in her house, where there were fourteen ladies, young and old, busy as bees, making shirts, drawers, and other clothing, for the soldiers.

She was also distributing money and tobacco to the soldiers. Judging probably from my rags that I too was in a destitute condition, she benevolently desired to take me in hand and replenish my entity throughout, but of course I declined, and though I could not help smiling at the ingenuous oddity of the proposition, a tear at the same time stole down my cheek at the thought of the sufferings which these noble-hearted ladies must have endured to prompt the unselfish generosity by which they endeavored to express their delight in our presence.

Though thousands of soldiers are now roaming through the town, there has not been a solitary instance of misdemeanor. I have heard no shouting, no clamor of any kind, and seen but a single case of intoxication—a one-legged Yankee prisoner.

All who visit the city are required to have passes, and the only persons arrested are those who are here without leave. This quiet behavior of our men contrasts so strongly with that of the Federals when here as to excite the favorable comment of the Unionists. None of the latter have, to my knowledge been interfered with, and, as far as I can learn, it is not the policy of our commander to retaliate. We shall, on the contrary, pursue a conciliatory course, and by kindness endeavor to show these misguided people that our home should be their home, and our God their God.

One of these Union men frankly confessed to me that he feared his own neighbors more than he did our troops, and he should regret to see us depart.

The only outrage, if outrage it can be called, which has taken place, was committed by the citizen Secessionists, who entered the office of the Frederick Examiner, a Black Republican newspaper of the darkest dye, and tore it to pieces, the editor himself fleeing on the first symptoms of our advance.

We pay for every thing as we go, the farmers being compensated for all damage by the burning of rails, use of forage, or destruction of crops, before we break up camp.

We are told by Marylanders that we shall have an accession to our ranks in this state of over forty thousand men, and that when we arrive within striking distance of Baltimore, twenty thousand men will rise in arms and join our standard. A gentleman from that city informs me that the excitement there is intense, the streets being blocked up by the crowds, and an armed force of cavalry and infantry constantly patrolling the city to keep down the increasing signs of a revolution.

Recruiting here goes on rapidly. Within two days five companies have been formed, and it is stated that from the surrounding country over seven hundred entered our ranks while *en route.*

Pennsylvania, the border line of which is only some twenty-five or twenty-eight miles distant, has sent us nearly a hundred recruits, who prefer service in the Confederate army to being drafted in that of the North.

Altogether, our movement has been thus far marked by the most gratifying success. Every detail has been successfully carried out, the troops are in

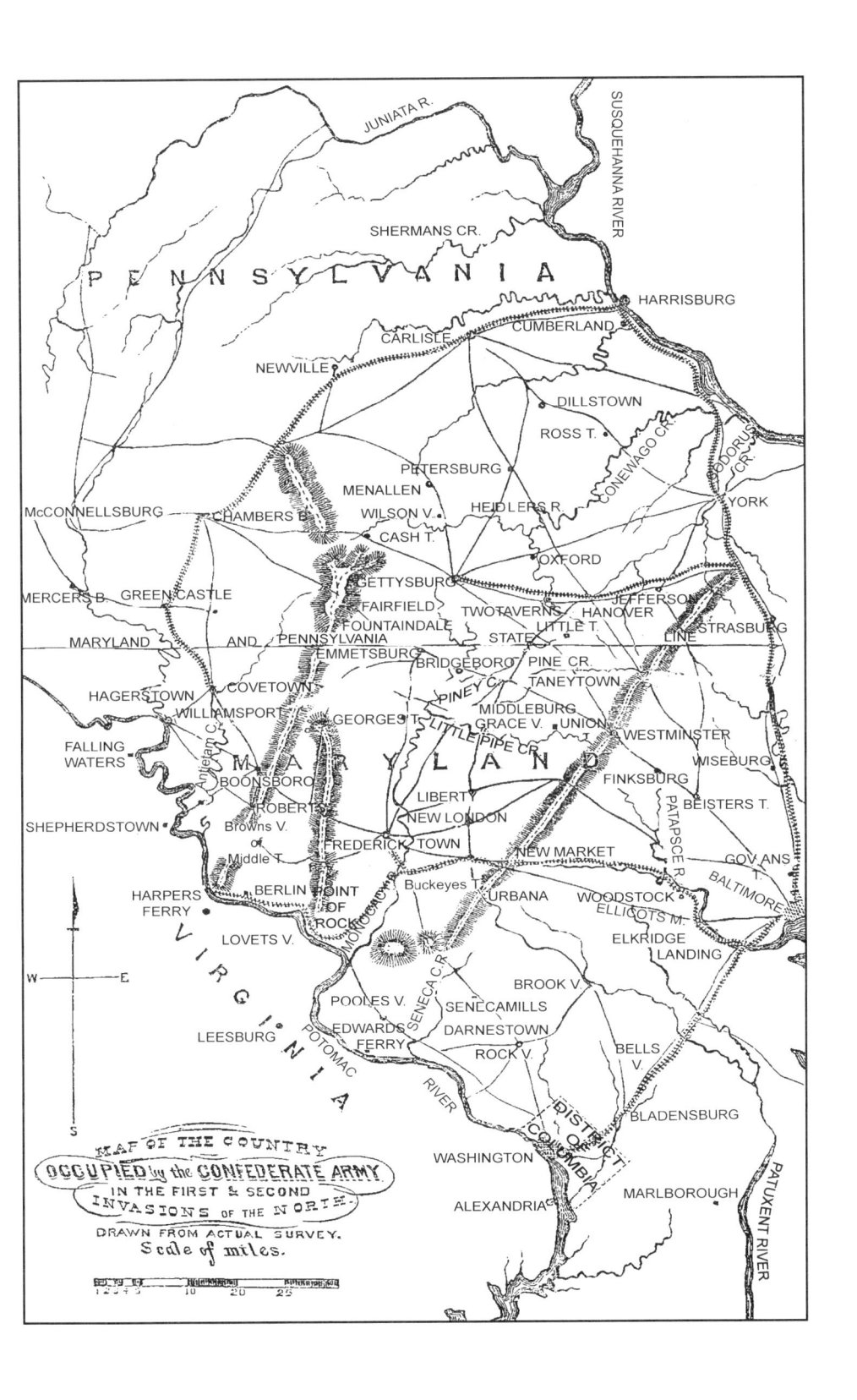

MAP OF THE COUNTRY
OCCUPIED by the CONFEDERATE ARMY
IN THE FIRST & SECOND
INVASIONS OF THE NORTH.
DRAWN FROM ACTUAL SURVEY.
Scale of miles.

good health, and full of enthusiasm, the commissariat is improving, and we wait for nothing more anxiously than the order to resume our march onward.

A Story of Shiloh

Brigadier-General Gladden, of South Carolina, who was in General Bragg's command, had his left arm shattered by a ball on the first day of the fight. Amputation was performed hastily by his staff surgeon on the field; and, instead of being taken to the rear for quiet and nursing, he mounted his horse, against the most earnest remonstrances of all his staff, and continued to command. On Monday he was again in the saddle, and kept it during the day. On Tuesday he rode on horseback to Corinth, twenty miles from the scene of action, and continued to discharge the duties of an officer. On Wednesday, a second amputation, near the shoulder, was necessary, when General Bragg sent an aid to ask if he would not be relieved of his command. To which be replied, "Give General Bragg my compliments, and say that General Gladden will only give up his command to go into his coffin." Against the remonstrances of his personal friends, and against the positive injunctions of the surgeons, he persisted in sitting up in his chair, receiving despatches and giving directions, until Wednesday afternoon, when lockjaw seized him, and he died in a few moments.

The Band in the Pines

(Heard after Pelham Died.)

By John Esten Cooke

Oh, band in the pinewood, cease!
    Cease with your splendid call;
The living are brave and noble,
    But the dead were bravest of all.

They throng to the martial summons,
    To the loud, triumphant strain;
And the dear bright eyes of long dead friends
    Come to the heart again!

They come with the ringing bugle,
>   And the deep drum's mellow roar;
Till the soul is faint with longing
>   For the hands we clasp no more.

Oh, band in the pinewood, cease!
>   Or the heart will melt in tears
For the gallant eyes and smiling lips,
>   And the voices of old years.

JACKSON'S PARTING WITH HIS OLD BRIGADE

Before leaving the army of the Potomac, Jackson took an affectionate farewell of the troops with whom he had been so long and so intimately connected. On the morning of the 4th of October, 1861, the gallant "Stonewall Brigade" was drawn up near its encampment at Centreville. All the regiments, except the fifth, which was on picket, were present. Drawn up in close columns, the officers and soldiers who had, on the immortal 21st of July, won such glory under the guidance of their gallant general, stood with sad hearts and sorrowful countenances to bid him farewell, while thousands of troops from other portions of the army stood by in respectful silence. In a short time, General Jackson, accompanied by his staff, left his quarters and rode slowly toward the brigade. He was received by them in silence. Until this moment his appearance had never failed to draw from his men the most enthusiastic cheers. But now, not a sound was heard! A deep and painful silence reigned over every thing; every heart was full. And this silence was more eloquent than cheers could have been.

As they reached the centre of the line the staff halted, and the general rode forward slowly to within a few paces of his men. Then, pausing, he gazed for a moment wistfully up and down the line. Beneath the calm, quiet exterior of the hero, there throbbed a warm and generous heart, and this parting filled it with inexpressible pain. After a silence of a few moments, General Jackson turned to his men and addressed them as follows:

"*Officers and Soldiers of the First Brigade!* I am not here to make a speech, but simply to say, Farewell. I first met you at Harper's Ferry, in the commencement of this war, and I cannot take leave of you without giving expression to my admiration of your conduct from that day to this, whether on the march, the bivouac, the tented field, or on the bloody plains of Manassas, where you gained the well-deserved reputation of having decided the fate of the battle. Throughout the broad extent of country over which you have marched, by your respect for the rights and the property of citizens, you have shown that you were soldiers, not only to defend, but able and willing both to defend and protect. You have already gained a brilliant and deservedly high reputation throughout the army of the whole Confederacy, and I trust in the future, by your deeds on the field, and by the assistance of the same kind Providence who has heretofore favored our cause, you will gain more victories, and add additional luster to the reputation you now enjoy. You have already gained a proud position in the future history of this our second war of independence. I shall look with great anxiety to your future movements; and I trust, whenever I shall hear of the *First Brigade* on the field of battle, it will be of still nobler deeds achieved, and higher reputation won."

Having uttered these words, Jackson paused for an instant, and his eye passed slowly along the line, as though he wished thus to bid farewell individually to every old familiar face, so often seen in the heat of battle, and so dear to him. The thoughts which crowded upon him seemed more than he could bear—he could not leave them with such formal words only—and that iron lip which had never trembled in the hour of deadliest peril, now quivered. Mastered by an uncontrollable impulse, the great soldier rose in his stirrups, threw the reins on the neck of his horse with an emphasis which sent a thrill through every heart, and extending his arm, added, in tones of the deepest feeling:

"In the army of the Shenandoah you were the *First Brigade!* In the army of the Potomac you were the *First Brigade!* In the second corps of the army you are the *First Brigade!* You are the *First Brigade* in the affections of your general; and I hope by your future deeds and bearing you will be handed down to posterity as the *First Brigade* in this, our second war of independence. Farewell!"

For a moment there was a pause, and then there arose cheer after cheer, so wild and thrilling that the very heavens rang with them. Unable to bear calmly such affecting evidence of attachment, General Jackson hastily waved farewell to his men, and gathering his reins rode rapidly away.

The Good Samaritan

During the day after the battle of Manassas, a Federal soldier, who had been separated from his regiment in the general rout of the day before, tried to reach the lines of Washington by going through the woods. Being slightly wounded in the leg his progress was somewhat slow, so that by Wednesday night, he had only reached the environs of Fairfax. Exhausted and completely dispirited, he espied a Confederate picket, and deliberately walked up and told the sentry who he was. To his grateful surprise the southern soldier poured out some whiskey, gave him food, told him where he could find a stack of arms, and where he could sleep in perfect security in a Negro hut. He added: "If we meet again in battle, I will not try very hard to shoot you, and mind you don't me." Truly a good Samaritan.

A Full Ration for Once

While General John B. Floyd was encamped on Cotton Hill, in Fayette county, Virginia, in the fall of 1861, very stringent orders were issued against the firing of guns without permission. The enemy were in close proximity, and the firing might lead to a false alarm, or it might produce indifference to such sounds, and permit a surprise on the part of the enemy. The rain fell for weeks in almost continuous torrents, the roads became almost impassable, supplies could not be procured, and we were forced to live on grated corn. In this time of trouble, Pat M——, was placed one night on picket. He got thoroughly drenched, of course, and what fretted him almost as much, he got his gun also full of water. Feeling the importance of having his gun in good order for a fight, Pat determined to fire it off on the sly, and then clean it out thoroughly. He accordingly went out of camp to a very suitable place, as he supposed, and fired it off, when, to his horror, he saw General Floyd riding up in the rainstorm.

General.—"What do you mean by firing your gun? Don't you know that it is against orders?"

Pat.—"And it's against orders is it, yer honor, for a man to clean out a dirty gun?"

General.—"Yes, you scamp, and you knew it. I've a mind to put you in the guard house on bread and water for a week."

Pat.— "Thank ye kindly, gineral, for the bread. It's meself that's been wanting the same for many a long day. But, gineral, you needn't mind the wather. I've got my ration of that rigularly ivery day, and night, too, for the likes of that, for this two months past."

General Floyd was too much amused to haul Pat up for his disobedience of orders.

The Man Who Swallowed a Drum

A very large citizen of a certain place in Georgia, who was blessed with an enormous abdominal protuberance, was standing by the roadside, watching the march of Joe Johnston's men, when he was suddenly surrounded by a crowd joyfully exclaiming: "We've found him! We've found him!" The captain of the company tried to get his men back in the road, and demanded what they had found. The reply astonished the fat man: "Oh! captain, *we've found the man who swallowed our bass drum!*"

The Burial of Stuart

By John R. Thompson

> We could not pause, while yet the noontide air
>   Shook with the cannonade's incessant pealing,
> The funeral pageant fitly to prepare
>   A nation's grief revealing.
>
> The smoke, above the glimmering woodland wide
>   That skirts our southward border with its beauty,
> Marked where our heroes stood and fought and died
>   For love and faith and duty.
>
> And still what time the doubtful strife went on,
>   We might not find expression for our sorrow,
> We could but lay our dear, dumb warrior down,
>   And gird us for the morrow.

The Grayjackets in Camp, Field, and Hospital

One weary year ago, when came a lull,
    With victory, in the conflict's stormy closes,
When the glad Spring, all flushed and beautiful,
    First mocked us with her roses—

With dirge and bell and minute gun we paid
    Some few poor rites, an inexpressive token
Of a great people's pain, to Jackson's shade,
    In agony unspoken.

No wailing trumpet and no tolling bell,
    No cannon, save the battle's boom receding,
When Stuart to the grave we bore might tell,
    With hearts all crushed and bleeding.

The crisis suited not with pomp, and she,
    Whose anguish bears the seal of consecration,
Had wished his Christian obsequies should be
    Thus void of ostentation.

Only the maidens came sweet flow'rs to twine
    Above his form so still and cold and painless,
Whose deeds upon our brightest record shine,
    Whose life and sword were stainless.

They well remembered how he loved to dash
    Into the fight, festooned from summer bowers,
How like a fountain's spray his sabre's flash
    Leaped from a mass of flowers.

And so we carried to his place of rest
    All that of our great Paladin was mortal,
The cross, and not the sabre, on his breast,
    That opens the heavenly portal.

No more of tribute might to us remain—
    But there will come a time when Freedom's martyrs
A richer guerdon of renown shall gain
    Than gleams in stars and garters.

I claim no prophet's vision, but I see
    Through coming years, now near at hand, now distant,
My rescued country, glorious and free,
    And strong and self-existent.

I hear from out that sunlit land which lies
    Beyond these clouds that gather darkly o'er us,
The happy sounds of industry arise
    In swelling, peaceful chorus.

And, mingling with these sounds, the glad acclaim
    Of millions, undisturbed by war's afflictions,
Crowning each martyr's never-dying name
    With grateful benedictions.

In some fair future garden of delights,
    Where flow'rs shall bloom and song-birds sweetly warble,
Art shall erect the statues of our knights
    In living bronze and marble;

And none of all that bright, heroic throng,
    Shall wear to far-off time a semblance grander;
Shall still be decked with fresher wreaths of song,
    Than this beloved commander.

The Spanish legends tell us of the Cid,
    That after death he rode erect, sedately,
Along his lines, even as in life he did,
    In presence yet more stately:

And thus our Stuart, at this moment seems
    To ride out of our dark and troubled story
Into the region of romance and dreams,
    A realm of light and glory—

And sometime when the silver bugles blow,
    That radiant form, in battle reappearing,
Shall lead his horsemen headlong on the foe,
    In victory careering!

The Last Six Days of the Army of Northern Virginia

The following article is by the Hon. Francis Lawley, the late Richmond correspondent of the *London Times:*

It is said by Coleridge, that no man thrown to the surface of human affairs, ever succeeded in simultaneously gaining distinction and affection, unless he possessed something of an epicene nature; that is to say, a mixture of masculine and feminine qualities. Without claiming for General Lee, in the highest sense, the title of "great," it is impossible to deny that his memory will be cherished by those who, in the crisis of his three years of trial, stood and suffered by his side, as an exceptionally dear and precious possession. Few soldiers, if asked whether they would rather have served under Lee on the one hand, or under Cromwell, Frederick the Great, Marlborough, or Napoleon, on the other, would hesitate to prefer the four famous generals to the discomfited Confederate. Yet it is doubtful whether any of the four, after they had passed away and had ceased to communicate the electric shock of their presence and contact—of eye, voice, character and influence—to others, possessed such hold on the affections and esteem as were inspired by Robert E. Lee.

The exceeding loveableness of Lee became more patent as your consciousness that, as a politician, he lacked vigor and self-assertion, became more irresistible. This loveableness was based on a never-tiring unselfishness, a contagious endurance of hardship and danger, a shrinking modesty, an abounding tenderness. The child and the young girl, who had never seen him before, ran to him instinctively as to a friend. His look spoke of honesty, directness, kindliness, courage. His smile was irresistibly winning. But the stuff which made Cromwell, Napoleon, William the Silent, greater as politicians than as soldiers, was lacking in Lee. All that there was of true and brave in the people whom he so nearly made into a nation, called on him, by signs that he who ran might have read, to put Congress aside, to control the press, to be Dictator indeed. And yet he would not! Nevertheless, in the belief that there is no more powerful stimulant to a noble ambition than the study of such a character as Lee's, I desire to throw my stone upon the cairn by gathering together a few notes—for the general accuracy of which I can entirely vouch—exhibiting the main features of those eventful six days which intervened between the evacuation of the Confederate lines around Petersburg and Richmond, on the night of April 2d, and the surrender of Lee's army on the morning of April 9th.

In order to understand rightly these six days, it should be premised that the Federal cavalry, massed under General Sheridan, numbering about fourteen thousand sabres, splendidly equipped, and converted by their able commander into a body of military horsemen upon whom an Austrian or French *sabereur* might have looked without disdain, moved southward down the valley of Virginia between the 1st and 10th of March, and encountered a scratch Confederate army of about three thousand men, under General Early, at Waynesboro. General Early, distrustful of his men, who were equally distrustful of him, planted them with their backs to a deep river, in order to make retreat impossible. The result is easily foreseen. General Sheridan bagged two thirds of his enemy's force, and most of his enemy's artillery. In the previous summer I remember that, as General Early kept losing gun after gun, great efforts were made to resupply his losses by sending up fresh guns from Richmond. Upon one of these guns some wag of a Confederate soldier had chalked, "General Sheridan, care of General Early." The transfer was probably effected at Waynesboro. Sweeping rapidly onward toward the James River, between Richmond and Lynchburg, Sheridan found himself confronted by a swollen and impassable stream. He fell back, rounded the left wing of Lee's army, crossed the Pamunky river at the White House (where he recruited his strength by picking up twelve hundred fresh horses which awaited him there), and upon the 25th of March joined General Grant in the lines before Petersburg. To Sheridan's untiring and sagacious activity in the subsequent operations, more than to the energy of any other man, is due the completeness of the Federal triumph, the seemingly inexplicable collapse of the Confederacy.

It was not long before Grant's accession of strength was felt by Lee.

Upon the evening of Saturday, April 1st, General Longstreet, who bad long defended Richmond by commanding the Confederate forces to the north of James River, received information from Lee that Grant had detached Sheridan's cavalry, and two corps of infantry (about twenty-five thousand men in all) to act against the Southside railroad.

Before communicating with Longstreet, Lee had dispatched Pickett's and Bushrod Johnson's divisions, Huger's battalion of artillery, and Fitzhugh Lee's division of cavalry (in all about seventeen thousand men) to meet the attack with which the Southside railroad was menaced. But in sending away these seventeen thousand men, Lee had so weakened his lines before Petersburg that there was but one Confederate left to every fifty yards.

Under these circumstances Lee called upon Longstreet for men. But at dawn upon the 2d of April, before Longstreet had had time to obey Lee's orders, Grant descried from his wooden towers of observation the weakness of the Confederate lines. Immediately he threw a very heavy column, consisting, I believe, chiefly of Gibbon's corps, upon the weakest spot. The Federals carried with very slight loss the outer line, thinly held by Heth's division of Confederates, and bulged inward until they struck two of the detached forts, whereof a string or system ran behind the whole length of the Confederate outer works. These two detached forts, which were of course designed to cover each other, were named Forts Gregg and Alexander.

The officer in command of Fort Alexander, which was farthest away from the on-coming Federals, deemed it more important to save his guns than to try and help Fort Gregg. Receiving no assistance from its twin brother, Fort Gregg, manned by Harris's Mississippi brigade, numbering two hundred and fifty undaunted men, breasted intrepidly the tide of its multitudinous assailants. Three times Gibbon's corps surged up, and around the work—three times with dreadful carnage they were driven back. I am told that it was subsequently admitted by General Gibbon, that in carrying Fort Gregg he lost from five to six hundred men; or, in other words, that each Mississippian inside the works struck down at least two assailants. When at last the work was carried there remained, out of its two hundred and fifty defenders, but thirty survivors. In those nine memorable April days there was no episode more glorious to the Confederate arms than the heroic self-immolation of the Mississippian in Fort Gregg to gain time for their comrades.

Fort Gregg fell about seven o'clock in the morning of the 2d. After a delay of two or three hours, the Federals swept onwards in the direction of Petersburg, taking the Confederate lines *en revers*. At this moment Longstreet, accompanied by Benning's brigade of Field's division, about one hundred and seventy bayonets strong, met the onpouring flood, and checked it long enough to enable fresh troops to hurry up in his rear, and to form a fresh line in front of Petersburg.

Simultaneously, in an attempt of Heth's division to reestablish their lines, General A. P. Hill (who commanded the corps to which Heth's division belonged) lost a life which for nearly four years he had unflinchingly exposed in a hundred of his country's battles. About the same moment was dispatched the memorable telegram which surprised President Davis in church, and announced that the last day of that heroic resistance which had made Richmond the most notable of beleagured cities had at length arrived. The delay purchased by the obstinate defence of Fort Gregg, and by Longstreet's bold handling of Benning's brigade, saved Petersburg until the tobacco and cotton stored in that city could be burned, and until leisurely preparation for its evacuation could be made. It is remarkable that no further onslaught was made by the Federals throughout the day, or during the evening, although the flames springing up in many parts of the town must have told their own tale. At nightfall on the 2d, all the Confederate troops, about four thousand strong, which remained under the command of General Ewell, to the north of James river, fell back from their lines and passed through the bewildered streets of Richmond, traversing before daybreak the bridges over the James River, which were so soon to be given to the flames. About eight on the night of the same 2d, the Confederate troops also commenced leaving Petersburg, their retreat being covered by Field's division under Longstreet. Pursuit there was none. It is probable that already Grant was bending all his energies to get round and cut off Lee's retreat. The Petersburg section of the Confederate troops, full of vigor and *elan*, crossed to the north of the Appomattox river on a pontoon bridge, and made sixteen miles during the first night of retreat. It would be difficult to conceive any thing brighter or more hopeful than the tone of General Lee's spirits on the morning of the 3d. "I have got my army safe out of its breastworks," he said, "and, in order to follow me, my enemy must abandon his lines, and can derive no further benefit from his railroads or from James River." There can be little doubt that Lee's design was to recruit his army with rations, which he hoped to find in abundance at Amelia Court House, and to fall in detail upon the Federals, who, breaking up into bodies of one or two army corps, were scattering all over the country with a view to a vigorous pursuit. Two days rations at Amelia Court House for forty thousand men would possibly have made a great difference in the immediate, though, as I believe, none in the ultimate history of the Continent of North America.

There is little satisfaction in dwelling in detail upon the five subsequent days, for which a parallel must be sought on the banks of the Beresina, or in other similar passages of military anguish. It is hardly necessary to state that at Amelia Court House, Lee found not a ration. I shall not pause now to distribute blame, or to investigate who was at fault. All that I have to state is that the fault was not Lee's, whose orders on this subject for a fortnight past had been urgent and precise. It became necessary for Lee to break nearly half his army up into foraging parties to get food. The country through which we was passing was a tract of straggling woods and pine barrens, with occasional little patches of clearings. The foraging parties had to go so far a-field in quest of food, that they were taken prisoners by wholesale. In the fact of such suffering as they left behind, it cannot be wondered at if some of the poor fellows courted capture. Those foragers who returned to Lee brought little or nothing with them. The sufferings of the men from the pangs of hunger have not been approached in the military annals of the last fifty years. But the sufferings of the mules and horses must have been even keener; for the men assuaged their craving by plucking the buds and twigs of trees just shooting in the early spring, whereas the grass had not yet started from its winter sleep, and food for the unhappy quadrupeds, there was none. As early as the morning of the 4th, Lee sent off half his artillery toward the railroad, to relieve the famished horses. This artillery making slow progress, thanks to the exhaustion of the horses, was captured by the Federals on the 8th, but not until General Lindsay Walker had buried many of his guns, which were, of course, subsequently exhumed (seventy of them at one haul) by their captors.

It is easy to see that the locomotion of an army in such a plight must have been slow, and slower. The retreat was conducted in the following fashion: About midnight the Confederates slipped out of their hasty works, which they had thrown up and held during the previous day, and fell back until ten or eleven o'clock the next morning. Then they halted, and immediately threw up earthworks for their protection during the day. It was not long before the wolves were again on their heels, and from their earthworks the Confederates exchanged a heavy fire with their pursuers throughout the day. Delayed by the necessity of guarding a train from thirty-five to forty miles in length, enfeebled by hunger and sleeplessness, the retreating army was able to make only ten miles each night. This delay enabled the active Sheridan to get ahead with his cavalry, and to destroy the depot of provisions along the railroad, between Burksville and Danville. Upon the 5th, many of the mules and horses ceased to struggle. It became necessary to burn hundreds of wagons. At intervals the enemy's cavalry dashed in and struck the interminable train here or there, capturing and burning dozens upon dozens of wagons. Toward evening of the 5th, and all day long upon the 6th, hundreds of men dropped from exhaustion, and thousands let fall their muskets from inability to carry them any farther. The scenes of the 5th, 6th, 7th and 8th were of a nature which can be apprehended in its vivid reality only by men who are thoroughly familiar with the harrowing details of war. Behind, and on either flank, an ubiquitous and increasingly adventurous enemy—every mud-hole and every rise in the road choked with blazing wagons, the air filled with the deafening reports of ammunition exploding, and shells bursting when touched by the flames, dense columns of smoke ascending to heaven from the burning and exploding vehicles—exhausted men, worn-out mules and horses, lying down side by side—gaunt famine glaring hopelessly from sunken lack-lustre eyes—dead mules, dead horses, dead men, everywhere—death, many times welcomed as God's blessing in disguise—who can wonder if many hearts, tried in the fiery furnace of four years' unparalleled suffering never hitherto found wanting, should have quailed in presence of starvation, fatigue, sleeplessness, misery—unintermitted for five or six days, and culminating in hopelessness.

    Yet there were not wanting occasional episodes which recalled something of the old pride of former memories, and reminded men that this hunted, famished crowd was still the same army which had won two Bull Runs, which had twice (in pursuit of a fatal policy) trodden its enemy's soil, and had written Fredericksburg, Chancellorsville, and a dozen other glorious names upon its banners. On the 6th, a large body of Federal cavalry, having got ahead of Lee's army and occupied Rice's Station, was attacked by some Confederate horse under General Rosser, who drove them off, capturing six hundred and eighty prisoners. On the 7th, a heavy attack was made upon Mahone's division, and the prowess of this active Confederate general, frequently exhibited during the last twelve months of the war, was maintained to the end, inasmuch as a Federal brigade, getting entangled in a ravine, was surrounded by Mahone's men, and literally disappeared. On the evening of the 7th, General Gregg, with six or seven thousand Federal cavalry, made a desperate attempt to capture all the wagon trains. He was gallantly met by two thousand horsemen under Fitzhugh Lee, and defeated. Gregg himself was captured.

Throughout these gloomy days, as an offset to the countless Confederates captured while foraging by Federals, numerous Federal prisoners were taken by the Confederates, and became participants of a hunger and suffering of which they had no previous conception. I may as well mention now that as the surrender became more inevitable, Generals Fitzhugh Lee and Rosser, with about two thousand Confederate cavalry, tacitly determined not to be included in it, and started off towards Lynchburg. On their road they fell in with a Federal supply train, and burned eight hundred and sixty wagons. The scanty and partial rations which, after the surrender, were issued on the night of the 9th to the starving Confederates by their captors, were apologized for by the Federals on the ground of the destruction of these eight hundred and sixty wagons by Fitzhugh Lee.

The reader will have gathered that, when General Lee found his depots along the Danville road destroyed by Sheridan, he had no alternative but to make for Lynchburg. He still hoped to get rations and to turn suddenly upon Grant, whose army was dispersed into many columns. The fatigue of the pursuit, though unaggravated by famine, was beginning to tell upon the pursuers. But in pressing for Lynchburg, Lee found himself in a dangerous predicament. He was on a strip of land, not more than seven or eight miles broad, between the James and Appomattox rivers. On the afternoon of the 7th Lee's situation seemed so unpromising that Grant, for the first time, sent to propose surrender. Lee at once replied that his circumstances did not seem to him such as to justify his entertaining such a proposal. On the morning of the 8th Grant renewed his solicitations,—Lee did not decline, but debated the matter, calling a council of war in the evening. No determination was arrived at on the 8th, and at midnight the usual dreary retreat was resumed. The springs of energy and will, unstrung by long want of food, had run down in the men like the machinery of a broken clock. Hitherto the retreat had been covered by Longstreet and Gordon alternately; but now the Federal force, which had got ahead of Lee, and was obstructing his retreat, had become so considerable, that Gordon was thrown out with two thousand men in front, while the "old bull–dog," Longstreet, whose pluck neither hunger, nor fatigue, nor depression, could abate or subdue; still covered the rear. At daybreak on the 9th, a courier from Gordon announced to Lee that a large body of Federal cavalry (in other words Sheridan's army) was across the road at Appomattox Court House. At the same moment a heavy force of infantry under Grant was pushing Longstreet vigorously in the rear. Between Gordon and Longstreet were the remaining wagons, and clinging to them thousands of unarmed and famished stragglers, too weak to carry their muskets. Lee sent orders to Gordon to cut his way through *conte qu' il coute.* Presently came another courier from Gordon, announcing that the enemy was driving him back. Lee had at this moment less than eight thousand men with muskets in their hands. The fatal moment had indisputably come. Hastily donning his best uniform, and buckling on his sword—which it was never his fashion to wear—General Lee turned sadly to the rear to seek the final interview with General Grant.

There is no passage of history in this heart-breaking war which will, for years to come, be more honorably mentioned and gratefully remembered than the demeanor on the 9th of April, 1865, of General Grant towards General Lee. I do not so much allude to the facility with which honorable terms were accorded to the Confederates as to the bearing of General Grant, and of the officers about him, toward General Lee. The interview was brief. Three Commissioners upon either side were immediately appointed.

In the mean time, immediately that General Lee was seen riding to the rear, dressed more gaily than usual and begirt with his sword, the rumor of imminent surrender flew like wildfire through the Confederates. It might be imagined that an army, which had drawn its last regular rations on the 1st of April, and harassed incessantly by night and day, had been marching and fighting until the morning of the 9th, would have welcomed any thing like a termination of its suffering, let it come in what form it might. Let those who idly imagine that the finer feelings are the prerogative of what are called the "upper classes," learn from this and similar scenes to appreciate "common men." As the great Confederate captain rode back from his interview with General Grant, the news of the surrender acquired shape and consistency, and could no longer be denied. The effect on the worn and battered troops—some of whom had fought since April, 1861, and (sparse survivors of hecatombs of fallen comrades) had passed unscathed through such hurricanes of shot as within four years no other men had ever experienced—baffles mortal description. Whole lines of battle rushed up to their beloved old chief, and choking with emotion, broke ranks and struggled with each other to wring him once more by the hand. Men who had fought throughout the war, and knew what the agony and humiliation of that moment must be to him, strove with a refinement of unselfishness and tenderness which he alone could fully appreciate, to lighten his burden and mitigate his pain. With tears pouring down both cheeks General Lee at length commanded voice enough to say:—"Men, we have fought through the war together. I have done the best that I could for you." Not an eye that looked on that scene was dry. Nor was this the emotion of the sickly sentimentalist, but of rough and rugged men, familiar with hardship, danger, and death in a thousand shapes, mastered by sympathy and feeling for another which they had never experienced on their own account. I know of no other passage of military history so touching, unless, in spite of the melo-dramatic coloring which French historians have loved to shed over the scene, it can be found in the *Adieux de Fontainebleau.*

It remains for me briefly to notice the last parade of an army whereof the exploits will be read with pride so long as the English tongue is spoken. In pursuance of an arrangement of the six Commissioners, the Confederate army marched by divisions, on the morning of April the 12th, to a spot in the neighborhood of Appomattox Court House, where they stacked arms and deposited accoutrements. Upon this solemn occasion Major-General Gibbon represented the United States authorities. With the same conspicuous and exalted delicacy which he had exhibited throughout these closing scenes, General Grant was not again visible after his final interview with General Lee. About seven thousand eight hundred Confederates marched up with muskets in their hands, and they were followed by about eighteen thousand unarmed stragglers, who claimed to be included in the capitulation. Each Confederate soldier was furnished with a printed form of parole, which was filled up for him by his own officers, and a duplicate handed to a designated Federal officer. By the evening of the 12th the paroles were generally distributed, and the disbanded men began to scatter through the country. Hardly one of them had a farthing of money. Some of them had from one thousand five hundred to two thousand miles to travel, over a country of which the scanty railroads were utterly annihilated. Many an interesting diary of the adventures of these individuals, as they journeyed from Eastern Virginia to Western Texas, or possibly to Mexico, may well have been written. It is hoped that one or two such narratives may yet be given to the world.

Shortly after noon on the 12th, General Lee, escorted by a guard of honor of Federal cavalry, mounted his horse as a soldier for the last time, and started for the city of Richmond. On his road he arrived about evening at the headquarters of his "old war–horse," General Longstreet, and the last and saddest of their many interviews took place. There are scenes which are too sacred and affecting for description, even though the pen were guided by a Macaulay or a Hoffman. If ever there were two genuine simple-minded men upon earth, to whom any thing melo-dramatic or theatrical is utterly abhorrent, they are the men of whom I am now writing. I close this brief chronicle with the remark that, in proportion to the reader's estimate of the sustained heroism with which Lee and Longstreet for four years bore up and stood erect under such a burden as never was yet laid upon man, will be his appreciation of the circumstances and emotions under which their parting interview took place.

GENERAL GREEN BELIEVES HE WAS SHOT AT

Brigadier-General Green, of Missouri, commanding the second division, was one of the most prominent men upon the field. His own brigade was the first to enter Corinth, and penetrated as far as the Tishomingo Hotel. This was the critical moment of the day. This brigade, forming Price's centre, had surmounted all obstacles in their way, carrying entrenchment after entrenchment, until they found themselves in the centre of the enemy's position. Lovell was to have encountered the enemy on the left, and thus to have compelled a withdrawal of a portion of his forces from the centre, while Green continued to force their centre back. For some reason, Lovell failed to do this, and the Federals threw their whole centre upon Green, and compelled him to retire, after having at such enormous sacrifices gained the position. Prior to his forcing the enemy from their position, he sent an aid to General Price, saying that there were heavy siege guns in front of him, which disputed his further progress. Price replied, "Then tell General Green to take them"; and take them he did—there being thirty in number—but being forced to retire after gaining possession of them, he was obliged to relinquish this heavy armament to its original owners. One of Price's staff—riding by, observed General Green covered with gore from head to heels, and asked him if he had sustained any injury. He replied, that his horse had been shot in the neck, and dismounted to stop the flow of blood, when another bullet pierced the animal again, but without fatal effect. The general was attempting to staunch the wound, when still another ball struck his steed in the forehead, and which after a few convulsive plunges, caused his death. The bullets continued to pour hot and heavy, cutting off twigs and branches, and one scraped the skin off of General Green's hip. He turned around to a bystander, and quietly remarked: "I believe those d——d scoundrels are trying to hit me!" If such was their intention, they certainly came as close to this brave officer as they possibly could without injuring him.

A Hero

General Van Dorn, while riding along the line on Friday, encountered a Missouri private with his face covered with blood and his hand pressed against his jaw. The general inquired if he was wounded and where he was going. He removed his hand, disclosing to sight a broken jaw, which he commenced working with his hand, and replied, as distinctly as he could, in broken sentences: "Only got my jaw broke—they're giving 'em hell back there—be back again soon as can get face fixed up—just go down there and see what hell these Yanks are catching"; and in half an hour afterwards, with bandaged face, he returned to his company to go with them through the balance of the bloody struggle.

The Most Extraordinary Marches on Record

The late marches of General Stuart and of General Pleasanton, as reported from Harrisburg—(the first, ninety-six miles in twenty-four hours; and the last, seventy-eight miles in the same time)—surpass any thing of military record. It is stated in General Halleck's work on military art and science, that Caesar marched the legions from Rome to the Sierra Morena, in Spain, at the rate of twenty leagues a day. In the campaign of 1800, Macdonald, wishing to prevent the escape of an enemy, in a single day marched forty miles, crossing rivers and climbing mountains. Clansel, after the battle of Salamanca, retreated forty miles in twelve hours. In 1814, Napoleon, wishing to form a junction with other troops for the succor of Paris, marched his army the distance of seventy-five miles in thirty-six hours.

It is said that the English cavalry under Lord Lake marched seventy miles in twenty-four hours.

The Kirby Smith brigade of cavalry, during the late advance into Kentucky, marched one hundred and sixty-five miles in seventy-four hours.

As a general rule, troops marching for many days in succession, will move at the rate of from fifteen to twenty miles per day. In forced marches, or in pursuit of a flying enemy, they will average from twenty to twenty-five miles a day. Only for two or three days in succession, with favorable roads, thirty miles a day may be calculated on. Where marches beyond this occur, they are the result of extraordinary circumstances.

All Quiet along the Potomac

"All quiet along the Potomac!" they say,
    "Except now and then a stray picket
Is shot, as he walks on his beat to and fro,
    By a rifleman in the thicket!
'Tis nothing—a private or two, now and then,
    Will not count in the news of the battle!
Not an officer lost—only one of the men—
    Moaning out, all alone, the death-rattle"

All quiet along the Potomac to-night,
    Where the soldiers lie peacefully dreaming;
Their tents, in the rays of the clear autumn moon,
    Or the light of the watch-fires, are gleaming.
A tremulous sigh, as the gentle night-wind
    Through the forest-leaves softly is creeping;
While stars up above, with their glittering eyes,
    Keep guard—for the army is sleeping.

There's only the sound of the lone sentry's tread,
    As he tramps from the rock to the fountain,
And thinks of the two in the low trundle-bed
    Far away in the cot on the mountain.
His musket falls slack—his face, dark and grim,
    Grows gentle with memories tender,
As he mutters a prayer for the children asleep—
    For their mother—may Heaven defend her!

The moon seems to shine just as brightly as then,
    That night, when the love yet unspoken
Leaped up to his lips, when low-murmured vows
    Were pledged to be ever unbroken.
Then, drawing his sleeve roughly over his eyes,
    He dashes off tears that are welling,
And gathers his gun closer up to its place,
    As if to keep down the heart-swelling.

He passes the fountain, the blasted pine tree—
    The footstep is lagging and weary;
Yet onward he goes, through the broad belt of light,
    Toward the shades of the forest so dreary.
Hark! was it the night-wind that rustled the leaves?
    Was it the moonlight, so wondrously flashing?
It looked like a rifle—"Ha! Mary, good-by!"
    And the life-blood is ebbing and plashing!

All quiet along the Potomac to-night!—
    No sound, save the rush of the river!
While soft falls the dew on the face of the dead—
    The picket's off duty forever.

Part III

Partisan Life and Adventure

The Guerrillas

By S. Teackle Wallus

Awake, and to horse! my brothers—
    For the dawn is glimmering gray;
And look! in the crackling brushwood
    There are feet that tread this way.

Who cometh? "A friend." What tidings?
    Oh! God, I sicken to tell,
For the earth seems earth no longer,
    And its sights are sights of hell!

There's rapine, and fire, and slaughter,
    From the mountain down to the shore;
There's blood on the trampled harvest,
    And blood on the homestead floor!

From the far off conquered cities
    Comes the cry of a stifled wail,
And the shrieks and moans of the houseless
    Ring out like a dirge on the gale!

I've seen from the smoking village
    Our mothers and daughters fly—
I've seen where the little children
    Sank down in the furrows to die.

On the banks of the battle-stained river
    I stood as the moonlight shone,
And it glared on the face of my brother
    As the sad wave swept him on!

Where my home was glad are ashes,
    And horror and shame have been there—
For I found on the fallen lintel
    This tress of my wife's dark hair.

They are turning the slave upon us,
    And, with more than a demon's art,
Have uncovered the fires of the savage,
    That slept in his untaught heart.

The ties to our hearth that bound him
    They have rent with curses away,
And maddened him with their madness
    To be almost as brutal as they.

With halter and torch, a bible
    And hymns, to the sound of the drum
They preach the gospel of murder,
    And pray for Lust's kingdom to come!

To saddle! to saddle! my brothers;
    Look up to the rising sun,
And ask of the God who shines there
    Whether deeds like this shall be done.

Wherever the vandal cometh,
    Press down to his heart with your steel—
And whene'er at his bosom ye cannot,
    Like the serpent go strike at his heel.

Through thicket and wood go hunt him,
    Creep up to his camp's fireside,
And let ten of his corpses blacken
    Where one of our brothers hath died.

In his fainting, foot-sore marches,
> In his flight from the stricken fray,
In the snare of the lonely ambush,
> The debts that we owe him, pay!

In God's hand alone is vengeance,
> But he strikes with the hands of men;
And his blight would wither our manhood
> If we smote not the smiter again.

By the graves where our fathers slumber,
> By the shrines where our mothers prayed—
By our homes, and hopes of freedom,
> Let every man swear, by his blade,

That he will not sheath nor stay it
> Till from point to heft it glow
With the flush of Almighty Justice
> In the blood of the felon-foe!

They swore! and the answering sunlight
> Leapt red from their lifted swords,
And the hate in their hearts made echo
> To the wrath in their burning words.

There's weeping in all New England!
> And by Schuylkill's banks a knell!
And the widows there, and the orphans,
> How the oath was kept can tell.

THE CAPTURE OF CATLETT'S STATION

An officer of General Stuart's staff gives the following account of this gallant exploit in a private letter, to a friend in Georgia:

We got to a camp of Pope's baggage train, at Catlett's Station, without their having the least idea of their danger. We reached the vicinity just at dark, and the scene was a most interesting one. There was our prey before us, laughing, talking, and cooking by the hundreds of campfires scattered around on every side. I rode down to within twenty yards of them, and passed along from one camp to another entirely unobserved in the darkness. It was very important to find out what to do, so we occupied the roads and caught passers by enough in a few moments to tell what was before us. They thought we were their own men, and an officer was very indignant, and asked what right the picket had to arrest him, but when our officer whispered that Stuart was about, he said no more. Among those caught was a servant of one of Pope's staff, who told us that the wagons and equipage of Pope and his staff were there, and some members of the staff. So we got directions where to find it and them. One party was to obstruct the track, one to cut the telegraph wire, and one to burn the bridge. All was soon ready to break loose, and two regiments, the first and ninth, went into it. Of all the scenes you ever imagined, this took the lead. The night was perfectly dark, the only light being afforded by the candles in the tents and the fires. When the order to charge was given, it made one's hair stand on end to hear the terrific yell that followed and the thunder of the rushing squadrons, the rattling of the pistol shots, and the occasional report of musketry as the soldiers got to their arms.

A train was at the depot, which we tried to stop but could not. I rode alongside of the locomotive and tried my best to shoot the engine driver as he moved off, catching a glimpse of him by the light of one shot by which to direct the next. I do not know whether I killed him or not, but one thing is certain, we lost the train, there not being time sufficient to obstruct the track sufficiently.

Now, the work of collecting the prisoners and destruction commenced. It was very hard, however, to get the men to work at the burning, when such rich plunder was scattered around. Pope's train received our especial attention. We burnt his private ambulance and took the four fine white mules attached to it, and all his private baggage, and much valuable correspondence. We found papers giving the exact strength of each division of his army. We caught his quartermaster and got his and commissary safes with a large amount of money in them. The quartermaster had been a good deal in Warrenton, and when we passed through the next day, a young lady of the place found out she had a good joke on him. He had bet her a bottle of wine that he would be in Richmond by the 1st of September; so when she heard he was coming, she had the bottle of wine at the gate ready for him, to the great amusement of all parties. The fellow took it very good-humoredly, and drank his wine to her very good health.

We got three hundred and ninety prisoners and hundreds of horses, I have not heard how many. We got all of Pope's staff horses, and two magnificent steeds, which the servant said were Pope's own. We have named one of them "Pope" anyhow.

I was so busy that I did not get any thing at all, but a supper I found neatly spread, and ate on horseback.

After the charge was over, the most terrible storm came up you ever saw—the rain poured down in torrents, the wind blew, and the thunder was like a hundred cannon with a musketry accompaniment. The rain wet everything, so the wood was hard to burn, and it was so dark you could not see your hand before you.

A regiment was ordered to perform some duty about a mile off, and the colonel and head of the column started, and the regiment remained standing in the road, neither party being aware of the separation until the colonel went to form his line, and found he had not twenty men. My oilcloth kept my shoulders dry, but my legs got very wet. We were on our horses the whole night, and had been on them all the day before.

IN THE WRONG PLACE

During the return of General Stuart's cavalry from the expedition to Pennsylvania, in the fall of 1862, as the head of the column was pushing toward the Potomac, a rockaway containing a gentleman in a fine suit of light colored oil cloth, drove up. The gentleman said politely: "Move aside, men—move aside; I am an officer of the seventy-ninth Pennsylvania, on recruiting service, and must get on." The men moved aside, but too slowly for the impatient gentleman. Stuart soon came up: "Are you the officer in command?" inquired the occupant of the rockaway. "I am," was the response. "Then be good enough to order your men to make way for me. I am an officer of the seventy-ninth, on recruiting service, and it is important for me to get ahead as rapidly as possible." "Very well," said Stuart, at the same time giving a significant look at one of his men, who at once dismounted and took a seat in the rockaway. "What do you mean, sir?" exclaimed the indignant occupant. "Nothing," said the man, dryly. "Who are you, sir?" thundered the officer of the seventy-ninth. "Nobody." "Who is that officer?" "General Stuart."

"What General Stuart?" "Jeb Stuart, Major-General of Cavalry in the Confederate army," was the calm answer. The officer of the seventy-ninth gave a long whistle, and exclaimed: "By——! I am procured." "I rather think you are," said the man, turning the rockaway southward. The captured officer managed to escape while our troops were crossing the Potomac, but his rockaway and horse were saved.

Lieutenant McNeill's Exploit

After the surprise and capture of New Creek, Virginia, by General Rosser, Major-General Crook, of the Yankee army, was assigned to the command of the department in which that station is embraced. Major-General Kelley, who previously commanded the department, still remained in Cumberland, having his headquarters at one of the hotels in the town. General Crook established his headquarters in the same town, at the other principal hotel. As soon as this state of affairs became known to Lieutenant Jesse C. McNeill, upon whom had devolved the command of McNeill's Rangers since the death of his father, the lamented old captain, he resolved to risk an attempt to surprise and bring off those two generals.

Having posted himself thoroughly in regard to the situation of affairs in and around Cumberland, he arranged his plan of operations, and with sixty trusty men, crossed Knobby Mountain to the North Branch of the Potomac. Reaching this stream at a point below the first picket post that overlooked the selected route of ingress into Cumberland, he crossed, and in a few minutes the Yankees on duty were relieved. "Your countersign," demanded Lieutenant McNeill, to a burly Dutchman, with such accompaniments as seemed to impress the fellow with the notion that to divulge it was a matter of self-preservation. "Bool's Kaah,"(meaning "Bull's Gap,") was the quick response.

Then on briskly down the county road toward town, near five miles distant, he moved. As the little band struck what is known as the old pike, soon, "Halt! who comes there?" rings out on the air, "Friends, with countersign," is the response. "Dismount, one, advance, and give the countersign," is the picket's next order to the lieutenant.

Having lately had his ankle crushed, the lieutenant was not in a condition to obey; and so urging his horse forward, he quickly heard from the astonished picket, "Don't shoot, I surrender."

On they rushed, and the reserves were gathered in. The first picket captured was cavalry, the next infantry. The former were brought along; the latter were disarmed, their guns smashed, and they were paroled to remain where they were until morning; were told that the town was surrounded, and it would be impossible for them to escape.

Entering town on the west side, they passed another picket on the right bank of the North Branch. By this picket they were not halted. Crossing Will's Creek, (which flows through the town,) at the Iron Bridge, coolly and deliberately up Baltimore Street they rode, some whistling, some laughing and talking, as if they were Yankees, at home among friends.

To and fro, on the street, by the gas-light, are seen walking Yankee guards. "Helloa, boys! whose command is that?" "Scouts from New Creek," is the response.

Presently here they are, between two and three o'clock in the morning, in front of the St. Nicholas Hotel, Kelley's headquarters. Down spring, quietly and calmly, the men who, by previous arrangement, are to visit Kelley's room. They entered the hall, and having procured a light, they entered the general's room. The general, aroused by the knock, rested on one elbow. "You know me, General, I suppose," says Joseph W. Kuykendall, who had charge of this party. "I do," said the general. "You are ——," giving his name. "General, you had me once; it is my honor to have you now. You are a prisoner." "But," says the general, "who am I surrendering to?" "To *me*, sir," was the emphatic response. "No place or time for ceremony; so you will dress quickly." The order was obeyed.

While this was going on at the St. Nicholas, another scene was transpiring at the Revere House. Thither went promptly a portion of the men, as per arrangement, under Lieutenant Welton. Reaching it they halt—five men, in charge of Joseph L. Vandiver, dismount, and "Halt!" is the greeting of the sentinel, standing in front of the entrance. "Friends, with countersign, bearing important dispatches for General Crook," is Vandiver's answer. "Advance, one," etc. In a moment, Vandiver had the sentinel's gun, and ordered him to stand aside under guard. The door is rapped at—a voice from within asks, "Who is you? I don't know you." "Open the door; I must see General Crook." The door is opened, and there stands a small darkey. "Is General Crook in?" "Yes, sir." "Show me his room." "I'm afeerd to; but I will, if you don't tell on me." Crook's room is reached; a rap given. "Come in." In obedience to the invitation, a tall and stalwart form, with light in one hand, and pistol undisplayed in the other, stands erect, cool and deliberate, before the general. "General Crook, I presume," says Vandiver. "I am, sir." "I am General Rosser, sir; you are in my power; you have two minutes to dress in." Then the general rubbed his eyes, as if he thought he dreamed: "Come, General, there are your clothes; you can either put them on, or go as you are." The general quickly arose and dressed.

The prisoner and his captors make their exit to their vigilant comrades without. The general is made to mount behind Vandiver. Off they start, soon rejoin the St. Nicholas party with their prize, and then they all commence to "evacuate" the city quietly, coolly, and in good order. Reaching Will's Creek Bridge, they turned to the left, and proceeded down the tow-path.

On the opposite side of the canal, encamped on the hills around the town, are many of Crook's and Kelley's soldiers, who dream not of the surprise the morning shall bring them; the sentinels too, as unconscious as their slumbering comrades of the proximity of a foe. A few are awake, and with curiosity aroused by the sound of horsemen moving, as it were, in midnight review before them, inquire, "whose command?" "Scouts going out," is the careless response. At length, they are about five miles below the town, where they intend to recross to "Old Virginia." A "Halt" greets the advance. "Friends, with countersign." The picket gives the usual command. "Bull's Gap," says McNeill; "no time to dismount; are in a hurry; the enemy are reported close; we are sent out by General Crook to watch his movements." "Go on, then; cold night, boys, to be out." "Yes, pretty cold." "Give the Johnnies h——l, boys." "O, yes, we are the boys to do that"; are some of the words interchanged, as McNeill and his boys file past the unsuspecting Yankees. A moment or two more, and McNeill is in Virginia!

> McGregor is on his native heath,
> With McGregor's clan around him.

On he pushes briskly, without any report of Yankees pursuing in the rear, to which a strict watch is kept. Romney, twenty-seven miles from Cumberland, is reached; the rear-guard report about sixty Yankees in sight, with some of whom they exchanged a few shots, but the Yankees exhibited no disposition to push on very fast. At about two o'clock in the day, McNeill is seen near Moorefield, moving up the South Branch of the Potomac, while up the pike, on the opposite side, move the Yankees, about two hundred strong, their horses the worse for having galloped from New Creek Station, some thirty-five miles off, from which point they started about eight o'clock in the morning, as we afterward learned. Tuesday night, McNeill camped on the South Fork of the South branch, with his prisoners all safe, but, like their captors, all tired. The next morning, five hundred Yankee cavalry entered Moorefield; a large force was also reliably reported to Lieutenant McNeill, going up Lost river, to intercept him; but they didn't, as the generals reached this city Sunday morning, about two o'clock, in charge of Lieutenant J. S. Welton, who rendered prompt, active, and efficient service in effecting the capture.

It is proper to say, that the entrance into General Kelley's room was through his Adjutant-General's apartment. An eye was kept to this gentleman, and he was brought off with four headquarter colors. His name is Major Melvin.

To have entered Cumberland, a city of eight or nine thousand inhabitants, (a majority of whom are bitterly hostile,) with, according to our best information, seven or eight thousand troops encamped in and around, is very strong evidence that Lieutenant Jesse C. McNeill is a chip of the old block, a worthy son of his gallant old sire, Captain John Hanson McNeill, who, and his eldest son, have already laid their lives upon their country's altar.

General Early, immediately on the receipt of the news of his exploit, advanced the gallant young officer to the rank of Captain in McNeill's Rangers.

A Dutchman's Opinion of Jackson

A gentleman residing in the Valley of Virginia relates that when Fremont and Shields thought they had entrapped Jackson beyond the possibility of escape, Siegel's Dutch soldiers passed his house singing "Shackson in a shug,"(jug) "Shackson in a shug," and when they returned crestfallen from Port Republic, they answered his inquiries as to what they had done with Jackson: "Py tam, de shtopper come out of de shug, he gone py tam; if de rebels don't make him de President, Siegel's men make him."

Insulting Women-Folks

Hood's Texans were hard cases. On their way to Chickamauga, a squad of them strolling about the streets of ——, came suddenly upon three nice young men, belonging to the "bomb-proof" class, as the soldiers called the Government employees, and others who had managed to raise technical objections to military service. Raising a wild yell, the soldiers charged upon the "bomb-proofs," surrounded and captured them. As usual in all such cases of teasing, the tormentors affected rustic manners and dialect.

1st Soldier.—"Mister, did you ever see a bumbsbell?"

1st Fop.— "Yes."

1st Soldier.—"Well, I hearn that you had a powerful lot of them in your 'bomb-proof.' Don't they fiz purty?"

2d Soldier.—"Mister, is you aid to the Guvnor?"

2d Fop.—"No."

2d Soldier.—"I kinder thought that you had them purty boots and store clothes to please the Guvnor's darters."

3d Soldier.—"Mister, is you a po-et?"

3d Fop.—"No."

3d Soldier.—"You looks like you was a rael po-et. I wants you to write some poetry to my old gran mammy. She's powerful on himes (hymns) and hot bricks to her feet."

At this juncture, a big soldier came up and interfered. Looking piteously upon the frightened captives, and then reprovingly upon their persecutors, he said to the latter: "Boys, hain't you got no more manners nor to insult the women-folks." Our informant does not tell us whether or not the women-folks thanked him for his interference.

Anecdote of John Morgan

Upon one occasion Captain John H. Morgan was sent on a scout with a detachment of his squadron near Laverno, and had a skirmish with the enemy's pickets, killing seventeen and taking about as many prisoners. Captain Morgan was entering the turnpike from a lane, and was alone, when he suddenly came in contact with a cavalier, who said to Morgan: "Halt, and dismount!" The reply was: "I am Captain John Morgan, and do not obey Federal commands. Draw your pistol, sir; we are upon an equality." The Federal replied: "We are not, sir," at the same time making a quick motion, with his hand to his side, when the valiant captain fired, and "down went a Federal meetin' house!" He fell dead, and turned out to be the veritable Captain Wilson, of Buell's staff, who planted the Federal flag on the capitol at Nashville! Morgan is certainly the intrepid Marion of the war.

The Marion of the War

A correspondent of the *Memphis Appeal,* (April 3d 1862,) vouches for the truth of the following exploit of Captain Morgan:

The heroic young Kentuckian is as full of stratagem as he is of daring. He disguised himself as a countryman and took a wagonload of meal to Nashville the other day. Driving straight to the St. Cloud Hotel, he left his wagon at the door in charge of a trusty follower, and went into the dining-room of the hotel about dinner, where he sat down opposite to General McCook.

"General McCook, I suppose," said the disguised partisan, bowing across the table.

"You are right, sir,"said McCook, "that is my name."

"Well, gineral, if thar's no seceshers about, I've got something to tell you right here."

Looking around, the general requested his new acquaintance to proceed with what he had to say.

"Well, gineral, I live up here close by Burk's mills, right in the midst of a nest of red hot seceshers, and they swear your soldiers shan't have a peck of meal if they have to starve for it. But, gineral, I'm all right on the goose, though I don't have much to say about it, about home, and so I got a wagon load of meal ground, and I've brung it down here to-day, and it's now out thar in the street, and you can have it if you want."

General McCook was highly delighted—expressed his gratitude to the plain-looking countryman for his kindness, praised his loyalty to "the old flag," etc. etc., and at once ordered the meal to be taken to the commissary of his brigade and paid for in gold and silver. This transaction accomplished, the counterfeit wagoner again repaired to General McCook's headquarters, where, after requesting a strictly private interview, he told, the "gineral" that if he would send out one hundred and fifty men to such a place, in such a neighborhood in Davidson county, he would guide them right into that "nest of seceshers and traitors," where they might "bag" a large quantity of meal and other "contraband of war," besides a number of the worst rebels that ever assisted in "bustin up" this "glorious Union." General McCook fell into the snare "as easy as falling off a log," and all the preliminary arrangements were made, and time and place agreed upon, for the one hundred and fifty Federal soldiers to meet their trusty guide.

McCook's detachment of one hundred and fifty men kept the appointment faithfully, and, of course, Captain Morgan, no longer disguised, was there to meet them; but, unfortunately for them, he was not alone—he had a sufficient number of well-armed horsemen to capture the whole Yankee force without firing a gun. So he took them quietly, and sent them swiftly "to the rear," to be exchanged "in due course"—all but one, an officer, whom he released on parole, and bade him return to General McCook with the compliments of his meal-selling acquaintance, who had the pleasure of meeting him at the St. Cloud a few days before.

INCIDENTS OF GENERAL MORGAN'S CAREER

One of Morgan's men gives the following account of his raid into Kentucky in the spring of 1862:

Colonel Morgan arrived at Cave City in time to stop a freight train—a splendid new engine and thirty-seven cars—from Louisville. I arrived soon after with our small army, when a detail of six men was sent up the railroad for the purpose of tearing up the track after a passenger train should have passed them, and which was soon due from Louisville. The freight train and engine were then destroyed. The passenger train soon coming into sight, the engineer discovered something wrong and tried to put back, but our men had performed their work in the rear of the train, and they were obliged to "halt," Major Coffee making his appearance and firing at the boys; but a bullet knocking splinters about his head, convinced the major that trifling would not do. The train was surrounded and ran down to the station. A scene of hysterics, confusion, and excitement was enacted in the ladies' car that is more easily imagined than described. Major Coffee, Elbetter, and a lieutenant, surrendered as prisoners of war. An affecting scene transpired at this juncture. A beautiful young lady, the wife of Lieutenant ——, her eyes red with weeping, came up to Colonel Morgan, begging him to be kind to her husband. Colonel Morgan replied that he did not know whether he should be doing her husband an act of kindness, but he was free to accompany her. The fair girl caught hold of Colonel Morgan's hands, covering them with tears and kisses. Other ladies came up, requesting their baggage to be saved. Morgan replied to their solicitations by saying that he represented a Southern soldier and gentleman, and that although the engine, one passenger and baggage car, were worth thousands of dollars to the Southern Confederacy they should have them to go back to Louisville. The expression of gratitude that came from fair women, who but a short time before had been blinded by prejudice; was sufficient compensation for the engine and car.

An incident also occurred of painful interest to Colonel Morgan. The conductor, an insolent fellow, approached him, not knowing that he was Morgan, and commenced the following conversation:

Conductor.—"Captain, one of your d——d rebels is out of the way, thank God."

Morgan.—"Who do you allude to, sir?"

Conductor.—"Morgan, the d——est of all the rebels. He was killed at Lebanon, and his mother and sister, from Lexington, came to Louisville to-day to receive his remains."

Morgan.—"Are you telling me the truth, sir?"

Conductor.—"Yes, by G——d, I am."

Colonel Morgan turning aside to hide his emotion, one of our men came up and addressed him as Colonel Morgan, asking what he should do with the prisoners. The conductor for the first time became aware that

Morgan was not dead, but in *propria personae* before him, and, in great trepidation, asked what would become of him. Morgan turned upon him, and in one of his characteristic, sarcastic, and searching looks when mad, told him that being worthless as a prisoner and too mean and contemptible to kill, he was free to go where he chose.

We took from the express $7,278 in Federal Treasury notes, being the large size notes with coupons attached, which were being sent to the army paymaster at Nashville. All private individual papers were left with the express agent, after having destroyed fifty-three cars, one engine, and some other government property, estimated in the aggregate to be worth over one million of dollars. Hearing by telegraph that the train from Nashville had been alarmed a few miles below and sent back, we commenced our march for a return to Sparta, well satisfied that we had given the Northerners proof positive that we were not very badly whipped at Lebanon.

On our return through Burksville, we surprised and captured eight of Wolford's cavalry, and took dinner with our loyal friends, who seemed very agreeably surprised to see Morgan and his men, whom they had supposed dead or prisoners; Morgan delivered a short lecture to the Union men which the court session had drawn together at this place, when we resumed our march towards Sparta, where we arrived in due time without further incident. Major Elbette was paroled here, Major Coffee having been paroled on the first day's march from Cave City. One interesting incident connected with Major Elbette is worth relating. The Louisville *Journal*, a number of which we got from the same train that brought the major as a passenger, containing an article relative to news being that morning received that the rebel Morgan had escaped, and his men were then rendezvousing at Sparta, and that Major Elbette had that day left Louisville to join his regiment (Wolford's) for the purpose of capturing the d——d rebel. Instead of capturing he was captured—a slight difference. The major evidently appreciated the joke. Stopping only long enough in Sparta to feed our horses, we marched for Chattanooga by a circuitous route for the purpose of misleading the enemy, who were after us in large force, they having been at Cooksville when we passed the White Plains,, two and a half miles distant.

And now, having labored through the recital of so much of our rather exciting adventure, let me mention a few incidents of devoted patriotism and heroism exhibited by our fair lady friends along the route. At Lawrenceburg and Pulaski we were greeted with the wildest demonstrations of joy. Handkerchiefs were waved from windows by fair hands—bouquets fell thick and fast upon us. Some came out to shake hands with the boys; while others, with a very commendable forethought, came with their servants, bearing huge baskets of provisions, etc. At Lebanon, also, we were received much after the same cordial fashion; and when, on the 5th instant, the fight was raging hottest, and missiles of destruction were flying in every direction, brave women came out on the street to cheer us on, exposing themselves to danger with as much coolness and nonchalance as did our own brave boys.

One little bright-eyed lad, not more than ten years of age, rushed out into the thickest of the fight, snatched up a gun, and, resting it upon a fence, sent its contents crashing through the brain of an approaching Yankee. Brave, noble boy! The next moment he had paid the forfeit of his daring with his own precious life. We saw him lay, with his bright sunny locks stained with his own warm gore; and the eyes that had flashed forth defiance, now looked blank up into Heaven. Does not the blood of such innocent martyrs cry aloud for vengeance ? And shall not the day of reckoning be a terrible one for our enemies?

A Brave Deed

After one of his raids, Captain Morgan was returning alone toward Murfreesboro, and, encountering a picket of six men, captured them and their arms. This is said to have been accomplished in this manner:—He discovered the picket in a house; and, having on a Federal uniform—or, perhaps, overcoat—assumed a bold front, and the confident air of a Federal *officer*; rode up to the picket, and rebuking the officer in command for not attending properly to his duty, ordered him to give up his arms, which he did. He then directed him, under penalty of death, to call out the men one by one, and surrender their arms—which was done, and all surrendered. One of Morgan's men, named Spalding, joined him with four prisoners, and they came up with Colonel Wood and his party next morning, and all returned to Murfreesboro with thirty-eight prisoners, who were sent on to Salisbury, North Carolina, for confinement.

HE WANTED TO SEE MORGAN

The operator at Lebanon, Kentucky, sat in his office silent and grum. He had just completed the forwarding of a dispatch from Louisville to Nashville, relative to Morgan's captured men, to the effect that they must be sent immediately to the former city by rail. The reason assigned was, that Morgan could at any time enter Nashville, and, with the assistance he would there obtain from rebel sympathizers, could force the prison and liberate the prisoners.

"Confound Morgan and his men!" said the operator to himself, biting his lips in rage; "I wish the last one of them was at Old Nick this very minute! They are always doing some devilment to make trouble. Who knows but what they may pounce down on me some of these days, and take me off to some of their cursed prisons? Confound the whole batch of them, I say. I wish I had Morgan here; I'd soon put an end to his villainy—the cursed rebel!"

Just at this juncture of the soliloquy, a horseman alighted in front of the door, and, with whip in hand, walled carelessly in. The surly operator scarcely raised his head to speak to the intruder as he caught a glimpse of his butternut suit, all bespattered with mud, and the old slouched hat with rim partly torn off. But the visitor was not to be repulsed by this very uncivil reception. Stepping forward toward a vacant chair, which stood beside the window in the further side of the room, he seated himself and asked for the news.

"No news!" was the curt reply.

There was a morning *Journal* on the desk. The stranger reached out his hand, and, with the most perfect *sang froid,* took the paper, and, opening it, commenced to read.

"John Morgan at work again!" he said, as he glanced down the first column; "great pity that that man can't be caught—he plays the wild with every thing!"

At the mention of Morgan's name, the operator, as if suddenly seized by his satanic majesty himself, sprang from his chair, doubled up his fist, and then with a sudden jerk withdrawing it again, as if practicing the pugilistic art on some hapless victim, and then thrusting his arm out at full length, while his eyes darted vengeful fire, exclaimed:

"Yes, the scoundrel, villain—I wish I had him here; I'd blow his brains out this very moment! I'd show him. Just let him come in reach of me, and he'll soon get a ball put through his cursed body. No more pranks from him, the mighty John Morgan, I tell you!" And the infuriated man went through all the gestures of shooting his hated foe.

"You wouldn't kill him, would you?" asked the stranger, quietly looking up from his paper, and lifting the torn brim of his old white hat.

"Kill him? Aye, and I would, sooner than I'd shoot a mad dog. I just dare him, at any time, to cross that door, and if he isn't a dead man in less than five minutes there's no truth in me."

The stranger rose, took off his hat, and stood before the bloodthirsty operator, and with a quiet mien, and voice gentle as a maiden's, said:

"I am John Morgan, sir; execute your threat! Here is a pistol—you are entirely welcome, to use it!"

As he spoke, he fixed his large piercing eyes steadfastly on the operator. Every feature of that noble face bespoke daring and defiance.

"Here is a pistol, use it!"

"Oh! thank you; I—I—didn't know—I hadn't any idea—that you were—Colonel Morgan, sir—indeed. I didn't—beg pardon, sir! So much annoyed to-day—every thing gone topsy-turvy. Man gets so fretted—excuse me!—really didn't mean what I said—wouldn't have any man's blood on my conscience—oh, no! Remember the commandment. Thousand pardons, sir; hope you'll forgive!" And the frightened man bowed himself quite back to the wall, where he stood pale and trembling.

"You have my pardon, sir," replied Morgan, in a firm, gentlemanly tone. "Another time I advise you to be less boastful of your courage and veracity. I have but little time to stay. Seat yourself, and send the messages that I shall dictate, to Louisville. Make no mistake; if you do, your life is the forfeit!"

The bewildered man, but too glad to escape so easily, obeyed the order of the colonel with alacrity.

"I understand this operation, sir; don't you attempt to give any information but what I instruct you to do."

Had the trembling man felt disposed to disobey the warning, the close proximity to his head of that formidable pistol would have forever lulled all such desire.

"Now," said Colonel Morgan, "show me all the dispatches that have passed through this office in the last twenty-four hours."

The man sprang from his seat and with a most obsequious air obeyed the bidding.

"That will do, sir," said Morgan, bowing politely, and bidding the pusillanimous wretch "good morning." Reaching his horse, he mounted and rode away, leaving the confused operator dumb with wonder and surprise at the strange and startling occurrence.

COLONEL MORGAN BUYS A HORSE

The *Columbus Republic* relates an amusing instance of Colonel Morgan coming it over a Tennessee tory, which is almost equal to Sergeant Jasper's exploits in the days of the old Revolution. Colonel Morgan and his squadron had not crossed the Tennessee river on his late scout over half an hour before two of Lincoln's gunboats came up, his men lining the bank watching them as they passed.

They then left, and after proceeding a few miles they came up; as it turned out, to the house of a Lincolnite "termed Union man." He gave them a cordial welcome, invited them to have something to eat, and asked many questions, how many troops came up with them, etc., supposing the squadron had just come off the boats that had passed, all of which were satisfactorily answered.

While stopping there, Morgan got his eye on a very fine horse. It was a splendid animal and he concluded to purchase. The old man didn't want to sell him much; he was young, a very fine animal, and thought a great deal of him. But he said he would contribute what he could toward the restoration of the Union, and if he would give him the modest sum of eight hundred and fifty dollars, he could have the horse. He did so, giving the old farmer *an order on General Buell for the amount,* signing his own name. The order was accepted, the old fellow believing him to be another Morgan, as the colonel explained to him the similarity of names. The colonel and his men then left, but it is not known at this time whether General Buell has honored the draft or not.

Quick Work

The *Chattanooga Rebel* says that Colonel Boone, of Kentucky, was in command of the Federal forces at Gallatin, Tennessee, when Colonel Jack Morgan made his morning call there last week, and had not shaken off the drowsy god at the time of the demand for the surrender of his forces. Mrs. Boone, however, was more wide awake, and aroused the sleeping colonel by exclaiming: "I surrender, and *so does the colonel!*" Of course, after that, the colonel had no more to say.

One of Morgan's Exploits

While General Morgan's command was at Gallatin, he received information that a large division of the abolition army was approaching Nashville' by the way of Tyree Springs. He accordingly selected three hundred men from the brigade for the purpose of ambushing them and capturing their wagon trains. He arrived at the road just as the head of the Yankee column was approaching, and, selecting a good position, succeeded in pouring a very destructive fire into them. The general arranged his men on the side of the road, and placing himself at the head of the line, instructed them to retain their fire until he gave the signal, which was to be the firing of his own pistol. The signal was given, and immediately three hundred double-barreled guns were discharged right into the midst of the Yankee hordes.

The effect can be imagined better than described. The whole column recoiled in great confusion, and it was some time before the enemy could regain their equilibrium. Our men had time to reload and discharge another volley before their artillery could be brought to bear on us. When we were compelled to retire, the general made a circuit to the rear, and placing his men in another good position, instructed them to await the approach of the next brigade, while he rode on with one of his officers toward Louisville, to ascertain how far it was behind.

In this ride he captured about a dozen prisoners, most of whom were officers. He was so much entertained by this amusement, that he was gone longer than he was aware. In the meantime, the enemy finding out that our men had taken a position in their rear, sent back two regiments of cavalry, and drove them from their position. The general not being aware of this, rode back to where he had left his men, but what was his surprise when he found himself in front of about two thousand "blue coats." The abolition officer immediately rode forward and ordered him to halt, and demanded the signal. The general replied: "What do you mean, sir, by demanding a signal from an officer of my rank? I'll teach you, sir, how to insult a government officer by demanding signals when you should be attending to other matters of greater importance."

He then ordered them to open the way for a column of infantry which he was going back to bring up. The officer touched his hat, and immediately gave way, while Morgan rode through their column. As he would ride along he would address the stragglers, ordering them to "move up," that they were no better than deserters, and only wanted Morgan to catch them. They would touch their hats and move up briskly. In the meantime, the prisoners, who were following the general, were convulsed with laughter, thinking, no doubt, that he was their prisoner, and they would see the fun out before giving him up. If this was their calculation they were sadly deceived, for the general, coming to a place in the lawn where the fence was low, put spurs to his horse, and bidding his captured officers good-day, was soon out of sight. What must have been their reflection when they beheld him disappear from their sight. I have no doubt they regarded him as a spirit. This is every word true. I have merely stated the facts. You can dress them up.

A Noble Deed

During his attack upon the Federal forces at Cynthiana, Colonel Morgan, while crossing the street of that town, had his attention arrested by a little girl who ran wildly along, shrieking with fright. He caught the child in his arms, and asked her what was the matter.

She laid her little bare head on his shoulder, and sobbed wildly. He smoothed her tangled hair, patted her stained cheeks, and with soothing voice endeavored to assuage her grief.

It was several moments before she could speak.

"Oh, my father—my dear father! They have got him! I will never see him no more!" And the little trembling creature burst into fresh paroxysm of tears.

"Where is your father, my child?" asked the colonel, in a soft tone, at the same time continuing his caresses.

"The Secesh has got him, sir. They'll put him in the big prison. Aunt Nancy told me so."

"And where is your mother, my child?"

"I haven't got no mother, sir. She's went up to heaven when I was a little baby."

Colonel Morgan felt the tears rush to his eyes. He thought of his own little girl and her mother now in heaven. He understood the whole case, and bearing the child in his arms, he moved into the midst of the prisoners.

"Whose child is this?" asked the colonel. "Is her father here?"

A man—one of the Home Guard—rushed forward.

"It is my child, colonel. Thank you—thank you for your kindness," said the grateful father, as the tears streamed down his face.

It was an affecting incident—such a one as sometimes occurs to relieve the horrors of dread-visaged war. And none of those who witnessed it were ever known to call Colonel Morgan harsh names after that.

Selling a Federal General

During one of his expeditions, Morgan reached a point on the railroad near Mumfordsville, Kentucky. His operator at once attached his instrument to the telegraph, and sent a dispatch to the Federal General Boyle, commanding at Louisville, as if from General Granger, the Federal commander at Bowling Green. This stated that Morgan was in the vicinity of Bowling Green, threatening an attack, and asked for aid.

General Boyle made answer that he could not give him any.

General Granger (Morgan) then asked if there were no troops in Louisville which could be sent to his aid.

General Boyle sent word that there were no troops in Louisville at all.

General Granger asked Boyle what disposition had been made of the troops.

General Boyle told him the force and position of his troops, spoke of their efficiency, etc., and gave all the information in regard to them that Morgan wanted.

Morgan then sent in his own name a dispatch to General Boyle, calling him a "very smart boy," and thanking him politely for the important information he had given him.

Exploit of One of Morgan's Men

The Decatur correspondent of the *New Orleans Picayune* relates the following:

I must mention a gallant exploit performed lately by Dr. Strader, of Captain John Morgan's command, which is worthy of record. Learning that a large quantity of knapsacks, etc., left by the army of Crittenden in his masterly retreat, was in the vicinity of Livingston, Overton County, Tennessee, he procured permission from Major-General Hardee to go after them. Proceeding alone, in citizens' dress, without even a pocket knife for protection, he collected at different places over seven thousand knapsacks, worth three dollars apiece, and got the people to loan their wagons to haul them to our army. At McMinville he also procured a quantity of saltpetre and sixty boxes of clothing. The services of such men are valuable, and deserve to be recorded.

The Kentucky Partisan

By Paul H. Hayne

Hath the wily Swamp Fox
    Come again to earth?
Hath the soul of Sumter
    Owned a second birth?
From the western hill-slopes
    Starts a hero-form,
Stalwart, like the oak tree,
    Tameless, like the storm!

His an eye of lightning!
    His a heart of steel!
Flashing deadly vengeance,
    Thrilled with fiery zeal!
Hound him down, ye minions
    Seize him—if ye can;
But woe worth the hireling knave
Who meets him, man to man!

Well done, gallant Morgan!
    Strike with might and main,
Till the fair fields redden
    With a gory rain;
Smite them by the roadside,
    Smite them in the wood,
By the lonely valley,
    And the purpling flood;
'Neath the mystic starlight,
    'Neath the glare of day,
Harass, sting, affright them,
    Scatter them and slay;—
Beard, who durst, our chieftain!
    Blind him—if ye can,—
But woe worth the Hessian thief
Who meets him; man to man!

There's a lurid purpose
    Brooding in his breast,
Born of solemn passion
    And a deep unrest:
For our ruined homesteads
    And our ravaged land,
For our women outraged
    By the dastard hand,
For, our thousand sorrows
    And our untold shame,
For our blighted harvests,

For our towns aflame—
He has sworn (and recks not
    Who may cross his path)—
That the foe shall feel him
    In his torrid wrath—
That, while will and spirit
    Hold one spark of life,
Blood shall stain his broadsword,
    Blood shall whet his knife:—
On! ye Hessian horsemen!
    Crush him—if ye can!
But woe worth your stanchest slave
Who meets him, man to man!

'Tis no time for pleasure!
    Doff the silken vest!
Up, my men, and follow
    Marion of the West!
Strike with him for freedom
    Strike with main and might,
'Neath the noonday splendor,
    'Neath the gloom of night;
Strike by rock and roadside,
    Strike in wold and wood;
By the shadowy valley,
    By the purpling flood;
On! where Morgan's war-horse
    Thunders in the van!
God! who would not gladly die
Beside that glorious man?

Hath the wily Swamp Fox
    Come again to earth?
Hath the soul of Sumter
    Owned a second birth?
From the western hill-slopes
    Starts a hero-form,

> Stalwart, like an oak tree,
>> Restless, like the storm!
> His an eye of lightning!
>> His a heart of steel!
> Flashing deadly vengeance,
>> Thrilled with fiery zeal!
> Hound him down, ye robbers!
>> Slay him—if ye can!
> But woe worth the hireling knave
> Who meets him, man to man!

An Honest Foe Better Than a False Friend

During one of the raids of John Morgan, an interesting incident occurred at Salem, Indiana. Some of his men proceeded out west of the town to burn the bridges and watertank on the railroad. On the way out they captured a couple of persons living in the country, one of whom was a Quaker. The Quaker strongly objected to being made a prisoner. The Confederates wanted to know if he was not strongly opposed to the South? "Thee is right," said the Quaker, "I am." "Well, did you vote for Lincoln?" "Thee is right; I did vote for Abraham," was the calm reply.

"Well, what are you?"

"Thee may naturally suppose that I am a Union man. Cannot thee let me go to my home?"

"Yes, yes; go and take care of the old woman," was the welcome answer.

The other prisoner was trotted along with them, but not relishing the summary manner in which the Quaker was disposed of, he said:

"What do you let him go for? He is a black abolitionist. Now, look here; I voted for Breckinridge, and have always been opposed to the war. I am opposed to fighting the South, decidedly."

"You are," said the Ranger; "you are what they call around here a Copperhead, ain't you?"

"Yes, yes," said the Butternut, propitiatingly; "that's what all my neighbors call me, and they know I ain't with them."

"Come here, Dave!" halloed the Ranger. "Here's a Butternut, just come and look at him. Look here, old man, where do you live? We want what horses you have got to spare, and if you've got any greenbacks, just shell them out!" And they took all he had.

General Morgan's Escape from the Ohio Penitentiary

General John Morgan was honored with an ovation on the 7th of January, 1864, on his arrival at Richmond. The following is an account of his escape from the Ohio Penitentiary, and subsequent adventures:

Their bedsteads were small iron stools, fastened to the wall with hinges. They could be hooked up, or allowed to stand on the floor; and, to prevent any suspicion, for several days before any work was attempted, they made it a habit to let them down, and sit at their doors and read. Captain Hines superintended the work, while General Morgan kept watch to divert the attention of the sentinel, whose duty it was to come round during the day, and observe if any thing was going on. One day this fellow came in while Hokersmith was down under the floor, boring away, and missing him, said: "Where is Hokersmith?" The general replied: "He is in my room sick"; and immediately pulled a document out of his pocket, and said to him: "Here is a memorial I have drawn up to forward to the government at Washington. What do you think of it?"

The fellow, who, perhaps, could not read, being highly flattered at the general's condescension, took it, and very gravely looked at it for several moments before he vouchsafed any reply; then, handing it back, he expressed himself highly pleased with it. In the meantime, Hokersmith had been signaled, and came up, professing to feel "very unwell." This sentinel was the most difficult and dangerous obstacle in their progress, because there was no telling at what time he would enter during the day, and at night he came regularly every two hours to each cell, and inserted a light through the bars of their door, to see that they were quietly sleeping; and frequently, after he had completed his rounds, he would slip back in the dark, with a pair of India-rubber shoes on, to listen at their cells if any thing was going on. The general says that he would almost invariably know of his presence by a certain magnetic shudder which it would produce; but, for fear that this acute sensibility might sometimes fail him; he broke up small particles of coal every morning, and sprinkled them before the cell-door, which would always announce his coming.

Every thing was now ready to begin the work; so, about the latter part of October, they began to bore. All were busy—one, making a rope-ladder by tearing and twisting up strips of bed-ticking, another making bowie-knives, and another twisting up towels. They labored perseveringly for several days, and, after boring through nine inches of cement, and nine thicknesses of brick placed edgewise, they began to wonder when they should reach the soft earth. Suddenly, a brick fell through. What could this mean? What infernal chamber had they reached? It was immediately entered; and, to their great astonishment and joy, it proved to be an air-chamber extending the whole length of the row of cells. Here was an unexpected interposition in their favor. Hitherto they had been obliged to conceal their rubbish in their bed-tickings, each day burning a proportionate quantity of straw. Now they had room enough for all they could dig. They at once commenced to tunnel at right angles with this air-chamber, to get through the foundation; and day after day they bored—day after day the blocks of granite were removed—and still the work before them seemed interminable.

After twenty-three days of unremitting labor, and getting through a granite wall of six feet in thickness, they reached the soil. They tunneled up for some distance, and light began to shine. How glorious was that light! It announced the fulfillment of their labors; and if Providence would only continue its favor, they would soon be free. This was the morning of the 26th day of November, 1863. The subsequent night, at twelve o'clock, was determined on as the hour at which they would attempt their liberty. Each moment that intervened was filled with dreadful anxiety and suspense, and each time the guard entered increased their apprehensions. The general says that he had prayed for rain; but the morning of the 27th dawned bright and beautiful. The evening came, and clouds began to gather. How they prayed for them to increase! If rain should only begin, their chances of detection would be greatly lessened. While these thoughts were passing through their minds, the keeper entered with a letter for General Morgan. He opened it, and what was his surprise, and I may say wonder, to find it from a poor Irish woman of his acquaintance in Kentucky, commencing:—"My dear Ginral: I feel certain you are going to try to git out of prison; but, for your sake, don't you try it, my dear Ginral. You will only be taken prisoner again, and made to suffer more than you do now."

The letter then went on to speak of his kindness to the poor when he lived at Lexington, and concluded by again exhorting him to trust in God and wait his time. What could this mean? No human being on the outside had been informed of his intention to escape; and yet, just as all things were ready for him to make the attempt, here comes a letter from Winchester, Kentucky, advising him not to "try it." This letter had passed through the examining office of General Mason, and then through the hands of the lower officials. What if it should excite their suspicion, and cause them to exercise an increased vigilance? The situation, however, was desperate. Their fate could not be much worse, and they resolved to go. Nothing now remained to be done but for the general and Colonel Dick Morgan to change cells. The hour approached for them to be locked up. They changed coats, and each stood at the other's cell door with his back exposed, and pretended to be engaged in making up their beds. As the turnkey entered they "turned in," and pulled their doors shut.

Six, eight, ten o'clock came. How each pulse throbbed as they quietly awaited the approach of twelve! It came. The sentinel passed his round—all well! After waiting a few moments to see if he intended to slip back, the signal was given. All quietly slipped down into the air-chamber, first stuffing their flannel shirts, and placing them in bed as they were accustomed to lie. As they moved quietly along through the dark recess to the terminus where they were to emerge from the earth, the general prepared to light a match. As the lurid glare fell upon their countenances, a scene was presented which can never be forgotten. There were crouched seven brave men, who had resolved to be free. They were armed with bowie-knives made out of case-knives. Life, in their condition, was scarcely to be desired, and the moment for the desperate chance had arrived. Suppose, as they emerged from the ground, that the dog should give the alarm—they could but die!

But few moments were spent in this kind of apprehension. The hour had arrived, and yet they came. Fortunately—yes, providentially—the night had suddenly grown dark and rainy, the dogs had retired to their kennels, and the sentinels had taken refuge under shelter. The inner wall, by the aid of the rope ladder, was soon scaled, and now the outer one had to be attempted. Captain Taylor (who, by the way, is a nephew of Old Zach), being a very active man, by the assistance of his comrades reached the top of the gate, and was enabled to get the rope over the wall. When the top was gained, they found a rope extending all around, which the general immediately cut, as he suspected that it might lead into the warden's room. This turned out to be correct. They then entered the sentry-box on the wall and changed their clothes, and let themselves down the wall. In sliding down, the general skinned his hand very badly, and all were more or less bruised. Once down, they separated—Taylor and Shelton going one way; Hokersmith, Bennett, and McGee, another; and General Morgan and Captain Hines proceeding immediately toward the depot.

The general had, by paying fifteen dollars in gold, succeeded in obtaining a paper which informed him of the schedule time of the different roads. The clock struck one, and he knew, by hurrying, he could reach the down-train for Cincinnati. He got there just as the train was moving off. He at once looked around to see if there were any soldiers on board, and, espying a Union officer, he boldly walked up and took a seat beside him. He remarked to him, that "as the night was damp and chilly, perhaps he would join him in a drink." He did so, and the party soon became very agreeable to each other. The cars, in crossing the Scioto, have to pass within a short distance of the penitentiary. As they passed, the officer remarked, "There's the hotel at which Morgan and his officers are spending their leisure." "Yes," replied the general, "and I sincerely hope he will make up his mind to board there during the balance of the war, for he is a great nuisance." When the train reached Xenia, it was detained by some accident more than an hour. Imagine his anxiety, as soldier after soldier would pass through the train, for fear that when the sentinel passed his round, at 2 o'clock, their absence might be discovered.

The train was due in Cincinnati at 6 o'clock. This was the hour at which they were turned out of their cells, and, of course, their escape would be then discovered. In a few moments after it would be known all over the country. The train, having been detained at Xenia, was running very rapidly to make up the time. It was already past 6 o'clock. The general said to Captain Hines—"It's after 6 o'clock; if we go to the depot, we are dead men. Now or never!" They went to the rear, and put on the brakes. "Jump, Hines!" Off he went, and fell heels-over-head in the mud. Another severe turn of the brakes, and the general jumped. He was more successful, and lighted on his feet. There were some soldiers near, who remarked, "What in h——l do you mean by jumping off the cars here?" The general replied,

"What in the d——l is the use of my going into town when I live here? and, besides, what business is it of yours?"

They went immediately to the river. They found a skiff, but no oars. Soon a little boy came over, and appeared to be waiting. "What are you waiting for?" said the general. "I am waiting for my load." "What is the price of a load?" "Two dollars." "Well, as we are tired and hungry, we will give you the two dollars, and you can put us over." So over he took them. "Where does Miss —— live?" "Just a short distance from here." "Will you show me her house?" "Yes, sir." The house was reached, a fine breakfast was soon obtained, money and a horse furnished, a good woman's prayer bestowed, and off he went. From there forward through Kentucky every body vied with each other as to who should show him the most attention—even to the Negroes; and young ladies of refinement begged the honor to cook his meals.

He remained in Kentucky some days, feeling perfectly safe, and sending into Louisville for many little things he wanted. Went to Bardstown, and found a Federal regiment had just arrived there, looking for him. Remained here and about for three or four days, and then struck out for Dixie—sometimes disguising himself as a government cattle-contractor, and buying a large lot of cattle; at other times, a quartermaster, until he got to the Tennessee river. Here he found all means of transportation destroyed; and the bank strongly guarded; but, with the assistance of about thirty others, who had recognized him, and joined him in spite of his remonstrances, he succeeded in making a raft, and he and Captain Hines crossed over. His escort, with heroic self-sacrifice, refused to cross until he was safely over. He then hired a Negro to get his horse over, paying him twenty dollars for it. The river was so high that the horse came near drowning, and after more than one hour's struggling with the stream was pulled out so exhausted as scarcely to be able to stand.

The general threw a blanket on him, and commenced to walk him, when suddenly, he says, he was seized with a presentiment that he would be attacked; and remarking to Captain Hines, "We shall be attacked in twenty minutes," commenced saddling his horse. He had hardly tied his girth, when "Bang! bang!" went the minie-balls. He bounced upon his horse, and the noble animal, appearing to be inspired with new vigor, bounded off like a deer up the mountain. The last he saw of his poor fellows on the opposite side, they were disappearing up the river bank, fired upon by a whole regiment of Yankees. By this time it was dark, and also raining. He knew that a perfect cordon of pickets would surround the foot of the mountain, and if he remained there until morning he would be lost. So he determined to run the gauntlet at once, and commenced to descend. As he neared the foot, leading his horse, he came almost in personal contact with a picket. His first impulse was to kill him, but finding him asleep, he determined to let him sleep on. He made his way to the house of a Union man that he knew lived near there, and went up and passed himself off as captain-quartermaster of Hunt's regiment, who was on his way to Athens, Tennessee, to procure supplies of sugar and coffee for the Union people of the country. The lady, who appeared to be asleep while this interview was taking place with her husband, at the mention of sugar and coffee, jumped out of bed in her night-clothes, and said: "Thank God for that; for we ain't seen any real coffee up here for God knows how long!" She was so delighted at the prospect, that she made up a fire and cooked them a good supper. Supper being over, the general remarked that he understood that some rebels had "tried to cross the river this afternoon." "Yes," said the woman, "but our men killed some of 'um, and driv the rest back." "Now," said the general, "I know that; but didn't some of them get over?" "Yes," was her reply, "but they are on the mountain, and cannot get down without being killed, as every road is stopped up." He then said to her: "It is very important for me to get to Athens by tomorrow night, or I may lose that sugar and coffee; and I am afraid to go down any of these roads for fear my own men will kill me."

The fear of losing that sugar and coffee brought her again to an accommodating mood, and she replied: "Why, Paul, can't you show the captain through our farm, that road down by the field?" The general says: "Of course, Paul, you can do it; and as the night is very cold, I will give you ten dollars (in gold) to help you along." The gold, and the prospect of sugar and coffee, were too much for any poor man's nerves, and he yielded, and getting on a horse, he took them seven miles to the big road.

From this time forward he had a series of adventures and escapes, all very wonderful, until he got near another river in Tennessee, when he resolved to go up to a house and find the way. Hines went to the house, while the general stood in the road. Hearing a body of cavalry come dashing up behind him, he quietly slipped to one side of the road, and it passed by without observing him. They went traveling after Hines, and, poor fellow!

he has not been heard of since. How sad to think that he should be either captured or killed after so many brave efforts, not only in his own behalf, but also in that of the general, for the general says that it is owing chiefly to Hines's enterprise and skill that they made their escape.

When he arrived at the river referred to above, he tried to get over, intending to stop that night with a good Southern man on the other side. He could not get over, and had to stop at the house of a Union man. The next morning he went to the house that he had sought the night previous, and found the track of the Yankees scarcely cold. They had been there all night, expecting that he would come there, and had murdered every body who had attempted to reach the house, without hailing them. In pursuing this brutal course, they had killed three young men, neighbors of this gentleman, and went away, leaving their dead bodies on the ground.

After he had crossed Okey's river, and got down into Middle Tennessee, he found it almost impossible to avoid recognition. At one time he passed some poor women, and one of them commenced clapping her hands, and said, "O! I know who that is! I know who that is!" but; catching herself, she stopped short, and passed on with her companions.

The general says that his escape was made entirely without assistance, from any one on the outside, and, so far as he knows, also without their knowledge of his intention; that the announcement of his arrival in Toronto was one of those fortuitous coincidences that cannot be accounted for; that it assisted him materially, no doubt. In fact, he says that his "wife's prayers saved him, and, as this is the most agreeable way of explaining it, he is determined to believe it."

THE DEATH OF GENERAL MORGAN

The *Abingdon Virginian* gives the following account of the death of General Morgan:

On Saturday, the third instant, accompanied by the brigades of Giltner, Hodges, and Smith, and a detachment of Vaughan's with four pieces of artillery, General Morgan and his staff approached the town of Greeneville, Tennessee. Scouts had brought the information that the enemy were not nearer than Bull's Gap, sixteen miles distant, and, in addition, a guard had been sent into the village to reconnoitre. Upon the report of the entire absence of the enemy, Cassel's battalion, commanded by Captain J. M. Clarke, together with the four guns, were posted some three or four hundred yards from the court house, when General Morgan and his staff entered and established headquarters at the residence of Mrs. Dr. Williams, near the centre of the town. Shortly after the advent of the guard in town, young Mrs. Williams (daughter-in-law of the lady at whose house General Morgan had his headquarters) disappeared; a scout was sent for, but could not find her, and as she returned with the enemy next morning, it appears she had ridden all the way to Bull's Gap and had given information of Morgan's whereabouts and the strength of the guard.

Precaution had been taken to prevent the egress of persons who might convey information to the enemy, and all the roads and avenues were picketed. After visiting the camps and seeing that pickets had been duly posted, General Morgan and his staff, at a late hour of the night, retired to rest. Being greatly fatigued, they slept very soundly, and were startled from their slumbers about six o'clock on Sunday morning by the elder Mrs. Williams, who informed them that the Yankees had surrounded the house. The general and his staff at once sprang from their beds, armed themselves, and rushed out at the opposite door to that at which the Yankees were thundering.

On the side of the house where they escaped there is a very large yard and garden, with a great deal of foliage and a vineyard. These, together with the basement of the old hotel at the southwestern extremity of the grounds, enabled them to conceal themselves for a time, but the Yankees by this time began to appear so thick and fast around them that concealment became hopeless, and they rushed out to fight their way through, in the hope of succor and assistance from the battalion so near at hand. The officers with General Morgan were Major Gassett and Captain Withers, Rogers, and Clay, and a young gentleman by the name of Johnson, a clerk in the office of the adjutant-general. At this time they were all, except Withers and Clay, in the basement of the old hotel occupied by Mrs. Fry (wife of the notorious bushwhacker and murderer, now in our possession), who was all the time calling to the Yankees, informing them of the hiding-place of the "rebels."

Seeing escape almost hopeless, General Morgan directed Major Gassett to examine and see if there was any chance of escape from the front of the basement into the street. Major Gassett looked, and replied that there was a chance, but it was a desperate one, which General Morgan did not hear, as that instant the Yankees charged up to the fence, separating the hotel from Mrs. Williams' grounds, when the general, with Major Gassett, Captain Rogers, and Mr. Johnson, sprang out in the direction of the vineyard, when the two latter were captured and the general killed. The latter had just fired his pistol, and was in act of firing again when he fell. Captains Withers and Clay had not been able to get out of the house, and had concealed themselves in or near it. Major Gassett, in the meantime, sought shelter in the basement and vineyard alternately, but could not elude the vigilance of Mrs. Fry, who was all the time directing attention to his whereabouts. Being the only rebel left—Withers and Clay having been discovered and betrayed by a Negro—Major Gassett's ingenuity was put to work to avoid capture. Mrs. Fry knew he was in the basement, and the Yankees were as thick around him as snakes in harvest. After passing to and fro several times between the basement and the garden, all the time under fire, he finally took shelter in the former, and at an auspicious moment sprang into the street, gave Mrs. Fry a parting blessing in his exit, mounted a horse hitched near by and made his escape. A great many shots were fired by the Yankees, but the only one that took effect was that which killed General Morgan, piercing his right breast and ranging through diagonally. Withers, Rogers, Clay, and Johnson are now, we presume, in a Yankee prison, and Major Gassett is again on duty with his command.

The general was determined never to surrender, and told members of his staff they must not give up. He was heard to say, "they have got us sure," when he drew his pistol and commenced firing.

After General Morgan had been killed, the unfeeling brutes who murdered him *threw his lifeless body across a horse and paraded it through the streets.* His body was subsequently sent through the lines by flag of truce.

A Patriotic Fellow

The committee appointed to collect metal for cannon for General Beauregard's army, applied to a planter of Adams county, Mississippi, for his bell. Not having such an article, he mentioned it to his wife, when she very patriotically offered her brass kettle. The little ones rather demurred to the sacrifice, and one of them, with a sweet tooth, said, "La, pa, what will we do for preserves?" "My daughter," said the wag of a father, "our whole duty now is to *preserve* our country." The kettle was sent.

Narrow Escape of Van Dorn

A letter to the *Charleston Courier,* from Columbia, Tennessee, gives an interesting account of a narrow escape made by Van Dorn from the capture of himself and whole command:

It appears that, on the 11th inst., he had taken an advantageous position to make a short opposition to the advance of a superior force of the enemy, and then retire across Duck river, over which a pontoon bridge was supposed to have been completed. Upon attempting to launch it, it was discovered to be impossible, as the river had overflowed its banks, and was sweeping on with the greatest rapidity, bearing on its bosom huge logs and driftwood, hurled down with such velocity as to render the laying down of the pontoon an utter impossibility. To render matters still worse, the rope, by means of which the ferry-boat was crossed, became submerged, and another one was with difficulty stretched across, by means of which they were enabled to cross a boat capable of carrying at each trip, occupying forty minutes, one wagon or eight or ten horses. The letter says:

Placed in this unfortunate position, we were completely covered by Federals in heavy force in the front and upon both flanks, without having any means of retreat in case of a superior force, which was certain, and which it was only our intention to engage and retire. Several plans of escape were suggested, among which the most plausible was to swim the horses across the stream and cross the troops by the ferry, but it was found that even this was impracticable. Our position was at the head of the peninsula formed by the junction of Carter's creek and Duck river, while the enemy's position was upon another peninsula directly opposite, formed by the junction of Rutherford and Carter's creeks, all of which streams were unusually high and well night impassable. Our forces were disposed on the south side of Rutherford's creek, our centre resting upon the Nashville pike, our left extending to Carter's creek, and our right, under Forrest, extending a mile or two to the right of the pike; and upon the border of

Rutherford's creek. The position was a very strong and commanding one, and King's battery was put upon the highest hill commanding the approaches from the pike. In front of our position, upon the centre, open fields stretched from Rutherford's creek back a thousand yards to a wooded hill upon the left of the turnpike, upon which the enemy mounted their artillery, but which was perfectly commanded by King's excellent position.

From the top of this hill the movements of the enemy might plainly be described. On the 10th, three brigades were plainly visible, and large wagon trains were moving in all directions. It was feared, from what could be seen of the enemy's movements upon our right, that he was about driving wagons into Rutherford's creek, upon which to place plank and cross his infantry, as the creek was too deep and rapid to be at all fordable. It soon became known to our troops that the pontoon bad proved a provoking failure, and being aware of the enemy's large force and his so perfectly covering our front and flank, and deeming escape improbable, their lack of confidence was plainly exhibited, and hundreds of stragglers attempted to cross by means of the ferryboats, but were prevented by the guard, who were ordered to permit none but couriers and ordnance wagons to cross. The night of the 10th was, indeed, a gloomy one, and the myriad camp fires of the enemy, seen through the rain and mist in the woods in front of our position, by no means reassured our disheartened forces. At ten o'clock at night a council of war was held, of which Forrest, Jackson, Crosby, and Van Dorn were members, and the plan of escape adopted. In the morning our troops were ordered to make an unusual noise and keep up a cheering, while buglers were ordered to sound "reveille" and "forward" from many more points than where we had troops.

At 8 o'clock A.M. the enemy's battery upon the left of the turnpike opened fire upon King's battery, and gave that officer the much desired opportunity to return fire and convince them of his whereabouts just before his battery was withdrawn. Several shells which be had taken from the battle-field of Spring Hill were returned rapidly to the enemy, to whom they originally belonged, and our battery was then taken to the ferry and crossed by the indefatigable exertions of the captain, and the horses swam across. Upon the previous evening the Texas brigade sent word that they were upon the same side of Rutherford's creek as the enemy, and were unable to cross. The next thing heard of them, the enemy commenced advancing, and it is said with a smile, that to see the Texas Rangers crossing the creek one would have thought that they were crossing a turnpike instead of a rapid stream, so hastily did they effect it. At 10 o'clock. A.M., this brigade and Crosby's, which had been upon our left, were withdrawn through the woods, so as to avoid being seen by the Yankee lookouts, leaving their usual outposts behind, and started upon a by-road running along the Duck river in a northeasterly direction. Forrest's command were upon another road running parallel with it, and Armstrong brought up the rear, with Van Dorn and staff, and escort immediately in the rear of Crosby, so as to be in a position to direct movements either in front or rear in case the enemy attempted to intercept us. Every thing was now under way, the artillery and wagon trains having been crossed upon the ferry, and the animals swam, the position completely evacuated, save by the outposts and pickets, who were directed to withdraw so soon as we got fairly under way, or the enemy should advance.

Jackson's Strategy

On the 16th of June, 1862, Jackson sent a note to Colonel Mumford, who had succeeded Ashby in command of the cavalry, and held the front toward Harrisonburg, to "meet him at eleven that night, at the head of the street at Mount Crawford, and not to ask for him or anybody." Mount Crawford is a small village on the valley turnpike, about eight or ten miles from Port Republic, and the same distance from Harrisonburg. Colonel Mumford received the note, set out alone, and, at the appointed hour, entered Mount Crawford, which, at that late hour of the night, looked dark and deserted. The moon was shining, however, and at the head of the street, in the middle of the highway, a solitary figure on horseback awaited him, motionless and in silence. The hand of the figure went up to his cap, and in the curt, familiar tones of Jackson, came the words:

"Ah, colonel! here you are. What news from the front?"

"All quiet, general," replied Colonel Mumford.

"Good! Now I wish you to produce upon the enemy the impression that I am going to advance."

And Jackson gave his orders in detail, after which the figures parted, and went different ways—Jackson back to Port Republic; Colonel Mumford to Harrisonburg. The following is the manner in which Colonel Mumford carried out his orders:

At Harrisonburg were a number of Federal surgeons, who had come with twenty-five or thirty ambulances to carry away the wounded officers and men who had been abandoned at that point by General Fremont in his retreat. These were informed by Colonel Mumford, that before he could give them permission to do so, he must ascertain the wishes of General Jackson; and, with this reply, he left them, to carry out the rest of the scheme. There was attached to his command, as an independent, a well-known gentleman of that region named William Gilmer; and to this gentleman, ever ready for a good, practical joke, was entrusted the execution of the plot. The Federal surgeons occupied an apartment next to the room used by Colonel Mumford for his headquarters, and only a thin partition divided them. Every word uttered in one room, could be heard in the other, and this fact was well known to Colonel Mumford, who gave Mr. Gilmer his instructions in a loud tone, dispatched him apparently to General Jackson, and then awaited the issue of his scheme.

Some hours having elapsed since they had been assured that General Jackson's wishes would be ascertained, the surgeons, all at once, heard a courier mounting the stairs, his spurs and sabre clanking as he ascended. They moved quickly to the partition, and placed their ears close to the cracks—as it was expected they would. The courier entered, the surgeons bent lower, and determined not to lose a word.

"Well," said Colonel Mumford, in a voice, which he knew could be heard, "what does General Jackson say?"

"He told me to tell you," replied Mr. Gilmer, in his loud and sonorous voice, "that the wounded Yankees are not to be taken away, and the surgeons are to be sent back with the message that he can take care of their wounded in their own hospitals. He is coming right on himself with heavy reinforcements. Whiting's division is up, Hood is coming. The whole road from here to Staunton is perfectly lined with troops, and so crowded that I could hardly ride along."

Such was the highly important dialogue which the Federal surgeons, listening with breathless attention, overheard. When Colonel Mumford sent for them, every man was on the other side of the room from the partition. They were ushered in, and briefly informed that they could return with their ambulances, that General Jackson had instructed him to say, that their wounded would be cared for in the Confederate hospitals.

The surgeons returned without delay, communicated the important intelligence they had overheard to General Fremont, and that night the whole Federal army fell back to Strasburg, where they began to intrench against the anticipated attack:

Jackson was, meanwhile, on his way to the Chickahominy. —*Cooke's Life of Jackson.*

A Thrilling Event

On Thursday, September 10, 1863, while General Forrest was at Lafayette, Georgia, he was ordered to Ringgold for the purpose of checking the enemy, reported to be marching in large force in that direction. Picking up about four hundred of his command, he marched off with all the promptitude of his ardent and enthusiastic nature. Here he found Vancleve's corps, consisting of seventeen thousand infantry and cavalry. Skirmishing immediately commenced, General Forrest fighting them at every step, as he slowly fell back. For two days did the unequal conflict continue, and notwithstanding the disparity of numbers, the loss on either side was about the same. General Forrest retired to Tunnel Hill about four o'clock, and in an hour the enemy was in sight, when one of the most gallant and thrilling incidents of the war occurred. The enemy's advancing column marched on—right on—and the cloud of dust, and the huge paraphernalia which they displayed, made them look indeed "terrible as an army with banners." On reaching the apex of the hill, a short pause was perceptible; but skirmishers being thrown out on the right and left, on they came. In every ambush, behind every knoll, and house, and tree, could be seen a blue coat, slyly, cautiously sneaking up like a hungry wolf in search of its prey. General Forrest leveled his trusty gun at the nearest one. The smoke from his gun seemed only to exasperate the infuriated foe, and to inspire them with anxiety either to capture or destroy the small but defiant squad of Confederates, and for this purpose a hundred guns opened upon them, while a dozen Yankees rushed across the railroad for the purpose of getting still closer. As they crossed the track, General Forrest looked still farther up, and he saw a couple of Confederate soldiers coming down the road, unaware of the approach of the enemy, and the immediate danger that surrounded them. The impudence of the Yankees that had crossed the railroad and were seen crawling in the woods, together with the peril that surrounded the two Confederate soldiers approaching, was more than General Forrest could stand. Hastily calling to his side five of his escort, he told them that his imperiled soldiers must be rescued, and that the insolent squad that had crossed the road must be captured. With coolness and self-possession, but with a loud and cheering shout, he ordered his little squad to the charge. In the midst of the iron hail that rained upon them, they rushed on. Every man forgot his own danger. The soldier stooped over his musket, or leaned upon his horse, absorbed in the scene. Dressed in a huge duster, General Forrest, as he dashed on in his fierce purpose, looked infernal. There was a sudden pause; then their heads were curtained in by the wreathing smoke of their own guns. The Yankees were seen retreating back across the road, and the Confederate soldiers rescued from death. From the hillside, a volley of musketry was now poured upon the small squad. Having accomplished their purpose, they turned to retreat, but three of the seven were wounded. A ball struck General Forrest near the spine, within an inch of the wound he received at Shiloh, inflicting a painful but not dangerous, wound; while two of his escort were wounded—one in the back of the head, the other in the arm.

Stuart's Ride around McClellan

It being determined upon to penetrate the enemy's lines, and make a full and thorough reconnoissance of their position and strength, General J. E. B. Stuart ordered the first (Colonel Fitz Hugh Lee), ninth (Colonel F. H. Fitz Hugh Lee), and fourth Virginia cavalry (Lieutenant Gardiner commanding), to hold themselves in readiness. These regiments, however, did not turn out more than half their usual strength; the fourth not having more than four companies in the field. The Jeff. Davis Troop were also incorporated in the detail, as also two pieces of Stuart's Flying Artillery—a twelve-pound howitzer and a six-pound English rifle piece—the whole force not numbering more than one thousand four hundred men, if even the total reached that number. On Thursday, at dawn, this column proceeded down the Charlottesville (Brook Church) turnpike, and had gone some distance without molestation, when the vanguard overtook some eight or ten adventurous Negroes journeying rapidly toward the Federal lines. These runaways were secured and sent to the rear, and as night was drawing near, pickets and videttes were placed, and the column camped for the night near Ashland, it being considered imprudent to progress further. Toward morning signal rockets were fired, and answered by our troops at the lines far to the rear, and as soon as day broke the cavalry column proceeded on its march. Carefully and cautiously journeying, the Federal lines were penetrated, when horse-pickets, discovering our videttes advancing, the videttes hastily retired, according to orders, upon the main body, concealed by woods and a turn in the road. Being near Hanover Court House, the Federals were wont to proceed thither daily for forage, as a captured picket informed the men, but on this occasion had orders to proceed as far as possible toward Richmond. It being thought possible to capture the whole detachment, dispositions were accordingly made, but upon the appearance of the second squadron of the ninth (composed of the Caroline Dragoons, Captain Swan, and Lee's Light Horse, Lieutenant Hungerford commanding), under command of Captain Swan, the enemy's outpost hastily galloped back, and their main body took to flight, Captain Swan's squadron dashing after them down the road, making a splendid race of two miles at a killing pace. Having proceeded thus far, and near the Court House, the enemy seemed to have been reinforced, and made a stand on the road, and in fields to the right and left of it. Thinking to flank them, and capture the whole force, Colonel Lee, of the first, proceeded round their position to cut off retreat, but the, movement occupying longer time than desired, the second squadron of the ninth prepared to charge. And as they trotted toward the enemy, the Federal leader could be plainly seen and heard haranguing his troops, urging them to act like men, and stand. His eloquence was of no avail, and as the second squadron of the ninth increased their pace and came near to them with flashing sabres, the Federal officer galloped toward them, thinking his men would follow. Not so, however, and as he wheeled his horse back again, our men were upon him; he fell, shot in the head; his men gave a feeble volley with pistols, and scampered off the field in ludicrous style, leaving killed and wounded behind, and many prisoners. Capturing outposts and pickets in great number, and overtaking wearied horsemen, it was ascertained that the force engaged were squadrons of the fifth United

States regulars, who had seen hard service in Texas and the Indian countries, and had never refused a charge before. Their camps were reported to be adjacent, and proceeding thither every thing was destroyed and put to the torch.

From several captured in and about these camps it was ascertained that several regiments were waiting for our advance up the road, and as their pickets were stronger and more numerous than usual, it was deemed advisable to halt. The second squadron of the ninth were dismounted and thrown to the front (on the skirts of a wood, to the right and left of the road), to act as skirmishers and defend the artillery, which was moved up and took position commanding a bridge in the hollow—the enemy's force and ours being screened from view by rising ground at either end of the road—our force being farther from the front than theirs. Appearing in considerable force, the enemy advanced in admirable order, but suddenly facing to the right about were quickly retreating, when the dismounted men poured a galling volley into them, emptying many saddles and causing much confusion. Reforming, they were a second time reënforced and came on to the charge up the rise in gallant style. Burning to distinguish themselves, the third squadron of the ninth (composed of the Essex Light Dragoons, Captain Latane, and Mercer County Cavalry, Lieutenant Walker commanding), under command of Captain Latane, had received orders to charge the advancing enemy, and putting spurs to their steeds dashed gallantly along the road, the brave Latane fifteen paces in front! "Cut and thrust," shouted the Federal commander. "On to them, boys," yelled Latane, and the meeting squadrons dashed in full shock together. The front men of either column were unhorsed, and the fight became instantly hot and bloody. Captain Latane singled out the Federal commander, and cut off the officer's hat close to his head; but the Federal, dodging the cut, rode past, and as he did so discharged two revolver loads at Latane, killing him instantly. The enemy rapidly giving way, our men shouted in triumph, and cut right and left, pistoling the foe with frightful accuracy and havoc; and seeing the Federal commander in pursuit of Adjutant Robins (who was himself in pursuit of an enemy), a private dashed after him and clove his skull in twain. The battle between these rival squadrons, though of short duration, was fierce and sanguinary in the extreme. Scattered in all directions and, apparently paralyzed by the relentless fury of this corps, the enemy fled in every direction, leaving killed, wounded, horses, accoutrements, etc., in profusion upon the dusty roads. Successful pursuit being impossible, their camps were visited and destroyed, wagons on the road were overtaken and burned, and the entire route from Ashland, by Hanover Court House and Old Church to Station No. 22 (Tunstall's, we believe), on the York River railroad, was naught else but a continuous scene of triumph and destruction. Commissary and quartermasters' stores were seized and burned at every turn, prisoners and horses were captured and sent to the rear, and by the time of their arrival at the railway station more than a million of dollars of Federal property must have been captured and destroyed, beside scores of prisoners riding in the rear.

Upon approaching the railroad, cars were heard advancing, and the whistle sounded. By orders, every man was instantly dismounted and ranged beside the track. Again the whistle blew, and thinking the force to be a friendly one, perhaps, the steam was stopped, when the Carolina troop, opening fire, disclosed the ruse—and putting on steam again, on sped the train toward the Chickahominy, and despite heavy logs placed on the track made good its escape; but the carriages, being but uncovered freight-trucks, and having soldiers on them, the slaughter that ensued was frightful. Many of the enemy jumped from the train and were afterward captured or killed, to the number of twenty or more. The engineer was shot dead by Lieutenant Robinson.

Still adding to their conquest at every step, a detachment was immediately sent to the White House, on the Pamunkey; and, discovering four large transports moored there, and some hundred wagons or more with teams, etc., in a wagon yard, all these were instantly seized, to the great fright and astonishment of the Federals, and the torch immediately applied to all things combustible. One of the transports escaped, and floated down the river. The contents of the other three were chiefly valuable commissary and quartermaster's stores, vast quantities of army clothing, grain, fruits, and sutlers' stores. Tempting as they were, all things were laid in ashes—the horses led off, and prisoners secured. Thinking that the enemy would send out an overwhelming force in pursuit, an unlikely route was selected, and the whole command proceeded in triumph to NewKent Court House. New Kent Court House being the rendezvous, the fourth squadron of the ninth, under command of Captain Knight (consisting of the Lunenburg troop and Lancaster cavalry), having burned the transports and wagons, joined the column on its route thither. "Hab we got Richmon' yet, boss?"

asks a slave in a corn-field, turning up his eyeballs in admiration of the "Maryland cavalry"; "well, if we ain't we soon shall, for McClellan and our boys is sure to fotch him." Others, however, proved keener-sighted than the Negro. Women run to the wayside cottage-door; a flush of triumph mantles their cheek; and, as the eye kindles into a flame of admiration, tears trickle down, and "God bless you, boys!" is all they say. Now and then an old man is met by the wayside, pensive and sad, but, recognizing the horsemen, he stops, looks astonished, and throws up his hat for the "Maryland cavalry" just arrived. Others wave handkerchiefs. It is useless to deceive them, for woman instinctively discovers friends or foes at sight. "Our cavalry here!" exclaim they, in wonder, and with hands clasped upon their breast, mutely but eloquently gaze. "Take care, men, take care! Heaven bless you, but take care—the enemy are everywhere!" Such is their gentle warning, given to the weary, dusty, chivalric column dashing through the country in the enemy's rear.

The advance guard having reached New Kent, and found an extensive sutler's establishment, some dismount and enter. Every description of goods that taste and fancy might require, are found in profusion here. Clothes of all descriptions and qualities, cutlery, sabres, pistols, shoes, preserves, conserves, boots, stationery, wines, liquors, tobacco, cigars, tea, coffee, sugar, tapioca, macaroni, champagne, sherry, and burgundy, in great quantity—in fine, all that men could buy for money was there discovered, while round the store lolled Federal soldiers, and the proprietor eloquently holding forth upon McClellan's wonderful genius as a commander and the speedy subjugation of the rebels. Our wearied horsemen called for refreshments, which the sutler handed to the "Maryland cavalry" with great alacrity. But when pay was demanded, our troopers roared with laughter, told the proprietor who they were, and, much to his surprise and indignation, pronounced them all prisoners of war! As the other troops arrived, it was found that a magnificent Federal ambulance had been captured on the route, containing very valuable medical stores. The vehicle and contents were burned where overtaken—the driver, good-looking well-dressed doctor and companions being accommodated with a mule each, and were at the moment to be found among nearly two hundred other nondescripts, sailors, soldiers, teamsters, Negroes, sutlers, etc. etc., in the motley cavalcade at the rear. Helping themselves liberally to all the store afforded, our troops remained at the sutler's until near midnight (Friday), when, being comparatively refreshed, and all present, the head of the column was turned toward the Chickahominy and home. Champagne, we are told, flowed freely while any remained—wines, liquors, and cigars, were all consumed. Yankee products of every description were appropriated without much ado; and with light hearts all quietly journeyed by a lonely road near to the main body of the enemy, and a little before dawn of Saturday were on Chickahominy's bank ready to cross.

Being far below all the bridges, and where deep water flows, they knew not how or where to cross! Here was an awful situation for our gallant band! Directed to Blind Ford, it was fifteen feet deep! The enemy had blocked up all the main roads, and had thousands scouring the country; eager to entrap or slaughter them!—but two miles from McClellan's quarters, within sound of their horse pickets—and without means to cross! Quietly taking precautions against all surprise, strict silence being enjoined upon the prisoners, first one horseman plunged into the flood, and then another, at different points—all too deep; no ford discoverable, no bridge! The horses, it was thought, would follow each other, and swim the stream—it was tried, and the horses carried away by the current! Breaking into small parties, the cavalrymen swam and reswam the river with their horses, and when some fifty or more had been landed, a strange but friendly voice whispered in the dark—"The old bridge is a few yards higher up—it can be mended!" 'Twas found, and mended it could be! Quietly working, tree after tree was felled, earth, and twigs, and branches, were carried and piled upon the main props,—old logs were rolled and pitched across the stream, yet after long and weary labor the bridge was built, and the long and silent procession of cavalry, artillery, prisoners, and spoils, safely and quietly passed this frail impromptu bridge, scarcely any sounds being heard but the rush of waters beneath. Once across, and in the swamp, all was industry and expedition. Artillery axles sunk low in the mire—ten Yankee horses were hitched to each piece, and as the first rays of morning crimsoned the tree tops, the long line rapidly sought the shade of woods away from the Federal lines. Yet our troops had not proceeded far when the advance were halted. "Who comes there!" cried the Federal horseman in the swamp; "Who goes there?" calls another, and quicker than thought our advance guard (by order) dashed away into the open ground; the Federals fire half a dozen shots, and rush in pursuit. Into the thicket some half dozen Federal horsemen dart after our men, and quicker than lightning are surrounded and prisoners.

Once more within our lines, all went merry as a marriage bell. Quickly the dirty, weary, gallant band sped along the Charles City road, dawn revealed them to our pickets, and they entered our camps faint and famished, but the noblest band of heroes that ever bestrode a charger, or drew a battle blade for their birthright as freemen.

The Mountain Partisan

I.

My rifle, pouch, and knife!
    My steed! and then we part!
One loving kiss, dear wife,
    One press of heart to heart!
Cling to me yet awhile,
    But stay the sob, the tear!
Smile—only try to smile—
    And I go without a fear.

II.

Our little cradled boy,
    He sleeps—and in his sleep,
Smiles with an angel joy,
    Which tells thee not to weep.
I'll kneel beside; and kiss—
    He will not wake the while,
Thus dreaming of the bliss,
    That bids thee, too, to smile.

III.

Think not, dear wife, I go,
    With a light thought at my heart;

'Tis a pang akin to woe,
    That fills me as we part;
But when the wolf was heard
    To howl around our cot,
Thou know'st, dear mother-bird,
    I slew him on the spot!

IV.

Aye, panther, wolf, and bear,
    Have perished 'neath my knife;
Why tremble, then, with fear,
    When now I go, my wife?
Shall I not keep the peace,
    That made our cottage dear;
And 'till these wolf-curs cease
    Shall I be housing here?

V.

One loving kiss, dear wife,
    One press of heart to heart;
Then for the deadliest strife,
    Of freedom I depart,
I were of little worth,
    Were these Yankee wolves left free
To ravage 'round our hearth;
    And bring one grief to thee!

VI.

God's blessing on thee, wife,
    God's blessing on the young;
Pray for me through the strife,
    Aid teach our infant's tongue—
Whatever befalls in fight,
    I shall be true to thee—
To the home of our delight—
    To my people of the free.

Anecdote of Mosby

One of the correspondents of the *New York Herald* tells the following story of this daring officer:

At a town, which shall be nameless, that we passed through, I was told the following circumstance about Mosby, which, as it has never found its way into print, I think worth giving, as illustrative of the bold and reckless audacity of the man. A squad of Northern cavalry got on the track of him and his men, pursued him into the village, captured some of his men, and hoped to take him captive. Guards were placed at the entrance of every street, and the search for Mosby began—a search up-stairs, down-stairs, in garret, in cellar, in beds, in closets, wardrobes, and every imaginable cuddy-hole big enough to hold a man. Mosby was not to be found. In quick time he had changed his military dress for the coarse spun habiliments of a non-combatant, and, while the search was progressing, passed for one of the curious throng of street lookers-on. He took ninety-nine chances out of a hundred of being captured, and fortune favored him, as it always does the brave. It is this bravery and this good fortune that make him and his exploits the theme of every tongue, and particularly tongues feminine, which, when they get to wagging about him, wag with a sneering sauciness, a vindictive exultation, indicating that the extent of their joy is only surpassed by one thing—the unending prolongation of their tongues.

Innocent for Once

"One night late in the fall of 1864," says an ex-cavalry officer of the C.S.A., "while our command was along the Opequan, a stampede was made among some horses, which ran to a point where some dismounted troopers were sleeping. Among them was a lieutenant, who had but recently received a severe reprimand from McCausland for a false alarm given by him. Hearing the maddened rush of the riderless horses, the gallant lieutenant thought a charge was being made by those fierce horsemen from Western Virginia, who, in Federal pay, shed such lustre upon Yankee arms. He did not wait till their flashing swords were over his head, but plunging into a creek just above a mill pond, he reached the opposite bank in safety, and was climbing the hill above it when a voice reached from the deserted shore, "Come back, lieutenant, it is nothing but some loose horses charging around." With teeth chattering with excitement and with cold from his recent bath, the youthful warrior shouted back, "Well, McCausland can't say *I* got up this infernal stampede, any way he can fix it."

A Natural Movement

One night General Adams, of Tennessee, on returning to camp, was halted by a sentinel on an outpost. After giving the countersign, and telling the sentinel who he was, he got to questioning the man about his duties as a sentry.

General.—"If you saw two men coming toward your post, what would you do?"

Sentinel.—"I would halt them, and then direct one to advance and give the countersign."

General.—"If three or four should approach, what would you do?"

Sentinel.—"I would do the same thing."

General.—"Suppose you saw a dozen coming, what then?"

Sentinel.—"I would do the same thing."

General.—"Suppose a whole regiment should come, what then?"

Sentinel.—"I would form a line as quick as possible."

General.—"What kind of a line could you form by yourself?"

Sentinel.—"A *bee* line for camp."

A Raid into Kentucky

The following letter appeared in the "*Knoxville* (Tenn.). *Register*," in August, 1863:

I have just been looking over a file of late papers. There is a perfect dearth of news. And thinking that you was rather "hard up" for something to fill up your columns, I have concluded to "kill the time" this morning in giving you an account of a recent raid into Kentucky by myself, accompanied by a fellow-soldier—the renowned Sergant S———s, of this command. And should I enter into details, and be rather prolific in statements, you must attribute it to the fact that I am in an excellent good humor this morning, and believe that you are most terrible out, on account of having no good reading—(dead gods of Greece! spare this communication!—) for your otherwise respectable paper! No offence intended, sirs!

We arrived here last Sabbath—I mean we, of Colonel Folks' cavalry—formerly seventh North Carolina battalion—the sixty-fifth regiment, now promoted to the sixty-sixth North Carolina regiment, on account of consolidation with Major Baird's fifth North Carolina battalion of cavalry.

Preparations were made on the evening of 18th inst., for a scout somewhere, with all the effective men of the command, to be accompanied by a detachment of infantry forces stationed here. Not being aware of the fact that the scout designed moving before next morning, at nightfall I felt so strongly wooed by Somnus that I "drew the drapery of my couch (a blanket and some hay) about me, and laid down to pleasant dreams." What those dreams were, I cannot now recollect, any more than that I was in a strange country, on a bed of sickness and suffering; and just as I was about giving over all hope of ever recovering, an angel came to me (she was my sweetheart, or rather one of them), and at the magical touch of her soft hand, the spirit of suffering was subdued—I was well, and would have arisen to kiss the soft hand of my love had I not found myself just at the moment looking up at our cook, who stood by me, with the admonition—"Captain, you had better get up for breakfast, the sun's away up yonder!"

"Where is the major?" I inquired, rubbing my eyes, and almost secretly cursing the cook because I didn't get that kiss.

"Oh! he went off with the scout last night at eleven o'clock, and left you asleep!"

"That's too bad, but I am going anyhow"; and as soon as breakfast was over we were moving.

Arriving at the headquarters of Colonel P———, commanding here, he entered a protest against my going alone, and assured me that we would certainly be either killed or captured by bushwhackers, if not Yankees.

I reflected that I had been in twenty conflicts, fights, and battles with the enemy—"are you certain that you have been in that many?"

Yes; let me count them: There's Vienna—ah, Vienna! most memorable of all memorable days—the first fight, first victory, the first blood, and my first prisoner! Then Drainsville, Pollocksville, North Carolina, three days during the memorable "seven" around Richmond, Fairfax, and Flint Hill, Virginia, Arbania, Crampton's (?) Gap, Middletown, Brownsburg, Boonsboro', Sharpsburg, and Williamsport, Maryland, then Barbee's X roads, Gaines' X roads (where I killed my first man, certainly, and either killed or wounded another the same day), then Anisville (where I killed another man and two horses after a duel's fight of an hour's duration), and last, but not least, was the interesting little fight at Duggin's Ferry, Carter county, Tennessee, with the bushwhackers. Here was the scene of our first *hanging*!

"But this is only nineteen times! You said you had been in twenty fights?" Well—perhaps I have omitted one time—when I skedaddled. Never mind that now—egotism and blowing your own trumpet enough for once. I had concluded that after having passed through *there,* I should not be deterred from taking a little raid into Kentucky, just to gratify my own curiosity, and to learn something about "Uncle Sam's nephews" over the line. So "nothing daunted nought afraid," we sat out, and by one P.M., were in the valley of Clear Fork river—having passed through the series of mountains without greeting a solitary bushwhacker.

The first event worthy of record in these pages occurred just over the civilized borders. An innocent looking damsel, aged, I should suppose, thirteen years, was conveying a quantity of unthreshed rye upon a colt of some two summers, which was being led by a lady of matronly appearance. The *novelty* of the thing consisted in the mother's *face,* and the *masculine attitude* of the aforesaid damsel on the horse. The mother looked (to use my friend Smith's language), like *she didn't care a d——n.* (It wasn't *we* that swore.) I passed them; giving an officer's salute—that is, by elevating my hand, etc.—which the good woman returned by elevating her *nose.*

Eight miles down the valley, I learned that a scouting party of Yankees had passed up in the evening before, and returning that morning, were only some three or four miles in advance of the force that had preceded us during the night. At four o'clock in the evening, I met a gentleman just from town. I had a long interview with him, which proved of interest. From him I learned a very significant and remarkable fact. Our scout left Big Creek Gap at eleven o'clock during the night of the 18th, *and by eleven o'clock next morning, the enemy, in Williamsburg, thirty-five miles distant, had information of it!*

"The rebels are coming! The rebels are coming!" was shouted through the streets; and then came skedaddling and rushing to and fro. Business houses closed up—valuables were hid—doubtful characters sought abodes of safety, and the blue columns of the enemy's cavalry, stationed beyond the river, came pouring over in terrible haste to meet the advancing host— a handful of jolly rebels.

But the rebels were gone—where? A convenient pathway stretched from a point on the main highway, six miles from Williamsburg, and led across the Patterson mountain, in the direction of Loudon—and this the rebels had taken, and were several hours in advance of their enemy when they started in pursuit. I arrived at this diverging path about five in the evening—the main force had passed on about one.

Now for a budget of incidents.

We had stopped a young gentleman of a countenance indicating great anxiety, and a footstep indicating greater haste.

"Well, my friend, are you just from town?" I inquired.

"Yes, sir."

"And what have you in your sack there?"

"Only a little coffee, sir."

"Eh? Coffee? Coffee, did you say? And how much?"

"Yes, sir; coffee—only four pounds?"

"Well, sir, *it's the very thing I want.* I am very fond of good coffee, and we can't get it over in Dixie—what do you pay for it?"

"Fifty cents, sir" (anxieties increasing).

"That's cheap. I believe I'll take what you have! Sergeant, can you carry it? Have you two dollars in change?"

Just here the anxieties of our strange friend seemed rapidly, fearfully on the increase.

"Don't be alarmed, sir," I remarked, "we will *pay* you for your coffee; and you shall not be hurt, if we are rebels."

"Can't you pay a little more than that, sir—it's very scarce, and hard to get, and I had rather not let this go. My wife is *sick,* and I have walked all the way to town for a little coffee for her" (considerably troubled).

"I am *sick,* too, and must have the coffee; hand it up."

"Well, mister, I think that hard. Can't you—but yonder comes Mr. John Jones, he will tell—"

"Who is Mr. John Jones?" I inquired.

"Well—but here he is—"

"How d'y do, boys" (I supposed this was Mr. Joshua Jones that spoke).

"Good evening, gentlemen." (There were two of them; and the Mr. Jones was mounted on a magnificent horse that immediately "struck my fancy," and I forgot the coffee.) He, Mr. Jones, spoke with nervousness and troubled emotion:

"Boys; I'll swear you had better be getting away from here, the Yankees are right down the road!"

"They are! Would you sell that horse? What would you ask?"

"Yes, sir; a hundred and fifty dollars."

"Will you let me try him?"

"Yes, sir; but I'll swear you had better be taking care of yourselves, the Yankees have just played h——ll with some of your men down here."

"Eh? what's the matter, what's up?"

"Why, by G——d, they've killed one of your men; shot him all to pieces, shot his chin off, shot six holes through him, and have got two others, and taking them on to—"

"What's become of the rest of our men; have you seen them?"

"No; they took out this road, here, you see (pointing to the pathway mentioned), and the Yankees are after them now; some of them's right down the road, and I'll swear, boys, you had better get out of here just as fast as you can—*make tracks!*"

"Well, let's trade about that horse first; I'm interested about him just now."

I tried him; found him "all right," and very desirable; oh how I did want him! "I've pressed me a splendid horse," I confidently whispered as I rode along in trying his speed. "He is really superb!"

"Well, sir, I'll take your horse," I observed as I returned. "You'll take Southern money, I suppose?"

"No, sir! I've got more now than I know what to do with. I'll take State money that's good, or gold or silver, or 'greenbacks'; have you got any of them?"

"Yes; some of Jeff Davis' 'greenbacks,' which I will pay you."

"Can't take them, sir; can't take them, sir. Maybe you'd like a little whisky? I've got some in a little 'tickler,' here; just got it in town as the Yankees were coming over the river."

"Yes, I'll take a little, and much obliged to you; but I want that horse."

We drank with Mr. Jones, and left his bottle pretty low. Mr. Jones then mounted his magnificent horse, and would ride away—I insisting on a trade. I tried to swap, I tried to beg, I tried to press, but the good old man would not listen to any thing; and all he seemed to think about was for us to "get away from there." I could not prevail on him to surrender the horse, and so he rode abruptly away, wishing us a "good evening, boys."

"That's too bad, S——," I remarked, "we ought to have that horse."

"Yes; and you ought to have made him leave the tickler of whisky with us. Hello, mister, won't you let us have the balance of the whisky, *just to remember you?*"

And the sergeant shouted as loudly as his throat would let him; the response was:

"You'd better get away from here!"

"Never mind, S——, you've got too much whisky already, for your good; let us go. Where's the coffee?"

"Good heavens, captain! didn't you see the fellow running up through the woods as soon as old Jones came up. You never saw a lizard or a wild turkey make tracks through the brush faster. He just *humped* himself."

"Got neither horse nor coffee! Let's halt old Jones yet and have the horse or die."

"Agreed!" and we went dashing out the road after him.

"Stop! Mr. Jones—stop!" but he raised his elbows and put the hickory to his fine gray, and away he went—we after.

"Halt! halt!" I cried. "Halt! or I shall fire on you."

I drew my pistol, and Mr. Jones' comrade took up, and soon thereafter I was beside the old gentleman very indignant, and told him, in very sharp tones, that I must have that horse.

"Come—dismount, quickly, or I shall *lift* you off," one of us said.

The old man was very obstinate and determined. He called very loud for "John!" "Oh, John!" We were then at a house here I had seen some men that evening, and I guessed rightly that there were bushwhackers there.

So I pulled down my *valor,* and concluded the horse would not do for cavalry service anyhow, and that Mr. Jones might keep him. I did not want him—he was a sour grape! We expected to be captured anyhow; and I knew, if ever caught with the pressed horse, that our doom would be the more terrible. We left them and rode back rapidly, and took the trail of Major —— in the direction of Patterson. Just as we passed into the path we met two women running rapidly, with frightened countenances, who told us the "Yankees were fixing for us right down the road, and they thanked God they would get us!"

"Captain, I think we had better ride up as fast as possible," said the sergeant.

"Come, Charley, we'll lope a mile or so, so that old Jones, and John, the bushwhacker, will not overtake us."

Crossing "Clear Fork" river five miles from town (Williamsburg), we met a young man with a haversack on, accompanied by three young ladies. I supposed him to be a soldier, and asked him where he belonged. He remarked that they had been to school, and that his haversack was used for carrying his books in. The girls corroborated his statements. Two of them appearing *interesting,* I remarked to the sergeant that he was "luck in leisure," and that if the young ladies had no objection we would stop, dismount, and talk awhile. I had a "good time" for nearly an hour. I made the discovery that one of the ladies was a young widow. I have a passionate fondness (or *particular love*) for widows, and have had two adventures in addressing that class of mourning unfortunates. But of all honest enemies I have ever met, this last widow acquaintance proved the most frank and sincere. She professed to have seen me before, without any doubt. She *couldn't be deceived* in "that face!" She had looked into "that eye" before! We were much fatigued, and hungry, so were our horses. Expressing this fact, she remarked that if we would stay (the dwelling was just inside the rail fencing) we should have supper, and have our horses fed on the best they had.

"Well, we will have to remain some place until morning. We can't follow the trail of our forces through the mountains to-night; the Yankees are in our front anyhow, and we will never turn back. Now, if we consent to remain, and the Yankees come to the house, what will you do? Will you betray us, or will you conceal us and let them pass on?"

"Sir," said she, "we will treat you kindly, but if the Union soldiers come, *I should betray you!* Don't you think it would be my duty? I am not a secessionist."

"Look me in the face. You would betray us, would you?"

"I certainly will."

"Captain, I think we had better *travel* anyhow," the sergeant remarked.

He was becoming very restless, and considerably alarmed. They had told us of the horrible death one of our comrades had met, and the fate of two others certain, and of the force in pursuit of the remainder; and told us we would certainly be bushwhacked by *some* persons, if they knew we were on the road.

The honesty of the widow in assuring me that she would betray us, saved us, as will be shown soon. I remarked that we would ride on, and that it being "bad luck to turn back," we would push on through the mountains, and that *I knew the road* (but I *didn't*; and so the moralist may philosophize on the sin, if I *lied*).

A mile's travel brought us into a small mountain, and it was determined that we conceal ourselves off the road some distance, rest, and feed our horses on the corn rations we were carrying with us; and then, in the darkness of the night, make the effort to escape by retracing our steps. We came very near being discovered by making our retreat too near an obscure house in the mountain dell. The noise of the geese gave the alarm, and "we changed our base." I reflect now that the cackling of a goose once saved Rome—perhaps it saved *me!*

Ah, many, many were the thoughts that came to me as we sat beneath a huge maple tree in our lonely, wild retreat! I felt a deeper interest just then in my life than I have ever known before. Why? There was a vision that flitted before my silent memory—a dream of *her love* laid its touch upon my heart, and I slumbered in hesitation and despondency no longer. The last night's dream of the angel had now its interpretation! The soft hand that once lay gently in mine, as we fixed the day of our nuptials (not "June" this time, my friend Tease!) like a magical wand drove away all doubts and fears; and infusing new courage and new hope into my spirit, *I vowed I never would be taken;* but must return, despite all the schemes the enemy might devise for my capture—*must* return for the fulfillment of our vows, and the consummation of our happiness—if for nothing else.

If we perished at the hands of civilization, "bushwhackers"—Who would ever know my doom? Could *she* hear it? If we surrendered as prisoners, the walls of the despot's bastile might encircle me for months and years, and *that* happy day roll around with iron fetters and chains binding me instead of

"Hymen's silver strings!"

Woman's love always ennobles and nerves the hearts of men of soul—their vows to make us happy come to us in the hour of peril and care, and scattering light, and incense, and flowers, around our pathway, strengthen the spirit, and prompt deeds that otherwise only oblivion might have claimed.

Night and darkness had encircled the dreary waste of mountains around, when we emerged from our hiding places and started on our return. We had nearly reached the house where we had spent an hour with the ladies that afternoon, when the clatter of horses' hoofs on the road ahead warned us of danger. We withdrew into a dark thicket some distance off to let any troops or persons passing go on without observing us. We dismounted that we might keep our horses the more quiet—but I have never known mosquitoes to mark men and horses half so badly in my life.

Discovering that the horses had been stopped just opposite the house, and hearing much animated conversation, I gave the horses to the sergeant, with orders to keep as still as death, while I advanced as far as prudent to reconnoitre, and ascertain what was the situation.

I approached unobserved to within thirty or forty yards; and taking my position in a clump of bushes, heard every word of the conversation going on. It seemed there was a party in pursuit of us, whether they were regular Yankees, or "home guards," I could not tell. Stopping at the house the same woman had come out, and such another clattering of tongues never was heard by a doomed eavesdropper. A complete "report" was given of their interview with the "rebel captain, and the man with him." Oh! what a nice time they are going to have catching us and bushwhacking us. Yes, they talked with the very identical phrase, "bushwhack,"—they were going to bushwhack us.

For an hour their jabber was ceaseless and so confused in its element that won over I couldn't recollect a single thing, only that our "doom was fixed." It was enough for me to know this much, and to devise plans to thwart theirs.

They concluded, however, at the urgent advice of an old man who came out and counseled in their schemes, "to send off and get some more of the boys—it would do no harm— but make the thing sure."

So off rode part of the crowd in the direction of town, and left the remainder. This was my time for action, I felt. I returned as promptly as practicable to the sergeant holding the horses, who had overheard enough of the conversation to bring on a *chill*. He was very taciturn and greatly excited.

I made known my plans and told him he must obey my order, and I would get out of there yet.

"Captain, let's don't go that way, let's pull down the fence and go through the fields and woods, and get across the river into the road," he entreated.

But like a good general, I had concluded my plans, and resolved to have them executed or die in the effort.

We supposed they had a regular picket there, or at the river, and as more than two are hardly ever on post at a time, we were to charge them, I to shoot one and he the other, and once across the river, we could make our means of escape more effectual.

We mounted our horses, drew our pistols, and came dashing down as if for a charge—but not a solitary soul could be seen in the road. Not looking for us then—perhaps they had gone into the house, and by the time they could get out and get ready for us we were gone.

We pursued the same course at the river, and meeting with no one, moved rapidly on toward the main road. We got lost once by taking the wrong path, but I soon discovered the mistake, and got ourselves placed in the right track. But we were yet to pass the house where our friend Jones called so loudly for "John." The sergeant's alarm grew on him as we drew nearer the spot, and before we were within fifty yards, I heard his spurs rattling along the side of his mule, and discovered he was out-traveling me.

"Come on, captain!" he again entreated, "let's don't be in a hurry!"

As he passed the house, I heard footsteps proceeding rapidly in the direction of the door, and as I came opposite a female voice called out:

"What's the news?"

"Well, not much, I believe!" I remarked rather carelessly and dryly.

"Are you just from town?"

"Right from there." (Another fib.)

"What's going on now?"

"Well, they are after the rebels pretty strong," I returned.

"Are they! Oh!" and she gave her hands a clap together with a little shout for glory.

"Who are you?" she continued. I was "stumped," and hearing confusion in the house, and having seen horses hitched at the gate, and believing them to belong to those men who had gone after assistance to bush us, I thought it advisable to get away as promptly as possible, and forgot the answer I should have given to her question, and told her we were "home guards."

"Ah, yes!" she quietly retorted, "you are the d——d rebels yourselves."

Just then the men came rushing out of the house, and I galloped away, no little rejoiced that all danger was now behind me. We traveled briskly for several miles for fear of being overtaken; afterward more leisurely, until we had nearly reached the line, when reflecting that it would not look very valorous to be run out of the State the same day we went in, I concluded to pass the remainder of the night on the "old Kentucky shore." We withdrew from the road a respectable distance and appropriated a quantity of somebody else's green corn for our horses, and extending ourselves upon one saddle blanket inside the field, slumber chased the remaining fears away, with sweet dreams of my home and the angel again.

Next morning, at daylight, we resumed our journey to camp, took breakfast just over the line in Tennessee, and arrived at camp early next evening, communicating "official" intelligence and information gained to headquarters in due form. Some of which facts, of course, I omit in this narrative, for reasons best known in military circles, and am now ready to make another scout all alone.

P. S.—Major S—— and his detachment have arrived, having successfully passed through the mountains of Little's Gap—bringing out seventeen prisoners and sundry important informations, all safe except the one man killed, two captured.

Prompt Settlement of a Claim

Old Lady—"Is this where Captain Bragg lives?"

Colonel Brent.—"Yes, madam. Can I do anything for you?"

Old Lady—"Well, you see, Mister, I lives over where the fitin' was, and when Captain Bragg's company skeered the Yankees, they ran rite peerst my house—rite peerst—when up comes Captain Forrest with his crittur company [cavalry] and makes a line of fight rite through my yard and oversets my ash hopper, and treads—"

General Bragg (sitting near).—"Colonel Brent, see that the lady's claim is settled *immediately!*"

Not Wounded

Jim A—— and John B——, two ragged and waggish boys in gray, while traveling on the South Carolina railroad, noticed on the train a portly gentleman, dressed in a style of magnificence that Count d'Orsay or Beau Brummell might have envied. Determining to have some sport out of him, they approached him. Assuming a rustic air and the drawling tones of the backwoods settlements, Jim A—— asked, "Mister, mout I be so bold as to ax you in what are battle you got wounded?"

Portly Gentleman (astonished).—"Me, sir, what do you mean, sir?"

John B.—"Axin' your pardon, Jim wants to know whar you got wounded."

Portly Gentleman (sharply).—"I have not been wounded at all. What makes you think that I have been?"

Jinn A. (drawling slowly).—"Well, you, see, mister, I didn't know but as how a bomb mout a bust in your belly, and kinder swelled you up so."

John B.—"And you smell like the regimental surgeon had been givin' on you kloreform or assefediddee to sorter fix you up a bit."

The Return

Three years! I wonder if she'll know me?
   I limp a little; and I left one arm
At Petersburg; and I am grown as brown
   As the plump chestnuts on my little farm:

And I'm as shaggy as the chestnut burs—
But ripe and sweet within, and wholly hers.

The darling! how I long to see her!
    My heart outruns this feeble soldier pace,
For I remember, after I had left,
    A little Charlie came to take my place.
Ah! how the laughing, three-year old, brown eyes—
His mother's eyes—will stare with pleased surprise!

Surely, they will be at the corner watching!
    I sent them word that I should come to-night
The birds all know it, for they crowd around,
    Twittering their welcome with a wild delight;
And that old robin, with a halting wing—
I saved her life, three years ago last spring.

Three years! perhaps I am but dreaming!
    For, like the pilgrim of the long ago,
I've trudged, a weary burden at my back,
    Through summer's heat, and winter's blinding snow;
Till, now, I reach my home; my darling's breast,
There I can roll my burden off, and rest.

*   *   *   *   *   *   *   *   *

When morning came, the early rising sun
    Laid his light fingers on a soldier sleeping—
Where a soft covering of bright green grass
    Over two mounds was lightly creeping;
But waked him not: his was the rest eternal,
Where the brown eyes reflected love supernal.

A KIND OF A SENTINEL

The colonel of an Alabama regiment was famous for having every thing done up in military style. Once while field officer of the day, and going his tour of inspection; he came on a sentinel from the eleventh Mississippi regiment sitting flat down on his post, with his gun taken entirely to pieces, when the following dialogue took place:

Colonel.—"Don't you know that a sentinel while on duty, should always keep on his feet?"

Sentinel (without looking up).—"That's the way we used to do when the war first began; but that's played out long ago."

Colonel (beginning to doubt if the man was on duty).—"Are you sentinel here?"

Sentinel.—"Well, I'm a sort of a sentinel."

Colonel.—"Well, I'm a sort of officer of the day."

Sentinel.—"Well, if you'll hold on till I sort of git my gun together, I'll give you a sort of salute."

A Friendly Warning

As a cavalry courier was dashing along the Winchester turnpike, after the bloody battle of Sharpsburg, he was suddenly halted by a barefoot infantry soldier, who, looking curiously at his big spurs, said, "Excuse me, mister cavalryman, but it's my duty to warn you not to ride along this 'ere road."

"Why should I not ride on this road?" asked the gay trooper.

"Well, you see," answered the footman, "it's all along of the interest I feels in you, for you see the old general (Lee) has offered a thousand dollars to any one who will find a dead man with spurs on, and I was kinder 'fraid some rascal would knock you over to get the money."

The bold dragoon evinced, by language more energetic than Chesterfieldian, his sense of the well-meant kindness.

Preferred to Die on the Field

During the battle of Gettysburg a poor fellow, who looked the very image of death, hobbled out of the ambulance in which he had been lying, and, shouldering his musket, was just starting forward, when the surgeon in charge stopped him with:

"Where are you going, sir?"

"To the front, doctor," and the brave fellow tried hard to stand firm and speak boldly as he saluted the surgeon.

"To the front! What! a man in your condition? Why, sir, you can't march half a mile; you haven't the strength to carry yourself, let alone your knapsack, musket, and, equipments. You must be crazy, surely."

"But, doctor, my division are in the fight," (here he grasped the wheel of an ambulance to support himself,) "and I have a younger brother in my company. I *must* go."

"But I am your surgeon, and I forbid you. You have every symptom of typhoid fever; a little over-exertion will kill you."

"Well, doctor, if I *must* die, I would rather die in the field than in an ambulance."

The doctor saw that it was useless to debate the point and the soldier went, as he desired. But on the evening of the next day he was buried where he fell—for fall he did,— his right arm blown off at the elbow; and his forehead pierced by a minie ball.

The Death of Ashby

Scarcely had he ordered his baggage train to proceed before the enemy opened fire upon his camp. With but two companies of his old cavalry he prepared to meet them; seeing this they immediately withdrew. The command was then moved slowly through Harrisonburg, and drawn up three hundred yards from the opposite end. Soon a regiment of "blue coats" came charging through town, around the bend, in full sight of Ashby's men, who stood upon their trained chargers as if fixed to the ground. When within a very short distance, they commenced to slacken their speed, only giving us time to tender the salute due them. Soon their ranks were broken and in confusion they fled through the streets.

Never before had I heard our noble general utter such a shout. It was not one caused by victory over a brave foe, after a hard contested fight, but only seemed designed to shame an ignominious band for running before they were hurt. We had begun to entertain a high opinion of this body of cavalry. Upon one instance it flanked and charged upon a battery, which was left without a support—a *most daring* feat for them. (Here General Ashby stood by the guns, fired every load from his three pistols, and brought every thing away safely.) Soon we were moving along the road to

Port Republic, the enemy pressing closely. Ashby's eagle eye was upon them, as if watching for an excuse to give them battle. An excuse, and even the necessity for a fight, soon became evident. The road was very bad, the train moved slowly, and the main body of the enemy's cavalry was only a mile from its rear. They gave us no time to prepare to meet them. Ashby had but begun to form his men, before three regiments, with colors flying and music rare, emerged from a woods three fourths of a mile distant. Bearing to our right, they charged, presenting a beautiful sight. Ashby could contain himself no longer. Gently drawing his sabre, and waving it around his head, his clear, sounding voice rang out his only command—"FOLLOW ME." The dash was simultaneous. Fences were cleared, which at any other time would have been thought impossible. The enemy came to a halt. It was but for a moment. As they heard the strange whiz of the sabre around their heads they broke and ran. The work of slaughter had commenced. At every step Ashby, followed closely by his men, cut them down, or sent them to the rear. For two miles and a half the chase continued, and the scene became more bloody. Never before did our general or his men use their sabres to such an extent.

None but those who have witnessed a similar scene can imagine the spectacle. Enraged by deeds too horrible to mention—led by a general whose presence exerted a mystic influence over every heart—the bravery of the men knew no limit, and seldom was a summons to surrender heard. The scattered fragments of the three regiments hid themselves behind their column of infantry three miles beyond the point of attack; and the pursuit ended not until this infantry opened fire. Here Ashby drew up his men, and remained beneath their fire, and waited for reënforcements from Jackson. In this fight, Major Green, of the sixth Virginia cavalry, was slightly wounded; also another, name unknown. We took forty-four prisoners, among them the colonel commanding the brigade of cavalry. The infantry having arrived, Generals Ashby, Ewell, and Stewart (of Maryland), led them to the fight. Here Ashby's gallantry could not have been excelled. Having led the first Maryland regiment in a charge which sent the enemy flying from that quarter, he sought the fifty-eighth Virginia, and, still between the two fires, he ordered the charge. His horse fell dead. He rose, beckoned to the men, and whilst in the very act, a ball entered low in his left side, came out near the right breast, and shattered his right wrist. He fell—he died. Not even a groan or a sigh was uttered by the dying hero. He was brave whilst living, but braver in dying. The men were not discouraged, but pressed on, and soon the victory was ours. Night closed the fighting. The noble Ashby fell between six and seven in the evening. The news went like a flash through our lines. Every heart was wounded. The aged, the young, and the hard-hearted wept. Nature made deeper the gloom; and soon the darkness of the night made still darker the region of the mind. He now sleeps in the University burying-grounds near Charlottesville.

THE ROMANTIC MOSBY

A correspondent of the Philadelphia *Press*, writing from Warrenton, Virginia, October 22d, 1863, pays the following compliment to the daring Mosby: a high compliment, inasmuch as it shows how he made his name a terror to the enemy:

Last Sunday I rode from Alexandria to Bull Run. It was my good fortune not to be captured. I was gaily galloping along the turnpike, thinking of this very individual, little thinking him to be the very devil that would soon appear. As I mounted my horse, I observed upon the newly white washed wall of the building a notice, written in great scrawling letters, similar to what a boy would compare the autograph of Jack Sheppard, written upon the parlor-wall of a plundered mansion. The writer "begged leave to inform the people of Alexandria" that he had this day "dined at the Marshall House." On the same line with the date, "September 30th, 1863," was plainly written, "Major Mosby."

Wondering very much if this bandit had been here, and if he had slept in the room on the same landing where Ellsworth was killed, I failed to notice an excited cavalryman, who was hastily telling me that the individual who now troubled my mind so much might trouble me for my purse, my watch—nay more, myself. I paid less attention to this information than did Lochiel to the forewarnings of the plaided and bonneted seer. Soon I came to a company of the second New Jersey cavalry, and was quietly passing, when twenty-five men in gray homespun sprang from the bushes, shot a sergeant through the thigh, and captured Captain

Gallagher, after shooting his horse. They affected their escape. The men were not drilled, but one or two had pistols, and I think they should have rescued their captain. They did not. Two or three trains turned back, and I was almost persuaded that it would be impossible to get through to Fairfax. I started, however, and galloped through in a short time. Mosby has a den in the forest. He captured a man in the one hundred and sixth Pennsylvania the last time the second corps crossed the Rappahannock.

The man wandered off into the woods about one hundred and fifty yards, when a little man stepped adroitly from behind the cover of a huge oak, presented a revolver to the soldier's head, and intimated for him to keep quiet. All this time the second corps was slowly filing along the road, within sight of Mosby and his prisoner. He led him by secret and unknown paths to a lair in the mountains, where were other prisoners, sutler's wagons, and other scamps engaged in the same nefarious calling. Every one living in this portion of Virginia would die to serve this man. They are his lookouts, his pickets, his videttes. Nothing passes their doors but is seen by them, and information sent to Mosby. He gives them a share of the plunder. A few miles from Anandale, on the road leading to Fairfax, stands a comfortable frame building, with the usual Southern outbuildings.

It is but little over two months since one of our soldiers stood at the front door of this house and shot Mosby. Every one thought the wound fatal. A friend took him to Upperville, where he was carefully nursed by Mrs. Mosby, and now he is waylaying people on this same road. He can never be captured by cavalry. All last winter Stahl's cavalry was busily engaged in hunting him. We could attend to a brigade of Stuart's cavalry much easier than he. His haunt is Upperville. One hundred good men marched there after night, and stationed around the building, would be sure to take him. In the daytime his friends in the different farm houses are alert and watchful; he is warned, and immediately flies to some place inaccessible to cavalry.

The Bare-Footed Boys

By the sword of St. Michael
    The old dragoon through!
By David, his sling,
    And the giant he slew!
Let us write us a rhyme,
    As a record to tell,
How the South on a time
    Stormed the ramparts of hell
        With her bare-footed boys!

Had the South in her border
    A hero to spare,
Or a heart at her altar,
    So its life-blood was there!
And the black battle grieve.
    Might never disguise
The smile of the South,
    On the lips and the eyes
        Of her bare-footed boys!

There's a grandeur in fight,
    And a terror the while,
But none like the light
    Of that terrible smile—
The smile of the South,
    When the storm cloud unrolls
The lightning that loosens
    The wrath in the souls
        Of her bare-footed boys!

It withered the foe
    Like the red light that runs
Through the dead forest leaves,
    And he fled from his guns!
Grew the smile to a laugh,
    Rose the laugh to a yell,

> As the ironclad hoofs
> Clattered back into hell
> From our bare-footed boys!

Harry Gilmor Attacks the Enemy*

I had just heard that a great number of refugees from the Valley were at Burner's, and had possession of the cabins and stables. Thinking that good fat farm-horses were better able to stand the weather than my poor cavalry nags, I soon hit upon a plan that would empty the stables and cabins. They had heard that Boyd was coming; so I took ten men, dressed them in blue overcoats, and started for the Springs about a mile off. The road comes in sight half a mile from the buildings, and the refugees were all out, wondering who we were. I made a feint as though we were going up the mountains, then suddenly wheeled to the left, gave a yell, drew pistols, and charged for the buildings. Every man, black and white, broke off and ran for the mountains near by, and we took quiet possession, turning all the horses out into the meadows, and putting our own in their places to eat the blue-grass hay with which their racks were filled. Some of these men staid out in the mountain all night, and came back in the morning almost frozen, but mad as hornets at our innocent little ruse.

Soon after we arrived, a Negro hid in the hay crawled out, and, seeing none but friends about, called out to his companions, and soon we saw twenty or more coming from under the barn and every imaginable hiding-place. I immediately sent all the men to the fires in the cabins, and put the Negroes to work unsaddling and cleaning the horses. I then gave each man half a pint of apple brandy to prevent their taking cold, which, strange to say, none of them did, after lying out two days and nights in sleet and rain, in wet and frozen blankets, besides swimming a creek filled with ice.

Next morning my scouts reported the enemy moving up the Valley, and, I moved too, encamping at the Caroline Furnace, twelve miles off, the first night; sent scouts into the Valley, and went myself to a high peak, from which I could plainly see Boyd's cavalry, artillery, and infantry, with

---

* From *"Four Years in the Saddle."* By Colonel Harry Gilmor.

wagons in the centre, passing up the Valley turnpike, their advance having already entered Newmarket. They had every thing too well arranged for me to attack the trains, but they had left a squadron on picket at the bridge over the north branch of the Shenandoah, which I determined to attack if they remained during the night. Accordingly, I sent fresh scouts to ascertain whether any change had taken place, or if they had been reënforced. At eleven P.M. they returned, reporting every thing unchanged, but that fires were seen a mile off, where they supposed the first New York cavalry were doing duty.

The night was bitter cold, and, as the weather had suddenly turned from sleet and rain to bright and clear, every bush, and tree, and blade of grass was glittering and loaded down with ice. In going through the gap there was a mountain stream to cross at least ten times, and the water, splashing over our feet and legs, froze instantly, making it very disagreeable.

When we got through the gap I took a by-path to the right, which brought us out into the Mount Airy estate, owned by Dr. A. R. Meem. Many of our friends know the doctor, and have partaken of his princely hospitality; and hundreds of our soldiers will tell in after years how the fair hands of its mistress have washed, dressed, and bound up their ghastly wounds, and that a Southern soldier was never turned away hungry, even after the "immortal" Sheridan had burned every stack, and fence, and building, and carried off all the provisions. What pleasant evenings we spent at Mount Airy in the delightful society of its beautiful young mistress and the fair visitors always to be found there. Can I ever forget that it was my Virginia home, and where, sick or wounded, I was nursed and treated as a son or brother?

As my route lay by the door, I called up, and found the ladies fully attired before a rousing fire in the grate, as if waiting our arrival. But the clock warned me to be off, after telling them we were about to attack the squadron on the bridge, in full view from the house.

At the foot of the hill, and just a mile from the bridge, ran a creek, much swollen, which we crossed with difficulty. Having tied four horses together, and leaving three men to guard them all, we started off on foot, intending to advance up the river under cover of the trees. My object was to give the men a rapid walk, to thaw them thoroughly before the fight commenced, and also to avoid being seen, for the night was bright and clear, though we had no moon. On reaching the river I turned to the left, moving in single file to prevent noise by trampling on the grass, for each blade was covered with ice, and made a crushing sound under foot.

The enemy had built shelters of cedar boughs and fodder, and their fires, being heaped up with seasoned rails, threw a bright light all around. These were built on either side of the turnpike, and on the opposite side from us was a two-story log house and a weather-boarded blacksmith's shop. The horses were chiefly tied along the yard fence.

Having approached within two hundred yards of the camp, I halted the men, and crawled up to reconnoitre the position, and was just in the act of getting on the bridge when I heard a sentinel dancing to warm his feet. I stepped back to the men, and moved cautiously up to within fifty yards of the shelters, when I put them in line fronting the camp without being discovered, though there was a sergeant moving about all the time.

All being ready, I gave final instructions, placed Lieutenant Kemp on the right, Captain Burke on the left, took the centre myself, and advanced on the shelters with drawn pistols. Treading on a pile of dry corn husks that lay in our way, the sergeant pricked up his ears and stooped down to look under the glare of light. I saw that he discovered us, and forthwith fired upon him and then charged the camp. The cry was, "Surrender or be killed!" and the yelling and firing were quite lively. I must do them the justice to say that they fought desperately, firing from their blankets as they lay behind their shelters, and it was with difficulty that any could be secured. We set fire to the shelters, but they fought their way into the log house, and opened fire upon us from the doors and windows. Up to this time we had taken about fifteen prisoners, and several were killed and wounded. The fires around the house shone brightly, and the soldiers within could see every one of us distinctly. Three of our men were shot. To finish the business, we charged the house, hoping to take all prisoners, but the door was barricaded and could not be forced. My cousin Willie was by my side nearly all the time. A bullet struck his right arm, and knocked the pistol from his hand. He cried out, "Major, I'm shot!" I asked him if he was much hurt. He replied, "No; but I'm bleeding." I told him to mount his horse, cross over to Doctor Meem's, and get the ladies to dress his wound. The brave boy looked up as if puzzled to know whether I was in earnest, and said, "But, major, I've got two loads left!" I told him then to "blaze away," and I thought that his first shot took effect. He remained with us to the last.

At length I determined to set fire to the house, and force them out in that way; so I gathered up an armful of fodder, and calling to a man named Hancock for a fagot, I started for a window in the southern gable. As I advanced, two shots were fired at me from the window; but I had determined to accomplish my object, and that nothing short of a wound should stop me. I had got within a step of it, and was about to throw in the fodder, when a ball struck the window-sill and glanced off, throwing a quantity of splinters in my face, one of which struck my nose, and hurt me so much that I involuntarily dropped he fodder and felt my face, thinking the ball had entered. In doing this I ran behind the corner, and just as I discovered the wound to be not serious, two men came out of the back door. My revolver was exhausted. I had two "Derringers" in my pocket, but, strange to say, forgot all about them. When within a step of one of them, I ordered him to surrender. "I'll be damned if I do," said he, and at the same instant presented his pistol. Quick as thought, I seized the barrel and turned it aside. It went off, and the leakage between the cylinder and the barrel burned my wrist. I tried to wrench the pistol from him, but he managed to cock it again, determined to make the muzzle bear upon me. The other fellow ran off, saying, "Give him hell, Captain!" We were standing on a sheet of ice, my foe being the stouter man. After be had discharged two more loads, my hand still upon the barrel, my feet slipped, and I fell to the ground. The captain took as good aim as he could, in the night, and under the excitement of the moment, I moved not a muscle, though I seemed to feel the ball crashing through my brain. I closed my eyes. He fired, and my face was covered with an avalanche of mud and ice. The ball had entered the ground two inches from my skull! The whole scene occupied but a few moments—it seemed an age to me.

The captain thought me dead, and fled into the weeds and willows on the river's bank, while I jumped up and ran back to the men. We made one more attack on the house, which failed, and then secured their horses, of which we captured twenty-six. I found the captain's mare tied to the wagon. They had five horses killed by random shots.

When out of range, Captain Burke informed me that he heard cavalry coming up the turnpike rapidly from Mount Jackson, and we started for the place where we had tied our horses. After getting a short distance, I was told that one of my best men, Debril, was left behind severely wounded. The night was bitter cold. Taking another with me, we went back and found him lying on the ground, suffering terribly. I dismounted, put him on my horse, and carried him slowly to the ford. After getting all the men together, I directed Captain Burke to take them back to our old camp in the gap, and wait for me there, while I took Debril up to Mount Airy, and put him in charge of those who would give him proper care until a surgeon could be procured. A bed was made ready for him with little delay, and soon the servants were building a fire in his room.

General Hardee and the Arkansas Soldiers

"In July, 1861," writes an Arkansas soldier, "our regiment was ordered into Missouri, where, with the other regiments, it was formed into a brigade and placed in command of General Hardee. None of the command had ever seen Hardee, and all were on the *qui vive* to see a live brigadier who had been in the old United States army. Hardee, on his arrival, was dressed in a very plain, faded uniform, which looked rather seedy in the eyes of those who thought he would be covered with buttons and gold lace. When he came out to the camps, he found a guard-line stretched around the regiment; and on the post to which he advanced, was stationed a backwoods specimen of humanity, who, being from the swamps of Arkansas, had never before been ten miles away from home. The sentry paced his post backward and forward, his gun slung across his shoulder in a devil-may-care style, and with an independent strut that denoted that he felt the importance of his duties. Hardee stopped within a few feet of the sentry, probably to study this soldier, who whistled away as he walked his post, not paying attention to any one either to the right or left of him. Hardee concluded to try him by crossing his line; but, as he started across, the sentry threw his gun to his shoulder and yelled to him to stop. 'Stop thar, stranger! and don't you cross that ar line or I'll blow your head off!' Hardee told him who he was, and that he intended taking command of the troops at that place. 'Oh!' said the sentry, 'you are General Hardee, are you?' and dropping his gun on the ground, he grasped the general's hand very heartily—'How are you, General Hardee? I am very glad to see, you, General! I hope you and your family are well, sir! Come down to-day and take dinner with me. My name is Tom Simpkins, and I belong to the H—— Guards. Come down, general, and I'll give you a good dinner!'

"The General thanked him kindly, and walked off, thinking no doubt that our Arkansas boys were a rich set if this was a fair specimen."

Charging Endways

An Alabama colonel, who was as good, true, and brave, as he was ignorant of tactics, was marching his men by the flanks when a hot fire was opened on them. General Rhodes dashed up, and gave the order to charge. The colonel looked embarrassed, not understanding that the general, of course, intended him to first throw his men into line before making the charge. The order being again repeated, the colonel said: "General, do you mean for me to charge endways?"

Mosby in the Federal Lines[*]

When General Lee was pressing Hooker toward the Potomac, Mosby called to see Stuart, who was at Middleburg, with his command thrown forward toward Aldie. After a short conference with the general, he returned to the party who had accompanied him, and started again for the neighborhood of Seneca. We had not proceeded more than two miles, when firing was heard in the direction of Aldie. The cause of it, as we soon learned, was a collision between Kilpatrick and Rosser, who had met unexpectedly at that place. Mosby, with sixty men, moved around by Oatlands, so as to gain a position in rear of Kilpatrick on the Little River turnpike.

A corps of infantry had reached Green Spring, another had gone to Leesburg, and Mosby thus found himself interposed between the cavalry and infantry of Hooker's army. With this information a courier was sent to General Stuart, who, for the first time, learned where Hooker was.

It was dark before we reached the turnpike, and on our march thither we had captured a number of prisoners.

Leaving the command concealed in the woods, Mosby, accompanied by Charlie Hall, Joe Nelson, and Norman Smith, proceeded to the road, where they espied three horses fastened near a dwelling, with an orderly standing by them. He rode up to the man, and was informed by him that

---

[*] From *"Partisan Life with Mosby."* By Colonel John Scott.

the horses belonged to Major Sterling and Captain ——. In a whisper, he then said to the orderly, who was an Irishman:

"My name is Mosby; keep quiet."

The man understood him to say that he (the Irishman) was Mosby, and very indignantly replied:—

"No, sir, I'm as good a Unionman as ever walked the earth."

"Those are the very sort I am after," replied Major Mosby.

Just then the officers made their exit from the house. When sufficiently near, Hall stretched out his hand to take the major's arms. Supposing him to be an acquaintance, Major Sterling offered his hand, and was thunderstruck when he was informed that be was a prisoner. And well he might be, for he was the bearer of important dispatches from Hooker to Pleasanton, his chief of cavalry.

Mosby proceeded to a house near by, where, after procuring a light, he discovered what a treasure he had captured. The dispatches informed Pleasanton of all Hooker's plans, and all the information which he wanted to obtain.

This information, so important, was intrusted to the courage, the prudence, and the fidelity of Norman Smith. At twelve o'clock at night, Norman set forth, and just as the first faint dawn appeared, the dispatches were placed in General Stuart's hands.

After the prisoners had proceeded a short distance, they were informed by Hall that Mosby was their captor. At this they were highly amused, and when asked the cause, replied: "We have laughed so much at our men for being gobbled up by Mosby, that we cannot help laughing at being caught ourselves."

We slept that night in the woods within half a mile of the camp of the fifth corps, and early the next morning moved lower down the turnpike, near Pleasant Valley, where further important information was obtained about the disposition of Hooker's army. Here we captured two well stored sutler-wagons, drawn by six horses, which we gutted in the woods. One sutler was indeed a prize, for he had six hundred dollars in greenbacks on his person, and was leading a very fine mare, which belonged to the lieutenant-colonel of the seventy-third Ohio. The mare was at once dedicated to the partisan service.

With thirty prisoners and horses, Major Mosby returned to report in person to Stuart, and crossed Bull Run Mountain by an unfrequented bridle-path, as Hancock's corps was at Thoroughfare Gap, and Pleasanton still at Aldie.

Jackson

By Harry Flash

Not 'midst the lightning of the stormy fight,
Not in the rush upon the Vandal foe,
Did kingly Death, with his resistless might,
    Lay the Great Leader low.

His warrior soul its earthly shackles broke
In the full sunshine of a peaceful town;
When all the storm was hushed, the trusty oak
    That propped our cause went down.

Though his alone the blood that flecks the ground,
Recording all his grand, heroic deeds,
Freedom herself is writhing with the wound,
    And all the country bleeds.

He entered not the nation's Promised Land
At the red belching of the cannon's mouth,
But broke the House of Bondage with, his hand,
    The Moses of the South!

O, gracious God! not gainless is the loss;
A glorious sunbeam gilds thy sternest frown;
And while his country staggers with the cross,
    He rises with the crown!

He Saw Jackson

    After Sharpsburg, an old and hardened offender in D. H. Hill's division was brought before that commander for burning fence rails, and despairing of producing any reform in him, General Hill sent him to Jackson, who asked him why he persisted in burning rails.

    "Well, General," returned the reprobate, "you see I've been enlisted now eight months in General Hill's division, and in all that time I never could get a good look at you, so I thought I would steal some fence rails. I knew they would take me up, and then send me to you, so I would see you."

A grim smile greeted this impudent excuse, and reading his man at a glance, Jackson turned to the guard and said:

"Take this man and buck him, and set him on the top of that empty barrel in front of my tent. The front is open and he can look at me as much as he likes."

The order was obeyed to the letter, and for several hours, while Jackson was engaged upon his official correspondence, the rail-destroyer had an excellent opportunity of gratifying his curiosity.

Part IV

The Grayjackets on the High Seas

THE NAVAL FIGHT ON THE MISSISSIPPI RIVER

The Stars and Stripes are floating over Memphis! The Federals now occupy the city, and Yankee rule is about to shed its beauties upon a people who through the trying scenes of the past twenty-four hours have proven themselves as loyal as any community in the Southern Confederacy. Fort Pillow was evacuated on Wednesday and Thursday, every thing of value being removed and the troops transported down the river.

THE NAVAL BATTLE

On Thursday night the Federal fleet made its appearance five miles above the city, where its presence was signaled by a rocket from one of our scout boats, which was immediately chased, and burned to prevent capture. Our own fleet of rams, which had arrived only six hours previously, at once prepared for action; but the night passed without any demonstration. At early dawn the Federals advanced, steaming slowly down in the following order: First, a series of eight rams, then the heavy, black, iron-clad gunboats, and behind a swarm of transports, mortar boats, and tugs. Altogether, the number of the fleet was about thirty-five. Our own force consisted of the following rams, seven in number, and was under the command of Commodore Montgomery and his associate steamboat captains: General Van Dorn, General Price, General Bragg, Jeff Thompson, General Lovell, General Beauregard, Sumter, and Little Rebel.

The flag ship of the commodore was the Van Dorn, but as she was on the present occasion loaded with over one hundred thousand pounds of powder, and other valuable stores, he transferred his flag to the Little Rebel, with instructions to the other to remain in the rear of his squadron and await his signal, when she was to make her way with all possible dispatch down the river to a place of safety.

Such were the immense odds against which our little fleet were about to contend—twenty boats to six, and eighty-four guns to fourteen, our rams, with the exception of the Jeff. Thompson, which had four, having only two guns each. Public opinion may question the propriety of attempting resistance in view of such disadvantages, but the commodore had no other resource. His fuel had given out, and notwithstanding his repeated applications he was enabled to secure only eight hundred barrels—enough to last his fleet about two hours. Had he drifted toward Vicksburg, the enemy would have pursued and captured him without a blow. Had he run, public sentiment would have written him down a coward. His only resource, therefore, was to fight or disgrace himself. He promptly determined upon the former. Calling a council of his officers, he imparted his views and received their hearty co-operation. At the same time it was unanimously agreed that no boat should be surrendered, and no flag struck; but when disabled or surrounded, every craft was to be sunk, blown up, or set on fire. The sequel will show how firmly this heroic resolution was carried out, though not an officer or man went into the fight expecting to survive.

As soon as the Federals were discovered approaching, Commodore Montgomery gave the signal—"prepare for action"—and the little fleet moved up abreast of the city. Fire was first opened by the Jeff. Thompson, and several shots discharged without eliciting a response. Soon, however, the cannonade commenced from the Federal gunboats, and for an hour and thirty-five minutes continued without intermission, the Federal fleet never halting, and (with the exception of the rams) never changing its battle array. When opposite the city one of the Yankee rams made a bold dash at the General Lovell as she was making a turn, and striking her amidships the latter sank on the Tennessee shore. Boats put off to rescue the survivors struggling in the water, when a whole broadside of grape and canister was fired from one of the gunboats, killing and maiming several as they swam. Yankee sharp-shooters, concealed behind bales of hay, also poured in a destructive fire, picking off the men wherever they were visible—a characteristic illustration of the baseness and cowardice which has from the beginning marked their side of this contest. Among those killed in this manner was Captain William Cable, of the Lovell.

The ram now made a dash for the Beauregard, but missing her, the latter sheered around, and, striking her antagonist, tore an immense hole in her side. She barely succeeded in reaching the Arkansas shore, when she sunk. Another ram now made for the Beauregard, when the latter, in conjunction with the Price, prepared to reciprocate. The Federal being in the diagonal of the two, however, by a skilful manoeuvre, managed to escape collision herself, and, the two Confederates coming together, the Price received a damaging blow, which also drove her ashore on the Arkansas side to prevent sinking. Meanwhile the fight was briskly going on between the other boats—our little fleet falling back with their bows to the enemy, and firing as rapidly as their small armament would permit.

The Little Rebel, with her signal flags, now became the target of both rams and gunboats. Shot and shell fairly rained around and upon her, and no less than three attempts were made to run her down without success. Finally a heavy hundred and twenty-eight pound ball struck her at the water line and passed completely through her machinery. The pilot had barely time to head her for the shore, when a Yankee gunboat laid alongside and poured a broadside into her, which, to use the expression of one of the men, "blew her bottom out." At the same time the sharp-shooters did their fearful work, and eight or ten men fell pierced with bullets. Six or seven were drowned.

Commodore Montgomery and Captain Fowler took to the water, and swimming ashore, escaped in the swamps of Arkansas. Both these officers, I have since learned, endured untold torments. For thirty hours they alternately swam and waded through the deep sloughs, a prey to mosquitoes, insects, and the cold of the night, which was intolerable. Soon they became separated, and the commodore was discovered by three Federal pickets. They had discharged their guns at him as he was swimming a swamp, all of which fortunately missed their object. As he landed, they demanded his surrender. "Certainly," said he, at the same time thrusting his sword through the body of one of the men. His revolver being wet would not go off, but he drew it on the remaining two, when they took to their heels and disappeared. The commodore then made his way to a point some miles below, where he met a couple of gentlemen, one of whom took him on his horse and carried him to a crossing on the river. He then succeeded in reaching the Tennessee shore, and arrived at this place. He is now safe at Grenada. Captain Fowler also came upon the Yankee pickets, but was undiscovered by them, though for two hours he lay concealed in the bushes within thirty feet of the rascals. I have since met him but he is scarcely recognizable, from the mosquito bites, which cover his person, wherever exposed, from head to foot.

I should here remark that previous to the engagement the Federal commander had taken the precaution to land three or four regiments on the Arkansas shore, who stretched their lines for a distance of four miles or more below the city.

The fight was now a thoroughly one-sided affair. Our gunboats were all more or less disabled. The Beauregard was in a sinking condition, and had been run ashore; the Bragg and Sumter were maintaining an unequal contest; the Jeff. Thompson had been blown up by the officers, and the Van Dorn, with her valuable cargo, was flying down the river toward Vicksburg. A few moments more and the battle was ended. The Bragg and Sumter were run ashore and set on fire, but before the work of destruction could be completed, they had fallen into the hands of the Federal pursuers. The fire was extinguished; those of the crew who could not escape were captured, and the Federal fleet slowly returned to the city and dropped anchor.

The unequal battle was witnessed by thousands upon the bluff, many of whom were women and children, and, though no one expected a victory, many a heartfelt prayer went up from that throng for the safety of the gallant officers and men. Our loss in killed and drowned may be thirty or forty. The enemy claims in prisoners about one hundred.

THE CRUISE OF THE ALABAMA

NARRATED BY HER OFFICERS

It was the 13th of August, 1862, that we left Liverpool in the chartered steamer Bahama; to the Western Isles, where we were to meet the Alabama, which had gone out before us to receive her armament, officers, and crew, for service. Our party consisted chiefly of the former officers of the Sumter— the gallant little vessel which created so much terror amongst the Yankee bottoms on the American coast, and although pursued by all the Federal fleet, crossed the Atlantic in winter with safety, and found a harbor refuge under the guns of Gibraltar. There, however, she was blockaded, and was sold on account of the Confederate States government. She was re-purchased privately, and her hull was taken over to England, where she was to be refitted. Her officers followed their captain, ready to obey his orders, for all admired him as a skilful seaman, a good tactician, an excellent diplomatist, and a brave man. They spent a short time in England, when the Alabama, or "Two hundred and Ninety," as she was then named, was purchased, and Captain Semmes at once prepared to take command of her, under commission from President Davis, with the object of doing as much damage as possible to the enemy's commerce on the sea.

At Porta Praya, in the Island of Terceira (Azores), we found our ship taking in guns, ammunition, etc., which had been brought to this place by chartered vessels. The Alabama pleased us all. She is a fine ship of one thousand and forty tons; the length of keel, two hundred and ten feet; breadth of beam, thirty-two feet; depth of hold, seventeen feet and three, inches; has two engines combined of three hundred horse power, and three furnaces, each below the water line; the diameter of her propeller is fourteen feet, with two blades three feet in width and twenty-one feet pitch; and is capable of running fourteen knots. She mounts eight guns—one rifled seven inch Blakeley's patent, and one eight inch shell or solid shot gun (pivots), and six thirty-two pounders of forty-two hundred weight (broadsides). Her motto is: *Aide toi et Dieu t'aidera.* The officers numbered twenty, and the crew at this time only eighty—and the terms which the latter insisted upon on engaging, called forth the remarks of Captain Semmes, that the modern sailor has greatly changed in character; for he now stickles for pay like a sharper, and seems to have lost his former love of adventure and recklessness. The ordinary seamen get as much as £4 10s per month; petty officers £5 to £6; firemen 7£. All the officers hold commissions from the Confederate States government, and receive pay according to the regular scale, varying from £150 to £800 per annum.

On the 24th of August, the command of the Alabama was formally handed over by Captain Bullock (who had brought her out from Liverpool), to Captain Semmes; and the "Stars and Bars" were flung to the wind amid the cheers of all hands. The captain called all the crew and explained to them the risks and dangers they would have to undergo, and the inducement of prize money; furthermore, he said he did not intend to rush headlong into battle with a whole fleet of the enemy, but that he did not intend to run away if he met with any, and that he would give battle to the last, so that he expected every man to do his duty. He did not wish to deceive or entice any one to go, and they were free to judge for themselves, either to stay in the Alabama or return with the Bahama to Liverpool. This speech had a good effect, and was loudly cheered, and very few left with the Bahama, which then parted company with us.

After leaving Terceira, several days were devoted to putting our ship in order and drilling the crew, who were mostly good seamen, but unacquainted with naval discipline. On the 5th of September we caught our first prize, the Ockmulgee, off the Azores, and continued to cruise in that vicinity for about ten days, capturing and destroying several ships of the enemy. From the Azores we proceeded to the banks of Newfoundland, and cruised thence in the direction of New York, capturing and destroying several other valuable ships. Among our seizures were the Starlight, on board of which we found some dispatches for Secretary Seward; the Tonawanda, bound from New York to Liverpool, with seventy-five passengers, forty of whom were women; and the T. B. Wales, from Calcutta, with an American consul and his lady on board. We provided for them as well as possible—two of the wardroom officers giving up their rooms for them. The consul, however, got so troublesome and intermeddling, that Captain Semmes had to tell him that he was only tolerated there on account of his lady; but if he again spoke to the men or his crew, he would be put in double irons and tied to the gun rack—which threat had its intended effect on the Yankee. The fate of the vessels captured was to be destroyed by fire, and the night effect of this spectacle at sea was sometimes very striking. One of the doomed vessels, the Levi Starbuck, was set on fire at six o'clock in the evening, and was one of the grandest sights ever witnessed by us. After the decks took fire, the flame sprang to the rigging, running from yard to yard, until it reached the royal truck, leaving half the canvas-head burnt away, and forming one mass of glittering stars; in a few minutes afterward, the powder charges exploded, tearing the vessel into a thousand pieces.

When within two hundred and fifty miles of New York, finding we had but four days' coal on board, Captain Semmes bore off for the island of Martinique, where he had ordered a coal ship to rendezvous. On the way we captured and destroyed two very valuable ships. We reached Martinique on the 18th of November, where we were received with enthusiasm by the inhabitants; but finding that our coal ship had been there a week or ten days, and that the object of her visit was well known, Captain Semmes sent her out to sea again, appointing a new rendezvous. It was well that he did so, for she had not been gone twenty-four hours when the United States frigate San Jacinto arrived. Immediately she was seen, all our hands were called to quarters, ready for action; thinking the enemy would put his threat into force, of running into us wherever he found us; but, as usual, it turned out to be their mode of gaining a victory. The San Jacinto kept moving in and out so long, that the governor of the island boarded her, and ordered her either to come to anchor or proceed to sea, three miles clear of the land, which she obeyed, and lay to, blockading the port. Captain Semmes determined to go out and fight her; but was advised against this by the French officer who came on board of us, who said she was too heavy, as she carried twelve eight-inch broadside guns, and two eleven-inch pivots, with a crew of two hundred and fifty men. The governor said that if we desired to take in coals, we must get under the guns of his fort, and he would protect us against Admiral Wilkes and his fleet; but as the bark with coals was sent off the day before, we concluded it was best to go to sea. So at eight o'clock that night, we got ready for action, and steamed out of harbor without any molestation from the enemy, who was keeping watch and ward a marine league off. We coaled at the Island of Blanquille, on the coast of Venezuela, the new rendezvous appointed; and here we found a United States whaling schooner, but forbore to capture her, because of the claim of Venezuela to the barren little island—a claim as barren as the island, for there was no settled population on it, and, of course, no vestige of government. There were only two or three fishermen's huts on the place; and we put ashore, with the brand of infamy, a seaman named Forest, who had deserted from the Sumter, and was captured on board one of our prizes; he was found guilty of inciting the crew to mutiny.

Desiring to strike a blow at the enemy, the Alabama, after coaling, sailed for the east end of Cuba, in the track of the California steamers. On our way we captured and destroyed a bark from Boston for Aux Cayes; on the 7th of November, after lying off Cape Maise for several days, we captured the United States steamer Ariel—unfortunately outward, instead of homeward bound. She was brought to by a shot, which struck her mizzenmast. She had on board eight thousand dollars in United States treasury notes, and fifteen hundred dollars in silver; and as there was no certificate or other papers on board claiming it as neutral property, it was taken possession of as prize of war. There were one hundred and forty marines on board, with six officers, all of whom were disarmed and paroled, as was also Commander Saston, U.S.A., who was on board. As this ship had some seven hundred passengers and crew, many of whom were women and children, and it was alike impossible to take her into a neutral port, or to receive the passengers in the Alabama, there was no alternative but to release her under a ransom bond of two hundred and fifty thousand dollars; and as we parted company, the passengers gave three cheers for Captain Semmes.

After this the Alabama hove to on the north side of Jamaica, to repair some damage which had happened to one of our engines, and then set out for the Accas Island, Gulf of Mexico, where we refilled with coal, and caulked and repaired ship. Here some of our men erected on the island an epitaph in black, "To the memory of Abe Lincoln, who died January, 1861, of negro fever of the head," with a card on which was written; in Spanish, instructions to those who visit the island to forward the board to the nearest United States Consul.

On board the Ariel we found some New York papers, containing accounts of an intended expedition by General Banks, which we concluded was destined for Texas, and we presumed would rendezvous at Galveston. As it was said that the expedition was to consist of twenty thousand men, we knew a large number of transports would be required: many of these vessels would have to lie outside the bar, and we determined upon making a night attack upon forty or fifty of them, laden with troops, sink and set on fire many of them, and escape before our vessel could be pursued by a superior force. As it afterward turned out, we found the expedition of General Banks took another direction, and landed at New Orleans.

After coaling at Accas, however, the Alabama set sail for Galveston, and arrived there on the 11th January, and before nightfall made out the enemy's fleet lying off the bar, consisting of five ships of war. One of their steamers we observed to get under way, and come in our direction. Captain Semmes ordered steam to be got up, but kept sail on our vessel as a decoy, to entice the enemy's ship sufficiently far from the fleet to give battle. We wore ship, and stood away from the bar, permitting the enemy to approach by slow degrees. When she was sufficiently near we took in all sail, and wearing short round, ran up within hail. It was now dark, about nine o'clock. The enemy hailed, "What ship is that?" We replied: "Her Majesty's steamer Petrel." The reply was, "I'll send a boat on board."

We now hailed in turn, to know what the enemy was, and when we received the reply that she was the United States steamer Hatteras, we again hailed and informed him that we were the Confederate steamer Alabama; and at the same time Captain Semmes directed the first lieutenant to open fire on him. This fire was promptly returned, and a brisk action ensued, which lasted, however, only thirteen minutes, as at the end of that time the enemy fired an off-gun, and showed a light; and on being hailed to know if he surrendered, he said he did, and was in a sinking condition. We immediately dispatched boats to his assistance, and had just time to rescue the crew, when the ship went down. The casualties were slight on both sides, although the action was fought at a distance of one hundred and fifty to four hundred yards. Our shot all told on his hull, about the waterline, and hence the small number of killed and wounded on the part of the enemy— two of the former and three of the latter. We had none killed, and only one wounded, although the Alabama received several shot-holes, doing no material damage. The Hatteras mounted eight guns, and had a crew of eighteen officers and one hundred and eight men. The Alabama had also eight guns, with a small captured piece (a twenty-four pounder, too light to be of any service), and a crew of one hundred and ten men, exclusive of officers.

Four of the Hatteras's guns were thirty-two pounders, the same calibre as our broadside guns, but our pivot guns were heavier than theirs. This was the only disparity between the two ships. The United States frigate Brooklyn and another steamer came out in pursuit soon after the action commenced, but missed us in the darkness of the night. The Alabama then proceeded to Kingston, Jamaica, where the prisoners were landed on the 20th January, and we repaired damages and coaled, and on the 25th proceeded again to sea.

We touched at the island of St. Domingo, on the 28th, to land two enemy's crews we had captured; sailed again next day for the equator, and remained for some days at the island of Fernando de Noronha. From thence we put into Bahia, where we landed more prisoners. The government at this place demanded explanations of our proceedings at Fernando de Noronha, as the American consul represented that we had made captures there in Brazilian waters; but as we clearly showed that no vessel had been taken within a prescribed distance from the island, the authorities were satisfied, and we were allowed to remain ten days, refitting.

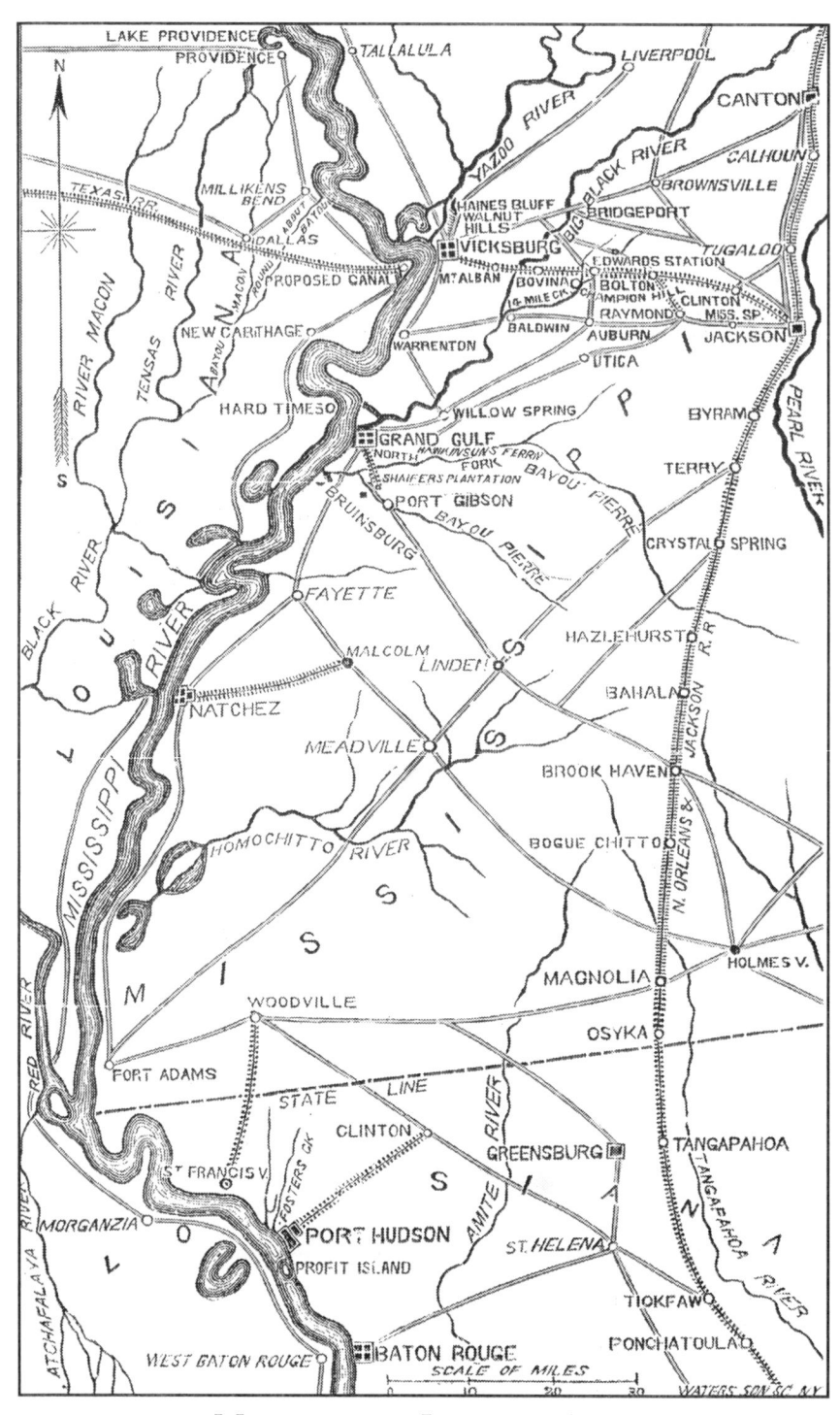

MISSISSIPPI AND LOUISIANA AREA

Meanwhile, the Castor, a coal ship, ostensibly bound for Shanghai, entered the port, and we commenced coaling from her. The American consul again protested, and wrote to the president of Bahia, stating that the Castor had on board guns and sailors for the Confederates. The president next day forwarded this complaint to the English consul at Bahia, inviting him to accompany the custom-house officers on board the Castor, to see whether the complaint had any foundation. The English consul returned the following reply:

"The denunciation of the American consul is devoid of foundation. The facts he has put forward are quite inexact. The opinion he expresses is entirely illusive. The English consul has been on board the Castor; has ascertained that she does not carry arms; that her crew consists only of the men upon the ship's books; and that the only real fact of those alleged is her delivery of coal—a proceeding which it is the sole aim of the American consul to prevent. The consul is ready to be present at the visit proposed by the president. The captain of the Castor is perfectly willing to permit such visit, but the consul, in any case, protests against every act assuming the character of the right of search or of requisition by the consul of the United States. He (the English consul) entertains grave doubts of the American consul's right, owing to the mere supply of coal, to raise any claim against an English ship, belonging to a neutral nation, at anchor in the harbor of Bahia, a neutral port. The neutrality resulting from the independent exercise of its right by a state cannot obstruct commercial relations, and a belligerent power is not entitled to demand their cessation in a neutral port between its opponent and the subjects of a neutral nation. Toleration by the president of the province of the supply of coal, by an English ship, to the Confederate cruisers in this port, cannot (without infringing common sense and international law) be considered a hostile act, contrary to the strict neutrality of Brazil."

The proposed visit on board the Castor took place, accompanied by interrogation of captain and crew. The result showed no proof whatever of the allegations, although it seemed pretty clear that the cargo of coal had no other original destination than the Confederate privateer. The captain of the Alabama, indeed, admitted the fact, plainly declaring that be had a perfect right to purchase coal in England, and to provide for its discharge taking place out of a neutral ship, within a neutral port. Captain Semmes, at the same time, requested the president's authorization to continue taking in his coal. The president replied that the coal must be put on shore and sent to the market, where Captain Semmes could buy as much as he pleased. He added that his instructions forbade him to allow the delivery of any kind of goods coming direct from another country, where the sale had taken place abroad. Under these circumstances, Captain Semmes directed the coal ship to meet him at Saldanha Bay, Cape of Good Hope, and we left Bahia. On our passage to the Cape, we captured the S. Gildensleeve, the Justina, Jabez Snow, Amazonian, Talisman, Conrad, A. F. Schmidt, and Express—all valuable prizes, except the Justina, which, being a Baltimore ship, was ransomed, and a number of the crews of the other vessels were transferred to her. The Amazonian attempted to elude us, but we gave chase, and while five miles distant from her, fired our rifle-gun, with a reduced charge of seven pounds powder and a one hundred pound shot, at an extreme elevation, which crossed her bows, and she soon clewed her courses and hove to.

The Conrad, which we captured, was a fine bark, and we fitted her out as a tender to the Alabama. The vessel was named the Tuscaloosa, and commissioned at sea on the 21st June. The command was given to Lieutenant Lowe, an excellent officer, with fifteen men; she was provided with two brass rifled twelve-pounders, pistols, rifles, and ammunition, and having provisions for three months, was ordered to cruise in the direction of the Cape. We then made for Saldanha Bay, where we anchored and repaired ship, expecting to meet the coal vessel; but nothing could be seen of her, and we supposed she must have met with some mishap.*

From Saldanha Bay we came round to Table Bay, and spied the American bark Sea Bride, standing into port, outside of all headlands, and at a distance from the main land. As we approached her, our officers were directed by the captain to make observation of the distance; and all agreed that the capture was made from two to three miles outside of the marine league.

---

* If the Castor was the vessel expected, it is very probable that some mishap occurred to her; for by Rio papers we learned that after the Alabama left, the Federal steam frigate Mohican put in at Bahia, and a report was immediately circulated that she intended to seize the Castor. The captain of the English vessel attempted to leave the port without having complied with the forms required by the customs. He was brought to by the guns of the forts, and put back, and went through the accustomed formalities preparatory to setting sail anew. Before the Castor was outside the harbor, the Mohican got up steam and went in pursuit. Perceiving himself chased, the captain of the Castor determined not to leave the port, but to place himself under the protection of Brazilian ships until the arrival of an English man-of-war. Thereupon the Mohican left Bahia to look after the Confederate privateers.

The total number of our captures has been fifty-six ships, by which we estimate the damage to the enemy to be not less than four millions of dollars, to say nothing of the indirect results of the cruise in the way of loss of freights, high war insurance, and numerous sales of enemy's ships, to put them under neutral flags. In no instance, however, have we destroyed a ship where the proof was complete that the cargo was neutral, though there have been some awkward attempts on the part of unscrupulous merchants to cover property—but when such were destroyed the proof of the fraud was apparent on the papers.

The following is a complete list of her captures: Ockmulgee, Starlight, Ocean Rover, Alert, Weathergauge, Altamaha, Benjamin Tucker, Courser, Virginia, Elisha Dunbar, Brilliant, Emily Farnum, Wave Crest, Dunquerque, Manchester, Tonawanda, Lamplighter, Lafayette, Crenshaw, Lauretta, Baron de Castine, Levi Starbuck, T. B. Wales, Chastalaire, Palmetto, Golden Eagle, Olive Jane, Washington, Betha Thager, J. A. Parker, Punjaub, Morning Star, Kingfisher, Charles Hill, Nora, Louisa Hatch, Lafayette, Kate Corey, Nye, Dorcas Price, Lelah, Union Jack, S. Gildensleeve, J. Snow, Justina, Amazonian, Martha, Union, Ariel, mail steamer ; United States gunboat Hatteras, Golden Rule, Talisman, Conrad, A. F. Schmidt, Express, Sea Bride.

The Alabama had the usual quota of wits and fun-makers among her crew. An Irish fiddler on board is the life of the forecastle. When the men are off duty he sets them dancing to his lighter strains, or, dividing them into Northerners and Southerners, like a true Irishman, he gets up a sham-fight to the spirit-stirring strains of a march, in which fight the Northerners are, of course, invariably beaten. Another sailor, Frank Townshend, is no mean poet, as will be seen from the verses which here follow. He had sung the exploits of their beloved ship to his messmates in rude and vigorous strains.

The Fight of the "Hatteras" and "Alabama"

Off Galveston, the Yankee fleet secure at anchor lay
Preparing for a heavy fight they were to have next day;
Down came the Alabama, like an eagle o'er the wave,
And soon their gunboat Hatteras had found a watery grave.

'Twas in the month of January; the day was bright and clear;
The Alabama she bore down; no Yankee did we fear
Their commodore he spied us; to take us long he burned;
So he sent the smartest boat he had, but she never back returned!

The sun had sunk far in the west when down to us she came;
Our captain quickly hailed her, and asked them for her name;
Then spoke our first lieutenant, for her name had roused his ire,
"This is the Alabama; now, Alabamas, fire."

Then flew a rattling broadside, that made her timbers shake;
And through the holes made in her side the angry waves did break;
We then blew up her engine, that she could steam no more–
They fired a gun to leeward, and so the fight was o'er.

So thirteen minutes passed away before they gave in beat;
A boat had left the Yankee's side, and pulled in for their fleet;
The rest we took onboard of us, as prisoners to stay;
Then stopped and saw their ship go down, and then we bore away.

And now, to give our foes their due, they fought with all their might;
But yet they could not conquer us, for God defends the right;
One at a time the ships they have to fight us they may come,
And rest assured that our good ship from them will never run.

―――――◆●◆―――――

THE RIVER DEVILS

A Federal writer tells the following amusing story:

The principal diver employed at Port Royal for cleaning the bottoms of the monitors, was named—and quite appropriately—Waters. A man of herculean strength and proportions, he became, when clad in his submarine armor, positively monstrous in size and appearance. A more singular sight than to see him roll or tumble into the water and disappear from sight, or popping up, blowing, as the air escaped from his helmet, like a young whale, could scarcely be imagined. Remaining for five or six hours at a time under water, he had become almost amphibious.

Waters had his own ideas of a joke, and when he had a curious audience would wave his scraper about as he bobbed around on the water, with the air of a veritable river-god. One summer day, while he was employed scraping the hull of a monitor, a Negro from one of the up-river plantations came alongside with a boatload of watermelons. While busy selling his melons, the diver came up, and rested himself on the side of the boat. The Negro started at the extraordinary appearance thus suddenly coming out of the water, with alarmed wonder; but when the diver, with gigantic motion, seized one of the plumpest melons in the boat and disappeared under the water—the gurgling of the air from the helmet mixing with his muffled laughter—the fright of the Negro reached a climax. Hastily seizing his oars, without a thought of being paid for his melons, he put off at his best speed, nor was he ever seen in the vicinity of Station Creek again. Believing that the Yankees had brought river devils to aid them in carrying on the war, no persuasion could tempt him again beyond the bounds of the plantation.

Cheer Up, My Lads

By E. King

Cheep up, my lads, a brisk breeze is blowing,
    And swiftly our ship glides through the rough sea;
Unfurled is our banner, and gallantly throwing
    Our star begemmed cross wide over our lee.
Draw hither, my lads, fill your glasses right cheery,
    In red wine we'll drink to the land that I name,
And when duty calls may we never be weary
    Of fighting for freedom, for honor, and fame,
Then drink to the South, dear home of the free,
    And success to her arms on land and on sea!

Should down-trodden nations e'er ask, as a blessing,
    A haven of rest on our own peaceful shore,
We'll lend them a hand, as a parent caressing
    The wandering child that seeks bread at his door.
No higher ambition than this do we cherish,

>   No high sounding titles our names to adorn;
>   The battle we'll brave, or triumphantly perish
>   In defending our flag till it outrides the storm.
>   Then drink to the South, dear home of the free,
>   And success to her arms on land and on sea!
>
>   If war's dread alarms drive peace from your pillow,
>   And we've tyrants to meet upon the wide main,
>   Remember poor Jack, who, rocked on the billow,
>   Is defending the land he may ne'er see again.
>   Then a cheer, boys, we'll give in our rough seaman manner,
>   As we launch forth our fire with unerring eye,
>   And so long as a star shall remain on our banner,
>   With courage we'll fight, or sink boys and die.
>   Then drink to the South, dear home of the free,
>   And success to her arms on land and on sea!

The Attack on the Ironsides

One of the most daring and gallant naval exploits of the war, distinguished by the greatest coolness, presence of mind, and intrepidity of the brave men associated in the enterprise, was performed Monday night, October 6th, 1863. This was no less than an attempt to blow up the United States steamer New Ironsides, lying off Morris Island. Though not fully meeting the expectations of those who conceived the plan, and those who carried it into execution, it called forth unbounded admiration for the brilliant heroism of the actors in their dangerous but patriotic and self-sacrificing undertaking.

The torpedo-steamer David, with a crew of four volunteers, consisting of Lieutenant William T. Glassell, J. H. Toombs, chief engineer, and James Sullivan, fireman of the gunboat Chicara, with J. W. Cannon, assistant pilot of the gunboat Palmetto State, left South Atlantic wharf between six and seven o'clock in the evening, for the purpose of running out to the Ironsides, exploding a torpedo under that vessel near amidships, and if possible blow her up. The weather, being dark and hazy, favored the enterprise. The boat, with its gallant little crew, preceded down the harbor, skirting along the shoals on the inside of the channel, until nearly abreast of their formidable antagonist, the New Ironsides.

They remained in this position for a short time, circling around on the large shoal near the anchorage of the object of their visit. Lieutenant Glassell, with a double-barreled gun, sat in front of Pilot Cannon, who had charge of the helm. Chief engineer Toombs was at the engine, with the brave and undaunted Sullivan, the volunteer fireman, when something like the following conversation ensued:

Lieutenant Glassell.—"It is now nine o'clock; shall we strike her?"
Pilot Cannon.—"That is what we came for; I am ready."
Engineer Toombs.—"Let us go at her, then, and do our best."
Sullivan, Fireman.—"I am with you all, and waiting; go ahead."

The boat was now put bow on, and aimed directly for the Ironsides. As the little steamer darted forward, the lookout on the Ironsides hailed them with—"Take care there, you will run into us; what steamer is that?" Lieutenant Glassell replied by discharging one barrel at the Yankee sentinel, and tendering the gun to Pilot Cannon, told him there was another Yankee, pointing to one with his body half over the bulwarks, and asked Cannon to take care of him with the other barrel.

The next moment they had struck the Ironsides, and exploded the torpedo about fifteen feet from the keel, on the starboard side. An immense volume of water was thrown up, covering the little boat, and going through the smokestack, entered the furnace, completely extinguishing the fires.

In addition to this, pieces of the ballast had fallen into the works of the engine, rendering it unmanageable at that time. Volley after volley of musketry from the crew of the Ironsides and from the launches began to pour in upon them. Lieutenant Glassell gave the order to back, but it was found impossible. In this condition, with no shelter, and no hope of escape, they thought it best to surrender, and hailed the enemy to that effect. The Yankees, however, paid no attention to the call. It was then proposed to put on their life-preservers, jump overboard, and endeavor to swim to the shore. All but Pilot Cannon consented. The latter, being unable to swim, said he would stay and take his chances in the boat. Lieutenant Glassell, Engineer Toombs, and Sullivan the fireman, left the boat, the first two having on life-preservers, and the latter supporting himself on one of the hatches thrown to him by the pilot. Engineer Toombs, becoming embarrassed with his clothing in the water, got back to the boat, and was assisted in by Cannon.

The boat was then rapidly drifting from the Ironsides. He now fortunately found a match, and lighting a torch, crept back to the engine, discovered and removed the cause of its not working, and soon got it in order. Engineer Toombs and Cannon reached their wharf in the city about midnight, fatigued, and presenting a worn-out appearance, but rejoicing at their fortunate and narrow escape.

THE CRUISE OF THE FLORIDA

Arriving in Brest, by way of Quimper and Chateaulin the first thing I heard on getting on board the steamer which navigates the picturesque little river Elorn from the latter place to Brest, was the arrival of the Confederate States cruiser Florida; and on crossing the glorious Rade de Brest for the mouth of the harbor, I had no difficulty in making out this now celebrated vessel, as she lay at anchor among some of the giants of the French navy—a long, low, black, rakish-looking craft, not over smart in appearance, yet useful, every inch of her—a pigmy among these monsters, and yet a formidable pigmy, even to the unpracticed eye, the Palmetto flag flying proudly from her mizzen. We happened to have a French vice-admiral, a Russian vice-admiral, and a senator of the empire on board; and you may imagine there was an infinity of gossip, but no reliable information.

When we landed at the Cale in the harbor, the crowd which usually assembles to welcome or pester new comers was full of *"La Floride"* and her doings. *"Elle a,"* cried an enthusiastic *commissionaire* to me, *"elle a, Monsieur, je vous assure sur ma parole d'honneur, près deux millions de livres sterling à bord, tout en or, je vous assure."* *"Eh! mon Dieu! c'est beaucoup!"* cried a smart little *mousse* from the Turenne. I could not help agreeing with the *mousse* that the sum was certainly a great deal.

That evening (aided by my fellow-traveler, Mr. Henry Tupper, vice-consul of France in Guernsey and one of the jurats of that island) I found some of the officers of the Florida at the Hotel de Nantes (Rue d'Aiguillon). Lieutenant Lingard Hoole (a young man, who apparently did not number more than twenty-three years) received us courteously, and gave us his card to assure us admission on board. He stated, however, that his superior officer, Captain Maffit, was generally to be found on board his vessel, and would be glad to see us. The frankness, courtesy, and total absence of boasting manifested by this young officer, impressed us most favorably.

All next day it blew a gale of wind in the Rade, and we could not find a boat to venture out. To-day, however, the weather was most propitious, and early morning found us alongside of the Florida. We sent our cards to Captain Maffit, and were immediately admitted on board, the captain himself coming to the top of the companion to receive us. Directly Captain Maffit understood that we were British subjects, he invited us below into his little cabin, and when I told him that there were many people in England who regarded his career with great interest, he entered very freely into a recital of his adventures.

I will here subjoin a copy of some notes which Captain Maffit subsequently handed to me, relative to the career of the Florida, promising, at the same time, a continuation, which has not yet arrived. They are as follows:

"The C. S. steamer Florida, Commander J. N. Maffit. This steamer was built in Liverpool, and sent to Nassau in April, 1862; was put in the Admiralty Court; cleared on the 6th of August, when her present commander took charge with eighteen men; went to sea; met her tender, and received guns, etc. On the 16th of August the yellow fever appeared on board, and Captain Maffit had to perform surgeon's duty, until necessity forced the vessel into Cardenas. There she lost nearly all her crew, her paymaster, and third engineer. She ran the blockade off Havana, in and out; and on the 4th of September appeared off Mobile. The entire blockading fleet put after her. Captain Maffit was brought up from a bed of sickness (yellow fever) to take her in. For two hours and forty-eight minutes she was under a close fire. All the crew were sent below, and the officers only remained on deck, for she had but eleven men on duty, and her guns were not furnished with rammers, quoins, beds, or sights; in fact, she was almost helpless. Three heavy shots struck her hull. One shell struck her amidships, and passed through, killing one man and wounding seven. Her standing rigging was shot away, and some fifteen hundred shrapnel shot struck her hull and masts."

So far the notes which Captain Maffit has as yet found time to send me. Of the captain himself, I may say that he is a slight, middle-sized, well-knit man, of about forty-two—a merry-looking man, with a ready, determined air, full of life and business; apparently the sort of man who is equally, ready for a fight or a jollification, and whose preference for the latter would by no means interfere with his creditable conduct of the former. His plainly-furnished little state-room looked as business-like as a merchant's office. The round table in the centre was strewn with books and innumerable manuscripts, and on the shelves were formidable-looking rows of account books, charts, etc. I may observe of the cabin, as of every part of the Florida, that none of it appeared to have been built for ornament—all for use. "You see," said the captain, pointing to the heaps of papers, letters on files, account books, etc., which literally littered the table, "you see I've no sinecure of it. Since my paymaster died I've had to be my own paymaster. There's a young man named Davis—no relation to our President—who does paymaster's duty; but he's not yet quite up to the work."

Captain Maffit forthwith began an animated recital of his career and adventures. He is forty-two years old, and is the oldest officer on board. All the officers were born in the Confederate States, and most of them were officers in the United States navy before the outbreak of the war. The oldest of the officers is not more than twenty-three. The men are more mixed. There are about one hundred able seamen on board the Florida, and about thirteen officers. Four fine fellows are from the neighborhood of Brest. Captain Maffit says that he has hardly ever taken a prize but what some of the crew of the prize have come forward to say—"Should like to serve with you, sir." Generally speaking, he has to refuse; but sometimes, when he sees a very likely fellow, he takes him on.

Captain Maffit was a lieutenant of the United States navy before the outbreak, and in that capacity distinguished himself greatly. In 1858, he commanded the brig Dolphin, when he captured the slaver Echo, with four hundred slaves on board, and took her into Charleston. For this feat his health was drank at a public dinner at Liverpool; and it is a curious fact, for those who maintain that the civil war in America is founded upon the slave question, that the commander of this important Confederate cruiser, should be the very man who has distinguished himself actively against the slave trade. In 1859, Captain Maffit commanded the United States steamer Crusader, and captured four slavers.

The captain had a great deal to say about his successful feat at Mobile. In his opinion, it has been the greatest naval feat of modern times. He dwelt long and warmly upon the incidents of the affair, and pointed proudly to the marks of shrapnel, which were numerous enough, upon the masts and smoke-stacks. The Florida was struck with three heavy shots on the occasion, and one can easily perceive in the side of the ship where the mischief caused by the eleven-inch shell has been repaired. The Florida made no endeavor to reply to the fire which she received, the sea running too high to admit of steady aim, and her small crew being too much occupied in the management of the ship. The captain showed us a water-color sketch (very well drawn by one of the midshipmen) of the Florida running the blockade. It would not have disgraced a professional artist.

The only broadside which the Florida has fired in anger was against the Ericsson, an armed merchantman, which she encountered some forty miles from New York. The Ericsson, a very large vessel, did not reply, but made the best of her way off, and succeeded in escaping. When they ventured within forty miles of New York, they did not know that the arrival of the Tacony, one of their "outfits," had put the New Yorkers on their guard, and they soon found that there were about seventy armed vessels out searching for them, and so were glad to retreat. "We never seek a fight," said Captain Maffit, "and we don't avoid one. You see, we've only two vessels against fifteen hundred; so we should stand a poor chance. Our object is merely to destroy their commerce, so as to bring about a peace. We have taken altogether seventy-two prizes, and estimate the value at about fifteen million of dollars. The Jacob Bell alone was worth two million one hundred thousand dollars." The captain exhibited a book in which all the prizes were regularly entered, and all particulars relating thereto. He explained that their mode of procedure was to burn and destroy the property of the Northern States wherever they found it. I asked if they took gold and precious articles, and the reply was, "Pretty quick, when we get them."

The papers of the burned prizes are all kept, and a valuation is made before the destruction of the vessels, in the expectation that when peace is restored, the Confederate government will make an appropriation of money equivalent to the claims of the captors. In consequence of this arrangement there is very little actual treasure on board the Florida; the officers and crew are working mainly on the faith of the future independence and solvency of the Confederacy. "Any way," said Captain Maffit, "we have cost the government very little, for we've lived on the enemy; O, yes, we've served them out beautifully." In reply to some questions as to the method of capture, the captain said, "We only make war with the United States government, and we respect private property. We treat prisoners of war with the greatest respect. Most of those whom we have captured have spoken well of us. To be sure, we have met with some ungrateful rascals; but you meet with those all the world over. The best prize we took was the Anglo-Saxon, which we took in the English Channel, the other day, in mid channel, about sixty miles from Cork. She had coal on board, and we burned her.

"The pilot was a saucy fellow, and maintained that he was on his piloting ground. He insisted on being landed in an English port; but we could not do that. I brought him and twenty-four men here (to Brest), and sent them to the English consul. If the pilot has any just claim upon us, it will be settled by the Confederate government. That's not my business. My business is to take care of the ship."

When the Florida came into Brest, she had been at sea eight months without spending more than four entire days in port. Before entering the port of Brest, she had not been more than twenty-four hours in any one port, although she had visited Nassau, Bermuda, Pernambuco, and Sierra (Brazil). "Yes, indeed, sir," said the captain, "two hundred and forty-five days upon solid junk, without repairs or provisions." During all this time, they have only lost fifteen men, including those who were killed and wounded at Mobile, the paymaster (who died of consumption), and one officer who was accidentally drowned. They have come into Brest to repair the engines, which are somewhat out of order, the shaft being quite out of line. The emperor has given orders that the Florida is to be admitted into the port for all necessary repairs, and is to be supplied with every thing she may require except munitions of war.

In the course of conversation, Captain Maffit gave me an account of what he called the "outfits" of the Florida. These have been three in number. The Clarence was captured off Pernambuco on the 5th of May, and Lieutenant Reed was put on board with twenty men and one gun. These were afterward changed to the Tacony, a better vessel, which was captured shortly after, and (to borrow Captain Maffit's expression) "she captured right and left." Finally, she took the revenue cutter off Portland harbor. The other "fit-out" was the Lapwing, on board of which Lieutenant Avrett was put to cruise on the equator. He made several captures, and has now returned to his ship.

Captain Maffit showed us over his ship, which was in pretty good order, considering the eight months' almost interrupted cruise, and he presented us both with a photographic picture of her, which was taken at Bermuda. The Florida mounts only eight guns—six forty-eight pounders of the Blakely pattern, made at Low Moor, and stern and bow chasers.

On taking our leave, I asked Captain Maffit whether he expected to be intercepted on leaving Brest, pointing at the same time to the Goulet, the narrow passage which affords the only ingress and egress to and from the Rade. "Well," replied he, "I expect there will be seven or eight of them out there before long, but I'm not afraid. I've run eight blockades already, and it'll go hard but I'll run the ninth."

Use for Them

A gentleman standing at the navy yard, in Richmond, one day, and looking at one of the new gunboats then in progress of construction, asked a sailor who was lounging near:

"What are they going to do with that vessel?"

"Why, don't you know?" responded the sailor. "Why, blow her up to be sure. It's d——d expensive, but it's the way to get along with the government."

Dixie's gallant tars never ceased to resent the destruction of their brave old "Virginia."

Two Things That Sounded Alike

There was a laughable story frequently repeated at Fortress Monroe, says an exchanged prisoner, concerning a certain high Federal commander, who was pious enough in creed, but on certain occasions, when his dander was up, could do full justice to his feelings by giving them mouth. When, therefore, the Virginia came down, the high official in question was all motion; he was highly excited, and now and then he eased his feelings by certain forcible ejaculations in the shape of solid balls of nouns substantive. A contraband, who heard him, gave a very good description of how the white haired old man moved about in the storm of shells. "By golly, boss," said he, "but de way dat old mass' off'cer moved about dat day war a caution. He went dis way and dat way; he went hea' and he went dar; but to hab hearn de old mass' swar!—Boss, it's de solemn truf, dat de way de old un swar war plumb nigh like preaching."

A Daring Feat

On Friday, July 25th, 1862, some half-dozen men, attached to the Prince George cavalry, conceived the idea of destroying one or more of the Federal vessels, which for several days past have literally covered the surface of the river in front of General McClellan's camp. Having procured a boat (the largest accessible), Corporal Cocke, Thomas Martin, William Daniel, Alexander Dimitry, and William Williams, embarked from Coggins's Point about one o'clock Saturday morning, and pulled off quietly for a very fine-looking schooner, of one hundred and sixty-three tons burthen, lying in the stream some half a mile from the southern shore. The Petersburg *Express* says:

As they neared the vessel, a small dog on board discovered their movements and commenced barking furiously. Two gunboats were lying but a few hundred yards distant, and many steamers and sail vessels in close proximity; but the enterprise had been undertaken, and the brave boys could not think of returning without accomplishing their object. Making fast to the vessel, they endeavored to seize the dog and stop his mouth by sending him to the bottom; but the animal would not allow a stranger's hand to be placed upon him. His barking had now aroused the captain of the vessel, who came upon deck and desired to know the cause of the untimely visit. He was answered by Martin, who quickly sprang to the deck of the schooner, and informed the captain that he had come at the bidding of General McClellan to effect his arrest. The captain expressed great surprise, declared his innocence of crime, and wished to know what were the charges against him. He was told by Martin that he was not there to decide upon his guilt or innocence, nor to prefer charges of any sort, but to effect his arrest, as General McClellan had ordered. The captain then consented to submit, and, manifesting no disposition to resist, was allowed to get into the boat untied. In the meantime the other five soldiers had reached the deck of the vessel, and gone into the cabin. Here they found a straw bed, which was ripped open, set on fire, and the cabin door closed. The party speedily disembarked, leaving the crew behind, who, it is supposed, escaped on the small boat belonging to the schooner. They were not taken because the boat used by the boarding party had a hole near its top, and could carry but seven men. As the surprise party pulled off for the southern shore, the captain of the schooner had his suspicions aroused as to the arrest having been made by order of McClellan, and remarked to his captors that the general's headquarters were not on that side of the river. He was told to "hold his peace"; that his captors knew what they were about; that they had changed their mind, and intended taking him to a Confederate instead of a Federal general. The captain now became greatly alarmed, and besought the clemency of his captors, stating with tears in his eye that he had a wife and children in New York; who would be not only deeply distressed at his loss, but greatly impoverished. His fears were quieted by the assurance that he would not be harmed, but that, as he was a subject of the Lincoln Government, he must consider his capture as entirely legitimate, and himself a prisoner of war.

Upon reaching the shore, the captain declared that, had he seen his captors approach from the southern bank, the ruse adopted would not have availed; for he had arms aboard—Enfield rifles—and would have only surrendered with his life.

In the passage from the vessel to the shore, not a ray of light, save the lamp in the rigging, was to be seen, and our boys had made up their minds that the vessel would not burn, and that the arrest of the captain was the only result of their enterprise. But they were soon most agreeably disappointed; for as they ascended the bank, the fire suddenly burst out, and in a few minutes the flames were licking the sides of the vessel from bow to stern. She burned slowly, but brightly, and the flames illuminated the river and the country around for miles. Our informant states that it was quite amusing to witness the commotion among the fleet of Old Abe, consisting of some two hundred steam and sailing craft. Steam was crowded on gunboats and transports, and the sailing craft were quickly towed out of the reach of the burning schooner. She continued to burn from half-past one until the dawn of day, when only such portions as were below the water's edge remained.

The schooner was nearly new, called the Louisa Rives, and commanded by Captain John A. Jones, of New York. She was one hundred and sixty-three tons burthen, loaded with corn and provisions, and valued at eight thousand dollars exclusive of cargo. Captain Jones was brought to Petersburg Saturday and lodged in jail, where he doubtless ruminated on the dating of the rebels and lamented over the fortunes of war.

Just above the Louisa Rives, several schooners were moored, but a gunboat lying alongside, it was considered somewhat imprudent to attempt to burn them. Another batch of vessels lay not far below the Louisa Rives, but a gunboat was near these also. Between the destroyed vessel and the Berkeley shore the water was studded with vessels, but the Confederate force was too small to venture in their midst.

The light from the burning vessel reflected brightly on the north bank of the James, and for miles and miles the tents of the Federal army were distinctly visible.

Praise from an Enemy

A Federal writer says:

Beverly Kennon, who was in command of the Governor Moore, one of the gunboats opposed to our fleet in the battle on the Mississippi below New Orleans, whatever his political and moral errors may be, is a thoroughly brave and gallant man.

When his craft was actually sinking, riddled like a sieve by the ordnance of the Oneida and other vessels, Lee, who was in command of that gunboat, shouted out to him, pointing as he did so to the stars and bars, which were still streaming upon her deck, "I say, there, haul down that d——d rag, will you?" "I'm d——d if I do," yelled Beverly Kennon in return. "I will see you in hell first!" Improbable as the meeting thus proposed may be, none can deny that the sinking rebel showed his possession of considerable "grit," or will be disposed to regret that he had a chance presented him, albeit against his will, of improving the acquaintance so agreeably commenced, in his subsequent compulsory visit to our fleet.

Semmes Outwitting the Vanderbilt

The intelligence that the Confederate war steamer Alabama was cruising about the Cape of Good Hope, created much excitement among the Federals. In the Straits of Sunda she captured some United States merchant vessels, and was put upon her speed by the Vanderbilt. When night came on, the Alabama was about twenty miles ahead of her pursuer, and, under cover of darkness, she unshipped her funnel, put out her fires, and set sail.

The ship was then put about, and stood in the direction of where they had last seen the Vanderbilt. At daybreak she was within only a mile of her enemy, who actually bore down and inquired if they had seen a large steamer standing to the northward. Captain Semmes graciously replied, "Yes; she was going ahead, full speed, and must be one hundred miles away by this." At this information, so opportunely obtained, the Vanderbilt immediately put on all steam, and went on a wild goose chase, while Semmes quietly shipped his funnel and bore away in an opposite direction.

Pleasant Hoax All Round

After the battle between the Kearsarge and Alabama, there was great excitement in Liverpool at the expected arrival there of Captain Semmes, and for several hours the neighborhood of the Exchange was crowded with persons anxious to get at least a glimpse of the famous sea raider.

About one o'clock, a double hoax was played in a highly successful manner. A middle aged man, who had passed several years in tropical climates, and delighted in sporting a white blouse and a Panama hat during the summer time, was often to be found lounging about one of the landing stages, having some connection with the shipping. Possessing a bronzed complexion, clean shaved cheeks and chin, and a pair of fierce moustaches, some mad wag contrived the idea of palming him off upon the public as "Captain Raphael Semmes, Confederate States Navy." Accordingly he was got hold of, treated very hospitably, and then asked to go on 'Change, in order to see the redoubtable hero of the Sunday's sea-fight arrive. One or two out-door officials connected with the underwriter's room were also got in tow, and under some pretence or other the fictitious Captain Semmes was taken through Brown's building, where the Southern clubs headquarters were, and was then brought out at the entrance which abuts on the Exchange flags.

This ruse was quite enough. Coming from such a neighborhood, followed by the underwriter's officials, and making across the flags in the direction of the newsroom, the expectant crowd at once made up their minds that this was the man they were on the lookout for, and they clapped their hands, waved their hats and caps, and cheered vociferously.

The object of all this demonstration was rather nonplussed at first; but readily catching the drift of the joke, he raised his straw hat, "bobbed around," and by his extemporized gracious demeanor, after the manner of "lions," raised the enthusiasm to fever heat—a special cheer rewarding a reverential obeisance that he made on passing Nelson's monument. He disappeared, not at the main entrance to the newsroom, but at the foot of the stairs leading to the underwriter's room, and in a little time it leaked out that the public had been hoaxed, that the object of their ovation was not Captain Semmes at all, but a "highly respectable" sailor's boardinghouse keeper, living in Leeds street, of the name of ——. But never mind, if he is allowed to be nameless.

A Bold Dash

Captain Lynch, in his report to the C.S. Navy Department, relates the following occurrence, which took place off Newport News:

The water being too low in the Chesapeake and Albemarle canal, for this vessel (the Sea Bird) to proceed to Roanoke Island, we last evening steamed down and anchored in the bight of Craney Island. This morning, a little before daylight, we weighed anchor and stood across to Newport News. About 7.30 A.M. an enemy's steamer passed out of James river, with a schooner in tow, and steered for Fortress Monroe. We immediately gave chase, when she cut the schooner adrift, and carried a heavy head of steam, in order to get under the cover of numerous men-of-war lying off the Fortress. We were fast closing in with her, however, when the explosion of our second shell set her on fire. Believing her destruction was certain, knowing that her crew could be rescued by boats from the vessels not far distant from her, and it being unusual for this vessel to approach her, we steered for and took the abandoned schooner in tow. In the meantime one large steamer from Newport News, and ten others from Hampton Roads and the Fortress, were making their way toward us, when an exciting scene took place; we endeavoring to carry the prize into port, and they making every effort to intercept, and by constant firing, disable us. Many shells from the ships and the Fortress exploded quite near us, and four or five passed immediately over the deck. We succeeded in fighting our way through, with the prize in tow, without the slightest injury to either, and gratefully attribute our escape to something more than chance or human agency. We know that a large steamer was struck once and a smaller one twice, by our shot; the former was reported to be seriously injured. The prize is a large schooner, her hold coated with zinc and filled with water for Fortress Monroe.

Anecdote of Stonewall Jackson

At a council of generals early in the war, one remarked that Major —— was wounded, and would not be able to perform a duty that it was proposed to assign him. "Wounded!" said Jackson. "If it really is so, I think it must have been by an accidental discharge of his duty."

Vicksburg—A Ballad

By Paul H. Hayne

I.

Fox sixty days and upwards,
   A storm of shell and shot
Rained 'round us in flaming shower
   But still we faltered not
"If the noble city perish,"
   Our grand young leader said,
"Let the only walls the foe shall scale
   Be the ramparts of the dead!"

II.

For sixty days and upwards
   The eye of heaven waxed dim,
And even throughout God's holy morn,
   O'er Christian's prayer and hymn,
Arose a hissing tumult,
   As if the fiends of air

Strove to ingulf the voice of faith
  In the shrieks of their despair.

III.

There was wailing in the houses,
  There was trembling on the marts,
While the tempests raged and thundered,
  'Mid the silent thrill of hearts;
But the Lord, our shield, was with us
  And ere a month had sped
Our very women walked the streets
  With scarce one throb of dread.

IV.

And the little children gambolled,
  Their faces purely raised,
Just for a wondering moment,
  As the huge bomb whirled and blazed,—
Then turned with silvery laughter
  To the sports which children love,
Thrice mailed in the sweet, instinctive though
  That the good God watched above.

V.

Yet the hailing bolts fell faster,
  From scores of flame-clad ships,
And about us, denser, darker
  Grew the conflict's wild eclipse,
Till a solid cloud closed o'er us,
  Like a type of doom and ire,
Whence shot a thousand quivering tongues
  Of forked and vengeful fire.

VI.

But the unseen hands of angels
  Those death-shafts turned aside,

> And the dove of heavenly mercy
>   Ruled o'er the battle tide;
> In the houses ceased the wailing,
>   And through the war-scarred marts
> The people trode, with steps of hope,
>   To the music in their hearts.

THE WRECK OF THE VESTA

The following account of the wreck and destruction of the blockade-runner Vesta is taken from a letter written by the correspondent of the *Richmond Dispatch*, "Bohemian," who was a passenger on board upon his return from abroad:

* * * * Sunday was wearing rapidly away as we lay off the town of St. Georges, steam was up, and every thing in readiness for departure when the order should be given. It was a little after four o'clock before the anchor was weighed, but in a short time thereafter we passed along the town, winding among the little islands, down by the scowling black-mouthed guns of the fortress, straight through the narrow pass which opened out into the broad Atlantic. On we went over the heaving waves, farther and farther from the fast receding shores; dusky night shadows gathered over the sea, deepening every moment, until the land grew dim and indistinct, and the "still vexed Bermoothes," was hidden from our view. When the stars came out there was nothing but sky and water; and then our "homeward bound" sea voyage was begun. Two days and nights of good sailing followed, with scarcely a sail to turn us from the proper course. The third day out, however, our troubles began. The weather grew heavy, the sea rough, and several sail were seen and ran from. The next day, and the next, were both stormy, and the sun was not a moment visible. We had then reached the cruising grounds and were chased here and there in every direction.

The Vesta was a new iron steamer, with double engines and screw, well fitted up for blockade running, and had on board a valuable cargo belonging to the government. Under full steam she could make twelve or fourteen knots, and I am confident the latter speed was made for two or three hours when chased by Yankee cruisers. A sister ship to the Ceres, she was an admirable craft, and upon all occasions conducted herself with marked propriety, walking rapidly away from all strangers who offered any uncalled-for attentions. Saturday, January 9th, we had a serious chase, and were driven far to the southward before night came and gave us an opportunity of heading again toward the land. This we expected to make before day—in time to run in under the guns of Fort Fisher before it was light—but after running in till nearly sunrise no land appeared. We had gone too far during the chase to make the return distance in time. Heading out again, we ran some half an hour, and then no cruiser being in sight, the engines were stopped and the ship hove to. The sun came out and a chance offered to get our position, but the captain was asleep, and the first officer (Tickle) made an attempt with the sextant, but nothing definite came of it. It was supposed we were some five and forty miles off Cape Lookout, but whether we were or not may be classed among "historical doubts." Well not to make my story too long, here we remained until about midday, when a steamer came in sight and immediately bore down upon us. Scarcely had we got under steam before two more steamers had discovered us and joined in the chase. Of course we now had to run for it. It was impossible to go at full speed without showing a black cloud of smoke, and, as soon as this became visible, we had the whole blockading fleet down upon us. They sprang up upon every side, as if by magic, and in half an hour we were completely surrounded. Capture seemed certain, and there was no chance of escape except to run the gauntlet. This was determined upon and on we bowled! straight through the fleet, eleven steamers fast closing in upon us. Three or four ahead were running across our bows, trying to cut us off, as many more on either beam, bearing down upon us, and the rest coming up astern.

  At length they opened fire at a distance of nearly a mile, firing their bow guns, still keeping on their course. The shots fell all around us, but for a long time none struck the ship. Nearer and nearer they came, and then, when only half a mile away, two, on the bows, veered around and gave us a broadside. This was repeated every few moments, and this in reality proved the means of our escape; for the time lost in turning gave us the lead, and slipping between the two ahead, we ran the gauntlet of their fire, and in a short time every one of them was left astern. The firing still continued, and one shot passed through the ship, but doing little damage. Dark came on, slowly enough it seemed to us, and finally we were hidden sufficiently to change the course. All our pursuers passed by us, and, completely doubling on them, we turned as was supposed again toward Wilmington. It was a hot fire for a time and for over two hours we were a target for Yankee gunners. Eighty-seven shots were fired from all the ships, but, providentially, no one on board was injured. Captain Eustace managed the ship well, and during the hottest fire ran up his flag to show defiance.

Free once more, another attempt was made to run in; but now, I am sorry to say, our greatest trial came. Captain Eustace, during the action, had visited the lockers a little too often, and just in the first moment of our triumph became quite under the influence of drink. The pilot, Adkins, was very drunk, hopelessly so, and Mr. Tickle, the first officer, completely stupefied with liquor. It was a sad state of things, and in a short time thereafter occasioned the loss of the poor little Vesta. Putting the ship upon a course, the captain sat in a chair upon the deck and slept for over an hour. The pilot was in the cabin, and the first officer unfit for duty. The second officer was at the wheel, where he had been from early in the day, *and not one officer of the ship was on lookout.* When I went on deck they were not to be seen, and Mr. Perrin of the navy, and a few of the men, were watching for the enemy. When the captain woke he changed the course toward the land, and about two o'clock in the morning we came upon it. With great difficulty the pilot was got on deck, and put in charge of the ship, at the same time, he says, he asked the position, and was told we were ten miles north of Fort Fisher. "Then," said he, "I know where I am," and he gave a course. The captain's statement is, that he asked the pilot if he recognized the land, and his reply was that "he knew it well." I give both stories, leaving all inference as to the amount of knowledge either had of the position of the ship or of the coast. In fifteen minutes we were among the breakers, the vessel was headed directly into them, and in a moment we were fast in the sand. The engines were reversed and worked for some hours, with full head of steam, but this only imbedded her the more. After a time the ladies were sent ashore in the boat, and a portion of their baggage landed; but a boat was refused the passengers to save all their trunks and packages until quite too late.

Just before sunrise, Captain Eustace set fire to the vessel and afterward, began to save the baggage. At this time no sail was in sight, and not

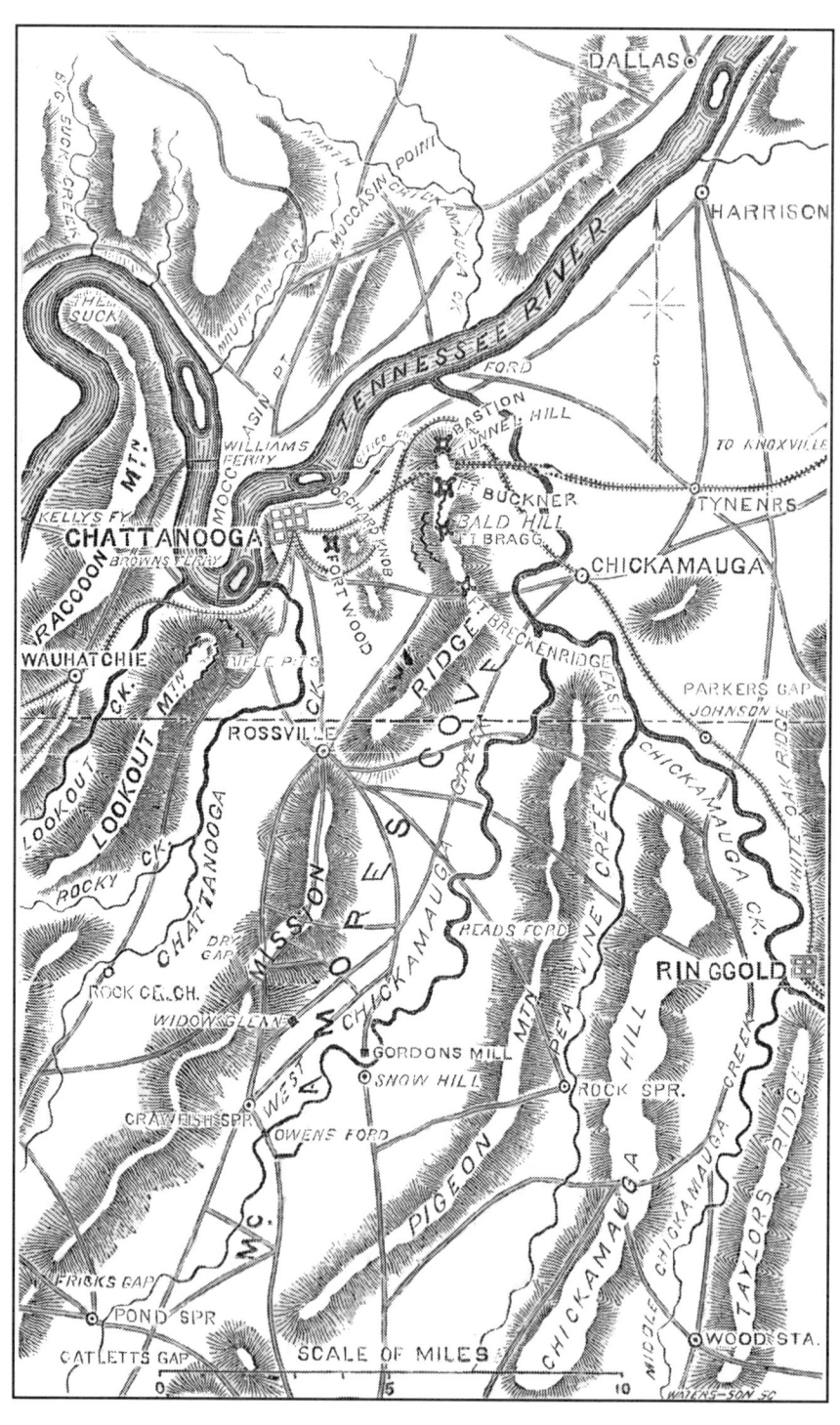

CHATTANOOGA, TENN., AND NORTH GEORGIA AREA

until some hours after, when attracted by the smoke of the burning ship, did one come in view, and it was quite two in the evening when she ranged alongside. Then all that remained of the Vesta was an empty, useless shell. Scarcely any thing was saved, the passengers losing a portion of their baggage. A splendid suit of uniform, sent as a present to General Lee, was also burned, and beside a large cargo of shoes and army goods belonging to the government. It was a total loss.

A Burial at Sea

A correspondent at Nassau, N. P., wrote as follows:

A melancholy incident occurred upon the steamship Fannie, while being chased by a Yankee man-of-war. One of the passengers on board, Captain Frank Du Barry, late chief of ordnance on General Beauregard's staff, C.S.A., died. Preparations had to be completed for his burial, which took place amid all the excitement of the chase. A burial at sea is a ceremony at all times full of solemnity, but it is when coupled with such events as this that war assumes its most repulsive aspect. In that frail little steamer, quivering with her efforts to escape the relentless fate bearing down on her with frowning guns and the ferocity of a tiger, while every living heart on board was throbbing with anxiety for safety they were suddenly called upon to render the last and most solemn rites known to our existence. No time then to stop in mid-ocean, while words that consigned "dust to dust," "ashes to ashes," went up in presence of the grim destroyer, but still dashing onward through the waves—a short and hurried service, a heavy splash, and a body sank to its eternal resting-place in the broad ocean's bosom, while all that was dear to it in life sped from it on its way like the arrow from the bow.

Capture of Gunboats in the Rappahannock

A correspondent of the *Richmond Dispatch*, writing from Port Royal, Aug. 28, 1863, gives the following sketch:

Some two weeks ago a party of seamen, armed to the teeth and accompanied by four splendid boats, left the city of Richmond on the Mechanicsville road. Their destination was a matter of conjecture, and more than one anxious *quid nunc* puzzled his brain over the problem. The quickened imagination of a curious man soon works out a troublesome secret, and before half the day had elapsed I was regaled with a dozen different accounts, each of them undoubtedly correct. It may seem singular that when the Secretary of the Navy gave me orders to join the party, he did not take me into his confidence, and I was therefore as ignorant about the matter as about the plans of General Lee. I must confess, then, to a certain amount of interest in the stories confidently whispered into my buttonhole, and I listened attentively to the recital of disasters about to befall me, and saw work marked out that would occupy several months, and finally consign me to Fort Delaware or to somewhere else. It was a cheerful prospect—but beyond a doubt. My orders came late in the day, when I was on liberty in the city, enjoying the luxury of leisure and white linen. I was to start at daylight in the morning, but owing to the difficulty of obtaining a passport from the courteous officers of that delectable office on Ninth street, I was delayed until meridian the following day. My command was then some eighteen hours ahead of me, and I had to overtake them upon as sorry a piece of horseflesh as one could well imagine. That animal was nearly the death of me: he was some what *rough,* and shook me until every joint in my body was loose and my teeth rattled in their sockets. Complaining did no good, and I determined to let no trials ruffle my good nature. By careful inquiry along the road I was enabled to trace the party across the Pamunkey, the Mattaponi at Mantua, on through Essex, half-way through the adjoining county. Toward evening of the third day I was fortunate enough to strike the trail, and in three hours after reached the end of my equestrian journey.

That night we bivouacked on the Piankatank, some twenty-five miles from its mouth. The boats were in the water in readiness for sailing, while the men, secreted between two hills, lounged about upon the grass, or cooked their rations by the bivouac fire. Lieutenant Wood, the commander of the party, was off on a reconnoissance, and did not return until the following evening, at which time immediate preparations for departure were begun. We knew then, for the first time, that our object was to capture one of the Yankee blockaders by boarding her in the night. At four o'clock the men were called to quarters, arms inspected, and ammunition distributed, and after prayer by Mr. Wood, the boats were manned. The crews were in fine spirits, and with muffled oars rowed rapidly and silently down the stream, sending out no noise save the rippling of the waves around the cutters' bows as they ploughed their way through the water.

About ten o'clock the mouth of the river was reached, and the boats were halted for an hour to rest the men and issue instructions for the attack. Toward midnight we were again in motion, pulling cautiously toward the spot where the gunboats usually lay. It was a warm, quiet, starlight evening, with hardly a breath of wind afloat. Upon reaching the mooring ground the steamer was nowhere to be seen, and no trace of her was visible. As we were searching for her, however, a signal light some mile or so away showed us her position, and soon afterward the sound of machinery told us she was in motion. This was contrary to her usual custom, and seemed evidence that our coming had been made known by spies and traitors on the shore, and, as it was impossible to board her while under way, nothing remained but for us to return and wait a more favorable opportunity.

Turning up the river, keeping out of sight under the wooded banks, we pulled some fifteen miles and entered the mouth of a creek with high shores on either side. Here the boats were secreted, and men and officers, thoroughly exhausted, threw themselves down on the ground to sleep. Daylight soon came, and with it the sound of an approaching steamer, making her way directly toward us. From this Lieutenant Wood naturally supposed we had been seen, and that the steamer was in pursuit of us. His plan of battle was quickly formed, and was an excellent one. Sending the boats high up the creek for protection, he ordered Lieutenant Hoge, with the main body of men, to follow them on land, keeping about a dozen men with him at the mouth of the creek. The Yankees, if in pursuit of us, would undoubtedly follow the boats, and we could thus get them between two fires and possibly cut off their retreat. Upon reaching the creek the steamer came to anchor, and sent ashore five boats, containing some eighty men. Our men lay ambushed in a small coppice, some five or six yards from the water; but, unfortunately, just as the first boat came abreast of them, one of them incautiously exposed himself and drew the attention of the Yankees. They immediately fired upon him, shouting from boat to boat, "Shoot him—kill him don't let the d——d rebel get away," firing their rifles rapidly and at random. After the first shot Lieutenant Wood, with all his coolness, was unable to restrain the men. They were bound to fire, and immediately poured a volley into the boats. This produced a great consternation, and all that were able pulled away as rapidly as possible—not waiting to load their muskets after the first discharge. The foremost boat was now aground, and to this our men turned their fire. The Yankees dropped into the bottom of the boat, and the captain, the only brave man in the party, shouted and cursed to make them point their oars and shove off. Two or three of the men were wounded before this could be accomplished, and just as the boat got out into the stream the captain also received a fatal shot. At the same time the flag was shot down, but was instantly replaced upon a shorter staff. The steamer also commenced shelling the woods, and the fire was kept up until the boats were in, when she, too, hastily retreated down the river. From the Philadelphia *Inquirer,* of the 20th, received since, we learned that the Yankee captain, Hotchkiss, was killed, and several of the men wounded "by guerrillas." We have ascertained also that the Yankees were ignorant of our presence, and came up the river to destroy the house of Mr. Jones, now a prisoner in the Old Capitol prison. On the way up, early in the morning, they had desolated the home of Mr. Hutchins, carrying off every thing possible, and shooting his stock in the field.

That evening we pulled up to our original starting point, and by dark had the boats again out of the water. When the wagons came they were put upon them, and we started across the country for a new scene of operations.

Worn out by hard marching and severe labor, it was necessary to give the men a day of rest, and it was not until the 19th that we reached the Rappahannock. The boats were again launched in Meachum's creek, just inside of Gray's Point, and about ten miles from the Chesapeake. Just at the mouth of the river is a small bay or cove, called Butler's Hole, in which the blockaders usually run at night for a safe anchorage. The river is some three or four miles wide. Upon the opposite side is Stingray Point, from which the land runs down into Mobjack bay and the mouth of the Piankatank. There are two sets of blockaders here. Off the mouth of the latter mentioned river the steamers belong to the "North Atlantic Squadron," while at the Rappahannock they are from the "Potomac Flotilla." They communicate with each other, however, and are near enough to signal at night with blue and red lights. At this time three steamers were off the Rappahannock—the Currituck, the Reliance, and the Satellite. One or all of these we were determined to have.

It was about six o'clock in the evening of the 19th, when the boats were again manned, and started down the creek. The sun was just setting as we entered the Rappahannock, and at dark we were running under the dim shadow of the wooded shore. It was a beautiful night. The land loomed up in the dark, the river ran calm and placid to the bay, and the stars shone in the sky, and in the west brighter than all hung the crescent moon. Added to the picture was a line of black boats filled with armed men, creeping snake-like over the water, prepared to spring upon the foe whenever he came in sight. Late in the night Lieutenant Wood called the boats alongside his own, and gave instructions for the attack; then, after a fervent prayer, we pushed out into the bay. From pickets on the point we learned the steamers lay some three miles out toward Butler's Hole, but after a careful search they were not to be found, and we were forced to return without accomplishing any thing.

It was daybreak when we entered Meachum's creek, and in half an hour after the boats were moored in their former hiding-place. The next night we tried it, but with no better success. Friday, the next day, we remained inactive, but Saturday night resolved to try again.

It was late in the night when we hauled out into the stream, and once more ran down toward the bay. It was just such an evening as before, but there were signs of an approaching storm. As we rounded Gray's Point the air was still and sultry. The crescent moon, blood red and clouded, stood upon the tops of the trees, the stars shone dimly, the dark pines threw a solemn shadow upon the water, and from the shore came the thousand night sounds of bird and insect. Presently the sky became obscured, and a northerly storm rose rapidly. Behind us a black cloud towered into the sky, from which came frequent flashes of lightning, and short gusts of wind began to agitate the waters. Before reaching the bay the storm had come, and we were tossing upon the waves like children's boats, while the wind whistled with fury around our ears.

Upon reaching Butler's Hole a flash of lightning showed the blockaders a short distance ahead, their black hulls rising from the water, some two or three hundred yards apart. The boats were now ranged alongside each other and the plan of attack made known. There being two of them, it became necessary to divide our forces, and consequently Lieutenant Wood, in the second cutter, and Lieutenant Hudgins, in the first, were to attack one, while Lieutenant Hoge and Midshipman Gardener, in the third and fourth cutters, were to take the other. Each man had a white badge around his arm to distinguish him from the enemy. Every thing being in readiness, the four boats pulled toward the steamers in line of battle. I was in Mr. Wood's party, in the boat with Lieutenant Hudgins. We pulled slowly and silently on. When within about fifty yards the sentinel on deck sang out his "boat ahoy." Mr. Wood answered in some unintelligible words, and then we gave way strong toward them. We had the starboard bow, Mr. Wood the port. It was a moment of anxiety—almost of misgiving. If the Yankees were aware of our approach, destruction was certain. There was no retreat now—death lay in the silent guns ahead and in the mad waters around. The waves had increased; the sea was fast lashing itself into fury. Long black lines started from the horizon, ran toward us like some huge leviathan, for a moment raised us in the air, then rolled away in the dusky distance. The sentinel's hail was the signal to give way, and every man put his whole strength to the oars. Our boat nearly sprang out of the water at every stroke, and shot over the waves with the velocity of an arrow. In a few seconds the dark hull rose before us, the boat struck its sides, there were a few shots; and as quick as thought, twenty of us were climbing over the nettings, upon her decks. The watch fired their rifles at us and gave the alarm, and immediately the Yankees came pouring from below, grasping cutlasses and side arms as they ran up the hatch. They fought well considering the circumstances, but it was of no avail; in a few minutes the vessel was ours and the crew had surrendered. Lieutenant Wood, followed by Midshipman Goodwin, was first upon the decks upon their side, while Lieutenant Hudgins and Mr. Wilson led the way on ours. The whole was over almost with the rapidity of thought.

Just as the decks were ours, sharp firing was heard upon the Reliance. We watched for a moment, but not seeing the preconcerted signal, were anxious about the other party. Our boat was immediately manned, and we pulled over to his assistance; but Lieutenant Hodge had done the work well before our arrival. He had met with more determined spirits, and had to encounter two or three deserters from our army, who fought well. Captain Walters, of the Reliance, was also a brave man, and did every thing possible to save the ship. Upon the first alarm he sprang forward to slip the cable, but was met by Lieutenant Hoge, who ran forward to encounter him, and was almost instantly shot through the body with a pistol. At the same time, Lieutenant Hoge received a dangerous wound through the neck, and fell beside the water-tank. Although wounded, Captain Walters sprang to the pilot-house and blew the whistle to get help from the Satellite, but he was soon secured. There was sharp firing on the decks, both with rifles and revolvers, during which Midshipman Cook, who was foremost in the fight, received a wound in the side, and one of the seamen was shot through the arm. Several wounded Yankees lay around the decks, and one Negro was stiff in death.

In fifteen minutes after the attack both vessels were secured. The prisoners were put in irons until they could be confined, and the wounded taken below. The new crew went to their work readily—the engineers got up steam—the firemen took their places—the pilot was at the wheel—the quartermaster on the deck—and the officers at their posts. Every thing was made ready for sailing, the boats were hauled alongside, the anchor raised, and just as day was dawning, the Confederate States steamers Satellite and Reliance got under way and stood up the Rappahannock. About sundown the anchors were dropped off Urbanna.

Civille Bellum

A Federal officer, at the battle of Belmont, Missouri, marked out a Confederate soldier who was conspicuous for his gallantry, and shot him. He noticed where he fell, and the next day when sent back by the defeated Federals, with a party to bury their dead, he sought out his victim, and upon turning the body over, found, to his horror, that he had shot his own brother.

Such was the war waged upon the South.

The Confederate Cruisers

I.

Though winds are high and skies are dark,
And the stars scarce show us a meteor spark;
Yet bouyantly bounds our gallant barque,
   Through billows that flash in a sea of blue;

We are coursing free, like the Viking shark,
    And our prey, like him, pursue!

II.

At each plunge of our prow we bare the graves
Where, heedless of roar, among winds and waves,
The dead have slept in their ocean caves,
    Never once dreaming—as if no more
They hear, though the Storm-God ramps and raves
    From the deep to the rock-bound shore.

III.

Brave soldiers were they in the ancient times,
Heroes or pirates—men of all climes,
That had never an ear for the Sabbath chimes,
    Never once called on a priest to be shriven;
They died with the courage that still sublimes,
    And, haply, may fit for heaven.

IV.

Never once asking the when or why,
But ready all hours to battle and die,
They went into fight with a terrible cry,
    Counting no odds, and, victors or slain,
Meeting fortune or fate with an equal eye;
    Defiant of death and pain.

V.

Dread are the tales of the wondrous deep,
And well do the billows their secrets keep,
And sound should those savage old sailors sleep,
    If sleep they may after such a life;
Where every dark passion alert and aleap
    Made slumber itself a strife.

VI.

What voices of horror, through storm and surge
Sang in the perishing ear its dirge,
As, raging and rending o'er Hell's black verge,
    Each howling soul sank to its doom;
And what thunder-tones from the deep emerge,
    As yawns for its prey the tomb!

VII.

We plunge the same sea which the rovers trod,
But with better faith in the saving God,
And bear aloft and carry abroad
    The starry cross, our sacred sign,
Which, never yet sullied by crime or fraud,
    Makes light o'er the midnight brine.

VIII.

And we rove not now on a lawless quest,
With passions foul in the hero's breast,
Moved by no greed at the fiend's behest,
    Gloating in lust o'er a bloody prey;
But from tyrant robber the spoil to wrest,
    And tear down his despot sway!

IX.

'Gainst the spawn of Europe, and all the lands,
British and German—Norway sands,
Dutchland and Irish—the hireling bands,
    Bought for butchery, recking no ride,
But flocking like vultures, with felon hands,
    To fatten the rage of greed.

X.

With scath they traverse both land and sea,
And with sacred wrath we must make them flee,
Making the path of the nation free,
    And planting peace in the heart of strife.
In the star of the cross, our liberty
    Brings light to the world, and life!

XI.

Let Christendom cower 'neath the Stripes and Stars,
Cloaking her shame under legal bars,
Not too moral for traffic, but shirking wars,
    While the Southern cross, floating topmast high,
Though torn, perchance, by a thousand scars,
    Shall light up the midnight sky!

Capture of the Underwriter

"Bohemian," the correspondent of the *Richmond Dispatch,* writing from Kingston, North Carolina, February 7th, 1864, gives the following account of this gallant exploit:

Just where the Trent river joins its waters with the Neuse, situated on a point of land which borders either stream, lies the little town of Newbern, a place of some note in North Carolina. Soon after the fall of Roanoke Island, on the 14th day of February, 1862, it fell into the hands of the Yankees, since which time it has been in their possession, and has been the seat of some of their most important military operations. Immediately after occupation extensive fortifications were erected, and the line extended over some twenty miles of surrounding country. The regiments stationed here have been composed principally of men from Massachusetts and New York, the blackest of abolitionists, full of schemes and plans for Negro emancipation, equalization, and education; Negro regiments have been organized; companies of disloyal Carolinians put in service against us; the most tyrannical rules established; and both men and officers have been guilty of the greatest outrages and atrocities. For many months they have occupied the town securely, retaining undisturbed possession, scarcely dreaming of the possibility of an attack. In the river, some two or three gunboats are generally lying, either anchored off the town, or cruising up and down the Neuse or Trent, to the great terror of the inhabitants living near their banks. The largest of these gunboats was the "Underwriter," the capture of which forms the subject of my brief sketch.

On the morning of Sunday, 31st of January, our boats were launched in the Neuse river, and in an hour's time we were pulling down toward the appointed rendezvous, some forty miles above Newbern. One by one the boats came in, and at midday we only waited the arrival of our commander, Captain Wood. About two o'clock his boat rounded the point, and he stepped ashore into the brigandish looking bivouac we had established. Without delay the arms and ammunition were distributed, the boats made ready, every thing put ship-shape for the night, and between two and three o'clock, we hauled out into the stream.

The boats were arranged in two divisions, the first under command of Captain Wood, the second under Lieutenant B. P. Loyall, and the two forming parallel to each other, we pulled rapidly down the stream. The trip was one of some little interest, but it would exceed my limits to give a detailed account of it. The river is wide and deep, the banks low and bordered with gnarled cypress trunks, whose branches hang over the water's edge, forming a wall on either side; woodlands unbroken, forest upland giving place only to swampy lowlands with dense undergrowth and *debris* of fallen logs, huge junipers, and dead trunks, which waved their Titan-like arms against the deep blue of the sky. Winding and curving in many a turn, the river seemed a succession of little lakes; wild ducks rose at our approach, and flew with rapid wing into the forest coverts, and from the oozy banks sprung the startled muskrat and otter into the depths below. Silently the two black lines of boats filed down the stream with muffled oars, issuing no sound but the steady dip as they fell into the wave. Sometimes fallen logs obstructed the way; and the monotony of the hour was varied by a boat aground, with those astern crashing into them, piling one into the other before the line could be stopped. Night came on, and the shores grew dim, dusky shadows fell upon the water, and the red tints of the west faded as the stars appeared from zenith to horizon. Just before dark the boats were hauled alongside each other to receive instructions, and this done, Captain Wood offered up fervent prayers for success, asking God to judge between us and our enemies, and once more we were winding down the Neuse. The night was very dark, and it was with great difficulty the way could be traced, the only bearings being taken from the faint light of the sky seen through the treetops above. About three o'clock we came into the open country above Newbern, where the river widened, and the shores grew low and marshy. The night was foggy and thick; some rain fell.

To get a fair understanding of the plan of attack, I may say briefly that it was intended General Pickett should open upon the Yankee lines early in the morning to divert their attention and drive them back into the town. He had with him two brigades only—Clingman's and Hoke's—while General Barton had been sent up the Trent to fall upon the town simultaneously with those in front. In addition to this, Colonel Dearing, with a small force of infantry, a battalion of cavalry, and two pieces of artillery, had been sent across the Neuse to threaten Fort Anderson, and prevent reinforcements from Washington. This was the position of affairs at an early hour this morning.

It was hard on to four before we came opposite the town, and so dark and foggy we could see but a short distance beyond our bows. The day before it had been ascertained the Yankee gunboats were in the Neuse, but upon reaching the position formerly occupied, they were nowhere to be seen. For an hour we cruised around from point to point, trying in vain to make their lights, and at last, daylight being close at hand, we were forced to give up the search and return up the river. There were no gunboats in the Neuse.

Meantime General Pickett had opened fire upon the Yankee lines, and while we were pulling again up the stream we heard his guns booming through the mist, varied at times with the rattle of musketry.

Going some four or five miles up the Neuse, we entered a small creek, and landed upon an island covered with tall grass and a few stunted shrubs. We were still in sight of Newbern, but the boats were hauled close in upon the bank, and the men completely hidden. The firing on the opposite shore was now at its height, and we could tell by the sound of the guns that General Pickett was driving the enemy, and that the fight gradually turned toward the town. Worn out by a sleepless night and the fatigue of pulling fifty miles, the men threw themselves down upon the ground, and were soon fast asleep; and I, too, would have slept, but was selected for other duty, an account of which will be given hereafter.

All day long the land fight was going on; but at length night came, and we prepared to go down again after the steamers. Two launches, under Lieutenant Gift, had now joined us, and about eleven o'clock we hauled again into the Neuse and pulled down toward the town. Completely worn out by the fatigue of the day, I had fallen asleep in the boat, and had slept for upwards of two hours, when the hail of "boat ahoy!" roused me from my slumber, and I knew we were close upon the enemy. "Boat ahoy!" again shouted the watch as he sprang the rattle which called the men to quarters. All abreast, about four hundred yards away, our boats were bearing down upon the steamer, which loomed up largely ahead of us. "Give way," shouted Captain Wood; "Give Way, boys, give way," repeated Lieutenant Loyall, and give way they did, until the boats nearly sprang out of the water. The instructions were that one division should board forward, the other astern; but, through some mistake, all but two of the boats went forward, Lieutenant Loyall's alone going aft and Captain Wood's amidships. I was in the boat with Mr. Loyall, and could see the Yankees had all gathered in the ways, just aft, the wheel house, and as we came up they greeted us with a volley of musketry, which flashed in our very faces, the balls whistling unpleasantly into the boat or into the water beyond. The men gave way strongly, and as soon as the boat struck the side the grapnel was thrown on board the steamer and we were fast alongside. Still the firing continued with great rapidity, and, having no support, we got the heaviest of it, only dividing with Captain Wood's boat, a few feet from us. Hot and fast goes the firing; the Yankees, having all gotten on deck and armed, were pouring it into us with remarkable rapidity. The flashes came full in our faces, lighting them up with a deathly pallor, while the sulphurous smell of burning powder pervaded the air. Struck by a splinter, the first fire, bringing a profusion of blood from my face and nose, I could scarcely see or comprehend all the rapid movements of our little fleet; but I knew our boat was first at the side, Captain Wood's close after, then came Lieutenants Hoge, Kerr, Porcher, Gardner, Roby, and Wilkinson, while a short distance away, slackened up to prevent running down the other boats, was Gift with his launches. Our boat once fast, Lieutenant Loyall and Mr. Gill, engineer, sprang forward to lead the men on board. At this time the fire was the hottest I have ever seen even in three years' experience in war, and I hardly dared hope one half our number would come out alive; Mr. Wood, especially, I looked every moment to see fall. Standing upright in his boat, he gave the orders as coolly as he had done an hour before the enemy were in sight. Finding I had sustained but a slight splinter scratch, I went forward to follow Mr. Loyall, when a marine, shot through the heart, fell heavily upon me and crushed me down over the thwarts. Extricated from this, I found the ship was ours, and Mr. Wood, upon the hurricane deck, was endeavoring to stop the fight, as the Yankees had called for quarter. It ceased in a moment, and the prisoners sent aft and secured, and the wounded gotten where the surgeons could attend to them. Poor Gill was lying in the gangway, shot in four places and mortally wounded, and midshipman Palmer Saunders, cut down in a hand-to-hand fight, was breathing his last upon the decks.

The fight was now ended; the boarders were successful. And here, I should say that the Underwriter was moored, head and stern, to the shore, under three of the largest batteries, and hardly a stone's throw from the wharf. The flash of the guns and the report of musketry had aroused the soldiers on shore, and they were now witnesses of the scene, but determined not to be inactive ones; for, regardless of their own prisoners on board, they fired a shell into us, which, striking the upper machinery and exploding on the deck, produced a terrible shock. I was in the cabin at the time, and thinking the vessel had been blown up, rushed on deck like others. Another shell exploding over the deck explained the cause of the commotion, and told us the shore batteries had opened fire. To spare the prisoners and wounded, Captain Wood ordered them to be put into the boats and the ship made ready for firing. But for them the shots would have been returned, for Lieutenant Hoge had opened the magazines, and had stationed the men at the guns. As the steam was down, it was found it would be impossible to take time to get it up, under the heavy fire of batteries not one hundred yards away; and so, the wounded and prisoners being put into the boats, the vessel was fired. In five minutes after our boats had left the side, the Underwriter was one mass of flame, burning up the dead bodies of the Yankees killed in action; also, three or four dead Negroes in the coal bunkers.

BELLE BOYD RUNS THE BLOCKADE[*]

On the 8th of May, 1864, I bade farewell to many friends in Wilmington, and stepped on board the Greyhound. It was, as may well be imagined, an anxious moment. I knew that the venture was a desperate one; but I felt sustained by the greatness of my cause—for I had borne a part, however

---

[*] From *"Belle Boyd in Camp and Prison."*

insignificant, in one of the greatest dramas ever yet enacted upon the stage of the world. Moreover, I relied upon my own resources, and I looked to Fortune, who is so often the handmaid of a daring enterprise.

At the mouth of the river we dropped anchor, and decided to wait until the already waning moon should entirely disappear.

Outside the bar, and at the distance of about six miles, lay the Federal fleet, most of them at anchor; but some of their light vessels were cruising quietly in different directions. Not one, however, showed any disposition to tempt the guns of the fort over which the Confederate flag was flying.

There were on board the Greyhound two passengers, or rather adventurers, beside myself—Mr. Newell and Mr. Pollard; the latter the editor of the *Richmond Examiner*. We laughed and joked, as people will laugh and joke in the face of imminent danger, and even in the jaws of death.

Gentle reader, before you accuse us of levity, or of a reckless spirit of fatalism, reflect how, in the prison of La Force, when the reign of terror was at its height, the doomed victims of the guillotine acted charades, played games of forfeits, and circulated their *bon-mots* and *jeux d'esprit* within a few hours of a violent death. Remember also that the lovely Queen of Scots, and the unfortunate Anna Boleyn, met their fate with a smile, and greeted the scaffold with a jest.

About ten o'clock orders were given to get under way. The next minute every light was extinguished, the anchor was weighed, steam was got up rapidly and silently, and we glided off just as "the trailing garments of the night" spread their last folds over the ocean.

The decks were piled with bales of cotton, upon which our lookout men were stationed, straining their eyes to pierce the darkness and give timely notice of the approach of an enemy.

I freely confess that our jocose temperament had now yielded to a far more serious state of feeling. No more pleasantries were exchanged, but many earnest prayers were breathed. No one thought of sleep. Few words were spoken. It was a night never to be forgotten—a night of silent, almost breathless anxiety. It seemed to us as if day would never break. But it came at last; and, to our unspeakable joy, not a sail was in sight. We were moving unmolested and alone upon a tranquil sea, and we indulged in the fond hope that we had eluded our eager foes.

Steaming on, we ran close by the wreck of the Confederate iron-clad *Raleigh*, which had so lately driven the Federal blockading squadron out to sea, but which now lay on a shoal—an utter wreck, parted amidships—destroyed, not by the Federals, but by a visitation of Providence.

At this point we three passengers began to experience those sensations, which, although invariably an object of derision to persons who are exempt from them, are, for the time being, as grievous to the sufferer as any in the whole catalogue of pains and aches to which flesh is heir. Reader, may it never be your lot, as it then was mine, to find seasickness overcome by the stronger emotion inspired by the sight of a hostile vessel bearing rapidly down with the purpose of depriving you of your freedom.

It was just noon, when a thick haze which had lain upon the water lifted, and at that moment we heard a startled cry of "Sail ho!" from the lookout man at the mast-head. These ominous words were the signal for a general rush aft. Extra steam was got up in an incredibly short space of time, and sail was set with the view both of increasing our speed and of steadying our vessel as she dashed through the water.

Alas! it was soon evident that our exertions were useless, for every minute visibly lessened the distance between us and our pursuer. Her masts rose higher and higher, her hull loomed larger and larger, and I was told plainly that unless some unforeseen accident should favor us, such as a temporary derangement of the Federal steamer's steering apparatus, or a breaking of some important portion of her machinery, we might look to New York instead of Bermuda as our destination.

My feelings at this intelligence must be imagined—I can describe them but inadequately. "Unless," I thought, "Providence interposes directly in our behalf, we shall be overhauled and captured; and then what follows? I shall suffer a third rigorous imprisonment." Moreover, I was the bearer of dispatches from my government to authorities in Europe; and I knew that this service, honorable and necessary as it was, the Federals regarded in the light of a heinous crime; and that, in all probability, I should be subjected to every kind of indignity.

The chase continued, and the cruiser still gained upon us. For minutes, which to me seemed hours, did I strain my eyes toward our pursuer, and watch anxiously for the flash of the gun that would soon send a shot or shell after us, or, for all I could tell, into us. How long I remained watching I know not, but the iron messenger of death came at last. A thin white curl of smoke rose high in the air as the enemy luffed up and presented her formidable broadside. Almost simultaneously with the hissing sound of the shell, as it buried itself in the sea within a few yards of us, came the smothered report of its explosion under water.

The enemy's shots now followed each other in rapid succession: some fell very close, while others, less skillfully aimed, were wide of the mark, and burst high in the air over our heads. During this time bale after bale of cotton had been rolled overboard by our crew, the epithet of each, as it disappeared beneath the waves, being, "By ——! there's another they shall not get."

Our captain paced nervously to and fro, now watching the compass, now gazing fixedly at the approaching enemy, now shouting, "More steam more steam! give her more steam!" At last he turned suddenly round to me, and exclaimed in passionate agents—

"Miss Belle, I declare to you that, but for your presence on board, I would burn her to the water's edge rather than those infernal scoundrels should reap the benefit of a single bale of our cargo!"

To this I replied, "Captain H., act without reference to me—do what you think your duty. For my part, sir, I concur with you: burn her by all means—I am not afraid. I have made up my mind, and am indifferent to my fate, if only the Federals do not get the vessel."

To this Captain H. made no reply, but turned abruptly away and walked aft, where his officers were standing in a group. With them he held a hurried consultation, and then, coming to where I was seated, exclaimed:

"It is too late to burn her now. The Yankee is almost on board of us. We must surrender!"

During all this time the enemy's fire never ceased. Round shot and shell were ploughing up the water about us. They flew before, behind, and above—everywhere but into us; and, although I knew that the first of those heavy missiles which should strike must be fatal to many, perhaps to all, yet so angry did I feel that I could have forfeited my own life if, by so doing, I could have balked the Federals of their prey.

At this moment we were not more than half a mile from our tormentor; for we had luffed up in the wind, and stopped our engine. Suddenly, with a deep humming sound, came a hundred-pound bolt. This shot was fired from their long gun amidships, and passed just over my head, between myself and the captain, who was standing on the bridge a little above me.

"By Jove! don't they intend to give us quarter, or show us some mercy at any rate?" cried Captain H. "I have surrendered."

And now from the Yankee came a stentorian hail: "Steamer ahoy! haul down that flag, or we will pour a broadside into you!"

Captain H. then ordered the man at the wheel to lower the colors; but he replied, with true British pluck, that "he had sailed many times under that flag, but had never yet seen it hauled down; and," added he, "I cannot do it now." We were sailing under British colors, and the man at the helm was an Englishman.

All this time repeated hails of "Haul down that flag, or we will sink you!" greeted us, until, at last, some one, I know not who, seeing how hopeless it must be to brave them longer, took it upon himself to execute Captain H.'s order, and lowered the English ensign.

Capture of a Blockade Runner

The Ella and Annie left Bermuda for Wilmington on the 5th of November, 1862, in company with the R. E. Lee, having on board the heaviest cargo ever tried by a blockade-running ship—three hundred and ninety four tons of dead weight, all on government account. Captain Bonneau publishes the following highly interesting narrative of the capture of his vessel:

At sunset we were eighty-five miles from Wilmington bar. At seven o'clock the wind, which had been light from the north and west, suddenly sprang up and in the course of one hour blew a gale, causing an ugly cross sea, and reducing the speed of our ship from eleven knots to five and a half, which was the utmost we could get out of her with thirty pounds of steam.

Things began to look squally as to our being able to make the run in time, but it was too late to think of turning back. We were, too, at this time passing two suspicious lights, which we took for the outer vessels of the blockading squadron. At eleven I hauled her into Masenboro' inlet, as I found if I did not get smooth water I could not save my time, and it was not until four and a half o'clock that I made the land. About noon, while to the southward and eastward of the inlet, as soon as I got fairly under the beach and in eighteen feet of water, I sent word to Mr. Gray and Mrs. Nicholson, my two passengers, that it would be impossible for me to get by dark to the fort, and that at daylight, we would be subjected to a very heavy fire (in all probability) from the fleet, as I was determined to try to run along the beach (I had, however, no other chance), and that if they would get ready I would land them in the little bay of Masenboro' inlet. This they bravely refused, saying it would take too much time, and that if I could stand the fire of the fleet they could too. I therefore prepared for the worst, and ordered the anchors taken in on deck, unstocked, and lashed down, the colors set, and all hands but the officers of the watch and the two men at the wheel sent below, determining, if I had to lose her, to make it cost the enemy dearly.

Just as day was dawning we touched the beach slightly, but did not stop, and while hauling away from it saw a gunboat standing directly across our bow (she must evidently have heard our wheels), and steering so as to cut us off from the beach. We being in three fathoms of water, I was much surprised to find a boat running so boldly for us. To pass outside of him would be to lose my ship, for he would then cut me off from the support I expected from our own batteries in a few miles more. To run my ship ashore at this point would have been madness, for the beach here is an *outer one*, the sound extending inside of it for miles, and consequently I could expect no protection, and my whole ship company would either be destroyed on this bold beach or taken by the enemy prisoners. To turn back and run to sea was to give the ship to the enemy without an effort to save her. I therefore determined to try and pass inshore of the bend or over him (not dreaming that he would dare run into eighteen feet of water). This matter was soon decided, as we approached each other rapidly, and I could hear the noise of his men preparing for action, etc., and when about one hundred and fifty yards from him I hailed him, telling him he would be afoul of me, hoping to induce the thought that I was one of their own ships, but was soon made aware of my mistaken opinion by a broadside of grape and canister, accompanied by a volley of musketry. I then ordered my ship pointed for her, and hoped to strike her just forward of her waist boat. Unfortunately he perceived this move of mine, and shifted his helm, causing his vessel to swing away from me, and making it impossible to strike fair.

Our ships came together the next moment with a fearful crash, carrying away his starboard boat rail and part of his stem and cutwater. My engine was kept working to its full capacity, as I had but one chance of getting clear of him in case I failed to sink him, and that was to force my ship past him before he could board, as I distinctly heard him call away his boarders. In this last attempt I failed, as the ships were both going ahead, and had now swung broadside on, and he firing broadside after broadside into us while in this condition, and almost at the same time boarding us on the port quarter and wheelhouse guard. Then ensued a scene which none but an eye-witness would believe. Officers and men rushing along our deck, shooting and cutting at every thing that came to sight, and even shooting, in their mad career, one of their own men—and in the case of Jany, of my ship, shooting him as he was coming up the hatchway to give himself up. Having satisfied themselves with this (courageous charge) they went below and broke open every thing that came to sight, state-rooms, trunks, boxes, etc., officers and men quarreling over trunks for the contents and the owners standing by. This robbery and carouse were kept up until the arrival of Commodore Ridgely, in the flag-ship Shenandoah, when it was quickly put a stop to by the appearance of Lieutenant Skerritt, to whom it was reported. (Lieutenant Skerritt is an officer and gentleman of the old navy.) Not one of the officers of the capturing ship—the Niphon—belonged to this class of officers.

The ship was then plugged (having received forty-one shots in her hull), and sent to Beaufort, N.C., where we landed our passengers and wounded, and then proceeded north, destination Boston, having on board the two cooks, two stewards, and myself. The crew otherwise were sent north in the transport Newburn.

Thus ended the fate of the favorite ship Ella and Annie. A more cowardly and murderous fire a vessel was never subjected to, and the conduct of the boarding was the most unheard of barbarity upon record. The officers of my ship behaved—as we all had a right to expect of them—cool, determined, and at their posts all of them, as they had often said if they were killed their bodies would be found at their stations in their engine-room. Strange as it may appear, her engine was not struck, although the balls are to be seen sticking in the wood-work of the gallery frame.

Had I been successful in the destruction of the Niphon, I presume I would have been considered deserving at least of a "well done"; but the reverse shows angry, false and calumnious opinions, which are generally heaped upon the heads of those who "try," by those who stay at home afraid to try, having heard even in this lonely prison that a voice had gone forth in "Dixie," condemning all of the captains of the vessels captured on the 8th and 9th of November.

I thought it proper to say, that for the discharge of my duty, and for the responsibility of all that occurred on that day, I am responsible, and to none but my country and my conscience.

Rily, fireman, mortally wounded by grape; Joseph Jany, dangerously in groin; Barre, fireman, shot in shoulder; —— (name forgotten), fireman, shot in neck; two of the cabin boys cut severely with cutlasses.

Lucky Moment on Board the Sumter

One of the officers of the C.S. steamer Sumter, gives the following account, in his private journal, of an hour of trepidation on board that craft. Under date of August 18, 1861, he writes:

After leaving Cayenne the vessel's course was shaped for Paramaribo, Dutch Guiana, off which port she signaled for a pilot until sundown; none having arrived at that hour she came to anchor. About twilight a sail was seen in the distance approaching the Sumter. It was soon apparent that she was a steam war-vessel. Steam was raised, the anchor hove up, all hands beat to quarters, the guns manned, the old charges drawn and fresh ones put in their places. By the time all these preliminaries had been arranged it was ascertained by the aid of the night telescope, that the strange vessel had anchored. The Sumter followed suit, but a vigilant lookout was kept upon the movements of the supposed enemy.

Early on the morning of the 19th, the lookouts had reported that the steamer outside was under way. Slowly she steamed toward the Sumter, seeming to have made every preparation for attack. She had not yet hoisted her flag, neither had the Sumter—each commander being apparently desirous of learning the nationality of the other first, and of letting him know, by a death-dealing broadside, that an enemy was at hand. The stranger looked like an American-built vessel, having long mast-heads and a sharp overhanging bow. Yes, there was no mistaking her—she must be one of the gunboats sent in search of the Sumter. When she was near enough for the number of her guns to be determined, we were glad to find that she carried but one gun more than the Sumter, and that the disparity was no greater.

Slowly and cautiously the vessels neared each other. When not more than a cable's length off, our first lieutenant hailed her in a loud voice:

"Ship ahoy!"

"Hallo!" was promptly answered.

"This is the Confederate States steamer *Sumter*—what vessel is that?"

After waiting about half a minute, which seemed an age, the "enemy" replied:

"The French steamer *Abbeville!*"

Here was a disappointment—after all this preparation for mortal combat, to find at last that the supposed enemy was a friend! There was not a single man who would not freely have relinquished all the prize money then due to him, could he have transformed the Frenchman into a Yankee. She was nearer the equal of the Sumter than they ever expected to meet again, and the Sumter had captured so many merchantmen that it might be said she did not care to meet any other class of vessels.

Part V

Home Life in Dixie

SCENE IN THE SOUTH CAROLINA CONVENTION—RATIFYING THE ORDINANCE; STARTLING SCENE

On the ratification of the South Carolina ordinance of secession, Rev. Dr. Bachman was selected by the convention to offer a prayer before them, in religious observance of the act. The scene was one that partook alike of the startling and the impressive. Most of the men there assembled to commit the highest and gravest act in the history of their State, were those upon whose heads the snows of sixty winters had been shed—patriarchs in age—the dignitaries of the land—the high priests of the church—reverend statesmen—and the judges of the law. In the midst of deep silence an old man, with bowed form and hair as white as snow, the Rev. Dr. Bachman, advanced forward, with upraised hands, in prayer to Almighty God for his blessings and favor on the great act about to be consummated. The whole assembly at once arose to its feet, and with hats off, listened to the prayer. At the close of this performance, the president advanced with the consecrated parchment upon which was inscribed the decision of the State, with the great seal attached. Slowly and solemnly it was read until the last word—"dissolved"; when men could contain themselves no longer, and a shout that shook the very building, reverberating, long continued, rose up, and ceased only with the loss of breath.

Prepared for It This Time

The late General Doles, of Georgia, used to relate the following story, with much relish:

While posted near Suffolk, a six-foot Georgian from the up country of his State, and a member of the "Fourth Georgia," attempted one morning to cross a little stream when the tide was in. Encumbered with his clothes, the poor fellow had to swim for his life, and narrowly escaped being drowned.

The regiment in the afternoon saw him sit down on the opposite bank of the creek, deliberately take off his shoes and socks, next his clothes, and tie them up carefully in a bundle for his back. All these preparations being made, he hesitated before proceeding any further; but at length having made up his mind like a gallant soldier, as he was, he *plunged boldly into the water, which was nowhere more than two feet deep, the tide having gone out.* The cheers, with which he was received by his regiment, when his perilous feat was safely accomplished, were prolonged, enthusiastic, and somewhat vociferous.

The Fredericksburg Exiles

The sufferings of the people of Fredericksburg, Va., just previous to and after the battle in December, 1862, were equalled only by the heroic fortitude and true patriotism with which they were endured, a devotion so grand that it drew tears from the eyes of General Lee when he spoke of it. The *Richmond Examiner* contained the following letter in reference to these unfortunates:

Fredericksburg, March 11, 1863.

Your correspondent has endeavored, in previous communications, to present your readers with some idea of the pecuniary losses and destruction of property to which the people here have been subjected.

The personal suffering remains to be told. Much of it, perhaps the greater part, will never be known, save to the afflicted individuals themselves or their families, for the parties are naturally slow to acknowledge their privations and necessities. Indeed, your correspondent, although fully acquainted with the population, was not aware of the facts of their condition until he had made investigation. The inquiry was prompted by his observation of the return of many of the fugitives to their ruined homes. A ride through the region where they have sought refuge revealed the reason. The day was raw, and the roads one mass of mud, of such consistency and depth as rendered it perfectly impassable, even on horseback. The hog-paths presented the only practicable passage. Yet, on such a day, and along such a road, your correspondent met a lady of this place on foot, who before the bombardment had lived in affluence, and whose house had been the very home of hospitality. She was only attended by her child, of eight or ten years, and the faithful house-dog. The group was thus wending its way to Fredericksburg, having already walked some five or six miles, and was then about the same distance from their destination. The want of food had driven them to undertake the journey.

This is not a single instance, for in the district which bore the brunt of the enemy's late devastation, those who were possessed of a competence and enjoyed every comfort are, in many instances, reduced to absolute indigence, whilst many who have lived in opulence suffer all the pangs of poverty. The late inhabitants, for the most part, are temporarily domiciled in the houses, Negro cabins, and shanties of the surrounding country within a radius of twelve or fifteen miles. In some cases, as many as four or five families have taken refuge under the same roof. Your correspondent, attracted by the curling smoke ascending from one of the chimneys, visited a hut, for such it really was, which was inhabited by some of the involuntary exiles. He found it consisting of a single room, and occupied by five children, two females, and an aged man. They were citizens of Fredericksburg, whose homes had heretofore been cheered by comfortable circumstances. They were now huddled around a few burning sticks, which had been gathered by the old man's trembling fingers, and the feeble flame flickered, and they shivered with each blast of the wintry wind that blew its chilling breath through many a crevice of their humble abode. The interior of the room showed the cleanliness of female care, but the slender clothing of the inmates and their sparse supply of food were painfully apparent. Their whole reliance was the provision made by public charity, and the inclement weather and impassable roads had precluded them from the procurement of their regular supplies. The country around affords no subsistence.

In a conference with the mayor, your correspondent was informed that the relief fund is rapidly diminishing, and the number and necessities of the applicants increasing. The despoiled population number about six thousand. Of these, about one fourth are destitute. This proportion has been fed for some twelve weeks. The contributions aggregate $200,000.

Your readers can readily estimate how soon starvation will stare a multitude in the face, unless this purse is replenished.

The generosity of the army, and of Virginia generally, has been unexampled, but the urgency and occasion of suffering here should commend itself to the charitable consideration of every Southern community.

A correspondent of the *Richmond Enquirer* thus refers to the citizens who remained in the city during the Battle:—

The Yankee generals were almost thunderstruck at finding so many persons through a shelling lasting twelve hours, and carried on without intermission, with one hundred and forty-three guns. General Sturgis told a lady that the women of Fredericksburg ought to be handed down to the latest posterity as model heroines. He then said to the same lady—"Madam, it is too dangerous for you to remain longer, General Lee will shell the town; go over to the other side, I will assure you protection and a return whenever you choose to come back." The lady's reply was quite significant—"No, sir," said she, "I have no more business across that river than a Yankee has in heaven; I shall stay and take the best care I can of my property." He then asked if she had a husband in the Southern army. "No, sir, I have a son; but if my husband does not now enlist and avenge the vandalisms you have committed on my town and its people, I shall get a divorce." Said Sturgis, "I admire your pluck, madam, and, from this time forward, as long as I remain, you shall be protected." In another instance, a gentleman had been arrested, and was being carried before an officer, when his daughter, one of the most beautiful and accomplished girls in the city, seized an old sword lying near, and following the guard, who was conducting her father, and who was abusing him, bade him desist, threatening him with instant death if he should harm her father, accompanied him to the presence of the officer, when both were released. A Yankee officer, who witnessed this scene, said he would rather fight the best regiment of the South than encounter the women of Fredericksburg.

One of the most gratifying of the many interesting incidents of the occupation of Fredericksburg was the faithful conduct of the slaves who remained. In several instances they saved, amid the perfect rain of shot and shell, houses and indeed squares from destruction. In other instances, they claimed and secured protection for the property of their owners; whilst in not a few instances they asked to be permitted to share the plunder with the thieving soldiery, and getting the permission, took care to save, for those who had left, many valuable articles.

Lines

Written on the Back of a Confederate Note[*]

I.

Representing nothing on God's earth now,
    And nought in the waters below it;—
As the pledge of a nation that's dead and gone,
    Keep it, dear friend, and show it!

II.

Show it to those who will lend an ear
    To the tale this paper can tell;—
Of liberty, born of the patriot's dream,
    Of the storm cradled nation that fell.

III.

Too poor to possess the precious ores,
    And too much of a stranger to borrow,
We issued to-day our promise to pay,
    And hoped to redeem on the morrow.

IV.

The days rolled on—the weeks became years,—
    But our coffers were empty still;
And coin was so rare, that our treasury quaked
    If a dollar should drop in the till.

V.

But the faith that was in us was strong indeed,
    And our poverty well we discerned:
And these poor little cheques represented to pay
    That our suffering volunteers earned.

---

[*] The above lines were written by a gallant soldier of the C.S.A.

VI.

We knew it had scarcely a value in gold,
    Yet as gold our soldiers received it;
It gazed in our eyes with a "promise to pay,"
    And each patriot Confederate believed it.

VII.

But our boys thought little of price, or pay,
    Or of bills that were over due;
We knew if it bought us our bread to-day,
    It was all our poor country could do.

VIII.

Keep it, it tells our history all over,
    From the birth of our dream, to the last;—
Glorious, and born of the Angel of hope,
    Like the hope of success, it has passed.

A Spartan Dame and Her Young

"We were once," says General D. H. Hill, "witness to a remarkable piece of coolness in Virginia. A six-gun battery was shelling the woods furiously near which stood a humble hut. As we rode by, the shells were fortunately too high to strike the dwelling, but this might occur any moment by lowering the angle or shortening the fire. The husband was away, probably far-off in the army, but the good housewife was busy at the wash-tub, regardless of all the roar and crash of shells and falling timber. Our surprise at her coolness was lost in greater amazement at observing three children, the oldest not more than ten, on top of a fence, watching with great interest the flight of the shells. Our curiosity was so much excited by the extraordinary spectacle, that we could not refrain from stopping and asking the children if they were not afraid. 'Oh, no,' replied they, 'the Yankees ain't shooting at us, they are shooting at the soldiers!'"

THE ARREST OF MARSHAL KANE;

OR, HOW IT TOOK EIGHTEEN HUNDRED MEN TO CAPTURE ONE MAN

Immediately after taking command at Baltimore, General Banks determined to capture Colonel George P. Kane, the marshal of police of that city, who had become obnoxious to the "loyal" element of the beautiful city. A Federal writer gives the following account of this great achievement:

Eighteen hundred men marched from Fort McHenry into Baltimore with loaded muskets. The men wore their cartridge boxes, in which were a few rounds, but no knapsacks. They had marched a square, when a policeman, in his cool summer uniform, and swinging his long baton, was observed crossing the street ahead. Instantly the head of the column opened, the body swept on, and the policeman, riveted to the ground in astonishment at this manoeuvre, unknown to the tactics of either Matsell or Vidocq, found himself swallowed up and borne along in the resistless advance! Two squares ahead, another policeman was discovered. Again the column opened, and he was engulfed. By the time the column reached the residence of the marshal, not less than fifty-seven of the vigilant guardians of the night had been thus swallowed up; but when they found that their captors had halted at the door of the marshal's house, they began to smell a rat of the largest possible dimensions. An officer now rang the bell. After some delay, a night-capped head popped out of the window, and the well-known voice of Marshal Kane inquired, in a rather gruff tone,

"What is wanted?"

The officer blandly replied, that he himself was the article just then in demand.

"Hum, hum," said the marshal, never at a loss for a joke, "I'll supply that demand!"

Did the vision of escape cross the marshal's mind? Possibly. It is certain that he skipped with agility to a back window, raised the curtain, and looked out. Alas! the moonbeams played upon five hundred glittering bayonets in the yard below. The game was up! and the marshal knew he must submit to his inevitable fate. He descended the stairs and opened the front door.

"Good God!" he exclaimed to the officer in command, "why did you not bring five or six more regiments, and some artillery? If you had sent me a note and a carriage, I would have come without all this fuss."

It was even then daybreak; the column moved briskly forward, and the marshal enjoyed the rare sight of sunrise from the ramparts of Fort McHenry.

A Baltimore Unconquerable

The *Charleston Mercury* contained, during the war, the following spirited sketch:

A Mrs. W——, of Baltimore, about to pay a visit of a few days to the country, to some relatives, was driving through the city in her own carriage, with her trunks strapped behind. Suddenly, the vehicle was stopped by a policeman, who assured the lady she was under arrest, and would be obliged to repair immediately to the office of the provost-marshal. Mrs. W., somewhat indignant at the request, refused to go, alleging as an excuse that such a public place was unfit for a lady to frequent. She said that she would go to the commanding general, Dix, at Fort McHenry; but if the policeman attempted to take her to the provost-marshal she would shoot him.

"As you please, madam; I will get into the carriage and go to the fort with you."

"You are mistaken," replied Mrs. W., "this carriage is mine, and if you attempt to get into it I will immediately fire upon you."

The policeman took a seat with her coachman, in whom Mrs. W. confided as her protector, and they drove to Fort McHenry. On reaching the fort she sent for General Dix, and seeing her he said:

"Madam, I do not know how to address you."

" It is time you did, sir, since I am arrested, I suppose, by your authority."

"Madam, you look wearied; walk into my office."

Ordering some regulars to bring in the trunk and search it, the general remarked to Mrs. W.:

"This is a military necessity, madam. I would these things were not; but the government must be supported. 'United we stand,' you know. Madam, have you any sons in the Confederate army?"

"I have three, sir."

"Did you aid and encourage them to enlist in that service?"

"General Dix, are you a married man?"

"I am, madam."

"Then ask your wife what she would have done under similar circumstances."

"Madam, you look faint and weary; let me order you some refreshments."

"What! eat here? I, a Southern woman, break bread with the *Yankees?* Never! while they are the miserable foes they have proved themselves. Every day I see more clearly the necessity of an eternal separation. And where the dividing line is fixed I want a wall built so high that a Yankee can never scale it!"

The trunk breakers having satisfied themselves that nothing objectionable to the administration could be found, reported the same to General Dix, who, on consultation, determined to have the person of Mrs. W. searched. The gallant general remarked:

"Madam, it is necessary now that your person be searched; you will not object, I hope?"

"Oh, no, sir, if the person to perform that ignoble office is a female."

"Oh, yes, madam, a lady, your equal."

"Sir, you are mistaken—not a lady, nor my equal. Were she either, she would not do the degrading work you assign her."

Mrs. W. was taken to a private apartment, and the search was begun. Finding the woman delinquent, Mrs. W. threatened to report her, if she did not perform her duty faithfully. "Pull off my shoes," she continued: "look well into them; make a thorough search, and see if you can find a combination of red and white, or any thing inimical to the Union-savers; look well, or I will report you."

The woman finding nothing treasonable upon Mrs. W., returned with her to the gallant general, telling him she would not search another lady for five hundred dollars: that such a persevering character she had never encountered.

General Dix, shocked, no doubt, at Mrs. W.'s agitated appearance, again proposed refreshments, saying:

"Madam, do have a glass of wine."

"Only on the condition, sir, that you will drink with me to the health and success of General Beauregard!"

The wine, it is believed, was not taken Mrs. W. then, turning to General Dix, said:

"Sir, I hope you are satisfied that I have nothing traitorous to your righteous (!) cause. You thought to find the Confederate flag in my trunk, or on my person; indeed, you are not good at hide and seek. Your soldiers are too little interested in your righteous cause to serve you faithfully. They searched my house a fortnight since for the flag. Both you and they have been foiled. I sent that flag to Virginia ten days since under a load of wood; it now waves over the glorious Confederates at Manassas. Sir, it seems the Yankees' peculiar pleasure is to try to frighten women and children. They cannot gain battles, so they revenge themselves in this ignoble manner. And now, sir, I imagine you have done."

"I regret, madam, that we should have met under these unfortunate circumstances. I will detain you no longer."

"Sir, I demand one thing of you, before I depart. I have been arrested, on suspicion. I desire now an honorable discharge."

"Oh, madam, that is unnecessary; it is a mere form, and therefore useless."

"I like forms, General Dix, particularly when connected with official documents."

The general, seeing Mrs. W. determined, ordered the secretary to write the discharge, and, handing it to Mrs. W. said:

"Madam, I believe that is all."

"No, sir, not all yet. I wish your name added. I believe that is essential to such a document."

The general, more reluctant to sign his name than to grant the discharge, was finally brought to the point.

"And now, General Dix," said Mrs. W., "do you know what I intend doing with this discharge? I shall send it to my sons at Manassas, and if they have any of the spirit of their mother, they will one day make you rue this encounter."

After Mrs. W. left, they say the general vowed he would not see another woman for three years, three months, and three days, calling no doubt to mind Richard Coeur de Lion's famous truce with Saladin.

Proof against Federal Gallantry

A certain Union colonel, a staff officer, noted for his talent at repartee, and for the favorable opinion which he entertained of his own good looks, stopped at the house of a farmer, and discovered there a fine milch cow, and, still better, a pretty girl, attired in a neat calico dress, cut low in the neck and short in the sleeves. After several unsuccessful attempts to engage the young lady in conversation, he proposed to her to have the cow milked for his own special benefit. This she indignantly refused. The colonel, not wishing to compromise his reputation for gallantry, remarked that if all the young ladies in Virginia were as beautiful as the one he had the pleasure of addressing, he had no desire to conquer the Confederacy. With a toss of her pretty head, and a slight but most expressive elevation of her nose, she answered thus: "Well, sir, if all the gentlemen in your army are as ugly as you are, we ladies have no desire to conquer *them!*"

Charleston Women under Fire

During the shelling of the city of Charleston, there was a moral sublimity exhibited in many cases by the female portion of that imperiled community, which could but challenge the heart-feeling even of the Federals, whose object it was to destroy or capture that city. An instance of the calm heroism to which women can rise is thus given:

A lady, dressed in deep mourning, was seated in the front verandah of her dwelling, sewing, when a Parrott shell came screaming up the harbor, and burst, with an unearthly sound, just above, and in front of the position where she was sitting, throwing its fragments in every direction. But this "mother of Gracchi," as she may be called, remained tranquil in her seat, slowly and sadly raising her eyes toward the point where the shell had burst. She was observed to thoughtfully gaze for an instant upon the deadly scattering missile, and then as calmly to resume her womanly employment in serene silence. From her mourning apparel it was judged she had felt before the horrors and desolation of war. Perhaps her only son had fallen at Wagner, at Sumter, or on James Island. Or perhaps the "loved one of her bosom" had fallen, and the angel of death had no more terror for her.

QUEER DRAFTING IN MARYLAND

The Yankee enrolling officer for Salisbury District, Maryland, was very active and thorough in the performance of his duties. One day he went to the house of a countryman, and finding none of the male members of the family at home,, made inquiry of an old woman about the number and age of the "males" of the family. After naming several, the old lady stopped. "Is there no one else?" asked the officer. "No," replied the woman, who was a full-blooded Dixieite, "none, except Billy Bray." "Billy Bray, where is he?" "He was at the barn a moment ago," said the old lady. Out went the officer, but could not find the *man*. Coming back, the worthy officer questioned the old lady as to the age of Billy, and went away, after enrolling his name among those to be drafted. The time of the drafting came, and among those on whom the lot fell was the veritable Billy Bray. No one knew him. Where did he live? The officer who enrolled him was called on to produce him; and, lo and behold, Billy Bray was a *jackass!*—(not a human one, like the enroller, but with four genuine legs, and ears of the usual length)—regularly recorded on the list of drafted men as forming one of the quota of Maryland.

A SOUTHERN SCENE

"O Mammy, have you heard the news?"
　Thus spake a Southern child,
As in the nurse's aged face,
　She upward glanced and smiled.

"What news you mean, my little one?
　It must be mighty fine,
To make my darlin's face so red;
　Her sunny blue eyes shine."

"Why, Ab'ram Lincoln, don't you know
　The Yankee President,
Whose ugly picture once we saw,
　When up to town we went.

"Well, he is goin' to free you all,
    And make you rich and grand,
And you'll be dressed in silk and gold
    Like the proudest in the land.

"A gilded coach shall carry you
    Where'ere you wish to ride;
And, mammy, all your work shall be
    Forever laid aside."

The eager speaker paused for breath,
    And then the old nurse said,
While closer to her swarthy cheek
    She pressed the golden head:

"My little missus, stop and res'—
    You' talkin' mighty fas';
Jes' look up dere, and tell me what
    You see in yonder glass?

"You sees old mammy's wrinkled face,
    As black as any coal;
And underneath her handkerchief —
    Whole heaps of knotty wool.

"My darlin's face is red and white,
    Her skin is soff and fine,
And on her pretty little head
    De yaller ringlets shine.

"My chile, who made dis difference
    'Twixt mammy and 'twixt you?
You reads de dear Lord's blessed book,
    And you can tell me true.

"De dear Lord said it must be so;
    And, honey, I, for one,
Wid tankful heart will always say,
    His holy will be done.

"I tanks Mas' Linkum all de same,
    But when I wants for free,
I'll ask de Lord of glory,
    Not poor buckra man like he.

"And as for gilded carriages,
    Dey's notin' 'tall to see;
My massa's coach, what carries him,
    Is good enough for me.

"And, honey, when your mammy wants
    To change her homespun dress,
She'll pray, like dear old missus,
    To be clothed with righteousness.

"My work's been done dis many a day,
    And now I takes my ease,
A waitin, for de Master's call,
    Jes' when de Master please.

"And when at las' de time's done come,
    And poor old mammy dies,
Your own dear mother's soff white hand,
    Shall close these tired old eyes.

"De dear Lord Jesus soon will call
    Old mammy home to him,
And he can wash my guilty soul
    From ebery spot of sin.

"And at his feet I shall lie down,
    Who died and rose for me;
And den, and not till den, my chile,
    Your mammy will be free.

"Come, little missus, say your prayers;
    Let old Mas' Linkum 'lone;
The debil knows who b'longs to him,
    And he'll take care of his own."

THE DEATH AND BURIAL OF STUART

No incident of mortality since the fall of the great Jackson has occasioned more painful regret than this, said the *Richmond Examiner* of May 13th, 1864. Major-General J. E. B. Stuart, the model of Virginia cavaliers, the dashing chieftain, whose name was a terror to the enemy, and familiar as a household word in two continents, is dead, struck down by a bullet from the dastardly foe, and the whole Confederacy mourns him. He breathed out his gallant spirit resignedly, and in the full possession of all his remarkable faculties of mind and body, at twenty-two minutes to eight o'clock, Thursday night, at the residence of Dr. Brewer, a relative, on Grace street, in the presence of Doctors Brewer, Garnett, Gibson, and Fontaine, of the general's staff; Rev. Messrs. Peterkin and Keppler, and a circle of sorrow-stricken comrades and friends.

We learn from the physicians in attendance upon the general that his condition during the day was very changeable, with occasional delirium, and other unmistakable symptoms of speedy dissolution. In the moments of delirium the general's mind wandered, and like the immortal Jackson (whose spirit, we trust, his has joined), in the lapse of reason his faculties were busied with the details of his command. He reviewed, in broken sentences, all his glorious campaigns around McClellan's rear on the Peninsula, beyond the Potomac, and upon the Rapidan, quoting from his orders and issuing new ones to his couriers, with a last injunction to "make haste."

About noon, Thursday, President Davis visited his bedside, and spent some fifteen minutes in the dying chamber of his favorite chieftain. The president, taking his hand, said, "General, how do you feel?" He replied, "Easy, but willing to die, if God and my country think I have fulfilled my destiny and done my duty." As evening approached the general's delirium increased, and his mind again wandered to the battle-fields, over which he had fought, then off to wife and children, and off again to the front. A telegraphic message had been sent for his wife, who was in the country, with the injunction to make all haste, as the general was dangerously wounded. Some thoughtless, but unauthorized person, thinking probably to spare his wife pain, altered the dispatch to "slightly wounded," and it was thus she received it, and did not make that haste which she otherwise would have done to reach his side.

As evening wore on, the paroxysms of pain increased, and mortification set in rapidly. Though suffering the greatest agony at times, the general was calm, and applied to the wound, with his own hand, the ice intended to relieve the pain. During the evening he asked Dr. Brewer how long he thought he could live, and whether it was possible for him to survive through the night. The doctor, knowing he did not desire to be buoyed by false hopes, told him frankly, that death, the last enemy, was rapidly approaching. The general nodded, and said, "I am resigned, if it be God's will; but I would like to live to see my wife. But God's will be done." Several times he roused up and asked if she had come.

To the doctor, who sat holding his wrist, and counting the fleeting, weakening pulse, he remarked, "Doctor, I suppose I am going fast now. It will soon be over. But God's will be done. I hope I have fulfilled my destiny to my country and my duty to my God."

At half-past seven o'clock it was evident to the physicians that death was setting its clammy, seal upon the brave, open brow of the general—and they told him so—and they asked if he had any last messages to give. The general, with a mind perfectly clear and possessed, then made disposition of his staff and personal effects. To Mrs. General R. E. Lee he directed that the golden spurs be given as a dying memento of his love and esteem of her husband. To his staff officers he gave his horses. So particular was he in small things, even in the dying hour, that he emphatically exhibited and illustrated the ruling passion strong in death. To one of his staff, who was a heavy-built man, he said, "You had better take the larger horse; he will carry you better." Other mementos he disposed of in a similar manner. To his young son, he left his glorious sword.

His worldly matters closed, the eternal interests of his soul engaged his mind. Turning to the Rev. Mr. Peterkin, of the Episcopal Church, and of which he was an exemplary member, he asked him to sing the hymn commencing:

> Rock of ages cleft for me,
> Let me hide myself in thee,

he joining with all the voice his strength would permit. He then joined in prayer with the ministers. To the doctor he again said, "I am going fast now; I am resigned; God's will be done." Thus died General J. E. B. Stuart.

His wife reached the house of death and mourning about ten o'clock on Thursday night, one hour and a half after dissolution, and was, of course, plunged into the greatest grief by the announcement that death had intervened between the announcement of the wounding of the general and her arrival.

The funeral services preliminary to the consignment to the grave of the remains of General Stuart, were conducted yesterday afternoon in St. James' Episcopal Church, corner of Marshall and Fifth streets, Rev. Dr. Peterkin, rector. The *cortege* reached the church about five o'clock, without music or military escort, the public guard being absent on duty. The church was already crowded with citizens. The metallic case, containing the corpse, was borne into the church and up the centre aisle to the altar, the organ pealing a solemn funeral dirge and anthem by the choir.

Among the pall-bearers we noticed Brigadier-General John H. Winder, General George W. Randolph, General Joseph R. Anderson, Brigadier-General Lawton, and Commodore Forrest.

Among the congregation appeared President Davis, General Bragg, General Ransom, and other civil and military officials in Richmond. A portion of the funeral services, according to the Episcopal Church, was read by Rev. Dr. Peterkin, assisted by other ministers, concluding with singing and prayer.

The body was then borne forth to the hearse in waiting, decorated with black plumes, and drawn by four white horses. The organ pealed its slow, solemn music as the body was borne to the entrance, and while the *cortege* was forming, the congregation standing by with heads uncovered. Several carriages in the line were occupied by the members of the deceased general's staff and relatives. From the church the *cortege* moved to Hollywood Cemetery, where the remains were deposited in a vault; the concluding portion of the service read by Dr. Minngerode, of St. Paul's church—and all that was mortal of the dead hero was shut in from the gaze of men.

Dr. Brewer, the brother-in-law of General Stuart, has furnished us with some particulars obtained from the general's own lips, of the manner in which he came by his wound.

He had formed a line of skirmishers near the Yellow Tavern, when, seeing a brigade preparing to charge on his left, General Stuart and his staff dashed down the line to form troops to repel the charge. About this time the Yankees came thundering down upon the general and his small escort. Twelve shots were fired at the general at short range, the Yankees evidently recognizing his well-known person. The general wheeled upon then with the natural bravery which had always characterized him, and discharged six shots at his assailants. The last of the shots fired at him struck the general in the left side of the stomach. He did not fall, knowing he would be captured if he did, and, nerving himself in his seat, wheeled his horse's head and rode for the protection of his lines. Before he reached them his wound overcame him, and he fell, or was helped from his saddle by one of his ever-faithful troopers, and carried to a place of security. Subsequently, he was brought to Richmond in an ambulance. The immediate cause of death was mortification of the stomach, induced by the flow of blood from the kidneys and intestines into the cavity of the stomach.

General Stuart was about thirty-five years of age. He leaves a widow and two children. His eldest offspring, a sprightly boy, died a year ago while he was battling for his country on the Rappahannock. When telegraphed that his child was dying, he sent the reply, "I must leave my child in the hands of God; my country needs me here; I cannot come."

Thus has passed away, amid the exciting scenes of this revolution, one of the bravest and most dashing cavaliers that the "Old Dominion" has ever given birth to. Long will her sons recount the story of his achievements, and mourn his untimely departure. Like the hero of the old song—

> Of all our knights he was the flower,
> Compagnon de la Marjolaine;
> Of all our knights he was the flower.
> Always gay.

A Girl Worth Having

"One of our fair countrywomen," says a correspondent, "the daughter of a rich and independent farmer of Rockingham, was married, the other day, to a gentleman who may congratulate himself upon having secured a prize worth having. She was what we should call 'an independent girl,' sure enough. Her bridal outfit was all made with her own hands, from her beautiful straw hat down to the handsome gaiters upon her feet! Her own delicate hands spun and wove the material of which her wedding dress and traveling cloak were made; so that she had nothing upon her person, when she was married, which was not made by herself! Nor was she compelled by necessity or poverty to make this exhibition of her independence. She did it for the purpose of showing to the world how independent Southern girls are. If this noble girl were not wedded, we should be tempted to publish her name in this connection, so that our bachelor readers might see who of our girls are most to be desired. If she were yet single, and we were to publish her name, her pa's house would be at once thronged with gallant gentlemen seeking the hand of a woman of such priceless value."

A Romance of the War

The following incident occurred at the capture of Courtland, Alabama:

The Federals had held Courtland for some time, and, as is their wont, inflicted many insults upon its unarmed citizens, without regard to sex. Among the abused and insulted of the fair sex was the belle of Courtland, a lady of high accomplishments, great amiability, and considerable wealth. Exasperated, and justly vindictive, the fair one announced publicly that whoever should either kill or capture the miscreant who had thus shamefully insulted her, should receive her hand and fortune. Not many days after this avowal, Frank Armstrong's command defeated the Yankees at Courtland, capturing the place, together with many prisoners, among whom was Captain Robertson, the dastardly villain whose little soul had permitted him to be insolent to a refined lady, and who had forgotten that "Hell hath no fury like a woman scorned" or insulted. This wretch, Robertson—faugh!—showed his cowardice early in the action, and surrendered his sword to Captain Champion, of Missouri, whose dauntless bravery in this, as on many former occasions, has made his name familiar to the army. Captain Champion was ignorant, until when about leaving Courtland, of the romance connected with his captive. The lady sent him a present of a splendid pair of holsters, accompanied by an earnest request to visit her. But, alas for romance, war is inexorable, and without being granted time to visit the fair charmer whom he had avenged, Captain Champion was obliged to leave the scene of his conquest. Since his return the captain has avowed his intention of returning to see his affianced, and we predict that his handsome figure will not prove uncomely to the lady's eyes. Robertson was imprisoned at Columbus, Mississippi.

A Brave Boy

A little son of Doctor B. J. Malone, of Holly Springs, Mississippi, one day heard a Yankee soldier address some insulting language to his mother.

"Sir," cried the boy, indignantly, "she is my mother."

"I don't care a d——n if she is," replied the Yankee; whereupon the boy seized a rock, and brought the fellow bleeding to the earth.

Quite the Youngest Recruit in the Service

At the outbreak of the war, a patriotic Irishman volunteered in one of the New Orleans regiments. His wife hearing of it, at once repaired to the company, headquarters and exclaimed to the lieutenant in charge:

"So, sir, you've clapped your dirty sojer trappings on my husband, have you?"

"Who is your husband?" asked the officer.

"Billy McCurtee, an' shure, an' a bould boy he is, so plaze ye. But it's a dirty thing of ye, my pretty man, to take him from his wife an' childers."

"Can't be helped," said the officer; "it's too late now."

"Then take the baby, too," she cried, as she forced the little one into the arms of Lieutenant Adams: "Take them all—I'll send ye four more to-day."

Off she ran at rapid pace, leaving the unfortunate officer with the squirming and squalling recruit in his arms. Doubtful of its services, he sent it home.

Each for His Own Side

While a long string of Federals were marching along the streets of Nashville, one day, a bright little fellow looked on very dolefully, and at last screamed out, "Hurrah for Jeff Davis." A Yankee said loudly, "Pshaw, hurrah for the devil." "All right," said the boy; "you hurrah for your captain and I'll hurrah for mine."

Home Life in the South

"There are many little things in which our daily life is changed," said the wife of a Confederate officer,—"many luxuries cut off from the table which we have forgotten to miss. Our mode of procuring necessaries is very different and far more complicated. The condition of our currency has brought about many curious results; for instance, I have just procured leather, for our Negro-shoes, by exchanging tallow for it, of which we had a quantity from some fine beeves, fattened and killed upon the place.

"I am now bargaining, with a factory up the country, to exchange pork and lard with them, for blocks of yarn, to weave Negro clothes; and not only Negro clothing I have woven, I am now dyeing thread to weave homespun for myself and daughters. I am ravelling up, or having ravelled, all the old scraps of fine worsteds and dark silks, to spin thread for gloves, for the general and staff, which gloves I am to knit. These home-knit gloves and these homespun dresses will look much neater and nicer than you would suppose. My daughters and I being in want of under garments, I sent a quantity of lard to the Macon factory, and received in return fine unbleached calico,—a pound of lard paying for a yard of cloth. They will not sell their cloth for money. This unbleached calico my daughters and self are now making up for ourselves. You see some foresight is necessary to provide for the necessaries of life.

"If I were to describe the cutting and altering of old things to make new, which now perpetually go on, I should far outstep the limits of a letter—perhaps I have done so already—but I thought this sketch would amuse you, and give you some idea of our Confederate ways and means of living and doing. At Christmas I sent presents to my relations in Savannah, and instead of the elegant trifles I used to give at that season, I bestowed as follows: several bushels of meal, peas, bacon, lard, eggs, sausages, soap (home-made); rope, string, and a coarse basket! all which articles, I am assured, were most warmly welcomed, and more acceptable than jewels and silks would have been. To all of this we are so familiarized that we laugh at these changes in our ways of life, and keep our regrets for graver things.

"The photographs of your children I was so happy to see. You would have smiled to have heard my daughters divining the present fashion from the style of dress in the likenesses. You must know that, amid all the woes of the Southern Confederacy, her women still feel their utter ignorance of the fashions, whenever they have a new dress to make up or an old one to renovate. I imagine that when our intercourse with the rest of mankind is revived we shall present a singular aspect; but what we shall have lost in external appearance I trust we shall have gained in sublimer virtues and more important qualities."

A Strange Resemblance

A citizen, with long hair, long whiskers, big moustaches, and grand imperial, had his head at a window in Richmond. The "human face divine" was so completely hidden by the hirsute covering, above it, under it, and around it, that the *tout ensemble* seemed to be an immense mass of hair stuck in the window, or pendant from it. A soldier passing by, stopped and gazed with much interest at the curious spectacle, and then calling to a comrade across the street, said:

"Ned, I've found my old mar (mare)!"

"Where?" replied Ned.

"Don't you see her tail sticking out of that window? I could swar to her tail anywhar. But how in the thunder did the old critter get up thar?"

The tail was promptly withdrawn.

The Rebel Sock

A True Episode in Seward's Raids on the Old Ladies of Maryland

By Tenella

In all the pride and pomp of war
    The Lincolnite was drest,
High beat his *patriotic* heart
    Beneath his armored vest.
His maiden sword hung by his side,
    His pistols both were right,
His shining spurs were on his heels,
    His coat was buttoned tight.
A firm resolve sat on his brow,
    For he to danger went,
By Seward's self that day he was
    On secret service sent.
"Mount and away!" he sternly cried
    Unto the gallant band,
Who all equipped from head to heel
    Awaited his command.
"But, halt, my boys—before we go
    These solemn words I'll say,
'Lincoln expects that every man
    His duty'll do to-day!'
"We will! we will," the soldiers cried,
    "The President shall see
That we will only run away
    From Jackson or from Lee!"
And now they're off, just four score men,
    A picked and chosen troop,
And like a hawk upon a dove
    On Maryland they swoop.
From right to left, from house to house,
    The little army rides,
In every lady's wardrobe look
    To see that there she hides;

They peep in closets, trunks and drawers;
    Examine every box,
Not rebel soldiers now they seek,
    But rebel soldiers' socks!
But all in vain—too keen for them
    Were those dear ladies there,
And not a sock or flannel shirt.
    Was taken anywhere.
The day wore on to afternoon,
    That warm and drowsy hour,
When Nature's self doth seem to feel
    A touch of Morpheus' power;
A farm-house door stood open wide,
    The men were all away,
The ladies sleeping in their rooms,
    The children at their play;
The housedog lay upon the steps,
    But never raised his head,
Though crackling on the gravel walk
    He heard a stranger's tread;
Old Grandma, in her rocking chair,
    Sat knitting in the hall,
When suddenly upon her work
    A shadow seemed to fall;
She raised her eyes and there she saw
    Our Fed'ral hero stand,
His little cap was on his head,
    His sword was in his hand;
While circling round and round the house
    His gallant soldiers ride,
To guard the open kitchen door
    And chicken-coop beside;
Slowly the dear old lady rose
    And tottering forward came,
And peering dimly through her "specks"
    Said, "Honey, what's your name?"

Then as she raised her withered hand
    To pat his sturdy arm—
"There's no one here but Grandmamma,
    And she won't do you harm;
Come, take a seat and don't be scared,
    Put up your sword, my child,
I would not hurt you for the world,"
    She gently said, and smiled,
"Madam, my duty must be done,
    And I am firm as rock!"
Then, pointing to her work he said,
    "Is that a rebel sock!"
"Yes, honey, I am getting old,
    And for hard work aint fit,
But for Confed'rate soldiers still,
    I thank the Lord can knit."
"Madam, your work is contraband,
    And Congress confiscates
This rebel sock which I now seize,
    To the United States."
"Yes, honey, don't be scared, for I
    Will give it up to you."
Then slowly from the half knit sock
    The dame her needles drew,
Broke off her thread, wound up her ball, ,
    And stuck the needles in—
"Here, take it, child, and I to-night
    Another will begin!"
The soldier next his loyal heart
    The dear-bought trophy laid,
And that was all that Seward got
    By this "old woman's raid."

Noble Southern Women

Much has been written about Spartan women of old—much about the noble Roman matron,—much about our excellent "foremothers of the Revolution"; but it has been reserved for the women of our sunny South to blend the virtues of these heroines all in one, and present to the world the brightest example of firmness, courage, and patriotism. Look at the hundreds of women all over our land—delicate ones, who have been reared in the lap of luxury; who have heretofore been shielded from every rough blast; women who, a year ago, were lingering over the ivory keys of their pianos, or discussing with their dressmakers the shade of silk which became their complexion best; and see how they have risen, without a dissenting voice, to meet the exigencies of the times. "What shall I wear?" is now a question seldom asked. The only attention that dress demands is the consideration, "Will it be a piece of economy to purchase this or that?" and daily we hear the remark, "I want homespun dresses,—they are the best for us now." Instead of finding our women at the piano, or on the fashionable promenade, we find them busy at their looms, busy at their wheels, busy making soldiers' uniforms, busy making bandages, busy in hospitals, busy girding up their sons, their husbands, and their fathers for the battle-field. Tell me, are they not a noble race? Luxury has not enervated them; adversity has not depressed them. There was once a French queen, who, surrounding herself by her maids of honor, wrought, day after day, on delicate tapestry, with which the churches in her realm were afterwards hung. It was thought to be an act of great virtue in her. The fact was registered upon the page of history; and she has been held up to her sex as a "shining example." But she did not, as the wife of our governor has done, set herself down to sew on heavy woollen goods for soldiers; she did not throw aside the silken robe and the golden chain, and apply herself, day after day, with unwearied assiduity, over stiff fabrics, which make the shoulders and the fingers alike ache. Nearly all the bandages that were used on the bloody field of Manassas, between the 21st and 23d of July, 1861, were made and forwarded by two Georgia women, Mrs. Robert Hardaway and her sister, who reside near Columbus. Southern matrons are indeed the jewels of our land.

THE LITTLE GIRL'S KINDNESS TO THE SOLDIERS

After the battle of Sharpsburg, we passsed over a line of railroad in Central Georgia. The disabled soldiers from General Lee's armies were returning to their homes. At every station the wives and daughters of the farmers came on the cars, and distributed food and wines and bandages among the sick and wounded.

We shall never forget how very like an angel was a little girl,—how blushingly and modestly she went to a great, rude, bearded soldier, who had carved a crutch from a rough plank to replace a lost leg; how this little girl asked if he was hungry,—and how he ate like a famished wolf! She asked if his wound was painful, and in a voice of soft, mellow accents: "Can I do nothing more for you? I am sorry that you are so badly hurt; have you a little daughter, and won't she cry when she sees you?"

The rude soldier's heart was touched, and tears of love and gratitude filled his eyes. He only answered: "I have three little children; God grant they may be such angels as you."

With an evident effort he repressed a desire to kiss the fair brow of the pretty little girl. He took her little hand between both his own, and bade her "good-by—God bless you!" The child will always be a better woman because of these lessons of practical charity stamped ineffaceably upon her young heart.

SPIRIT OF THE WOMEN OF VIRGINIA

A lady of Clark County, Virginia, whose husband had been during two years in Yankee prisons, and in exile from his home, and whose son (an only child, in his eighteenth year) was then in some northern bastile, as a prisoner of war, wrote to her husband as follows: "If it were possible, I should like you to be at home; but I do not want you or O. ever to give up the struggle for liberty and our rights. If your salary fails to pay your board, go at something else for the Confederacy; I will try and contrive a way to clothe you. I would love to be with you; but do not expect it now, in these times. I wish O. I was at home—I mean in his company; but I would rather he would be held a prisoner for the war, than have him at home dodging his duty, as some do. I am proud to think every man in my little family is in the army. If I have but two, they are at their posts of duty."

Traveling under a Flag of Truce[*]

On the first day of December, early in the morning, I started for Fortress Monroe, under the charge of Captain Mix and an orderly sergeant.

After being subjected to the annoying and ungentlemanly conduct of Captain Mix, who seemed to exert himself especially to make every thing as disagreeable as he possibly could for me, I arrived at Fortress Monroe about nine A.M. on Wednesday morning. Captain Mix immediately went on shore to report to Captain Cassels, the provost marshal and aide-de-camp to Butler, to whose care I was to be committed until the "exchange boat" should start for Richmond.

Meanwhile all the passengers had landed, and I was left in the charge of the orderly sergeant. Major (now General) Mulford, the exchange officer, returned on board with Captain Mix, and was introduced to me. I found him an elegant and courteous gentleman. In a short time I was escorted from the boat to the provost marshal's office, passing between a company of Negro soldiers, who were filed on each side. Thence I was taken into the fortress, to Butler's headquarters, and, after waiting a short time; I was conducted into his august presence.

He was seated near a table, and upon my entrance he looked up and said: "Ah, so this is Miss Boyd, the famous rebel spy. Pray be seated."

"Thank you, General Butler, but I prefer to stand."

I was very much agitated, and trembled greatly. This he noticed, and remarked: "Pray be seated. But why do you tremble so? Are you frightened?"

"No; ah! that is, yes, General Butler; I must acknowledge that I do feel frightened in the presence of a man of such world-wide reputation as yourself."

This seemed to please him immensely, and, rubbing his hands together and smiling most benignly, he said: "Oh, pray do be seated, Miss Boyd. But what do you mean when you say that I am widely known."

"I mean, General Butler," I said, "that you are a man whose atrocious conduct and brutality, especially to southern ladies, is so infamous that even

---
[*] From *"Belle Boyd, in Camp and Prison."* Written by herself.

the English Parliament commented upon it. I naturally feel alarmed at being in your presence."

He had evidently expected a compliment when I commenced to reply to his inquiry, but, at the close of my remarks, he rose, and with rage depicted upon every lineament of his features, he ordered me out of his presence.

I was conducted to the hotel, and felt for the time being exceedingly uneasy lest, by my Parthian shot at an enemy whom I thoroughly detested, I should have laid myself open to his petty spirit of revenge. I feared that I should be remanded to a dreary prison cell; for General Butler was all-powerful in the North about this period.

Events have since clearly proved this man, even to the Yankees themselves, to be but a meretricious hero and a political charlatan. Like others who render themselves rather notorious than great, he first pleased a fickle populace by his acts of brutality, and then disgusted his contemporaries, who feared that he might become to America what Robespierre had been to France. The tyrant of New Orleans, having failed most signally at Wilmington, was discovered to be a coward, and suspected of being a rogue. Well might the baffled New England attorney exclaim: "*Facilis desensus Averni!*" In the hope of being styled a modern Cincinnatus, lie retired to Lowell, to live upon the ill-gotten gains extorted by threats or force from southern people.

But to resume the thread of my story. I was obliged to give my parole that I would not leave the house until permitted to do so. Here I found the Misses Lomax, sisters of the Confederate General Lomax, and a Miss Goldsborough, of Baltimore, who were to be sent south. These ladies, however, were not the only sympathizers in the hotel; there were others whose names I dare not mention.

On Wednesday evening the order came for Miss Goldsborough and myself to be in readiness to start that same night for Richmond. The Misses Lomax, for some reason, were not allowed to proceed, but were sent back to Baltimore. When the time arrived for our departure, we were taken back to the provost marshal's office; and here I found my luggage, consisting of two Saratoga trunks and a bonnet-box. The keys were demanded of me, and I complied with the request.

A man and two women immediately set to work to ransack my boxes, although I assured them that they need not search, as I had just come from prison. This appeal, however, was ineffectual, and they still continued their examination. Imagine their astonishment and my chagrin when they pulled from the bottom of one of my trunks two suits of private clothes, a uniform for Major-General W——, a dozen linen shirts, etc. These things I had succeeded in smuggling into prison by means of an underground railway, of which Superintendent Wood, sharp as he imagined himself to be, was little aware. I was interrogated as to how I had obtained the articles in question, but they did not succeed in eliciting any thing by the queries.

All the goods considered contraband, including several pairs of army gauntlets and felt hats, with a pair of field-glasses which had formerly belonged to General Jackson, and which I greatly prized, together with much clothing, were taken from me. I entreated them to let me retain the glasses; but this was flatly refused; and they were, to my mortification, given to General Butler.

When I saw how these vandals were robbing me of nearly every thing, I strove in vain to restrain my tears; and my trunks having been thoroughly ransacked, I was informed that I must undergo a personal search. At this turn of affairs I began to feel very nervous, for I had concealed about me twenty thousand dollars in Confederate notes, five thousand in greenbacks, and nearly one thousand in gold, as well as the letters of introduction which I have previously mentioned. I earnestly appealed to their forbearance, assuring them that I had nothing contraband; for I did not consider my money contraband.

As it was getting late, the captain said, "Well, if you will take an oath to the effect that you have nothing contraband upon you—no letters or papers—you shall not be searched." As this was impossible, I told him that I could not make such a declaration, handing him my letters at the same time. He then asked if I had any money about me. To this I replied by giving him a roll of two or three thousand dollars in Confederate money, which I had placed in my pocket. This he regarded as valueless, and sneeringly informed me that I might keep "that stuff."

Upon opening my letters and finding mention of "my immense services to my country," "my kindness towards prisoners," "my devotion to the Southern cause," etc., he became very angry, and said, "I shall send this to General Butler in the morning. I would do so now, but it is after office hours."

Miss Goldsborough sat by meanwhile, a quiet spectator of the whole affair, she having undergone the ordeal of search in the morning. We were then conducted to the wharf, placed on-board a tug, and sent off to the exchange boat, the *City of New York*, which lay at anchor in the stream. Upon our arrival on board we were kindly received by Major Mulford, who conducted us to the saloon, and introduced us to his wife, a very charming, lady-like woman. Here we remained all night, and next morning, about seven o'clock, got under way. Shortly afterward we ran aground, and it was not until eight A.M. that we succeeded in getting the vessel off again. Then, under a full head of steam, we steered for City Point.

About this time the little steam-tug that had brought us alongside the City of New York quitted the wharf, apparently in chase of us. My heart sank, for I felt intuitively that this pursuit had something to do with me, and that General Butler must have given an order for my detention. But the larger steamer had already waited so long that Major Mulford, angry and impatient at the delay, took no notice of our pursuers, and, to my great joy and relief, kept steadily on our course.

I afterward learned that my fears upon this occasion were not unfounded. When General Butler, smarting with the remembrance of my farewell sarcasm, had beheld the letters that Captain Cassels had taken from me; he commanded that I should be followed, and, if recaptured, should be sent at once to Fort Warren, in Massachusetts Bay. As he issued this order, he remarked to those who surrounded him that he would take a "leading character in 'Beauty and the Beast.' " When the tug returned from her fruitless chase, he was almost beside himself with rage at being thwarted in his revenge. This I had from such good authority, that I am confident the general will not feel it worth his while to contradict the statement.

At the mouth of the James river we passed the Federal blockading fleet, and were here boarded by a boat from the flag-ship *Minnesota*, commanded by Admiral Lee. In a few moments we had entered the James, whose waters are distinguishable from those of the Potomac by a yellow streak on the surface.

As we wended our way up the river we could see the signal officers at the different stations busily announcing our approach, and occasionally we observed Confederate soldiers on picket duty. Every thing reminded me that I was once more drawing near to the capital of my own sunny South.

> Amate sponde!
> Pur vi torno a riveder,
> Trema in petto e si confonde
> L'alma oppressa dal piacer.

Though exceedingly happy that I was again permitted to breathe the pure air of my native State, I did not feel completely free, for I was still under the Federal flag, and could scarcely count upon my liberty as being yet fully assured to me.

We arrived at City Point late on Friday evening. This place, which could hardly be correctly dignified with the name of village, is situated in a bend of the river. It was used as a depot by the Confederates, for the purpose of forwarding stores to those of their unfortunate countrymen who were prisoners in the North.

Whilst the *City of New York* was coming to an anchor, Major Mulford, his wife, Miss Goldsborough, and myself, stood conversing on the hurricane deck. Major Mulford remarked, pointing to what was apparently the Confederate flag-of-truce boat approaching, "After all, ladies, you will not have to remain on board here to-night."

Looking in the direction indicated, we distinctly saw a steamer, which, judging from the distance between us, would in less than ten minutes be alongside. Ten minutes, however, passed in fruitless expectation; then followed twenty more of hope deferred; when Major Mulford, who began to grow very impatient, went on shore to inquire the reason of her remaining as she did—he even sent a boat to her to ascertain the reason of her detention. Major Mulford was so confident that he had seen her that the Confederate officer commanding the "Point" telegraphed the news to Richmond. Judge of our great surprise, when the telegraphic reply, brought to us on board shortly afterward, announced "that the Confederate flag-of-truce boat had left Richmond exactly at the hour we had seen her." As Richmond was more than twelve hours distant from us at the then rate of travel over that route, we could only consider that we had been deceived by a "mirage." How often must such phenomena have given rise to stories of phantom ships!

A French corvette, which had been up the river to Richmond, lay at anchor near us. This evening, in acceptance of an invitation from Major Mulford, the French captain and his lieutenant came on board to spend the evening with us; and we enjoyed their visit heartily. The next morning, when I awoke, I found that the flag-of-truce boat had arrived during the night. Captain Hatch, the Confederate exchange officer, presently, came on board. We were introduced to him, and very soon afterward were, with our luggage, safely ensconced in the snug little cabin of the ———. Here, under my own country's flag, I felt free and comparatively happy.

On our way up the river to Richmond we had to pass the obstructions situated between Chapin's and Drury's Bluffs. These places take their name from the bold appearance that the shore here presents. The obstructions designed to impede a hostile squadron became accidentally hurtful to our Confederate vessel. She ran foul of them, and it was found utterly impossible to continue the voyage.

At Drury's Bluff, therefore, we went on board a tug, in which we proceeded to Richmond. When we arrived, at eight P.M., I went immediately to the Spottswood House, and, tired and worn out with the fatigues of my journey, I retired to rest, refusing to see any one that evening.

THE INAUGURATION OF PRESIDENT DAVIS

The Richmond Dispatch gives the following account of the inauguration of President Davis, in February, 1862:

On Saturday, in the presence of an immense concourse of people, Jefferson Davis was inaugurated President of the permanent government of the Confederate States. The day was an inclement one, and exceedingly unfavorable for the exercises incident to an occasion so interesting. Notwithstanding the disagreeable weather, thousands were present to witness the accession to power of a president selected in the hour of strife, and amid the intensest struggle for constitutional freedom.

At half past eleven o'clock the two houses of Congress convened in their respective halls, and shortly after repaired to the hall of the House of Delegates of Virginia, the use of which for the occasion had been courteously tendered by the members of the legislature. The galleries were exclusively allotted to ladies, a large number of whom had gathered to participate in the proceedings, and to add encouragement by their presence and their smiles.

At a quarter before twelve o'clock, the President and Vice President elect, accompanied by the joint committee of arrangements, entered the hall, and were received by the assembly standing. Every available point in and about the capitol was jammed, and the whole crowd evinced a painful eagerness to see the distinguished chief magistrate, and to hear what he might have to utter in his first inaugural address. The arrangements made for the preservation of order were complete, and successfully prevented any attempt to interfere with the regular program of the committee. There was but one thing to mar the interest of the occasion, and that was the inclemency of the weather, heavy rains continuing to descend unceasingly throughout the entire day.

During the preliminaries to the formation of the procession, under the direction of the chief marshal, Colonel Dimmock, and his aids, the President occupied the speaker's chair in the House of Delegates, the Vice President elect that on the left of the President, and the President of the Senate that on his right and the Speaker of the House that on the left of the Vice President.

At half past twelve o'clock the procession moved from the hall by the eastern door of the capitol, to the statue of Washington, on the public square, in the following order, to wit:

1. The chief marshal.
2. The band.
3. Six members of the committee of arrangements, including their respective chairmen.
4. The President elect, attended by the President of the Senate.
5. The Vice President elect, attended by the Speaker of the House of Representatives.
6. The members of the cabinet.
7. The officiating Clergyman and the Judge of the Confederate court at Richmond.
8. The Senate of the Confederate States, with its officers, in column of fours.
9. The House of Representatives, with its officers, in column of fours.
10. The Governors of Virginia, and other States, and Staff.
11. The members of the Senate and House of Delegates of Virginia, and their officers.

12. The Judges of the Supreme Court of Virginia, and other States, in the city of Richmond.

13. The officers of the Army and Navy.

14. The Reverend Clergy.

15. The Mayor and corporate authorities of the city of Richmond.

16. The Masons and other benevolent societies.

17. Members of the press.

18. Citizens generally.

At the statue of Washington, the President elect, the Vice President elect, the President of the Senate, the Speaker of the House of Representatives, the officiating Clergyman, Confederate Judge, Governors of States, the Chief Marshal and his Aids, and six of the Committee of Arrangements, took their positions on the platform.

The exercises there were opened by a fervent, eloquent, and patriotic prayer, from the Right Reverend Bishop Johns, in which he earnestly invoked the guidance of Providence and the protection of Heaven, in our struggle for independence. The prayer of the Bishop was solemnly impressive, and caused many a tear to trickle from eyes unused to weep.

After the prayer, the President stepped to the front of the platform and delivered a beautiful address which was received with frequent rounds of patriotic applause, and the vast crowd gathered around the statue of the Father of his Country, seemed to catch the spirit of the Inaugural, and to be infused with renewed zeal to prosecute our struggles to a successful issue. The address occupied about twenty minutes in its delivery, and at its conclusion, the oath was administered to the President by Honorable J. D. Halyburton, of Virginia, Confederate Judge.

And thus was completed the organization of our new government; a government founded upon the devotion of a loyal and patriotic people, and, relying upon Providence for its permanent establishment and perpetual continuance. Its machinery is all now complete, and that it will work harmoniously, and to the best interests of the country, we do not mean to permit ourselves to doubt.

An Impudent Fellow

A nice young man, who couldn't go to war, rode up to a depot just as a train filled with soldiers arrived. He was soon surrounded by a group of "ragged rebels," coolly criticizing his person, dress, age, occupation, manner of life, political opinions etc., etc. A curious old soldier kept going round him in that beautiful elliptical curve, which *did* so well at Port Royal, but which *did not* do at all at Sumter. His curiosity seemed to be more and more excited by each revolution around the young hero; at length unable, to control himself, he cried out:

"Mister, woz you raised about here, or did you come out of a drove?"

Letter from a Brave Woman

The Montgomery, Alabama, papers publish a letter from Miss Emma Sansom, who so heroically guided General Forrest in his memorable capture of General Streight and his raiders. This letter is in response to one written by Governor Shorter, when transmitting the resolutions of the legislature to Miss Sansom. Streight and his men were captured in Cherokee county, Alabama, within a few miles of Miss Sansom's home.

Gadsden, Alabama, *December 20th*, 1863.

To his Excellency Governor Shorter:

Respected sir, I must acknowledge the receipt of your quite complimentary communication of November 27th, 1863, and in doing so, tender my gratitude for the more than expected respect shown me for having done my duty. At the time the duty was performed, it was a pleasure to be able to render some service to my country, and give aid to our noble cause. There are other duties that would seem more becoming and adapted to my sex, but feeling it my high privilege upon such an occasion, I went forward, inspired by a sense of duty, and of the purest motives, willing to hazard woman's timidity in giving aid to impede the onward march of the marauding foe.

In conclusion, I must acknowledge my profound gratitude for the very liberal donation by the State; and while I continue to live, I shall endeavor to render myself not more unworthy of your high respect than heretofore.

I have the satisfaction to be, very respectfully, your friend.

Emma Sansom.

Spoken Like Cornelia

A young lady of Louisiana, whose father's plantation had been brought within the enemy's lines, in their operations against Vicksburg, was frequently constrained by the necessities of her situation to hold conversation with the Federal officers. On one of these occasions, a Yankee official inquired how she managed to preserve her equanimity and cheerfulness amid so many trials and privations, and such severe reverses of fortune. Our army, said he, has deprived your father of two hundred Negroes, and literally desolated two magnificent plantations.

She said to the officer—a leader of that army, which had, for months, hovered around Vicksburg, powerless to take it with all their vast appliances of war, and mortified by their repeated failures: "I am not insensible to the comforts and elegancies which fortune can secure, and of which your barbarian hordes have deprived me; but a true southern woman will not weep over them, while her country remains. If *you wish to crush me, take Vicksburg.*"

The Desolation in Tennessee

The correspondent of a northern paper, writing from Tennessee, gives the following description of the sad condition of the country, which was held for so long by the Federals:

In years agone, and not long ago, Tennessee was a paradise. Peace and plenty smiled, law and order reigned. How is it now? After a week's journey, I sit me down to paint you a picture of what I have seen. To the east and to the west, to the north and the south, the sights are saddening, sickening. Government mules and horses are occupying the homes—aye, the palaces—in which her chivalric sons so often slumbered.

The monuments of her taste, the evidences of her skill, the characteristics of her people, are being blotted from existence. Her churches are being turned into houses of prostitution, her seminaries shelter the sick and sore, whose griefs and groans reverberate where once the flower of our youth were wont to breathe the poetic passion and dance to the music of their summer's sun. Her cities, her towns, and her villages are draped in mourning. Even the country, ever and always so much nearer God and Nature than these, wears the black pall. Go from Memphis to Chattanooga, and it is like the march from Moscow in olden time.

The State capitol, like the Kremlin, alone remains of her former glory and greatness. Let this point (Murfreesboro) be the centre, and then make a circumference of thirty miles with me, and we will stay "a week in the womb of desolation." Whether you go on the Selma, the Shelbyville, the Manchester, or any other pike, for a distance of thirty miles either way, what do we behold? One wide, wild, and dreary waste, so to speak.

The fences are all burned down; the apple, the pear, and the plum trees burned in ashes long ago; the torch applied to thousands of splendid mansions, the walls of which alone remain, and even this is seldom so, and where it is, their smooth plaster is covered with vulgar epithets and immoral diatribes. John Smith and Joe Doe, Federate and Confederate warriors, have left jack-knife stereotyping on the doors and casings, where these, in their fewness, are preserved. The rickets and the railings—where are they?

Where are the rosebushes and the violets? But above all, and beyond all, and dearer and more than all else, where, oh where, are the once happy and contented people fled, who lived and breathed and had their being here? Where are the rosy-cheeked cherubs and blue-eyed maidens gone? Where are the gallant young men? Where are all—where are any of them?

But where are they gone—this once happy and contented people? The young men are sleeping in their graves at Shiloh, at Corinth, at Fort Donelson, and other fields of so called glory. The young women have died of grief, or are broken-hearted; the children are orphans. Poor little things, I pity them from my heart as I look at them—black and white—for they seem to have shared a common fate, and like dying in a common destiny.

Their lives—I mean the master and slave, and their offspring—seem to have been inseparably blended. In many cases, I found two or three white children, whose parents were dead, left to the mercies of the faithful slave; and, again, I have seen a large number of little Negro children, whose parents were likewise dead, nestled in the bosom of some white families who, by a miracle, were saved from the vandalism of war.

Ben McCulloch and Joe Baxter

General Benjamin McCulloch was in many particulars a remarkable man. Though a very common looking person, he was very vain of his personal appearance and proud of his fame. When the general was returning from Richmond, not long before the fatal battle of Pea Ridge, a little incident occurred—such as, perhaps, he was more than once the subject of. The party consisted of the general, Captain Armstrong, his A. A. G., and Colonel Snyder, of the Missouri army, with two or three black servants, traveling in a four mule ambulance. They stopped for lunch by the wayside, about two days' travel from Fort Smith, in Arkansas, and were discussing the prospects of the Confederacy and the contents of a basket and a demijohn, when a stranger rode up and inquired the way to Colonel Stone's quarters. The stranger was a perfect specimen of the genus *"butternut."* He was dressed in bilious looking jeans, with a home-made hat and coarse boots, and wore his hair and beard very long. He was mounted on a good horse, and carried on his shoulder a long, old-fashioned rifle. Before there was any time to answer his inquiries he cast his eyes on General McCulloch, and seemed to recognize him. Dismounting at once, he advanced eagerly to the general, with extended hand and a hearty "Bless my soul, Joe! how do you do? What on earth are you doing here?" The general saw that the man was mistaken, but answered him pleasantly, and invited him to partake of the lunch, to which said lunch and demijohn the stranger did full and ample justice. He told the general (for to him he addressed all his conversation, as to an old friend) that he was a volunteer, and had joined Colonel Stone's regiment of Texan Rangers, and that he intended to fight with "Old Ben McCulloch until we had gained our independence." Old Ben enjoyed the man's mistake until they were about ready to start on, when he said to his Texan copatriot:

"My friend, I think you are mistaken as to whom you have been talking; I don't think you know me, and perhaps have never seen me before."

"You be darned!" said Butternut; "I would know you, Joe, if I was to meet you in Africa!"

"Well, now," said the general, getting tired of his new friend's familiarity, "who do you take me for, anyway?"

"*Take* you for?" retorted Texas, earnestly; "I don't *take* you for anybody; I *know* you to be Joe Baxter, what staid in the Perkins settlement, *in* Collins county, all last summer, *a sellin' chain-pumps and puttin' up lightnin'-rods!*"

THE EMPTY SLEEVE

By Dr. G. W. Bagby

Tom, old fellow, I grieve to see
    The sleeve hanging loose at your side;
The arm you lost was worth to me
    Every Yankee that ever died.
But you don't mind it at all;
    You sware you've a beautiful stump,
And laugh, at that damnable ball—
    Tom, I knew you were always a trump.

A good right arm, a nervy hand,
    A wrist as strong as a sapling oak,
Buried deep in the Malvern sand—
    To laugh at that is a sorry joke.
Never again your iron grip
    Shall I feel in my shrinking palm—
Tom, Tom, I see your trembling lip,
    How on earth can *I* be calm?

Well! the arm is gone, it is true;
    But the one that is nearest the heart
Is left—and that's as good as two;
    Tom, old fellow, what makes you start?
Why, man, *she* thinks that empty sleeve
    A badge of honor; so do I,
And all of us:—I do believe
    The fellow is going to cry!

"She deserves a perfect man," you say;
    "You not worth her in your prime?"
Tom! the arm that has turn'd to clay
    Your whole body has made sublime;
For you have placed in the Malvern earth
    The proof and pledge of a noble life—
And the rest, henceforward of higher worth,
    Will be dearer than all to your wife.

I see the people in the street
    Look at your sleeve with kindling eyes;
And you know, Tom, there's naught so sweet
    As homage shown in mute surmise.
Bravely your arm in battle strove,
    Freely, for Freedom's sake, you gave it;
It has perished—but a nation's love
    In proud remembrance will save it.

Go to your sweetheart, then, forthwith—
    You're a fool for staying so long—
Woman's love you'll find no myth,
    But a truth, living, tender, strong.
And when around her slender belt
    Your left is clasped in fond embrace,
Your right will thrill, as if it felt,
    In its grave, the usurper's place.

As I look through the coming years,
    I see a one-armed married man;
A little woman, with smiles and tears,
    Is helping as hard as she can
To put on his coat, pin his sleeve,
    Tie his cravat, and cut his food;
And I say, as these fancies I weave,
    "That is Tom and the woman he wooed."

> The years roll on, and then I see
> A wedding picture bright and fair;
> I look closer, and it's plain to me
> That is Tom with the silver hair.
> He gives away the lovely bride,
> And the guests linger, loth to leave
> The house of him in whom they pride—
> "Brave old Tom with the empty sleeve."

A Narrow Escape

An army correspondent gives the following narrative of the manner in which a Confederate soldier in Mississippi escaped the clutches of the Yankees:

While dwelling upon the subject of ladies and the purifying influence of ladies' society, I will take occasion to mention, for the benefit of the fastidious, an adventure of two nice and accomplished young ladies, together with a young gentleman well versed in gallantry. Not long since, *mon cher* M., of this brigade, while in the vicinity of the Federal encampments, took occasion to put up for the night at the house of an old acquaintance, where he had often called to enjoy a pleasant repast with the young ladies. During the night, the Federals, learning his whereabouts, approached the house, creating a bluster everywhere, save in our young hero's apartment. He soundly slept, and continued to sleep, as if on "beds of roses," unconscious of approaching danger, until the young ladies, panic-stricken on his account, rushed, *en dishabille,* into his room, and awoke him from his slumbers.

But the Federals had advanced too far for him to make his escape in the front, and there was no window or door in the rear. How then was his escape to be effected? Reader, the young ladies instituted a plan unprecedented in the history of military operations. When the old lady discovered he could not escape by running, she rushed in, crying, "Girls! we must do something—the Federals are already in the passage." No sooner said than done. The young ladies leaped in bed with our young hero, one on each side, completely concealing his head, and thereby causing the search of the Federals to be fruitless. They looked into every nook, and under every bed in the house, not excepting the one occupied by the hero; but the young Confederate scout was nowhere to be found. How much better than to have suffered him to be murdered or imprisoned for years in a felon's cell! So we say; but the mystery to us is, why they did not think of looking in the bed, as well as under it.

Graphic Picture of a Sacked City

A correspondent of the *Charlotte Carolinian,* writing from Columbia, gives a graphic picture of the destruction of that city. He says:

General Sherman entered about mid-day, accompanied by one Bergholtz, who formerly lived in Columbia, and was employed by Hon. G. A. Trenholm in laying out the grounds around his mansion. Notwithstanding the many tokens of kindness he had received, the villain was afterward instrumental in laying the house in ashes. Guards were placed around many of the dwellings, but without avail. As if by preconcerted action, robbery immediately commenced, and was continued until the enemy left. Words would fail to describe the frequent indignities and the brutality of the wretches who offered them. No house was safe from their pollution, no hiding-place secure from their search. The chamber of the sick and the sanctity of the church were nothing. Rev. Dr. Shand was robbed of his communion service in the street. The convent (the mother superior of which is said to have been instrumental in the education of the niece and daughter of General Sherman) was broken open and the innocent sisters of mercy and other inmates stripped of their all. The very altars were desecrated, and the lady superior, while appealing, with cross in hand, to the humanity of the soldiers, was rudely thrust aside. The building was afterward fired. The Methodist church—a humble edifice—was likewise entered, and, unable to do more, the scoundrels defaced the monument of the venerable Bishop Capers, and spoke of him as "the first damned secessionist." They then went into the parsonage, robbed it of every thing, abused the pastor's wife, stole the communion service, drank the consecrated wine, and blasphemed God and Jesus Christ in the most horrid manner.

The conflagration, which commenced in the evening of Friday, destroyed nearly four fifths of the city. The horrors of that night are as a dream. Pen cannot describe them. The city was like a sea of fire. Thousands of drunken brutes were rushing through the streets, with torches in their hands, shouting, shrieking, cursing, and even fiddling and dancing over our burning homes. Women and children were driven from their dwellings by the flames, only to be robbed of the few articles they had gathered in their flight. Little ones, with tiny bundles of their own in their arms, brought them forth only to see them thrown back into their burning home or scattered into fragments at their feet. Sick and dying went by on beds to seek shelter in the woods, and old men, whose white locks and venerable aspect should have spared them a reproach, received indignities that none but hearts utterly sunk in depravity could have prompted.

Saw the Elephant

Three Negro boys, one owned in Savannah, and another in Florida and the third in Charleston, all of the crew of the illfated Atlanta, determined, on the exchange at Fortress Monroe, to try their fortunes North. They proceeded as far as Fort Lafayette, New York harbor, delighted their eyes for several days in gazing on the magnificent city in the distance, but on the whole concluded that a southern master was better than a Yankee one; that they had (to use their own expressive language) "put their foot into it." They accordingly notified their intention to the officers in command, who no doubt pretty sick of the Negro themselves, offered no objection, but gave them passage back to Fortress Monroe, and thence by flag-of-truce boat to City Point and Richmond. Two of them arrived here Sunday afternoon, the other remaining over a day in Charleston, and reported themselves to their owners, perfectly satisfied with their short experience of Negro freedom at the North.

Banished from Home

The *Richmond Examiner* of June 10th, 1863, contains the following:—

Richmond, June 7, 1863.

To the Editor of the Examiner:

I received a letter this morning from a refugee, giving an account of the banishment of the secessionists of the town of Weston, from their homes by the Yankees, and I will give you a couple of short extracts which furnish fair specimens of the treatment which our unfortunate citizens of North Western Virginia are receiving at their hands. The writer says:

"All secessionists have been banished from Weston—those who had protectors this side were sent across the lines, the others were sent to Camp Chase." She then mentioned six ladies with families, and five young ladies who, with others, were sent within our lines. They were taken to Clarksburg in ambulances, thence sent by Winchester by rail and brought to Kingstown and set down on the road-side in the night and told to do the best they could. They were allowed to bring sixty pounds of baggage and one hundred dollars in Yankee money. The writer names a good many who were given their choice (how very *kind* to give them *such* a choice) either to go to prison or to Ohio, and names ten or twelve more who were sent to Camp Chase, and says: "The hardest of all was they were *compelled to leave their children*. Mrs. D., started without hers, but went back and took up her youngest, and told them they might kill her, but she would take her baby."

Such is a meagre sketch of their proceedings in one little town. Allow me to ask, Mr. Editor, is there no help for these helpless women and children? Is the *lex talionis* to be entirely ignored and our people to be left at the mercy of these worse than vandals, who have no mercy, nor justice, nor honesty, nor humanity.

A City under Fire

A writer in the *Jackson Mississippian* gives the following account of the bombardment of the city of Vicksburg:

When we reached Clinton, the first station on the road, we were informed that the enemy had that morning opened a heavy and incessant fire, and from daylight the guns have been distinctly heard. Indeed, when the cars stopped, and the noise of wheels and machinery had subsided, we ourselves began to hear the distant rumblings of that fearful storm of which we were ere long to be anxious, if not eager spectators.

We were occupants of the same car with General Van Dorn, who was then on his way to take command at Vicksburg, and our party had full opportunity of making his acquaintance, and studying somewhat his appearance and bearing. In stature he is not above the middle height, with well-set person; his hair is what in a lady you would call auburn, but in a soldier and, gentleman, sandy. He wears it flowing and uncut, and his beard full, though not bushy or neglected. His complexion is soft and blonde, almost like that of a woman, and I was told that he could, and at times actually did blush. If I had to choose the features of his face which most clearly indicate the soldierly qualities, earnestness, judgment, and courage, I should say they are found in his active, quick, keen (not soft) blue eye, his clean cut, chiseled nose (especially the nostril), and resolute, determined mouth. Being a native born Mississippian, and bringing with him here a high character as a soldier, our people generally, and our Vicksburg friends in particular, are restored to a degree of confidence which they have not felt under the recent military regime.

As we neared Vicksburg, more palpable evidences of the presence of the enemy became apparent both in sight and sound. "Grim visaged war" began to show "his wrinkled front." The cars were not permitted to go entirely to the depot, but were stopped at the machine shop, about one mile distant; and then on foot and in wonder, and even somewhat of awe, we entered the beleaguered city, amid the roar of cannon, and the sharp, hissing, hurtling sound of exploding shells.

I had often been there before, and, in years past, had been familiar not only with its localities, but with most of its worthiest and hospitable citizens. I had traversed its streets and entered its houses in happier and better days; and as our party made its way along into the town, the contrast became more and more obvious. Places which erst had shone glorious with peace and happy faces—homes made bright and lovely with all the adornments of art and the cultivation of nature, where families had gathered and clustered around worthy and noble mothers and sires; where wealth, and kindness, and hospitality, had been dispensed with a profuse and lavish hand the chosen and adopted home of Prentiss and his host of gallant compeers, rendered desolate, deserted, and abandoned, by a relentless and ruthless foe. Indeed, if you wish to see the greatest and best example of the self-devotion and longsuffering endurance of our people to our cause, go to Vicksburg! Traverse its deserted streets; enter the sacred precincts of its churches; roam, saddened and sick at heart, through its lovely and neglected gardens; seek admittance for trade or curiosity to its closed hotels, stores, and courtrooms, and you will see of what a brave and virtuous people are capable, when inspired by the noblest sentiment of humanity and true patriotism; and, yet, is not this a better fate and a nobler destiny than has befallen Memphis and New Orleans? Is it not safer, wiser, and better, to preserve freedom, faith, and honor, than to pander to a base enemy to preserve wealth in property or safety to person! Witness, now, the difference in the moral grandeur of the spectacle presented to the world. The two cities in the hands of enemies and tyrants—the little "queen city" of the great valley, devoted to certain destruction, and yet calm and undismayed amid the war of nations and of element.

At our outset from the cars, it was determined that we should make our way to some conspicuous point upon the river, where we could see the fleet of the enemy and witness his operations. This place we found on Washington street, in the establishment of our old friends Hardaway & White. In the upper stories of this house we had a fair opportunity of observing, in comparative security, the array of gun and mortar boats; most of them being engaged the whole of that day and night in sending shell and shot at our batteries and into the town. The effects up to the coming on of night had, however, been trivial, and comparatively harmless. From our point of view, we had in sight all of the enemy's gunboats, those lying around the point and against the Louisiana shore, and also most, if not all, his mortar boats. The latter had crept up during the night previous, and were lying just below the point and immediately under the bank on our own shore, thus getting nearer our batteries and commanding the town. Their masts, we observed, were wrapped with the limbs or foliage of trees, intended, we suppose, as a disguise to aid them in getting so closely in upon us.

About eight o'clock at night the enemy again opened a terrific and deafening fire. The scene was fearful and grand in the extreme. The air and sky at times seemed one sheet of living flame, while shells burst in mid-air, scattering their dreadful missiles of death around and over the devoted city.

This was kept up for at least two hours, when, it seemed to us, from sheer exhaustion of the combatants, the firing ceased, and stillness and midnight, like a pall, darkened and fell over the scene. Nothing but the light of morning could reveal the death and desolation which had ensued. When that morning came, more appalling and fearful still was the scene which it presented. Several of the principal gunboats, with the flag boat of the enemy, for some purpose, of course unknown to us, ran the gauntlet of our batteries, and at about four o'clock in the morning were at the landing, and directly under and opposite the town.

Here, in conjunction with about twenty of their mortar-boats and a concealed battery upon the opposite bank of the river, they all simultaneously opened fire. We were awakened from our dreams of peace by a report and reverberation scarce equaled in volume by the terrific peals of "Heaven's artillery." The whale broad bosom of the river was one sheet of liquid flame, the houses and hills seemed to rock upon their very foundations. First came the whirring, whizzing noise of the shell, awakening the echoes far and near, and then the booming sound of the report. To an uneducated ear, the peculiar sound made by the shell, when first projected from the mouth of the mortar, is terrible in the extreme. I still hear it in my ears, and every loud, crashing sound almost startles me into the belief that I am still "under fire."

After remaining within walls for some time, we at length determined to try the open streets, where, at least, was offered a better chance for dodging than in doors. When we reached the street, we then began to see the effects of the bombardment upon the few remaining inhabitants of the town, and upon the houses along our route. As we were merely amateurs, and our presence not absolutely essential to the safety or defense of the town, it was, upon a council of war, determined to make our way to the friendly protection of the hills on the outskirts. All along our way we found men, women, and children flying in every direction to seek shelter and protection somewhere. Here would be seen a mother and helpless children, hastened perhaps in their flight from their homes by a shell having fallen upon and through their roof, or in the yard adjoining. Here came first the hissing sound, and then the messenger of death plowed up the streets just before you, or went crashing into some house or grassy bank almost at your back. Here we saw a poor Irishman kneeling in profound reverence, with his face pressed to the very earth, and as we heard his earnest invocation, "*Ave Maria, ora pro Nobis,*" we were impressed with the thought that if the missile of death would strike him, it could not come at a better time.

We found the shells fell thicker and faster the further we went, as if the enemy sought to show how far their murderous engines would carry, or because they were "feeling" for the camps of our soldiers, which they supposed were in range. Thus, from four until six o'clock did this hellish work continue, and by an enemy whose proud boast is that they "never make war upon unoffending citizens, and helpless women and children!" God save the mark. We gradually found our way back to our stopping place, and after a good breakfast betook ourselves to ranging the city to learn the casualties and incidents of the fight. Compared with the "sound and fury," these were comparatively trifling. Within the whole bounds of the city we could hear of but one death; but this was a most estimable lady, Mrs. Gamble, who, we were told, had been one of the most active in acts of kindness and labor for our soldiers. She was struck with a splinter, and died instantly.

At the batteries, we had but two men killed and four or five wounded. An incident at one of our guns is worthy of recording, and should immortalize the actor in it. A soldier stationed with his finger at the vent while the gun was being loaded, had the hand he was thus using dreadfully mangled with a fragment of shell—and yet he nobly held it in position until the gunner had finished loading the piece! Because, if he had for an instant released his hold, death would have been inevitable to his companions. Can people exhibiting such traits ever be conquered?

A great number of houses were struck, and many of them entirely gutted and destroyed. The Methodist and Catholic churches were both struck, the former in the cupola and basement, with two shots. The small loss of life is perhaps attributable to the fact that most of the occupants were absent, and many had fled temporarily from their houses into the streets and open country.

Thus terminated for us the scenes of which I fear I have given but a faint idea, from my imperfect manner of description. Indeed, there were moments of time when the incidents occurring around me seemed forever daguerreotyped upon my mind. And yet, for all the chances of death around us, we all agreed that no earthly consideration would have induced us to have forgone the spectacle.

A Traveled Lady

While Hood was at Atlanta, a detachment was sent to the rear of Sherman's army under Colonel Hill, of Louisiana. An officer of the second Missouri regiment stopped one day to get dinner at the house of a very clever old lady with three fine looking daughters. At the table she asked the young man where he was from. "From Missouri, madam," was the reply. She looked over her spectacles, as though trying to gaze through illimitable space, and said slowly, "Missouri, Missouri, Missouri, why that jines Gwinnett, don't it?" Now Gwinnett was a county just across the Chattahoochee River. The officer choked down a laugh, and said, "Certainly, madam." The youngest daughter, a sweet girl of sixteen, in the innocence of her heartfelt infinite pride at her mother's wisdom; said, "Why, I declare, mammy knows every thing. She has been at all them places."

Impressment by Women—A Rich Scene

A correspondent of the *Petersburg Express,* writing from Salisbury, North Carolina, on the 18th instant, says that about twelve o'clock of that day a rumor was afloat that the wives of several soldiers now in the war, intended to make a dash on some flour and other necessaries of life belonging to certain gentlemen who the ladies termed *"speculators."* They alleged that they were entirely out of provisions and unable to give the enormous prices now asked; but were willing to give government prices. The letter adds:

Accordingly about two o'clock they met, some fifty or seventy-five in number, with axes and hatchets, and proceeded to the depot of the North Carolina Central road, to impress some there, but were very politely met by the agent, Mr. ——, with the inquiry: "What on earth was the matter?" The excited women said they were in search of "flour," which they learned had been stored there by a certain speculator. The agent assured them such was not the case. They still insisted on examining the depot, but after a while desisted and made their way up town to the store of one of the oldest and most respected citizens. They commenced a general attack on his lumber-room, in which was stored a large quantity of flour. The old gentleman, seeing their determination to have the flour, compromised the matter by saying if they would desist he would give them ten barrels, which he readily did.

They then went to the store of a large firm (one of them a Petersburger) to impress his flour. They heard he had been speculating, but were sadly mistaken, he only having seven barrels. But *he* like a good citizen made them a present of three barrels, and remarked that any soldier's wife could get any thing in reason from him. (What a great pity there are not more of the same kind.)

The word march was given, and onward they went to the government warehouse, under the superintendence of a gentleman from South Carolina, to see if they could impress any thing there. He very politely opened the door, and gave them every facility to examine the premises. They soon dispersed from there, not finding a thing they could impress.

They then met a gentleman on the street who, they had been told, had salt, on which they said he intended to speculate. He assured them most positively that such was not the case; that it was sent to him to sell. They insisted on having a bag. He reiterated what he had told them, but said, rather than have the salt impressed he would make them a present of a bag and a twenty dollar Confederate note.

Their cry was still for more, and they proceeded down the street to the store of another highly respectable merchant, who, I suppose, rather than be bothered gave them a barrel of molasses.

Finally, and now came the richest scene of all—they returned to the depot of the North Carolina Central road, and again demanded of the agent that they be allowed to go in. He still refused, but finally agreed to let two go in and examine the flour, and see if his statement was not correct. A restlessness pervaded the whole body, and but a few moments elapsed before a female voice was heard, saying, "Let's go in." The agent remarked, "Ladies, I hope you will desist from this course, for it is useless to attempt it, unless you go in over my dead body." A rush was made and in they went, and the last I saw of the agent he was sitting on a log blowing like a March wind. They took ten barrels and rolled them out, and were sitting on them when I left, waiting for a wagon to haul them away. While the agent was sitting on the log, a farmer came up and desired to know if he could ship some tobacco to Charlotte. Yes, was the reply, but if you store it in the warehouse, it will be at your own risk—don't you see the women have just pressed ten barrels of flour? The farmer, fearing they would learn to chew and press the tobacco, very speedily retired.

The Evacuation of Savannah

The *Charleston Courier* contains a letter giving a very interesting statement of the evacuation of Savannah. The writer says:

Our fortification extended from the Savannah river, some four miles above the city, on our right, to the Little Ogeechee river, near the Gulf railroad, some eight miles from the city, on our left. We held Fort McAlister, on the west bank of the Ogeechee, a few miles below the Gulf railroad. We also had strong batteries at Rose Dew, between the two Ogeechee, at Beaulieu, Thunderbolt, Causlin's Bluff, etc., and troops stationed on Isle of Hope and Whitmarsh islands. Our newly erected fortifications on the land side of the city were very strong, and capable of turning back almost any kind of assault, though they were not commenced till after Sherman had nearly reached Milledgeville. Sherman's army appeared before these works about the 8th or 9th instant, and on Saturday, the 10th, considerable fighting occurred. Several severe assaults were made, in which the enemy were signally repulsed. Early on Sunday morning, the 11th, a tremendous cannonading began and was kept up for half the day. It was supposed in the city that a heavy engagement was going on, but it proved to be only a general shelling from the heavy guns, on our lines. Sherman was in no condition to attack our works. He was scarce of ammunition and had no heavy guns, as well as other difficulties in the way of his giving battle. During the siege, severe assaults were several times made on particular points, with a view of storming our works and breaking through our lines, but all these were handsomely repulsed.

On Saturday, the 17th instant, a flag of truce was sent in by Sherman, demanding the surrender of the city; and on Sunday, the 18th, a reply was given by General Beauregard, refusing to comply with the demand. On Monday the evacuation commenced—the first squad coming out about mid-day; another came out at four P.M., and two others at night. How rapidly the evacuation was thereafter conducted, I know not, except from reports. It is said the evacuation took place on Tuesday night. I fear all our soldiers did not get out. Some of them were twelve or fourteen miles from the city, while many were eight miles off. The heaviest fighting of the siege took place on Monday evening and night, the 19th. The enemy were repulsed in all their attempts on our lines; so the soldiers must have been there, and not on the retreat. If so, I cannot perceive how it is possible for all to have come off by Tuesday night, though they may have done so. We had several boats, capable of carrying from five hundred to one thousand each, across the river at a trip, and a pontoon bridge besides.

Very few of the citizens left the city. Many would have done so if they could, but the realization of their condition came too late. It found them all unprepared, and escape impossible. There was no alternative but to submit to their terrible fate. It does seem to me that our military authorities should, by some means, have given some notice or hint to the people, or time allowed those who desired to do so, either to get away or set their houses in order if they intended to stay. Perhaps I am wrong in this conclusion—I will not say positively. As before stated, the people were in the dark as to what was going on. They hoped we would be able to force Sherman to the coast, either to the right or to the left, and save the city, and, in this belief, very little private property of any description was sent off. Neither of the newspaper offices was removed, and all the material of both, including a considerable supply of paper, fell into the hands of the enemy. If they remain there long, we may expect soon to have them issuing Yankee newspapers from the offices of these hitherto substantial southern journals.

The last issue of the *News* was on Saturday morning, the 10th instant. The enemy had cut all the railroads and telegraphic wires, thus cutting off any outside information by mail or otherwise, and the military authorities desired nothing concerning the situation, or what was there taking place, to be made public. Under these circumstances the paper was stopped, and the editors and printers went into service.

The *Republican* continued to issue a quarter sheet, but it contained no news, either local or from abroad, and was, under the circumstances, the most unsatisfactory newspaper that I ever tried to read. I never witnessed such a forcible illustration of the value of newspapers in a community.

Everybody was in a state of suspense. There was a pretty general hope that the city would be saved, but no one could give any substantial reason for this hope, having no certain grounds upon which to base it; and ignorance of the real condition kept them from arriving at a different conclusion and preparing for the worst.

All was uncertainty and doubt. Hope was mingled with fear, and it was difficult for any one to decide which preponderated in his own mind. Every man, when he met his neighbor, inquired, and was inquired of, after the news, and neither could gratify the other. All were the victims of every imaginable kind of rumor and opinion, from the best to the worst. I hope never to pass through such dreadful days again. Such suspense is worse agony than any reality, be it ever so dreadful.

Social Life in Baltimore during the War

The author of "*Emy Livingstone,*" in his entertaining volume, entitled "Border and Bastile," gives the following interesting account of life in Baltimore during the war:

The southward approach to Baltimore is very well managed. The railroad makes an abrupt curve, as it sweeps round the marshy woodlands through which the Patapsco opens into the bay; so that you have a fair view of the entire city, swelling always upward from the water's edge, on a cluster of low, irregular hills, to the summit of Mount Vernon. From that highest point soars skyward a white, glistening pillar, crowned by Washington's statue. I have seldom seen a monument better placed, and it is worthy of its advantages, The figure retains much of the strength and grace for which in life it was renowned, and, if ever features were created, worthy of the deftest sculptor and the purest marble, such, surely, was the birthright of that noble, serene face.

No one, that has sojourned in Washington, can be ten minutes in Baltimore without being aware of a great and refreshing change. You leave the hurry and bustle of traffic behind at the railway station, and are never subjected to such nuisances till you return thither. Even in the exclusively commercial squares of the city there reigns comparative leisure, for, except in the establishment of government contractors, or others directly connected with the supply of the army, business is by no means brisk just now. You may pass through Baltimore street, the main artery bisecting the town from east to west, at any hour, without encountering a denser or busier throng than you would meet in Regent street, any afternoon *out* of the season, and, about the usual promenade time, the proportion of fair *flâneuses*, to the meaner masculine herd, would be nearly the same.

I betook myself to Guy's hotel, which had been recommended to me as quiet and comfortable: for many people it would have been *too* quiet. The black waiters carried the science of "taking things easy" to a rare perfection; they were thoroughly polite, and even kindly in manner, and never dreamed of objecting to any practicable order, but—as for carrying it out within any specified time—*altra cosa*. After a few vain attempts and futile remonstrances, the prudent and philosophical guest would recognize resignedly the absolute impossibility of obtaining breakfast, however simple, under forty-five minutes from the moment of commanding the same; indeed that was very good time, and I positively aver that I have waited longer for eggs, tea, and toast. I never tried abuse or reproach, for I chanced, early in my stay, to be present when an impatient traveler voided the vials of his wrath on the head of the chief attendant insisting, with many strange oaths, on his right to obtain cooked food, of some sort, within the half-hour.

Years, ago, I was amused at the *Gaietés*, by a commonplace scene enough of stage temptation. *Madelon,* driven into her last intrenchments by the sophistries of the wily aristocrat, objected timidly, *"Mais, Monseigneur, j'aime mon mari."* For a moment the *Marquis* was surprised, and seemed to reflect. Then he said: *"Tiens—tu aimes ton mari? C'est bizarre: mais—après tout—ce n'est pas defendu."* As he spoke, he smiled upon his simple vassal—evidently wavering between amusement and compassion.

With just such a smile—allowing for the exaggeration of the African physiognomy—did "Leonoro" contemplate his victim, and me, the bystander, and then sauntered slowly from the room, without uttering one word. It was a great moral lesson, and I profited by it. But, in truth, there was little to complain of; the quarters were clean and comfortable, and one got, in time, as much as any reasonable man could desire. The arrangements are on the European system, *i.e.,* there are no fixed hours for meals, which are ordered from the *carte,* and no fixed charge for board. I should have remained there permanently, had it not been for one objection, which eventually overcame my aversion to change. The basement story of the house was occupied by a bar and oyster saloon; the pungent testaceous odors, mounting from those lower regions, gave the offended nostrils no respite or rest; in a few minutes, a robust appetite, albeit watered by cunning bitters, would wither, like a flower in the fume of sulphur. Half-a-dozen before dinner, have always satiated my own desire for these molluscs; before many days were over, I utterly abominated the name of the species; familiarity only made the nuisance more intolerable, and I fled at last, fairly *ostracised*. How the *habitués* stood it was a mystery, till I recognized the fact, that there is no accident of pleasure or pain to which humanity is liable, no antecedent of rest or exertion, no untimeliness of hour or incongruity of place, which will render an apple or an oyster inopportune to an American *bourgeois*.

My first visit in Baltimore was to the British consul, to whom I brought credentials from a member of the Washington Legation. I shall not easily forget the many courtesies, for which I have never adequately thanked Mr. Bernal: few English travelers leave Baltimore, without carrying away grateful recollections of his pleasant house in Franklin street, and without having received some kindness, social or substantial, from the fair hands which dispense its hospitalities so gently and gracefully.

On that same evening my name was entered as an honorary member of the Maryland Club. It would be absurd to compare this institution with the palaces of our own metropolis; but, in all respects, it may fairly rank with the best class of yacht clubs. You find there, besides the ordinary writing and reading accommodation, a pleasant lounge from early afternoon to early morning; a fair French cook, pitilessly monotonous in his *carte;* a good steady rubber at limited points, and a perfect billiard-room. In this last apartment it is well worth, while to linger, sometimes, for half an hour, to watch the play, if the "Chief" chances to be there. I have never seen an amateur to compare with this great artist, for certainty and power of cue. A short time before my arrival, at the carom game, on a table without pockets, he scored one thousand and fifteen on *one break. I* heard this from a dozen eye-witnesses.

I went through many introductions that evening; and, in, the next fortnight, received ample and daily proofs of the proverbial hospitality of Baltimore. There are residents—praisers of the time gone by, who cease not to lament the convivial decadence of the city; but such deficiency is by no means apparent to a stranger.

If *gourmandize* be the favorite failing in these parts, there is surely some excuse for the sinners. Probably no one tract on earth, of the same extent, can boast of so many delicacies peculiar to itself, as the shores of the Chesapeake. Of these, the most remarkable is the "terrapin"; it is about the size of a common land tortoise, and haunts the shallow waters of the bay and the salt marshes around. They say, "he was a bold man who first ate an oyster"; a much more undaunted experimentalist was the first taster of the terrapin. I strongly advise no one to look at the live animal, till he has thoroughly learnt to like the savory meat; *then* he will be enabled to laugh all qualms and scruples to scorn. Comparisons have been drawn between the terrapin and the turtle—very absurdly; for beyond the fact of both being testudineous, there is not a point of resemblance. Individually, I prefer the tiny "diamond-back" to his gigantic congener, as more delicate and less cloying to the palate. Then there is the superb "canvass-back"—peerless among water fowl—never eaten in perfection out of sight of the sand banks where he plucks the wild sea-celery; and, in their due season, "soft crabs," and "bay mackerel." Last of all, there are oysters (well worth the name) of every shape, color, and size. They assert that the "cherrystones" are superior to our own Colchester natives in flavor; for reasons before stated, I cared not to contest the point.

A dinner based upon these materials, with a saddle of five-year old mutton from the eastern shore, as the main *pièce de resistance,* might have satisfied the defunct Earl Dudley of fastidious memory. The wines deserve a separate paragraph.

For generations past, there has prevailed a great rivalry and emulation amongst the Amphitryons of Baltimore. They seem to have taken as much pride in their cellars as a Briton might do in his racing or hunting stables—bestowing the same elaborate care on their construction and management. The prices given for rare brands appear fabulous, even to those who have heard at home, three or four "commissioners" at an auction, with plenipotentiary powers, disputing the favorite bin of some deceased Dean or Don. But when you consider, what the lost interest on capital lying dormant for seventy years will amount to, the apparent extravagance of cost is easily accounted for.

That is no uncommon age for Maderia. No European palate can form an idea of this wonderful wine; for, when in mature perfection, it is utterly ruined by transport beyond the seas. The vintages of Portugal and Hungary are thin and tame beside the puissant liquor that, after half a century's subjection to southern suns, enters slowly on its prime with abated fire, but undiminished strength. Drink it *then*, and you will own, that from the juice of no other grape can be drawn such subtlety of flavor, such delicacy of fragrance, passing the perfume of flowers. Climate, of course, is the first consideration. I believe Baltimore and Savannah limit, northward and southward, the region wherein the maturing process can be thoroughly perfected.

These pleasant banquets began early, about five P.M., and were indefinitely prolonged; for cigars are not supposed to interfere with the proper appreciation of Maderia, and the revellers here cherish the honest old English custom of chanting over their liquor. Closing my eyes now, so as to shut out the dingy drab walls of this, my prison chamber, I can call up one of those cheery scenes quite distinctly: I can hear the "chief's" voice close at my ear, trolling forth the traditional West Point ditty of "Benny Havens," or the rude sea-ballad, full of quaint pathos:

'Twas a Friday morning when we set sail;

then—deeper and fuller tones, rolling out Barry Cornwall's sonorous verses of "King Death." It is good to look back on hours like these, though I doubt if the ill-cooked meats, whereof I hope soon to partake—not unthankfully—will be improved by the memory.

In spite of this large hospitality, instances even of individual excess are comparatively rare. I have seen more aberration of intellect and convivial eccentricity after a Greenwich dinner, or a heavy "guest night," than was displayed at any one of these Baltimore entertainments; a stranger endowed with a fair constitution, abstaining from morning drinks; and paying attention to the Irishman's paternal advice—"Keep your back from the fire, and don't mix your liquors"—may take his place, with comfort and confidence.

But my social recollections of Baltimore are by no means exclusively bacchanalian. British stock, lamentably at a discount in other parts of the Union, is perhaps a trifle above par here. The popularity of our representatives—masculine and feminine—may have something to do with this. At any rate, the avenues of the best and pleasantest circles are easily opened to any Englishman of warranted position and name.

If a traveler were to enter a drawing-room here, expecting to be surprised at every turn by some incongruity of speech or demeanor such as book-makers have attributed to our American cousins, he would not fill a page of his mental note-book. I had no such prejudices to be disappointed. After experience of society in many lands, I begin to think that well-bred and educated people speak and behave after much the same fashion all the world over. Few Baltimorean voices are free from a perceptible accent. It is more marked in the gentler sex, but rarely so strong as to be disagreeable. The ear is never offended by the New England twang, or Connecticut drawl, and some tones rang true as silver.

You hear, of course, occasional peculiarities of expression, and words somewhat distorted from our Anglican meaning, but these are not much more frequent or strange than provincial idioms at home. I was only once fairly puzzled in this wise.

It was at a public "assembly." I had just been presented to the

> Queen rose of a rosebud garden of girls,

a very gazelle, too, for litheness and grace. The music of the *sirène* had begun, and my arm had encircled my partner's willow waist, when I felt her hang back, and saw on her fair face a distressed look of penitence and perplexity. "I'm so sorry," she murmured, "but I can't dance *loose*." Perfectly vague as to her meaning, I assured her that she should be guided after as *serree* a fashion as she chose. But this evidently did not touch the difficulty. By the merest chance, I observed that all the cavaliers put themselves, as it were, in position, their left hand locked in the right of their *valseuse*, before making a start, omitting the preliminary, paces that get you well into the swing. It was all plain sailing then, and swift sailing too. The rest of the performance was completed with perfect unanimity, much to my own satisfaction, and, I trust, not to the discontent of my fairy-footed charge.

The freedom and independent self-reliance of the Baltimorean *demoiselles* is very remarkable. At home they receive and entertain their own friends, of either sex, quite naturally; and taking their walks abroad, or returning from an evening party, trust themselves unhesitatingly to the escort of a single cavalier. Yet you would scarcely find a solitary imitation of the "fast girls" who have been giving our own ethical writers so much uneasiness of late. It speaks well for the tone of society, where such a state of things can prevail without fear and without reproach. Though Baltimore breeds gossips, numerous and garrulous as is the wont of provincial cities, I never heard a slander or a suspicion leveled against the most intrepid of those innocent Unas.

From the *morale* one must needs pass to the *personnel*. On the appearance of a *debutante,* they say the first question in Boston is—"Is she clever?" In New York—"Is she wealthy?" In Philadelphia—"Is she well-born?" In Baltimore—"Is she beautiful?" And, for many years past, common report has conceded the golden apple to the Monumental city. I think the distinction has been fairly won.

The small, delicate features—the long, liquid, iridescent eyes—the sweet, indolent *morbidezza,* that make southern beauty so perilously fascinating, are not uncommon here, and are often united to a clearness and brilliancy of complexion scarcely to be found nearer the tropics. The upper ten thousand by no means monopolize these personal advantages. At the hour, of "dress parade" you cannot walk five steps without encountering a face well worthy of a second look. Occasionally too, you catch a provokingly brief glimpse of a high, slender instep, and an ankle modeled to match it. The fashion of balmorals and kilted kirtles prevails not here; and maids and matrons are absurdly reluctant to submit their pedal perfections to the, passing critic. Even on a day when it is a question of Mud *v.* Modesty, you may escort an intimate acquaintance for an hour, and depart, doubting as to the color of her hosen. But, conceding the justice of Baltimore's claim, and the constant recurrence of a more than *stata pulchritudo,* I am bound to confess that, with a single, exception; I saw nothing approaching *supreme* perfection of form or feature.

The exception was a very remarkable one.

I write these words as reverently as if I were drawing the portrait of the fair Austrian empress, or any other crowned beauty; indeed, I always looked on that face simply as a wonderful picture, and so I remember it now. I have never seen a countenance more faultlessly lovely. The *pose* of the small head, and the sweep of the neck, resembled the miniatures of Giulia Grisi in her youth, but the lines were more delicately drawn, and the *contour* more refined. The broad open forehead—the brows firmly arched, without an approach to heaviness—the thin chiselled nostril, and perfect mouth, cast in the softest feminine mould—reminded you of the first Napoleon. Quick mobility of expression would have been inharmonious there. With all its purity of outline, the face was not severe or coldly statuesque—only superbly serene—not lightly to be ruffled by any sudden revulsion of feeling; a face, of which you never realized the perfect glory till the pink-coral tint flushed faintly through the clear pale, cheeks, while the lift of the long trailing lashes revealed the magnificent eyes, lighting up, slowly and surely, to the full of their stormy splendor. It chanced, that the lady was a vehement Unionist, and "rose," very freely, on the subject of the war. Sincere in her honest patriotism, I doubt if she ever guessed at the real object of her opponent in the arguments which not infrequently arose. If there be any indiscretion in this pen-and-ink sketch from nature, I should bitterly regret the involuntary error, though its subject, to the world in general, remains nameless as Lenore.

There is another peculiarity of Baltimore society, which a stranger will only perceive when he has passed withinside its porches. It is divided, not only into sets, but, as it were, into clans. Several of the leading families, generally belonging to the territorial aristocracy (let the word stand) that took root in the State at, or soon after, its settlement, have so intermarried, as to create the most curious net of cousinship the meshes of which are yearly becoming more intricate and numerous. Yet there are no especial indications of exclusiveness or spirit of *clique;* rather it is the homely feeling of kinsmanship, which makes the intercourse of relations more familiar and unceremonious, than that of intimate acquaintances or friends.

Cadets from many powerful houses in all the three kingdoms were among the earliest colonists of Maryland. It is good to mark, how gallantly the "old blood" holds its own, even here; how the descendants of soldiers and statesmen have already attained the pride of place that their ancestors won at home centuries ago, by a like valiance of sword, tongue, or pen. Take one family, for instance, with whose members I was fortunate enough to be especially intimate.

For generations past, the Howards have been men of mark in Maryland. Wherever hard or famous work was to be done, in field or senate, one, at least, of the name was sure to be found in the front. The present head of the family sustains right well the reputation of the worthies who went before him. A staunch friend and an uncompromising adversary—valuing political honesty no more lightly than private honor—liberal and unsuspicious to a fault in his social relations—very frank and simple in speech—in manner always courteous and cordial—it would be hard to find, in Europe, an apter representative of the ancient regime. I believe, that those who really know General Howard, will not consider this sketch a flattery or an exaggeration. He was a candidate for the governorship at the last election, and so powerful was his acknowledged personal *prestige*, that, in despite of overt intimidation and secret influences, which made a free voting an absurdity, the Black Republicans exulted over his withdrawal as an important victory.

Though ordinary business is so slack in Baltimore just at present, almost every male resident, not engaged in law or physic, has, or supposes himself to have, something to do. Instances of absolute idleness are very rare. So, by ten A.M., all the men betake themselves to their offices, and there busy themselves about their affairs, after a fashion, energetic or desultory, till after two o'clock. The dinner hour varies from three to half-past five. Post-prandial labor is generally declined; wisely, too, for few American digestions will bear trifling with; though nature must have gifted some of my acquaintance with a marvelous internal mechanism. How, otherwise, could they stand a long unbroken course of free living, with such infinitesimal correctives of exercise? The evening is spent after each man's fancy—at the club; or at one of the many houses where a familiar is certain to meet a welcome, and more or less of pleasant company. The entertainments are often more extensive and formal, embracing, of course, music, and such are invariably wound up by a supper. I have heard certain of our seniors grow quite pathetic over the abolition of those social, if unsalubrious repasts. I wonder at such regrets no longer, if I cannot share them. There is surely a hilarious informality about these *medianochi* that attaches to no antecedent feast; the freedom of a pic-nic, without its manifold inconveniences: as the witching hour draws nearer, the "brightest eyes that ever have shone" glitter yet more gloriously, till in their nearer and dearer splendor a Chaldean would forget the stars; and the "sweetest lips that ever were kissed" sip the creaming Verzenay, or savor the delicate "olio," with a keener honesty of zest. The supper tables are almost always adorned by some of the pretty, quaint conceits of an artist, whose fame extends far beyond Baltimore. Mr. Hermann's ice imitations of all fruits and flowers are marvelously vivid and natural: I have never seen them equaled by any continental *glaciers*.

I have lingered, perhaps, too long over too trifling details; and yet, I wish I had done my subject more justice. Be it remembered, that I visited Baltimore at a season of unusual social depression. I do not speak of the stagnation in commerce, and the ruin of southern interests and possessions, from which many have suffered heavy pecuniary loss: the effects of the war come home to the fair city yet more sharply. For months past the best part of her *jeunesse doree* have been fighting—as only the daintily born and bred *can* fight, at bitter need—in the van of southern armies.

Every fresh rumor of battle adds to the crowd of pale, anxious faces, and every bulletin lengthens the list of mourners. There are few families, Federal or Secessionist, who have not relatives—none that have not dear friends—exposed to hourly peril, from disease, if not from lead or steel. The suspense felt in England during the Crimean or Indian wars, cannot be compared to that which many here are forced to endure. *We* knew, at least, where our soldiers were, and heard often how they fared: their sickness, wounds, and deaths were all recorded. But the scenes of this war's vast theatre are so often shifted, and communication with the remoter parts of the Southwest is so uncertain, that months will elapse without a line of tidings from the absent; the grass has grown and withered again, over many graves, before the weary hearts at home knew that the time was past, for waiting, and watching, and prayers.

Epilogue

Postbellum North and South

FOREWORD TO *DEFENDING THE SOUTHERN CONFEDERACY: THE MEN IN GRAY*

BY ROBERT CATLETT CAVE

When I delivered the oration at the unveiling of the monument to the soldiers and sailors of the Southern Confederacy, in Richmond, Virginia, on May 30, 1894, I supposed that the war was over; that the animosities engendered by it had been buried; that it might be discussed as freely as any other historical event; and that at the dedication of a monument to the Confederate dead a Southerner's attempt to free their memory from reproach by plainly stating the reasons that moved them to take up arms and justifying their action would be received by the people of the North with patience and kindly toleration, if not with approval. However it may have seemed to those who read extracts from it, the speech was not prompted by a malevolent spirit. Indeed, I think I can truthfully say that never, either during or after the war, was I moved by a feeling of enmity toward the brave men who fought under the Stars and Stripes in obedience to what they believed to be the call of duty. I deplored the fact that they had been deceived into taking up arms against what I regarded as the cause of truth, justice, and freedom; but toward them personally I had no feeling of ill will or hostility. I had friends among them—young men of admirable qualities, whom I had met before the war and esteemed highly, and whom I loved none the less because their uniforms were blue.

Not only was I conscious of no feeling of enmity in my own heart, but, so far as I knew, Southern men generally entertained no such feeling. We of the South believed most firmly that the North had unrighteously made war on us; but we credited the Northern soldiers with the same loyalty to honest conviction that we claimed for ourselves, and freely conceded to them the right to speak without restraint in justification of what they had done. We had so far allayed whatever of animosity we may once have felt that we could read misrepresentations of the South and her cause with an indulgent smile, and excuse them on the ground that those who made them believed them to be true.

Knowing this to be the attitude and feeling of the conquered, to whom the war had brought incalculable loss and suffering, I supposed that the conquerors, who had suffered and lost comparatively little, would be equally magnanimous. But I was speedily undeceived. The storm of unjust criticism and bitter denunciation which the speech called forth showed but too plainly that the embers of hate were still smoldering in some Northern hearts, needing but a breath to fan them into flame, and that the time was not yet come when plain speech in justification of the South would receive calm consideration or even be tolerated.

Deeming it unwise and unpatriotic to add fuel to the flame which I had unintentionally kindled, I did not reply to these animadversions; but I think it well to notice here the objection to the speech as a violation of Decoration Day proprieties. In the words of one of my critics: "Decoration Day in both sections belongs to the bravery of the dead. [May 30 has never been Confederate Memorial Day.] Old issues belong to other places of discussion." With this sentiment I am in full sympathy. When we meet where sleep the heroic dead, to pay a tribute of respect to their high courage and soldierly virtues, and, following a custom which originated with the women of the South, reverently to decorate the graves of Federals and Confederates alike, the calling up of the old differences that arrayed them in opposing lines of battle is a gross impropriety. Had I been speaking on such an occasion, I would have raised no question as to whether Federals or Confederates had fought for the right. But the speech was not made on such an occasion. Although delivered on National Decoration Day, it was not at the graves of any dead, but at the unveiling of a monument to the soldiers and sailors of the South. It was a ceremony which pertained not to both sections, but to the South alone—a ceremony in which the Southern people were formally dedicating a shaft that would bear witness to their appreciation of the worth of the men who fought under the flag of the Confederacy and to their desire to perpetuate the memory of those men. Since the highest courage, if displayed in defense of an unjust cause, cannot deserve a memorial, it seemed to me that this shaft was intended to commemorate not only the valor of the Southern soldiers and sailors, but also the righteousness of the cause in defense of which that valor was displayed. Hence I thought it appropriate to speak in justification of their cause, as well as in praise of their courage.

Many Northern orators seem to think it altogether proper to discuss the old differences between the sections, even in the usual exercises on Decoration Day. On the same day that the Confederate monument was unveiled in Richmond Judge J. B. McPherson, as a part of the Memorial Day services held at Lebanon, Penn., delivered an address from which I take the following:

> But, while our emotions give this anniversary its peculiar character, we must not forget that its more enduring value lies in the opportunity it affords to repeat and strengthen in our minds the truths of history for which this tremendous sacrifice was made. . . . Our school histories today are largely at fault because they do not tell the truth distinctly and positively about the beginning of the war. It is too often spoken of as inevitable. . . . This is not only not true, but it is a dangerous falsehood, because it tends to lessen the guilt of the rebellion and suggests that after all the South was not to blame. I would be the last to deny that a contest of some kind was inevitable between freedom and slavery until one or the other should prevail over the whole nation. . . . But I do deny that an armed conflict was inevitable; I do deny that it was impossible by constitutional means to find a peaceful solution. The solutions which other countries have found for similar problems were surely not beyond our capacity, . . . *but the opportunity to try them was refused by the action of the South alone.* . . . This, I repeat, was rebellion, and I am willing to call the Southern soldiers Confederates, since they prefer that title; and while I welcome the dying away of personal bitterness between the soldiers and citizens of both sections, I am not willing to speak of the war as the Civil War or the War between the States, or to use any phrase other than that which the truth of history demands, and that which ought to be taught to every child in our schools for all time to come—the War of the

Rebellion. A crime like this, a deliberate attack upon the nation's life, ought not to be glossed over by a smooth turn of speech or half concealed for the sake of courtesy.

The papers of the country had nothing to say of the impropriety of the speech of which the foregoing extracts are fair samples. On the contrary, it was published under double-leaded headlines and declared to be "especially appropriate to the occasion." Here and there in the North speeches containing such misrepresentations of the South are still made on Decoration Day without calling forth any expressions of disapproval from the press. And if it be especially appropriate in the "customary Memorial Day services" to charge that the South refused to give the country an opportunity to find a peaceful solution of the questions at issue by constitutional means, and was guilty of the "crime" of deliberately and causelessly drawing the sword and attacking the nation's life, how can it be especially inappropriate, when dedicating a monument to Southern soldiers, to attempt to refute the charge? Does the propriety of discussing the causes of the War between the States belong exclusively to Northern writers and speakers? Did the South, when she laid down her arms, surrender the right to state in self-justification her reasons for taking them up? If not, I fail to see how it can be improper, when perpetuating the memory of the Confederate dead, at least to attempt to correct false and injurious representations of their aims and deeds and hand their achievements down to posterity as worthy of honorable remembrance.

Other comments on the Richmond speech I do not care to notice. In no one of them was there a calm and dispassionate attempt to refute its statements. For the most part they consisted of invective—the means to which small-minded men are prone to resort when they can find no available argument. Apparently this invective proceeded from misconceptions of my meaning, resulting from a hasty and prejudiced reading of what I said; and I am not without hope that, published now with other matter, the speech may be considered more calmly, be better understood, and, perhaps, be more favorably received.

Surely now, when nearly half a century has elapsed since the flag of the Confederacy was furled in the gloom of defeat; when the loyalty of the

South has been placed beyond all question by the fact that her sons, in response to the country's call, have fought as bravely under the Stars and Stripes as they once did under the Starry Cross; when, of those who were engaged in the conflict between the sections, all save an age-enfeebled remnant are numbered with the dead; when new men, most of them too young to have taken part in the war and many of them unborn when it closed, have come to the front and are directing the affairs of the nation—surely now our Northern friends will be tolerant and charitable and magnanimous enough to concede to a Southerner freedom of speech in defense of his dead comrades and refrain from heaping abuse on him, even though they may wholly dissent from what he says.

It is said, however, that it is disloyal to maintain that the South was right. Disloyal to what? Certainly not to the existing government. The controversy does not involve any question of loyalty to the government as it now is, but only a question of loyalty to a theory of government which was enunciated by the leaders of the Republican party prior to the war, which, by an unfortunate combination of circumstances, triumphed at the polls and elected its representatives to power in 1860, and the triumph of which led to the withdrawal of the Southern States from the Union. That theory the existing government does not profess to uphold. I believe that no prominent statesman of any party will openly advocate it to-day. Has any President since the war been willing to say in his inaugural address that in shaping the policy of the government in regard to vital questions he would not be bound by the decisions of the Supreme Court? Has any Secretary of State since the war been willing to say that "there is a law higher than the Constitution," and that a pledge to administer the government according to the constitution as construed by the Supreme Court would be "treason"? I think not. The existing government, professedly at least, repudiates that unconstitutional and "higher law" theory. It professes to respect the Constitution as the supreme law of the land. Surely there can be no disloyalty to it in maintaining that fifty years ago the South repudiated and withdrew from the Union rather than accept what it repudiates now.

But is it consistent with loyalty to the existing government to claim that the secession of the Southern States from the Union was not rebellion? Most certainly. The war changed conditions. It established new relations and obligations. It nationalized States that were previously federalized. It changed the union of independent States, held together by mutual consent, into a union of dependent States, held together by national authority. It abolished State sovereignty and changed the federal government, which derived its powers from the States, into the national government, which exercises authority and power over the States. Some things that may not be lawful under the national government established by the war may have been altogether lawful under the federal government that existed before the war. Secession is one of them. To maintain that a State now has the right to withdraw from the Union may be disloyal to the existing national government; but there is no such disloyalty in maintaining that a State had that right under the old federal government, and hence that the secession of the Southern States was not rebellion.

But it may be asked, Why seek to revive these old issues? What good can possibly result from discussing them? Why not, as a well-known Southern editor puts it, "pay a tribute to the conspicuous valor of the Southern soldiers without a revival of bootless discussions?" Why not acquiesce in all that has been said and done and "take up the old, sweet tale of Bunker Hill and Yorktown, and pursue it, under God's blessing, to the end of time? What cause has the South lost which remains to be vindicated or which can be recovered?"

If, as this distinguished editor—somewhat to the discredit of his reputation as a well-informed thinker—affirmed, slavery and secession were the only issues involved in the War between the States, it must be admitted that the South has no cause which remains to be vindicated and has lost nothing that can be recovered. The war abolished slavery, and, with the exception of a few Negroes who found that freedom brought them cares and hardships such as they had not known in slavery, I never heard a Southerner say he regretted it. If the war did not abolish the constitutional right of a State to secede from the Union, it clearly demonstrated that the exercise of that right is altogether impracticable when the seceders are the weaker party. In the South slavery and secession are dead, and no discussion of old issues can possibly bring them back to life or excite in the Southern heart a desire to restore them.

Nor can a discussion of the old issues add in any way to the rights of citizenship now enjoyed by the Southern people. As the editor quoted above said, in all save pensions "it is one with the men who followed Grant and with the men who followed Lee. They sit side by side in Congress; they serve side by side in the Cabinet; they have represented the country and are representing it in its foreign diplomatic service with an ability and loyalty which, as between the two, cannot be distinguished the one from the other." The discussion of old difference is not expected to increase the number of Southern office holders, gain for the South any larger share of Federal patronage, cause any inflow of Northern capital to develop her resources and enrich her people, or add to her material wealth in any way whatever. From the viewpoint of one who has an eye for the "loaves and fishes" only, it must seem altogether bootless.

But there are some who do not see in "loaves and fishes" the only thing worth striving for, who think that unsullied honor is better than material wealth, and who are unwilling to prosper and grow fat by acquiescing in perversions of history that tarnish the fame of their heroic dead. In discussing the causes of the war they have no thought of restoring the *ante bellum* conditions of Southern life; they do not aim to recover any material wealth or political place and prestige that the South may have lost; they are not "seeking to raise up a generation of young vipers to undo the good that God has done"; they are not "seeking to make traitors of the fair lads whom we are sending to West Point and Annapolis." Their sole purpose is to state fairly the South's side of the case, to refute the false charge that she plunged the country into a long and bloody war without the semblance of just cause, to bring into prominence the real reason of her withdrawal from the Union, to present her action to the world in a truer and fairer light, and to free her from the reproach which unfriendly and calumnious writers have heaped on her.

I acknowledge to its utmost lawful extent the obligation to heal dissensions, allay passion, and promote good feeling; but I do not believe that good feeling should be promoted at the expense of truth and honor. I sincerely desire that there may be between the people of the North and the people of the South increasing peace and amity, and that, in the spirit of genuine fraternity, they may work together for the prosperity and glory of their common country; but I do not think the Southern people should be expected to sacrifice the truth of history to secure that end.

It has been truthfully said that "history as written, if accepted in future years, will consign the South to infamy"; and only by refusing to acquiesce in it as it is now written can we possibly prevent future generations from so accepting it. By keeping these politically dead issues alive as questions of history, freely discussing them, and reiterating the truth in regard to them, we may possibly counteract to some extent the effect of the misrepresentations found in history as it is now written, add something to the luster of the page that records the deeds of the men and women of the South, and hand their story down to posterity so that their children's children will think and speak of them with pride rather than shame.

With this end only in view and conscious of no feeling of bitterness, I delivered the speech at the unveiling of the monument to the soldiers and sailors of the South. With the same end in view and in the same kindly spirit, I now give this little book (*Defending the Southern Confederacy: The Men in Gray*) to the public. If it shall excite any feeling of enmity in the North or the least disloyal and traitorous feeling in the South, I shall be sincerely sorry; but if it shall give to any one a truer and juster conception of the South's motives, aims, lofty patriotism, and unwavering devotion to principle, I shall be very glad.

R. C. C.

Editor's Note

The men of the North, and the South, were mustered into service in the spring of 1861.

After decades of bitterness, and wrangling, it became impossible for the citizens of the commercial and industrialized states of the North, and those of the South, to live in harmony. This economic disparity was also a source of discord. The Southern people lived in a society largely agrarian in nature; and independent in thought and action. The struggle for independence by those living in Dixie land is brought into focus and is told simply and truthfully in the two hundred and forty-six diversified stories of heroic actions, and adventures, by people and members of the armed forces in the South.

These outstanding narratives of personal daring, and wartime adventure and conflict, have no equal in today's Civil War literature.